HUNTING AND THE

American Imagination

HUNTING AND THE | *American Imagination*

Daniel Justin Herman

SMITHSONIAN INSTITUTION PRESS
WASHINGTON AND LONDON

EDITOR: Ruth G. Thomson
DESIGNER: Amber Frid-Jimenez

Library of Congress Cataloging-in-Publication Data
Herman, Daniel Justin.
  Hunting and the American imagination /
Daniel Justin Herman.
     p.   cm.
  Includes bibliographical references.
  ISBN 1-56098-919-X (alk. paper)
     1. Hunting—United States—History.   2. Hunting—
  United States—Social aspects.   3. Hunting—United
  States—Philosophy.   I. Title.
  SK40.H47   2001
  799.2973—dc21   00—47004

British Library Cataloguing-in-Publication Data available

Manufactured in the United States of America
06 05 04 03 02 01   5 4 3 2 1

♾ The paper used in this publication meets the minimum
requirements of the American National Standard for
Information Sciences—Permanence of Paper for Printed
Library Materials ANSI A39.48-1984.

Vignettes on the title, contents, and chapter opening pages have
been drawn from illustrations appearing throughout the book.
For full credits for the following vignettes, please refer to the
captions on the following pages: title and contents pages, p. 186;
prologue, p. 14; chapter 1, p. 70; chapters 2 and 8, p. 108; chapter 3,
p. 207; chapters 4 and 14, p. 101; chapter 5, p. 73; chapters 6 and 12,
p. 220; chapter 7, p. 198; chapter 9, p. 192; chapter 10, p. 161; chapter
11, p. 238; chapter 13, p. 189; chapter 15, p. 202; chapter 16; p. 233;
chapter 17, p. 242; chapter 18, p. 267; and epilogue, p. 260.

For permission to reproduce illustrations appearing in this book,
please correspond directly with the owners of the works, as
listed in the individual captions. The Smithsonian Institution
Press does not retain reproduction rights for these illustrations
individually or maintain a file of addresses for photo sources.

To my teachers,
to my students,
and to Sande, who is both

Contents

Preface

"What is so . . . fascinating about" hunting, wondered a correspondent of the American sporting journal *Forest and Stream* in 1877, "that its lovers will travel thousands of miles, spend thousands of dollars, endure torrid heat and frigid cold, run risks that seem almost foolhardy, scale mountains, shoot rapids, cross arid deserts, thread trackless forests, and do a thousand other monstrous things to indulge their ruling passion?"[1]

No small number of Americans—hunters, animal rights activists, psychologists, anthropologists—have sought to answer that question. In this book I, too, seek to answer the question of why Americans hunt—or rather why historically Americans have or have not hunted. Neither my answers, however, nor my inquiries are what readers might expect.

Let me say at the outset that this book is not a defense of hunting or its legacy. It does not offer timeless answers for why men hunt. It does not suggest that men are instinctively killers or that men hunt because their prehistoric ancestors did. Nor does this book offer a comparative view of North American hunting traditions. Readers will find here only fleeting glimpses of American Indian hunters and none at all of Spanish, Mexican, French, Métis, African American, or Russian hunters of America.

A book could be written about the several hunting traditions of North America. My book, however, concerns the formulation of an Anglo-American (or, more simply, American) ethnic identity based on hunting. In this book I seek to answer the questions "why did Americans hunt?" and "why did Americans think they hunted?" from the perspective of cultural history.

In employing this methodology, I hope to show that hunting and ideas about hunting compose a shifting constellation that appears now in one part of the cultural sky, now in another. Consequently, my book contemplates hunting not as it was practiced and thought about in a single decade or century, nor hunting as a timeless, ahistorical phenomenon. Instead, my book contemplates hunting as it was practiced and thought about in America from the time of John Smith to that of Theodore Roosevelt.

This sort of history is no longer as fashionable as it once was. Most historians, particularly those in the early stages of their careers, mine discrete bodies of evidence on subjects and time periods equally discrete. I have embarked on a different course because I think that it is impossible to understand hunting in American culture without starting at the colonial beginning and proceeding to what was potentially the end of hunting in the Gilded Age. By surveying three centuries of American history, I have traced the origins of what might be termed America's hunting myth, the idea that Americans are (or were) a hunting people and that it was hunting that made them American.

The problem with this sort of history is the problem of abundance. Any diary, travel narrative, or cookbook—if it deals with hunting or hunters—becomes source material. How does one proceed up this Everest? And how does one record the climb? Obviously, it would be impossible to pore over all sources that deal with hunting in America since the founding of Jamestown in 1607; to do so would require more lifetimes than I have to give.

For purposes of focus I have concentrated on certain themes (hunting and farming, hunting and manliness, hunting and empire) rather than writing the thick description that anthropologists might recommend. I have also declined to reduce hunters to statistics by totting up ages, political affiliations, avocations, and incomes. I decline to do that not because I think quantification makes bad history (it is often indispensable) but because the sources speak for themselves. I realized at the outset that I was dealing with two populations of hunters: the backwoodsman/settler/farmer and the well-to-do sportsman. To count these men would be impossible and unnecessary, given that I was tracking their role in the American imagination rather than in discrete geographical and temporal locales (as, for instance, Kentucky in the 1760s).

I realize, however, that in describing sport hunters as urban and middle class—without quantifiable evidence to back up these labels—is a problematic exercise. Nineteenth-century Americans continually changed occupations as they shuffled from farm to town and from town to farm. Meanwhile, rural villages grew almost overnight into urban communities.

For purposes of my study, "urban" describes men who worked or resided in small towns as well as in major cities like New York, Boston, and Philadelphia. I would go so far as to say that in my study "urban" denotes not a community with a given population but an intensified set of social and market relations most characteristic of cities.

If pressed for a precise definition of "middle class," I would include those whose occupations fell within what historian Stuart Blumin labels "low non-manual" (schoolteachers, grocers, clerks, innkeepers, and ministers) as well as those whose occupations ranked among Blumin's "high non-manual" category (merchants, industrialists, bankers, government officials, and professionals). Yet the middle-class man of whom I write was defined not so much by vocation as by his aspiration for social advance through enterprise, thrift, and a genteel standard of behavior.[2]

I assume that such traits reflected the post-Revolutionary triumph of a middle-class consensus over an older social order that valued deference to one's betters, duty to community, and social and geographical stability (the sort of society that Gordon Wood labels "monarchical").[3] I would argue, by extension, that those who opposed this middle-class triumph were not necessarily members of a working class. Resistance to middle-class values came from landed men, often Federalists, and, more important for my study, from farmers who subscribed to the values of an older, less individualistic, less enterprising, and more geographically and socially static society. These were Jefferson's farmer-heroes who, although they were individualists and capitalists, were not fully indoctrinated into the competitive, atomistic, middle-class world that had taken shape by the Age of Jackson.

In arriving at my conclusions, I have quarried thousands of sources, ranging from sporting periodicals and hunting books to travelers' narratives, diaries, letters, newspapers, and works of art. The result is neither narrative nor social history, yet I hope that this book will be read and appreciated by both historian and layman. To compose a readable book, however, is not to compose a book that all will appreciate. Some Americans want the hunter praised; others want him vilified. I have steered a middle course, neither indicting hunters nor paying them tribute. Nevertheless, I have offered criticism and praise where I thought them due.

Another caveat may be appropriate here. When I use the term "American imagination," I am aware that there is no such thing. There were as many American imaginations in the past as there were Americans. Much of my book is about how the hunter became a contested figure in American culture, how he became a sort of politician running for the office of American icon (or American Native), opposed by some and supported by others. In the mid-nineteenth century, the hunter had won that election. He had critics, but admirers outnumbered them.

By the late nineteenth century, the hunter (as sportsman and backwoodsman) had become, in the phraseology of Antonio Gramsci, a "hegemonic" figure, a culture hero propagated by powerful members of American society to serve their ideological ends.[4] The hunter became the human banner for imperialism, laissez-faire individualism, and patriarchy. As that banner, the hunter triumphed in the American imagination. But hegemonic culture heroes play ambiguous roles as they wander across the prairies of history. If the hunter epitomized laissez-faire freedom and imperial conquest, he also became in the Gilded Age a symbol of the American common man (and, in some instances, woman) and the nation's democratic ethos.

I admit that I am not a hunter, which, I hope, has given me some critical distance from my topic. Yet I am not immune to the obsessions of hunters. I have longed to stalk a buck on a cool fall day high in the Colorado mountains, and if asked, I would not hesitate to go deer hunting today. Nothing could be more natural, or more American. That I think of hunting in this way is why I wrote this book. How, I wondered, had I come to see hunting as natural? Is the idea that hunting is natural, like most ideas about human nature, a social invention, a story we have told ourselves so many times that it has become true?

And how did hunting come to be American? I remember when as a boy of fourteen, dressed in a Pendleton shirt and holding a rifle, I pictured myself in another, more American, time and place. Seduced by images from *Boys' Life* and *Field and Stream,* I saw myself in the countryside, living close to the land, bringing home a rabbit or a duck for supper ("dinner" was too civilized sounding), or perhaps a real prize, a mule deer with four tines on each antler. This life, I thought, was the essence of Americanness. It was the life I thought my grandfathers had lived, and it was a life I wanted to share, despite finding myself marooned in a sea of tract homes called Phoenix, Arizona.

Years later, as a graduate student, I began to puzzle over the ingredients of this thing Americanness. What were the ingredients of my own Americanness and that of my forebears? More specifically, how was it that I, residing in what was once the territory of the Hohokam and O'Odham peoples, could feel indigenous, as though I belonged in this saguaro-studded terrain (though decidedly not in the built environs of Phoenix)? Having a grandmother who loved to observe (not to shoot) peccaries, bobcats, and Gambel's quail and who made Roger Tory Peterson's field guides my boyhood reading had something to do with my sensibilities. Studying nature (if through books) makes one feel part of nature; it gives one a sense of belongingness, even possession. Was the same phenomenon, I wondered, at work among my forebears? Did reading natural history and studying animals (if through a gunsight) instill in my ancestors a sense of belongingness in North America? In writing this book, I have addressed these questions as they are refracted through the image of hunters and hunting in the American imagination.

I confess to choosing this topic not only because it satisfied my curiosity but also because it offered me the chance to keep one foot—or eye, perhaps—outdoors. Though my decision to study hunting was hastened by my fear of humiliation—I had five minutes to come up with a topic in my first graduate research seminar—my choice could not have fit me better. Though graduate school would demand monastic devotion to library and study, I could at least read about exploration, adventure, and life outdoors. Now, after years of research and writing, I am still captivated by tales of backwoodsmen like Daniel Boone and scouts like Kit Carson, as well as tales penned by heroic sport hunters like "Hal A. Dacotah" (Henry Hastings Sibley) and "Nessmuk" (George Washington Sears).

As I argue here, these individuals were American Natives, men who seemed to live close to nature, absorb its virtues, and take on the aura of the indigene. We should remember, however, that none of these men were indigenes, at least in the fullest sense of the term. They were cultural ciphers who allowed Americans to "play Indian," as Philip Deloria has phrased it, and to portray themselves as heirs to the continent.[5] Even as hunters adopted American Indian names and personae, they remained the descendants of transplanted Europeans who took the continent by force, by trickery, and at times by treaty. I use the term "American Native" as an ironic label for a people who thought they were indigenes but who were in reality conquerors. Never should American Native be confused with Native American; the triumph of the former meant the dispossession of the latter, leaving both with a bitter history indeed.

If American Natives, in taking possession of the continent, displaced Native Americans, however, they also created a lasting and meaningful legacy of stewardship and a genuine appreciation for the wildlife and geography of the continent. It may seem contradictory that a socially constructed identity from America's imperialist past could create a hopeful as well as a maleficent legacy, but history is seldom a straightforward tale of good or bad. I hope that those who read this book will come away with a better understanding of both legacies.

Notes

1. H. W. De L., "Field Sports," *Forest and Stream* 9, no. 1 (August 16, 1877): 30, col. 2.
2. Stuart M. Blumin, *The Emergence of the Middle Class: Social Experience in the American City,*

1760–1900 (Cambridge, Mass., 1989), 44. On the evolution of the American middle class, see also Richard Bushman, *The Refinement of America: Persons, Houses, Cities* (New York, 1993); John Cawelti, *Apostles of the Self-Made Man* (Chicago, 1965); Karen Halttunen, *Confidence Men and Painted Women: A Study of Middle-Class Culture in America, 1830–1870* (New Haven, Conn., 1982); John F. Kasson, *Rudeness and Civility: Manners in Nineteenth-Century America* (New York, 1990); and Arthur Meier Schlesinger Sr., *Learning How to Behave: A Historical Study of American Etiquette* (New York, 1946).

3. Gordon Wood, *The Radicalism of the American Revolution* (New York, 1992; reprint, New York, 1993), 9–92 (page citations are to the reprint edition).

4. Antonio Gramsci's concept of hegemony is complex, but in part he refers to the uncanny ability of ruling groups to legitimate their rule even when economic conditions, theoretically, should make the ruled ready for change. So long as the ruled believe in such tropes as the self-made man (or, for that matter, the biological differentiation of the sexes—though Gramsci did not say so), they will support existing political, economic, and cultural arrangements, no matter how exploitative and artificial these might be. Ruling groups are thus said to exercise hegemony over their societies. See David Forgacs, ed., *An Antonio Gramsci Reader: Selected Writings, 1916–1935* (New York, 1989), especially pages 189–221 and 363–78. My argument is that frontier hunters, as American culture heroes, legitimated hegemonic social relations (including patriarchy, laissez-faire capitalism, and imperialism) that benefited ruling groups. To say, however, that hunter-heroes exerted an altogether conservative force on American society would be a distortion because they also represented America's democratic, egalitarian tradition.

5. Philip Deloria, *Playing Indian* (New Haven, 1998).

Acknowledgments

In writing this book, I felt at times like a hunter myself. Like any good scholar, I prey on the work of others. Indeed, the entire realm of scholarship is Darwinian. Everything feeds on everything else; the simple forms of one generation evolve into the more complex ones of another; and only the fittest survive (at least temporarily). What's the purpose? There isn't one, it often seems. It just happens.

I would add that scholarly arguments, although they mutate endlessly, enhance our social vision in the bargain. The richer our sight, the richer our world. There is purpose. Meanwhile, the operative paradigm for my work has been cooperation rather than competition. The encouragement, suggestions, and goodwill of others brought this book into being.

I especially wish to thank Gunther Barth, who shepherded me through the labyrinth of graduate school at the University of California at Berkeley. Gunther's reservoirs of wisdom, patience, and humor made him a model mentor. At Berkeley I also benefited from the perspicacity, energy, and encouragement of Jim Kettner and the anthropological expertise of Bill Simmons, both of whom read this project in its dissertation phase. My friend, fellow graduate student (now Ph.D.), and angler extraordinaire, Carl Sjovold, likewise read a draft and offered astute suggestions. Carl also knows how to catch crappie, a skill I lack.

When I began teaching, I wondered how I would ever have time to transform a swollen manuscript into the lean form of a book. Dick Orsi at California State University at Hayward insisted that it was possible, and—thanks in part to his encouragement and editorial suggestions on chapter 8—it was. Jim Ronda, Alan Taylor, John Mack Faragher, and Warder Cadbury also read and offered astute comments on later drafts of various chapters. Their experience, expertise, and willingness to help contributed immensely to the manuscript. Dan Flores read the manuscript in its mature form; his erudition, along with the graceful suggestions of Ruth Thomson at the Smithsonian Institution Press, were the enamel that covered the primer gray. Mark Hirsch, senior editor at the Smithsonian Institution Press, also came to my aid with unflagging enthusiasm and by awarding me a book contract.

I would also like to thank my sister, Luciana Herman, and my father, Justin Herman, who read and approved many chapters, and my ninety-three year old grandmother, Louise, who insists that I am the brightest young man on the planet. With that kind of send-off, one can hardly go wrong. It took, however, Mary Ann Jimenez, Alan Greenberger, and Werner Warmbrunn, my history professors at Pitzer College, to convince me that I would make a good historian—and to help make me one. And, finally, my partner in romance, Sande De Salles, read every word I wrote and never failed to fill my sails with advice, confidence, and conviction.

I also benefited from a Bancroft Library Fellowship and a Mellon Fellowship (as a graduate student). Without these awards, I could not have found the pearls within the oysters at the Bancroft Library or the Beinecke Library at Yale. In the book-writing stage, I benefited from a Smithsonian Postdoctoral Fellowship that gave me access to the troves of the Smithsonian Institution Archives, the Adirondack Museum, and the Hagley Museum and Library. In particular, I wish to thank Pam Henson and Paul Theerman (my advisor) at the Smithsonian, both of whom were consistently helpful, interesting, friendly, and enthusiastic.

To spend ten weeks in Washington, D.C., under the auspices of the Smithsonian Institution was one of the great pleasures of writing this book. But still greater pleasures awaited me at the Adirondack Library in Blue Mountain Lake, New York, where I plucked books freely from the shelves and exchanged ideas with Caroline Welsh, Jerry Pepper, and Jane Mackintosh.

My advice to young scholars: figure out a project that will get you to Washington, D.C., and then to the Adirondack Museum. And don't assume—at least where scholarship is concerned—that Darwin is right.

When Daniel Boone goes by, at night,
The phantom deer arise
And all lost, wild America
Is burning in their eyes.

Rosemary and Stephen Vincent Benet, *A Book of Americans*

Of one thing at least I am certain: that not to
take myth seriously in the life of an ostensibly
"disenchanted" culture like our own is actually
to impoverish our understanding of our
shared world.

Simon Schama, *Landscape and Memory*

Prologue

 When John Smith—explorer, historian, and founder of Jamestown—reported early in the seventeenth century that two of
his fellow colonists had killed 148 wildfowl with three shots, he
inaugurated the idea of America as a "hunter's paradise." Smith
did not report what sort of gun these nimrods employed; perhaps to do so would
have disabused readers of the fantasy he sought to create. The actual weapon
might have been a cannon loaded with grapeshot; it would be difficult to wreak
such havoc with a musket. Or, in the tradition of great hunting and fishing yarns,
the toll may have been exaggerated in the telling. True or not, the New World
must have appeared to be, as Smith proclaimed, a place where gentlemen would
find themselves "ranging dayly those unknowne parts" in search of game, much
as gentlemen ranged leisurely through the woods of England.[1]

Two centuries later, Americans would be fascinated by such tales. They would
devour stories of wildfowl hunts, bear hunts, panther hunts, wolf hunts, and deer
hunts. Their heroes—Meriwether Lewis, Daniel Boone, Davy Crockett, Kit Carson, Buffalo Bill—were hunters, men who seemed to fit the mold of their colonial forebears. By the late nineteenth century, Americans had come to see themselves as a hunting people, a people who could trace their cultural instincts to the
dim recesses of the colonial past.

To nineteenth-century Americans, even to modern Americans, it would seem
self-evident that Americans were destined to become a hunting people. Americans were products of the frontier; it was natural that the backwoods hunter had
emerged as American hero. As Smith testified, America had always been a land
of bountiful game and good hunting, a place intended by providence to lure those
of hardy and adventuresome spirit. Abundant game and Americans' skill in har-
vesting it seemingly had made possible the spirit of independence itself. If

Americans had not been a self-sufficient, liberty-loving, hunting people, what would have compelled them to stand up to King George III? And if Americans had not been skilled with rifle and musket, how could they have defeated the mightiest army in the world?

Not until the nineteenth century, however, did hunters dominate the canvas of American culture. In that century America's first hunter-heroes—Boone, Crockett, Natty Bumppo—were made famous by an urban publishing industry that catered to a burgeoning middle-class reading public. Nineteenth-century printing presses poured forth thousands of tales about hunters and hunting as if to slake an unquenchable public thirst, while sport hunting became a favorite pastime, a way to mimic frontier heroes (and the English elite), and a school of American virtue.

Why the celebration of hunters and hunting appeared in the nineteenth century—precisely when the tentacles of modernization reached into most aspects of American life—is the riddle this book explores. The answer, insofar as there is an answer in cultural history, is aswim in contradiction. At the same time that middle-class Americans became passionate about hunting, at the same time they embraced Daniel Boone and Natty Bumppo as culture heroes, they concerned themselves with domesticating their society. They learned etiquette and polite speech; they embraced the doctrine of temperance; they sought to reform prisons; they built almshouses and asylums; and they attended the recitals of "the Swedish nightingale," Jenny Lind. Some Americans also crusaded for peace and against slavery, created socialist and religious utopias, and even took up the cause of animal rights.

These trends bloomed among a specific segment of the American population, well-to-do Protestants who lived chiefly in the growing cities of the northeastern and midwestern United States. Ironically, sport hunting took hold in this same population. Sport hunters were not necessarily reformers, but they were middle-class or elite men. The growing ranks of sport hunters, commented Philadelphia author Elisha Jarrett Lewis in his 1851 *Hints to Sportsmen,* included "the student of science, the cunning expounder of Blackstone, the deeply-read follower of Galen, the shrewd devotee of commerce, as well as the most skillful and industrious artisans."[2] Together with elite southern planters, these men campaigned to make sport hunting respectable, to institute game laws, and to make hunting a cornerstone of American identity.

By the late nineteenth century, their campaign had succeeded. Hunting was identified with something one's father had done, and one's grandfather before him, and one's forefathers before him. Hunting was a sacred knowledge handed down from father to son since the age of heroes. To know this sacred knowledge—to know how to stalk and to shoot—identified one not just as a man but as an American. Arms manufacturers bolstered this legend by associating their mass-produced wares with the deeds of old: the conquest of the wilderness, the defeat of the British, and the winning of the Far West. Yet in so doing, arms manufacturers, together with America's writers and artists, transformed the American hunting myth into a tale of decline. According to this tale, Americans had once been a sturdy, independent, powerful, and noble people, a people of the gun. As America became urban and industrial, however, its men had become effeminate, luxury loving, retreating, and weak. Only through the gun and the hunt could Americans reclaim their heritage.

So the legend ran. In the twentieth century, the image of the hunter slipped a bit, along with the idea that Americanness came—or should have come—from guns and hunting. When D. H. Lawrence wrote in 1923 that the American male, as a descendant of frontier hunters, was in his soul hard, isolate, stoic, and a killer, he was attempting to exorcise the hunter from American consciousness. Exorcism was also the goal of Richard Slotkin when in 1973 he made the hunter the central figure in American myth. For Slotkin, the archetypal hunter-hero was Daniel Boone, the man who, armed with his Kentucky rifle, crossed the border between "civilization" and "savagery" to defeat buffalo, bear, and American Indian and, in so doing, to defeat the savage within. To conquer the savage was to conquer one's own savage urges for autonomy, indolence, and sexuality.[3]

Slotkin's frontier hunter was another incarnation of Joseph Campbell's hero with a thousand faces, the man who makes a risky pilgrimage beyond the known world to acquire the sacred knowledge that will rejuvenate his culture.[4] In equating the hero's pilgrimage with violence, however, Slotkin went beyond Campbell, for whom the hero was still heroic. In Slotkin's view, Daniel Boone—prefiguring countless Americans after him, right up through the Vietnam War—was the prototype of the malevolent man who employs racist violence to regenerate (one wants to say degenerate) American culture. Thus Slotkin's title *Regeneration through Violence.* Following this logic, Slotkin has spun out two more thick volumes that attempt to bring the story of the American killer in myth, literature, and American consciousness up to the present.

In a curious way, members of the National Rifle Association might take comfort in Slotkin's findings. Both see the hunter as a figure who emerges from the colonial frontier, a figure who expresses the American character in its purest form. For both, as for Frederick Jackson Turner, Americanness issues from the frontier. This Americanness may be reenacted, dramatized, and exaggerated in dime novels, movies, and television, but it must originate in the westering experience. The frontier is for Americans a certificate of cultural authenticity, as the Saxon woods once were for the English or the Hercynian forests for the Germans.

There is truth in the idea that the frontier made Americans a hunting people; hunting was a common frontier activity. When land had not yet been cleared and planted, or when there was blight, hunting could mean the difference between survival and starvation for backwoods families. The meat, skins, hides, and pelts taken by hunters could be used at home or traded for seeds, tools, and other useful goods. Hence a good hunter on the frontier was a respected man. At the same time, backwoodsmen tended to view hunting as a utilitarian skill rather than a source of moral virtue. "Killed a Doe Fawn and a Yearling Buck," noted New Hampshire farmer Matthew Patten in his diary on January 12, 1754; "carried the meat out to the path," he reported a day later.[5] For Patten, hunting was a temporary expedient, useful until crops could be planted and towns built.

Despite the assumptions of Slotkin and others, the idea that Americans were a hunting people was not so evident to our forebears (even those on the frontier) as to us. Far from being a widely celebrated pastime, hunting in the colonial and early national imagination was rife with contradiction. Hunting called up images of a paradise of game and plenty, where every man could find subsistence, making him beholden to none. Hunting also fueled the hope that every man might become genteel; in Europe hunting had long been the sport of the elite, the great men who ruled countryside and nation. At the same time, hunting in the New World called forth images of man fallen to a state of nature, the condition of savagery. If the New World was to be a hunter's paradise, what would prevent each colonist from becoming a force unto himself, a man who observed no law or authority but his own? As hunters, would colonists be reduced to the level of American Indians, men who seemed to renounce religion, gentility, and civilization? For two centuries these dilemmas worked against the apotheosis of hunters and hunting in American culture.

Yet at some point in American history, hunting became celebrated. Where do we locate this historical moment (or moments)? How and why did Americans embrace hunters and hunting? To comprehend the role of hunters and hunting in American culture requires us to follow many leads. Our story, however, has a tidy beginning: the American Revolution.

During and shortly after the Revolution, frontier hunters appeared in popular literature, in art, and even on colonial bills of exchange. In the memory of

Americans, courageous hunters had filled the ranks of militias and punished British regulars from Lexington to Yorktown. Yet here, too, truth blends with fiction in a powerful concoction of myth.

Frontier hunters did figure in the winning of the Revolution, though not so handsomely as Americans like to remember. Most backwoodsmen remained neutral, while others became Tories. The Revolution was won by Washington's regulars (who generally carried short-range military muskets, not hunting rifles) rather than militias.[6] Like our Revolutionary ancestors, however, we remember volunteers from the backwoods whose hunting experience made them ideal citizen-soldiers, while we forget impoverished regulars (from city and countryside) who had killed more hogs and chickens than deer.

Although Revolutionary era Americans came to praise frontier hunters, they did not do so wholeheartedly. The intellectual currents that ran together in the vortex of the Revolution—ascetic Protestantism, civil millennialism, republicanism, the Enlightenment—placed farmers, not hunters, on the pedestal of American virtue.[7] According to Revolutionary logic, farmers were the bricks with which a model society was to be built: farmers were pious, virtuous, industrious, self-sufficient citizens of nature.

One might argue that these farmers were hunters; America was a nation of farmer-hunters, and no sophistry should distinguish the two. If we are easy in our minds with the idea that our ancestors were both farmers and hunters, however, many of the founders were not. Influenced by Protestant and Enlightenment social thought, they believed that the farmer was the builder of civilization, whereas the hunter was its nemesis. Thus the Revolution—the event that catapulted the hunter to the rank of hero—simultaneously awarded him a marginal place in the American imagination. For decades the hunter rocked precariously on his pedestal of fame.

Although tributes to hunters came with the Revolution, the worship of hunters reached a crescendo only in the mid-nineteenth century. That crescendo came as part of a vast effort to define what it meant to be American. It is critical to note that seventeenth- and eighteenth-century colonists, far from remaking themselves in the image of the New World, had remade the New World in the image of themselves. "Well may New-England lay claim to the Name it wears," proclaimed Cotton Mather in 1700, its inhabitants having paved the land with familiar English names to "bear up the particular Places . . . from whence they came." The same judgment could have applied to the middle and southern colonies, whose citizens did not see themselves as a people whose cultural roots lay in the New World. Even at the time of the Revolution, commented patriot and naturalist Samuel Latham Mitchill, "the Mother Country and the Father Land were familiar terms" to describe England, and a voyage thither was "'going home.'"[8]

Only after the Revolution did the nation's writers and artists become fascinated by what was native, indigenous, and truly American. Writers James Fenimore Cooper, Washington Irving, and Ralph Waldo Emerson self-consciously styled an American literature. Artists Thomas Doughty, Thomas Cole, and Albert Bierstadt formulated an American art. Explorers and ethnographers Henry Rowe Schoolcraft, Lewis Henry Morgan, and Thomas McKenney, along with painters George Catlin, Seth Eastman, and John Mix Stanley, documented American Indian cultures.

The frontier society of the white man also had its chroniclers; George Caleb Bingham, Lyman Copeland Draper, John Shane, Timothy Flint, and John Mason Peck were among the foremost. Frederick Jackson Turner was a latecomer to this tradition. Most significant of all, American nature—including fauna, flora, geography, geology, and mineralogy—was cataloged, analyzed, and brought within the ken of an American public by a troop of patriot naturalists, including Thomas Jefferson, Charles Willson Peale, Alexander Wilson, and John James Audubon.

As Lee Clark Mitchell argues, the effort to define and to catalog all things American emerged from a profound ambivalence over progress and development.[9] Nineteenth-century Americans saw the continent's forests and fauna disappearing, its aboriginal peoples dying off, and their way of life forever changed. Artists, writers, and ethnographers urgently documented a vanishing America. Yet the juggernaut of empire rolled on; Americans worshiped progress even as they lamented the destruction in its wake.

From a different perspective, no great conflict existed between the America of progress and empire and the America of historic tradition. The effort to record and to participate in things American was more an attempt to establish and to conserve a state of mind than an attempt to conserve the physical world. A comprehensive knowledge of all that composed the American continent—animals, plants, peoples, and landscapes—became transformed into an American tribal identity that was to be salvaged and rendered impervious to progress through art, literature, and science.

Hunting became another vehicle for the expression of tribal identity. As one sporting journal explained in 1839, the panther was "in the American forest what the tiger is in Africa and India, a dangerous and savage animal, the terror of all other creatures," and the white man who hunted it ranked as an "almost aboriginal hunter." The image of the nineteenth-century hunter-hero—wearing moccasins and buckskins, carrying a Kentucky rifle, and educated in the school of nature—suggested a new aborigine. This man—the American Native—became the symbolic heir of the American Indian.[10]

In some respects, white hunters did resemble American Indians. For thousands of years, Indians had crisscrossed the continent, becoming expert on the natural world while subsisting on big game and small. Whether they killed mammoths, deer, or rabbits, Indian hunters took control of the natural world by gaining the favors of the animals themselves and their nonhuman keepers. The hunter ensured the survival of his people by becoming intimately familiar with geography, climate, fauna, and flora and by systematically burning the land to create conditions conducive to game propagation and growth. The hunter was a critical link between the tribe and its environment, the individual who rendered a nature that was impersonal or inimical into a nature that was controlled and beneficent. For Indians, to be a skilled hunter was to be a steward of nature and of the tribe.

Anglo-Americans, by contrast, celebrated the farmer. In the farmer's ability to make the earth fruitful, Americans found justification for claiming the lands of hunting peoples (forgetting that Indians were farmers too). By the early decades of the nineteenth century, however, Americans had begun to embrace hunters as culture heroes. The frontier hunter, like the Indian, learned the continent's geography, named its topography, and lived off the land. In times of danger, moreover, the hunter rushed to his people's defense. By the Age of Jackson, Americans had come to see frontier hunters as courageous men who, like Indians, had sprung from the American soil.

In an era of science, however, mastery of the land involved more than killing wild animals. Any man could shoot a deer. Hunting might make white Americans equal to American Indians but not superior. What was needed was a courage greater and a knowledge beyond those of Indians. Thus while Americans demonstrated their courage through ritualized hunting excursions into the wilderness, they demonstrated their knowledge through a scientific discourse called natural history.

To Americans of the eighteenth and early nineteenth centuries, natural history was science itself. It encompassed an array of modern disciplines: zoology, botany, geology, mineralogy, and medicine. Natural history was also a cultural discourse (to use an arrow from the quiver of Foucault) that located power and authority in the hands of educated Europeans.[11] Natural history's devotees—the most brilliant men of their age, men like Sir Joseph Banks, Karl von Linné,

Alexander von Humboldt, William Bartram, and Thomas Jefferson—gave natural history the cachet of universal truth. Through natural history they would create an encyclopedic and objectively true account of the earth, an account meant to supersede ideas about nature derived from folk wisdom.

On the imperial stage of the eighteenth and nineteenth centuries, natural history confirmed European dominion throughout the world. Plants, animals, and humans with dark skin pigments became the naturalist's quarry, all reduced to a bit of anatomical description and perhaps a hand-colored illustration on a few pages of parchment. Meanwhile, in London and New York City, learned gentlemen, books in hand, studied creation like so many lesser gods.

Amid this attempt to define and to catalog the world's natural productions, competing ideas about nature fell victim. "Silly" was how English ornithologist and botanist Mark Catesby, writing in the 1730s, described the belief of North American Indians that the coachwhip snake had magical powers, while in the early nineteenth century the American naturalist Thomas Say berated American Indians for believing that there had been a time when animals had conversed like humans.[12] No superstition was tolerated in the empire of natural history. Ignorance was to be effaced from the earth, while men trained in Latin and Greek became arbiters of order and truth.

Naturalists failed to realize that their technology itself was of mythic dimension. True, natural history was premised on empirical scrutiny and was subject to refutation and change. Yet before Darwin natural history served, like myth, as a way to understand the divine mind by understanding the variety and usefulness of God's productions. Natural history, like myth, prescribed the proper relationship between humans and nature. Natural history described the origins of the earth and its fauna and flora, recognized an epic past in which huge monsters battled for supremacy over the earth, and identified an anthropomorphic present in which birds and mammals had distinct personalities and distinct lessons to teach humans. Natural history told stories about mountains, seas, and rivers, stories that defined tribal cosmography and boundaries, albeit boundaries that might extend to the far reaches of creation.

To know natural history was to claim dominion over the earth; that is what made natural history so attractive to hunters. The hunter with his gun and the naturalist with his pen were Janus faces of the same man; often they were the same man. Indeed, the so-called Great Reconnaissance of nineteenth-century naturalists might be called the Great Hunt. Hunters and naturalists together entered nature to take command of it.

Centuries earlier, Romans had carted off elephants and lions from conquered lands as symbols of their far-reaching powers, while on the other side of the globe, and a few centuries later, Aztecs assembled the most fantastic collection of plants and animals the world had ever seen; Montezuma even imported bison from North America. Still later, English adventurers would ship antlers of Virginia Cervidae to Queen Elizabeth as symbols of her authority; individual English nobles had their own collections of the like. When naturalists of the eighteenth and nineteenth centuries collected the earth's fauna and flora, they transformed the ancient endeavors of kings, nobles, and hunters into a scientific pursuit worthy of an age of Enlightenment. The outcome, however, was the same: dominion.

In the nineteenth century it was a small step for hunters to adopt the costume of naturalists, just as naturalists adopted the costume of hunters. Hunters wished to be soldiers of science, eagerly engaged in the glorious task of knowing the world. Thus at the outset of the nineteenth century appeared the American hunter-naturalist, an ideal type embodied in explorer Meriwether Lewis and ornithologist John James Audubon, popularized through the sporting journals of the antebellum and postbellum eras, and culminating in Theodore Roosevelt. The hunter-naturalist took possession of the American continent by employing the canons of science to comprehend, catalog, and worship its natural productions. He, as much as Boone or Bumppo, became an American Native, a man who seemed to have both a scientific and a spiritual propriety over American nature.

To call such men American Natives is not to suggest that they shared the animistic worldview of American Indians. Yet they followed—in a real and symbolic sense—American Indian precedent.

Like white Americans, American Indians had not always been indigenous to lands they inhabited. Tribes moved gradually as their numbers grew or shrank; they displaced other tribes through warfare (and were in turn displaced themselves); and some migrated over great distances, settling in vastly different ecosystems and leaving behind long-established sacred sites. When a tribe remained in one place, however, that place—its fauna, flora, geomorphic features, weather, rivers, springs—became named, described, and integrated into a tribal system of belief. An intricate weave of folklore explained the origin and character of local animals and plants, their relationship to humans, their medicinal uses, and their religious significance, and a skein of myth and legend described earth-shaping culture heroes who had formed the tribal landscape. So closely attached were

American Indians to their tribal realms that many came to see themselves as autochthonous; they believed that they had sprung from the ground on which they stood (or, more commonly, from a lake, pond, or cave). Canasatego, a spokesman for the Iroquois Confederacy, reminded the governor of Maryland in 1744 that

> long before one hundred years, our ancestors came out of this ground, and their children have remained here ever since. You came out of the ground in a country which lies on the other side of the big lake; there you have claim, but here you must allow us to be your elder brethren, and the lands to belong to us.[13]

By the nineteenth century, American hunter-naturalists fancied that they had become as much heirs to the land as Canasatego's people. No longer were they foreigners from across the big lake. Through natural history and exploration, Americans had developed an intimate knowledge of the land, while through the teachings of hunter-heroes like Daniel Boone, they had developed aboriginal personae. Hunters had made themselves American Natives.

Yet how had the hunter become a model American? It was the farmer who provided Americans with moral justification for taking the lands of hunting peoples by mingling his sweat with the soil and making the earth bear fruit. In the nineteenth century, farmers continued to be thought of as ideal citizens of the republic; their virtue, piety, and self-sufficiency made them, as Jefferson had written, "the chosen people of God."[14]

In taking up sport hunting, thousands of American men—urban professionals, merchants, southern planters—sought to share, not to steal, the innate, manly virtues associated with spartan, self-sufficient farmers. To hunt was to engage in the rural pastime of yeomen farmers and frontiersmen. Though men of commerce and cities could hardly be expected to return to the field for good, they could return to engage in field sports. Having strayed from Jefferson's ideal republic of small farmers, having flirted with luxury, license, and effeminacy (evils that the founders associated with Europe's urban elite), nineteenth-century sport hunters sloughed off the sins of affluence like men converted.

As ideal Americans, however, sport hunters and farmers differed. Although sport hunters, like farmers, saw themselves as virtuous and self-sufficient—even pious insofar as they revered the sublime handiwork of the Creator—they identified themselves with the wilderness rather than the cultivated field. Like Boone, or Crockett, or knights of old, hunters took command of nature—and the continent—not by clearing and plowing but by doing noble battle with wild beast.

Even before the Civil War, hunters had burst onto the cultural stage to vie with farmers for the role of ideal citizens of nature, depicting themselves as men with a keen appreciation for the continent's fauna, geography, and sublime natural features. Soon the hunter shone as the ideal citizen of "Nature's Nation" (in the words of Perry Miller), the indigenous man whose virtues seemed rooted in the land.[15]

Yet within the hunter's heart was a paradox. In engaging in rural sport, middle-class hunters cast themselves as heirs to rustic frontiersmen, yet they also cast themselves as heirs to the chivalrous hunters of England. The antebellum popularizer of sport hunting in America, Henry William Herbert, was an English aristocrat. Two images of the hunter—one democratic and native, the other elitist and foreign—coexisted uneasily, epitomizing the classic dilemma of nineteenth-century Americans. What constituted Americanness in a society that looked to England for cultural precedent?

This dilemma grew more acute as wildlife populations declined throughout the century, causing hunters to worry about how to save game and whom to save it for. Should game be saved for men of affairs who could afford private hunting preserves or memberships in hunting clubs? In that case hunting would become an aristocratic privilege, as it was in England. Or should game be saved for all Americans? If so, hunting would remain a democratic practice, harking back to the egalitarian tradition of the frontier. In debating these questions, hunters debated the future of their nation.

Having made themselves model citizens of nature, sport hunters engaged in another conflict with vast implications. Time and again the sport hunter clashed with an earlier citizen of nature, a man who had once been the repository of American virtue, the farmer. The immediate issues were trespass and game laws. Farmers complained long and loudly of broken fences and trampled crops, yet the underlying issues were larger and less obvious than it would appear. At stake was not merely who would hunt but also who was the ideal citizen of nature. Would America remain a land of sturdy farmers and the rural, traditional culture they represented? Or would it become a land of chivalric hunters and the dynamic, commercial culture that many of them championed? In this conflict, sport hunters—among them the most wealthy and powerful men of their age—resembled not Boone or Bumppo but the nobility of England. For these men, to hunt was to demonstrate dominion over American society.

The trend toward aristocracy threatened everything Americans had revered. As elite men captured America's last buffalo, elk, and moose for private hunting parks, they also captured America's political and economic machinery. Soon, observers suggested, hunting would be the luxury of the rich; hunting could no longer be a democratic sport, and America would no longer be a democracy. As Progressives stepped in to regulate corporations and to protect workers, however, they—Theodore Roosevelt being conspicuous among them—also called on government to save America's game. Roosevelt, with his boyish, amiable, yet bullying personality, remembered what Gilded Age plutocrats forgot: the common man's right to hunt was a symbol of the common man's political rights, and to take away the right to hunt was to concede that America had lost its democratic vitality.

One might say that Roosevelt and his allies saved something not worth saving, that hunting epitomizes what is wrong with American culture: its celebration of machismo, weaponry, and death. One might also say that, in saving hunting as a democratic sport, Roosevelt and his allies saved the conquering, arrogant, atavistic mentality of the nineteenth century, a mentality unsuited to modern America. Finally, one might argue that Roosevelt saved the libertarian idea that American men, as sons of the pioneers, should rely on themselves alone. For Americans, hunting has long been a ritual of self-reliance, a reflection of the individualism they still cherish.

Historical crusades, however, have unintended consequences. To save hunting as an expression of individualism, hunters were forced to enlist the aid of government. In doing so, they made government the engine with which to abolish market and subsistence hunting and to protect game for middle-class and elite men. Though conservation temporarily compromised hunting as a democratic practice, it saved wildlife. In the twentieth century, Americans from every walk of life could take up sport hunting thanks to conservation campaigns waged by Roosevelt and his allies.

In enlisting government, moreover, sport hunters helped lay the groundwork for later efforts to save not only game species but also nongame species. Whether one opposes or supports hunting, it is important to recognize that Progressive era hunters left a legacy of stewardship over public lands, waterways, plants, and animals that continues today.

What is equally important to recognize is that Progressive era hunters bequeathed to modern hunters—as well as to environmentalists, who share with hunters a common cultural ancestry—an ethnic identity. So tightly did Roosevelt and his fellow hunters weave together stewardship and ethnic identity that it is all but impossible to separate them a century later. One hopes that to understand the origin of this ethnic identity is to take a step toward amending it, while continuing to practice the ethic of stewardship that emerged alongside it.

I
Paradise

There is no better place to start than the beginning and no better beginning than perfection. For Renaissance Europeans perfection lay in the New World. There, they believed, paradise could be regained. The New World was not just any paradise, however; it was a hunter's paradise.

The proposed colony of New Albion, according to a pamphleteer, would offer "pure aire, fertility of soile, . . . vallies of grapes, [and] rich mines" along with "millions of Elkes, Stags, Deer, Turkeys, Fowl, [and] Fish." Virginia, "Earth's only paradise," would likewise yield an "infinite store" of "land and water fowls," as well as "deer, kain, and fallow, stags, coneys, hares, with many fruits and roots good for meat." In 1656 one promoter rated venison "a tiresom meat," though he admitted that few Virginians hunted for fear of American Indian attack.[1]

Carolinians solved the problem of Indian animus by hiring Indians as hunters. One Indian, confided Samuel Wilson in 1682, could supply thirty colonists with deer and wildfowl for twenty shillings a year. This solution, however, compromised the idea of a hunter's paradise. Carolina, after all, was a place with "such infinite Herds that the whole Country seems but one continued [game] Park."[2] If only Indians hunted, how would colonists fulfill their fantasies of leisure?

In early New England a colonist could "ride ahunting in most places of the land," promised William Wood, but only "if he will venture himself for being lost." With Wampanoag Indians to guide them home, some men took the risk. In 1629 Francis Higginson of Massachusetts Bay reported to his friends in England that numerous "fat, sweet and fleshy" turkeys and hen-sized "partridges" (ruffed grouse) were taken in the woods, adding that "a great part of the winter" the colonists had "eaten nothing but roast meat of divers fowls which they have killed." The infamous Anglican of Merry Mount, Thomas Morton, who reveled

Colonial promoters depicted the New World as a hunter's paradise. This illustration, accompanying John Smith's account of Virginia, appeared in Theodor de Bry, *America*, part 10 (Oppenheim, 1618). Courtesy of Prints and Photographs, Library of Congress, Washington, D.C., LC-USZ62-49747.

with Indians until his Pilgrim neighbors banished him, also engaged in the delights of fowling, claiming to have seen one thousand geese at once before his gun. Such flocks were "not much frighted" by gunshots noted William Wood in 1634, who had seen more birds "living and dead the last year than I have done in former years." Wood himself had "killed twelve score at two shoots."[3]

The most astonishing abundance for New England hunters came in the form of "millions and millions" of passenger pigeons that migrated between roosting sites throughout eastern America. Seventeenth-century naturalist and traveler John Josselyn witnessed flocks of pigeons in New England that "had neither beginning nor ending, length nor breadth" and—like an eclipse—blocked the sun entirely.[4] Here was a wonder of Biblical proportion.

Such reports show that North America was a place of natural abundance. Unlike Europe, North America had not been lumbered and mined, plowed and fenced, and divided into parcels small and large for private gain. There were no cities in the European sense, nor were there aristocrats and monarchs to monopolize forests and game. Reports of a hunter's paradise in North America must have tantalized English commoners who—prohibited from hunting in their homeland—longed to begin anew in a land of plentiful game and easy shooting.[5]

Though few colonists realized it, Indians had altered the land by burning underbrush to create edge habitat for deer and other game. This burning left mature trees alive yet made the woods open, grassy, and parklike, accessible to hunters on foot or horseback.[6] Europeans did not explicitly note God's handiwork in this habitat, as they did in the plagues that wiped out seaboard Algonquian peoples, yet the expansive hunting parks of the New World seemed providentially intended for Europeans. North America seemed to be paradise on earth, where men would take their game and their ease together.

Seventeenth-century promotional tracts, to be sure, were less effusive than travelers' and explorers' narratives of earlier times. Before the era of exploration, cartographers had asserted that the Garden of Eden must exist somewhere in the world's netherlands. The Bible did not say that Eden had been destroyed, only that Adam and Eve had been driven out of it; surely it still existed on the periphery of creation. Thus, on reaching the Orinoco River in South America in 1498, Columbus believed he had located the Gihon, one of the four rivers that flowed from Eden.[7]

By the seventeenth century most Europeans had given up on the idea that Eden would be found, yet the trope of edenic abundance continued to resonate. There was a critical difference, however, between the Garden of Eden and the New World. In Eden Adam and Eve had subsisted on the fruits of the trees of paradise. Rather than hunting one another, human and beast had lived in harmony. One thinks of Alexander Pope's couplets,

> Pride then was not; nor Arts that Pride to aid;
> Man walk'd with beast, joint tenant of the shade;
> The same his table, and the same his bed;
> No murder cloath'd him, and no murder fed.[8]

In the New World, by contrast, Europeans, far from walking with wild beasts, felt compelled to exterminate them.

If New World reality failed to live up to the edenic idyll, perhaps another model—one equally steeped in Judeo-Christian utopianism—would better serve: Canaan, the promised land of the Jews. Colonial promoters trumpeted that another Canaan—a land overflowing with milk and honey—awaited the English in the New World.

Yet Canaan had been no more a land of hunters than Eden. The Old Testament forbade men to eat most forms of game and seldom spoke of hunting. One might cite in Genesis the example of that "mighty hunter before God," Nimrod, founder of Babylon and grandson of cursed Ham, or the example of Esau, who sought game for his father, blind Isaac, and found himself disinherited upon his return. Judaism and Christianity, however, were not religions of hunting peoples. Drawn from the pastoral histories of the Near East, the sacred texts of both religions exalted stable, patriarchal communities of worshipers. Insofar as the New World was a hunting paradise, it resembled the paradise of ancient Persians (from whose language the word "paradise" derives), an afterworld where bold hunters perpetually enjoyed the chase, yet the Christian paradise was the colonists' template.

Below the breezy tale of New World contentment, meanwhile, burned the coals of anxiety. Only after Adam's fall had God sanctioned hunting by turning man and animal against one another, remaking nature into a place of disorientation, confusion, danger, and anarchy. The name for this realm, wilderness, was what the New World often seemed to be.

The Biblical idea of wilderness was reinforced by medieval fears of dark forests where humans seldom ventured. Far from the recreational wilderness of today, the wilderness of medieval and early modern Europe was the abode of wild animals and wild people, where neither religion nor law could penetrate. The medieval wilderness teemed also with trolls, goblins, sprites, and fairies. By the seventeenth century, the English people had extirpated wolves and bears from their island, while Christianity had extirpated (with more or less success) the imaginary beings of the wilderness. Yet New World settlers retained the concept of wilderness as a place where evil resided.[9]

The idea of the New World as wilderness, together with its opposite, the New World as paradise, bespoke profound contradictions in colonial thought. Neither Eden nor Canaan could abide with a "hidious & desolate wildernes, full of wild beasts & willd men." If Europeans were to reign in the New World, they would do so by wedding themselves to a powerful instrument of authority, the gun.[10]

In the fall of 1621, four hunters from the Plymouth Colony returned from the woods with enough fowl to feed their people for a week. The Wampanoag, the Algonquian-speaking people who had entered into a league of amity with the Pilgrims, added to this five deer, and for three days the two peoples feasted together. Americans commemorate this as the first Thanksgiving.

Long celebrated in American history, Thanksgiving suggested the possibility of lasting friendship between American Indians and colonists. Within the chorus of good fellowship, however, sounded a note of distrust. Amid the festivities, re-called Edward Winslow, colonists "exercised our arms," in part to entertain the Indians but also to impress upon them the martial prowess of Englishmen.[11]

In truth English muskets were little better than bows and arrows for wood-land hunting or warfare, as Indians proved when they demonstrated their own weapons. Lead balls could shatter bone and muscle in ways that arrows seldom could, but muskets were heavy and unwieldy (some forty motions were required to fire a matchlock), inaccurate (most muskets lacked sights, and until the eigh-teenth century, all lacked rifling in the barrel), and they could be fired only once without reloading. Moreover, matchlocks, the most common firearm in the colonies until flintlocks replaced them in the late seventeenth century, were no-toriously unreliable in wet weather.[12]

In hunting, a man skilled with a bow could often outperform a man skilled with a musket, especially in marshes and dense forests, where muskets were awk-ward to carry, load, and aim. With their bows, noted William Wood, Indians "smite the swift running hind and nimble winged pigeon, without a standing pause or left eyed blinking." Yet the thunder of firearms had a powerful psycho-logical impact, striking terror into enemies unaccustomed to hearing it. Capi-talizing on this effect, Virginia's House of Burgesses in 1632 passed a resolution encouraging common men to hunt to give them practice with guns while simul-taneously warding off wolves and Indians.[13] Despite the musket's shortcomings, hunting with firearms seemed destined to become a core ingredient of colonial identity, the act of Renaissance Europeans who sought to master savage nature and savage men.

From almost the outset of colonization, several colonies had required white males to carry guns or swords when they ventured afield in case of Indian at-tack. In Virginia and Georgia freemen were even required to bring guns to church.[14] The gun, however, became a cornerstone of colonial society not only because it buttressed European martial authority but also because it expressed the worldview of the Renaissance.

In the medieval period, according to Carolyn Merchant, nature had been per-ceived as a living, sacred thing, not to be defiled by mining, lumbering, industry, and technology. By the 1500s, however, nature was identified increasingly as inert, a repository of raw material for exploitation; Max Weber referred to this shift as "the disenchantment of the world." Nature, as Sir Francis Bacon suggested in his *New Atlantis,* far from being respected and worshiped, must be manipulated and controlled; its secrets must be divulged and made to serve the purposes of men. Nature would be man's servant, not the reverse.[15]

This logic entered the rhetoric of promotional literature, which portrayed hunters dominating and controlling a disenchanted or hostile nature with firearms. The gun was, after all, the first flower—if so feminine and natural a word serves for such a masculine and unnatural artifact—of Baconian technology. The gun had helped revolutionize European society, transforming kingdoms into nation-states capable of conquering and colonizing distant realms, and had come to symbolize European patriotism, power, and pride.

The idea of a state, or colony, composed of gun-toting hunters, however, was a radical idea for Europeans. Hunting in England had never been a democratic practice—at least not since the early Middle Ages—but instead had served the English elite as the training ground for martial skill. Throughout Europe, and particularly in England, only the elite were legally eligible to hunt, and until at least the fifteenth century, only the elite constituted a martial class. Although by the late seventeenth century, all English Protestants had gained the constitutional right to bear arms, the game laws of England continued to prohibit commoners from carrying arms in public or using them to hunt.[16]

By confining hunting to the elite, the game laws ensured that the gentry and aristocracy remained preeminent as martial castes, prepared to wage war, put down rebellions, and maintain social order (and, when none of these duties required attention, create havoc by poaching one another's deer). "Hunters by their continuall travaile, painfull labour, often watching, and enduring of hunger, of heate, and of cold," explained Sir Thomas Cockaine in his sixteenth-century treatise, "are much enabled above others to the service of their Prince and Countrey in the warres, having their bodies . . . in much better health, than other men have, and their minds also by this honest recreation the more fit and the better disposed to all other good exercises."[17]

As a school of martial prowess, however, hunting was becoming outmoded by the seventeenth century. Although Englishmen still hunted deer *par force*, that is, riding horseback behind packs of dogs and delivering coups de grace with lance, pike, or sword, the feudal era of chivalry had ended. The *mano-a-mano* combat of knights, with its code of horsemanship, swordsmanship, and individual prowess—all recapitulated in the act of hunting—was rendered useless by the movements of cavalry, bowmen, pikemen, and musketeers. Rather than dying out, however, hunting—including its newest variant, shooting—became more popular in seventeenth-century England as newcomers to the ranks of the nobility and gentry reenacted (and reinvented) the chivalrous codes of old. If "a man have not skill in the hawking and hunting languages now-a-days," comments a character in a Ben Jonson play of the early seventeenth century, "I'll not give a rush for him. They are more studied than the Greek or the Latin."[18] The same phenomenon would hold true in America centuries later.

"There is a saying among hunters," wrote the author of an Elizabethan sporting manual, "that he cannot be a gentleman which loveth not hawking and hunting, which I have heard old woodmen well allow as an approved sentence among them. The like saying is that he cannot be a gentleman which loveth not a dog."[19] English gentlemen continued to love dog, hawk, and hunt right into modernity. Having taken lessons from French authors, Englishmen also made themselves into arbiters of a byzantine code of sportsmanship.

Said to have been set down by Sir Tristram, one of King Arthur's knights, the protocols of genteel hunters were so arcane that only select initiates could master them. The correct cry in rabbit hunting, for instance, was "how, how, that, that," whereas in deer hunting it was "how, how, that's he, that's he."[20] That sounds simple enough, yet the pronoun "he" could apply to any of six different classes of male red deer.

In its first year, the male red deer was a calf; in the second year, a brocket; in the third, a spayd; in the fourth, a staggard; in the fifth, a stag; and in its sixth year, a hart. Harts were further broken down into the hart proper, the hart royall, an animal hunted by king or queen, and the hart royall proclaimed, an animal that had escaped the king or queen's pursuit and was granted freedom from persecution. Equally arcane terms defined points of distinction in antlers, hoof prints, and deer sign. Those who failed to observe these conventions could be publicly spanked with the flat of a hunting knife.[21]

Finally came the breaking, or butchering, of the deer. "What pleasure [elite hunters] take to see a buck or the like unlac'd," wrote Erasmus.

> Let ordinary fellows cut up an ox or a wether, 'twere a crime to have [a deer broken] by anything less than a gentleman! who with his hat off, on his bare knees, and a cuttoe for that purpose (for every sword or knife is not allowable), with a curious superstition and certain postures, lays open the several parts in their respective order; while they that hem him in admire it with silence, as some new religious ceremony, though perhaps they have seen it an hundred times before. And if any of 'em chance to get the least peace of 't, he presently thinks himself no small gentleman.[22]

In royal hunts dogs were included in this ritual; their status, like that of men, was affirmed (or denied) by the order in which they received their bit of meat.

Venison was also distributed to members of the local gentry who had not participated in the hunt, as well as to clergy, and finally—during festivals and feasts—
to that other inferior breed, the commoner.[23]

These protocols transformed what might have been perceived as a barbarous
act into an act of gentility. Like American Indians, who employed complex protocols to honor the spirits of slain animals, English hunters saw themselves as kin
to the animals they hunted. Insofar as Englishmen deemed deer noble, majestic,
graceful, and regal, deer became reflections of the nobility itself. One need not
be Freud to identify the antlers of the adult male deer as a phallic crown, a symbol of masculine authority, or to argue that hunting deer was associated with eros
and power. Indeed, the English word "venery" refers both to hunting game and
to gratifying sexual desire. Its root, the Latin *ven*, which is derived from Venus,
the Roman goddess of love, forms the stem of the words "venerable" and "ven-
erate."

As a tableau of authority, deference, hierarchy, martial skill, and noblesse
oblige, hunting made elite Englishmen into a "venerable" caste, superior to
tradesmen, yeomen, and tenant farmers. Hunting, moreover, served as an appropriate recreation (literally a re-creation of the self) for elite men because it gave
them respite from their enormous responsibilities. Traders and farmers, with
their simpler tasks, required no such remedy. For them, to hunt was to engage in
idleness.[24]

Judging by the vigilance of Crown, aristocracy, and gentry in protecting their
monopoly on hunting in the seventeenth and eighteenth centuries, one might
conclude that hunting defined the English elite as much as the elite defined hunting. Many Englishmen considered game laws to be critical to the existence of
their society. Repealing or weakening these laws, they argued, would bring lev-
eling, vagrancy, and riot.[25] The repeal of game laws, however, was precisely what
took place—at least figuratively—in the colonies.

As early as 1624 John Smith—despite his pleas to "gentlemen" hunters—commented that Jamestown planters "do so traine up their servants and youth in
shooting deere, and fowle, that the youths will kill them as well as their Masters."
North Carolina, too, encouraged common men to hunt. In 1700 John Lawson, sur-
veyor general for the Lords Proprietors, explained in his diary that

> here property hath a large scope, there being no strict laws to bind our privileges. A
> qu[e]st after game being as freely and peremptorily enjoyed by the meanest planter,
> as he that is the highest in dignity, or wealthiest in the province. Deer and other

game that are naturally wild, being not immured, or preserved within boundaries, to satisfy the appetite of the rich alone. A poor laborer that is made master of his gun, & c., hath as good claim to have continued coarses of delicacies crowded upon his table, as he that is master of a great purse.[26]

Game and fish in west New Jersey, meanwhile, were "free and common to any Person who can shoot or take them, without any lett, hindrance or Opposition whatsoever." William Penn—who, as a Quaker, condemned wealthy Englishmen whose retinues included huntsmen and falconers—likewise guaranteed Pennsylvania settlers the right to hunt and fish. Even New York's royal proprietors awarded the right of fishing and fowling to colonists, regardless of rank, although the term "hunting" was absent from the promise, perhaps because the proprietors intended to restrict deer hunting at some future time.[27]

Not every male colonist availed himself of such privileges. According to Terry Jordan and Matti Kaups, most immigrants (English, Scottish, Irish, Welsh, German, and French Huguenot), having been forbidden to hunt in their native lands, were slow to take up hunting in North America. Only Finnish immigrants of the Delaware Valley, contend Jordan and Kaups, became full-fledged hunters in the early years of colonization, having been recruited by New Sweden because they were "more conversant with, and understand better than any other nation, . . . hunting and fowling." Soon these Finns added Delaware Indian hunting technologies to their own, including the Algonquian terms "skunk," "raccoon," and "opossum."[28]

To determine who among the colonists hunted first, or who hunted most, however, is no easy task. Grady McWhiney argues that it was the blustering "crackers" of southern frontiers whose Celtic traditions (whether Scot, Scots-Irish, or Irish) made them eager hunters and herders. One suspects, however, that these ethnohistorical interpretations understate the ubiquity of hunting on American frontiers while overstating the legacy of particular groups of hunters. According to an antebellum historian of frontier settlement, the Scots-Irish, being "thoughtful and austere, industrious and conscientious, . . . found no pleasure in the license of the hunter's life," engaging in the hunt only when necessity demanded.[29]

Finns and some Celts may have led the way in hunting, but where game was abundant, others took advantage. In 1705 Robert Beverley, a well-to-do Virginia planter, reported in his *History and Present State of Virginia* that "the People there are very Skilful in the use of Fire-arms, being all their Lives accustom'd to shoot in the Woods." As early as 1691, indeed, William Blathwayt, auditor general of the

American colonies, had noted that "there is no Custom more generally to be observed among the Young Virginians than that they all Learn to keep and use a gun with a Marvelous dexterity as soon as ever they have strength enough to lift it to their heads." Neither Blathwayt nor Beverley provided a demographic portrait of these gun-toting Virginians. Were such men sons of important planters who had taken up sport hunting? Or were they men of the frontier who used guns to hunt for food and to deter bobcats and foxes from killing chickens?[30]

According to Michael Bellesiles, both Blathwayt and Beverley were propagating a stereotype of the armed colonist rather than reporting reality (Beverley in particular wished to prove that Virginians could defend themselves and needed no English troops, who, he believed, would create tyranny instead of safety). In his controversial study, Bellesiles asserts that guns were hard to come by in colonial America. Even Virginia, the most populous colony in eighteenth-century America, was home to just eighteen gunsmiths during its first 150 years of existence. Because the great majority of firearms had to be imported from Europe—and because guns were handmade and therefore expensive—a minority of colonists owned them, a fact bolstered by probate records. In a few counties, most adult white males seemed to have owned a gun at the time of their deaths, but Bellesiles claims that in most locales gun ownership was exceptional, and nowhere was it close to universal.[31]

Rare or not, guns had cachet as symbols of English authority in North America. But did hunting for sport have equal cachet? In a chapter titled "Of the Recreations, and Pastimes used in Virginia," Beverley testified that colonists had "Hunting, Fishing, and Fowling, with which they entertain themselves an hundred ways," yet none of these hundred ways involved the rituals of sport practiced by the English elite. Beverley described smoking hares out of holes or hollows, hunting "Vermine" (raccoons, opossums, and foxes) at night with small dogs, trapping wolves and turkeys, and using weirs for fishing. He also described tricks used to take deer, including the placement of sharp stakes, points up, inside fences surrounding pea fields. When deer jumped the fences to eat the peas, they were impaled.[32]

The meat obtained from such hunts often ended up not on the tables of hunters but on the open market. In a chapter titled "Of the Edibles, Potables, and Fewel in Virginia," Beverley wrote that "the Gentry pretend to have their Victuals drest, and serv'd up as Nicely, as at the best Tables in London." Rather than supplying their tables through hunting, however, gentlemen bought game from others. In season, remarked Beverley, "Wild-Fowl" were "the cheapest Victuals" available, whereas deer carcasses were "sold for eight, ten, or twelve Shillings a Head, according to scarcity."[33]

Because game was an important food source, as well as a source of profit, colonists chose the cheapest and most efficient ways to hunt rather than the most sporting. Settlers snared birds and trapped beavers; netted pigeons, rabbits, and fish; set fire to woods to drive game into the open; and engaged in communal surrounds, in which dozens of men, women, and children would circumscribe an enormous swathe of land and proceed toward its center, driving game before them. Once trapped in this human noose, the game was netted, clubbed, or shot, whichever was convenient. Still cleverer farmers of the early national era—and probably earlier—practiced yarding, in which fields were sown with wheat to attract deer. Once deer had entered these fields via gaps left open in fences, farmers closed the gaps and trapped them. Bucks were slaughtered, while does were left alive to recruit new victims.[34]

Colonists also hunted wolves, cougars, bobcats, foxes, and bears for bounties, an enterprise that brought a good income as long as the hunter—whether Indian or European—conserved some breeding stock. Equally profitable was the deerskin trade. In the 1730s and 1740s, South Carolinians exported as many as 100,000 deerskins a year, most of them purchased from Indians. These skins were used to manufacture gloves, breeches, and vellum for England's burgeoning book trade. Deerskins (and other furs) were also used as substitutes for specie in colonial trades, so much so that, by the Revolutionary era, the term "buck" had become synonymous with "dollar," which was what a good buckskin was worth. Doeskins were worth half a buck.[35]

Colonists killed game for food, for market, for bounties, and for an escape from the drudgery of farming. Few hunted to create or to renew a traditional social hierarchy; hence few adhered to English nomenclature or codes of sportsmanship. Colonists described deer as "in the blue," "in the red," or "in the green," terms that defined seasonal changes in the coloration, texture, and marketability of a deerskin, but the general term for the male deer was simply "buck," or "stag" on occasions calling for formality.[36]

If hunting and shooting in the New World were open to men of every occupation, rank, and station, however, what would become of the ethic of sportsmanship? More important, how would an American elite define itself? If hunters refused to obey the codes of genteel hunting, would they refuse to observe gentility itself? Moreover, if hunting and shooting were for every man, what was to stop every man from becoming a force and empire unto himself, a man who observed no authority but his own?

One solution to these vexing questions appeared in plans for the Margravate of Azilia, an eighteenth-century colony proposed—though never established—

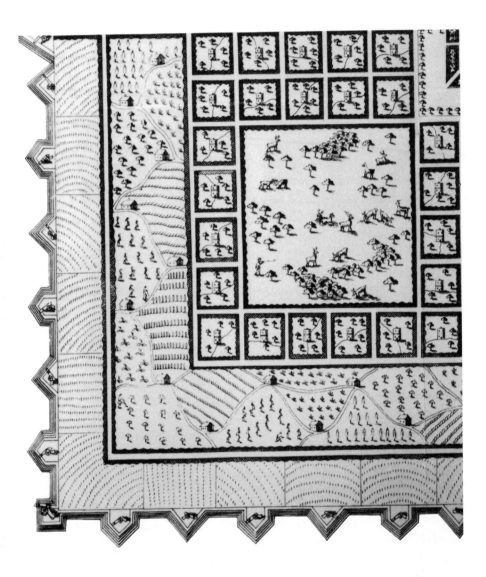

In this detail from a plan for the Margravate of Azilia, a hunter fires on a stag in a deer park. The walls of the Margravate were intended to protect not only colonists but also feudal tradition by confining hunting privileges to an elite. From Sir Robert Mountgomry, *A Discourse Concerning the Design'd Establishment of a New Colony to the South of Carolina, in the Most Delightful Country of the Universe,* in *Tracts and Other Papers relating principally to the Origin, Settlement, and Progress of the Colonies in North America . . .,* comp. Peter Force, vol. 1 (Washington, D.C., 1836; reprint, Gloucester, Mass., 1963), document no. 1, 8. Photograph by Terry Firman Jr.

for an area south of Carolina. A drawing of the settlement depicts an enormous, walled-in enclave with an administrative building at the center and four hunting parks arranged symmetrically around it. In one park a gentleman fires at a deer, while beyond him lie orchards, houses, cultivated fields, and walls bedecked with cannons.[37] The Margravate would stand as a feudal, fortified city, self-sufficient and easily defensible against American Indian, Spanish, or French attack.

It may seem odd that hunting was to occur within the walls when "Deer, and other Game," wrote the author of a pamphlet accompanying the map, "feed in Droves" in nearby forests burned free of undergrowth by American Indians.[38] If we assume that the deer parks within the walls were intended for the pleasure of a colonial elite, however, they reflected a common wish. Many English schemers dreamed not so much of egalitarian settlements as of feudal Englands in miniature, relics of a society that accorded rank in traditional ways.

To reconstitute English privilege, the occasional Chesapeake planter enclosed a private deer park in the manner of the English gentry. The legislatures of Virginia and Pennsylvania also exempted hunters who met property qualifications—six slaves in Virginia, fifty acres of land in Pennsylvania—from trespass restrictions during the chase.[39] This sort of legislation mirrored English custom that permitted propertied men to hunt, while discriminating against propertyless whites who roamed the frontier like savages, living off the land. Yet ownership of six slaves or fifty acres hardly made one a gentleman by English standards. Almost any male settler, apart from slaves and indentured servants, could acquire fifty acres by purchase or headright.

In most colonies all hunters—rich and poor—gained access to unfenced lands under the presumption that property owners invited hunters by neglecting to fence them out.[40] Such new freedoms from trespass were based on *ferae naturae*, the legal doctrine that made wild animals the property of those who took them in the chase, not the property of those on whose land they were taken. After all, landowners could hardly own deer that happened to stray onto their property.

In England this doctrine let wealthy men claim game they had killed on the lands of poorer neighbors yet seldom benefited common men, who were forbidden to carry arms on the game-rich lands of the wealthy.[41] For Americans, however, *ferae naturae* meant that poor men could hunt wherever they wished, as long as the land had not been enclosed. America was to be a place where every man could hunt.

Given the abundance of game, the lack of legal restraints on hunters, and the colonists' familiarity with, and celebration of, guns, hunting figured to become an American rite of passage from the moment of colonization. The American man—not just the gentleman but also the ordinary man—would be a great hunter, and America would be a hunter's paradise. Hunting was poised to become a discourse of mastery over the land and its native inhabitants, both human and faunal. What is surprising about hunting in the colonial era, however, is how seldom it figured as a badge of American identity, despite how celebrated it would later become.

2

Hunting as a Religious Problem

 Near Pomfret, Connecticut, in 1742, lived a wolf. She was sole survivor of her kind in the Pomfret area and perhaps the last wolf in southern New England. She in turn was pursued by the last of another kind—American Indian bounty hunters—who destroyed predators to make way for New Englanders of Puritan stock.[1]

The Pomfret wolf, however, refused to surrender. While "grave and reverend seigniors" met in Pomfret to establish a library for "propagating Christian and useful knowledge," the Pomfret wolf conducted her own sort of business. In a single night, the she-wolf of Pomfret killed seventy of Israel Putnam's sheep and goats, not counting "many lambs and kids wounded." Perhaps these numbers were inflated in the telling (though wolves, according to Barry Lopez, do at times kill more than necessary), yet to residents of Pomfret "there was not a farm or door-yard safe from [the wolf's] incursions. Little children were scared by her out of sleep and senses; boys and girls feared to go to school or drive the cows home, and lonely women at night trembled for absent husbands and children."[2]

Each spring the wolf roamed westward to mate, returning to Pomfret to bear her litter. In a matter of months, the pups would fall victim to human persecutors, but the old she-wolf always escaped.[3] The Pomfret wolf was bigger than life, a demon of medieval legend that lurked at the peripheries (and sometimes at the center) of colonial consciousness.

New England farmers were not easily bested, however, and resolved to hunt the wolf by turns. After a light snow, the men were able to track the wolf through the "savage fastness" outside Pomfret, an area "never before penetrated by a white man" (though only three miles from Putnam's home). Up an "icy crag" came at last the hunters, now preceded by a motley group of boys and dogs from town. Among "gnarled stumps and fallen tree-trunks," one of the boys discerned a small opening in the granite boulders.[4]

The wolf's cave had been found, but how to kill her? Fires of straw and brimstone were set at the mouth of the cave with which to smoke out the wolf, to no avail. Dogs were sent in to the cave but came back "cowed and wounded." Finally, Israel Putnam asked his black servant to enter, but the man declined.[5]

"Ashamed to have a coward in his family," Putnam—who in later decades would become one of the most storied generals of the American Revolution—removed his coat and waistcoat and fixed a rope to his body. Then, taking in hand a torch, he crawled into the "solitary mansion of horror" where "none but monsters of the desert" had gone before. Deep within, he spied the torch's reflection in the wolf's eyes. Putnam then signaled the men outside to hoist him out. Moments later he reentered the cave with his gun and killed the wolf with a single shot.[6]

Though the story of Putnam and the wolf seems to have been popular among Connecticut raconteurs for decades after the hunt, it gained national attention only after the Revolution. "Had Putnam remained obscure," noted a New England historian of the nineteenth century, "his wolf might have been long forgotten." After Putnam became a Revolutionary general, however, the story of his wolf hunt exploded into popular consciousness. "Every schoolboy," wrote a New York historian of the mid-nineteenth century, "has heard the story of Israel Putnam and the wolf."[7]

In many ways the Putnam tale typifies an American genre. The names have changed, but the plot has echoed through the centuries. The hero might be Israel Putnam, Daniel Boone, or Theodore Roosevelt, while the villain might be wolf, cougar, or bear. The drama of hunter versus predator (or hunter versus American Indian) has always represented the righteousness of the American cause. Good must triumph over evil, civilization over savagery, and courage over cowardice (it apparently occurred to no one that Putnam had been less than courageous in urging his servant to enter the cave first).

At closer glance, however, one finds not a timeless tale of hunting but a fable peculiar to colonial New England. Whereas later hunters—whether Boone, Crockett, or Roosevelt—professed to love wilderness, Putnam and his fellow hunters exulted in its destruction. The imagery of the tale—"savage fastness," "icy crag," "gnarled stumps and fallen tree-trunks," "mansion of horror," "monsters of the desert"—bespoke not the nineteenth-century trope of wilderness bliss but the Puritan trope of evil nature. Putnam's purpose was to destroy the vestige of savagery and evil—the wolf—to make way for godly persons and agrarian civilization.[8]

What is curious about the Putnam tale, finally, is its uniqueness. Though a few obscure hunting tales appear in nineteenth-century histories of Connecticut and New Hampshire, such tales are remarkable for their rarity in the lore of colonial New England.[9] Where were the wilderness-loving Daniel Boones of Massachusetts Bay? Where were the "half-horse, half-alligator" Davy Crocketts of Rhode Island or Connecticut?[10] And where were New England's sport hunters, men who hunted stags and foxes for pleasure? How was it that New England could be so full of game at the outset of colonization and yet produce so few tales of hunters and hunting?

Perhaps the answers to these questions lie in the soul-searching of John Winthrop, one of the first governors of Massachusetts Bay Colony and a hero to generations of Americans. In 1610 Winthrop, at age twenty-two, confided in his journal that "by muche examination" hunting "could not stande with a good conscience in my selfe." Winthrop enumerated eight reasons and allotted several hundred words to describe how he had come to such a resolution. First, hunting was "prohibited by the lawe of the land" and "spoiles more of the creatures than it getts." Winthrop added that hunting "procures offense unto manye," "wastes great store of tyme," "toyles a mans bodye over-much," "endangers a mans life," "brings no profite all things considered," and "hazards more of a mans estate by the penaltye of it, then a man would willingly parte with." Finally, hunting "brings a man of worth and godlines into some contempt."[11]

Interestingly, Winthrop spoke as a poacher. When he was the tender age of twenty-two, his income was apparently still insufficient to meet the property qualification for hunting. However, no such concern could have kept Winthrop—who, as scion of a well-to-do landowning family, attended Cambridge University and became a member of the Inner Temple in 1628—from hunting in later years. More interesting is the fact that Winthrop, in renouncing hunting, seemed to renounce the codes of gentility that defined the English landed elite.

Immediately apparent in Winthrop's dialogue with himself is the logic of cost and benefit. Hunting wastes time, money, and effort and brings no economic or moral gain. This is the logic of the bourgeoisie, not of the landed gentry whose lives revolved around fetes and festivals, leisure, and rituals of authority like hunting. By contrast, Winthrop became one of Max Weber's model Protestants, a man who defined his life around the moral axis of work to prove himself saved.[12] In short, Winthrop became a Puritan, a member of a radical offshoot of the Anglican church known for its distinction between the regenerate (sober, industrious, upright members of the community who could hope for salvation) and the unregenerate (lovers of luxury and indolence, some of whom might conform outwardly to the dictates of Christianity but were in all probability destined for hell).

Puritans led the first campaign against blood sports in the seventeenth century. They condemned not only sport hunting but also ratting, cockfighting, bear-baiting, and bullbaiting, as well as gambling and horse racing. Such pastimes were popular among aristocrats, gentry, rural commoners, artisans, and tradesmen, who mingled in tipsy conviviality at their local pub to cheer their favorite cocks and bulldogs.[13]

Puritans rejected blood sports—along with drinking, gaming, and pagan festivals and saints' days—because they were unproductive and un-Christian; God expected men to devote themselves to church, family, and calling, not pagan debauchery. Puritans "hated bear-baiting," wrote Lord Thomas Macaulay, "not because it gave pain to the bear, but because it gave pleasure to the spectators."[14] Though others denounced hunting for its cruelty, the fact that blood sports were forms of ritual torture was beside the point for most Puritans.

What Puritans did oppose was the traditional worldview of the English gentry. In the old scheme of things, the country squire and his tenants existed in a sort of organic equilibrium. Their lives followed the yearly rounds of planting and harvest, punctuated by cyclical fairs, festivals, and ritualistic hunts; life varied little from year to year. Rather than investing capital in new industries, squires invested profits from rents paid by tenants in ritual artifacts of high status: clothing, carriages, and estates, as well as horses, dogs, and arms for hunting. For their part, tenants could expect secure employment in farming or in domestic service and indulgence, if not philanthropy, when they became old and feeble.

The Elizabethan and Stuart worlds, however, were beset by rising population, unemployment, enclosure, and the birth of factories, all of which undermined the traditional lifestyle of squire and tenant. While some of those dispossessed (both gentry and commoner) by these revolutionary changes protested by poaching in the woods and chases of wealthier neighbors, others, like Winthrop, adopted the moral and personal standards of Puritanism. They became, to put a modern spin on it, productive individuals, men who repudiated diversions from work and worship because only work and worship could insulate one from social instability. Among Puritans, wrote Macaulay disapprovingly, "it was a sin to hang garlands on a Maypole, to drink a friend's health, to fly a hawk, to hunt a stag, to play at chess, to wear lovelocks, to put starch into a ruff, to touch the virginals, to read the *Fairy Queen*."[15] To be fair to the Puritans, they did not reject all entertainments, only those they regarded as excess.

Hunting was not foremost on the Puritan list of reprehensible acts, but it brought "a man of worth and godlines into some contempt," as Winthrop reminded himself. Especially offensive to Puritans was the hunting parson, the Anglican divine who rode with the gentry in deer hunts rather than attending to his duties to God. Hunting clerics, in fact, had come in for reproach since the Middle Ages. Hunter-monarchs also became targets for Puritan rebuke. James I, despite his hatred for them, probably did much to popularize his Puritan detractors by hunting obsessively, drinking heavily (especially during hunts), and showing unabated contempt for commoners. During the English Civil War of the 1640s—the war against the Stuart kings—the Puritans, once they controlled Parliament, managed to abolish sport hunting for a time by opening royal forests to common men who presumably hunted for subsistence rather than pleasure.[16]

Forged in the crucible of religious reaction, New England Puritans never became the great hunters prophesied by promotional tracts. The traveler and naturalist John Josselyn, who—true to his status as an English gentleman and an Anglican—took great interest in hunting, lamented in his 1674 narrative of travels in New England that despite "innumerable" bucks, stags, and "raindear," there were "but few slain by the *English*." Thomas Dudley, John Winthrop's successor as governor of the Massachusetts Bay Colony, likewise reported to Lady Bridget, Countess of Lincoln, in 1631 that "fowl and venison . . . are danties here as well as in England." Despite New England's "good stor" of wildfowl, one settler complained that "it is hardur to get a shoot then it is in ould eingland."[17]

The Pilgrims of Plymouth shot a weeks' supply of turkeys for the first Thanksgiving on December 11, 1621, yet after this signal success, the Pilgrims, like their Puritan brethren, seem to have been lackluster hunters. Combing through Plymouth trash heaps, archaeologists have turned up only small quantities of game animal bones and no turkey bones, although wild ducks appear in substantial numbers. The archaeologists also unearthed more fowling pieces than muskets, indicating that Pilgrims who did hunt preferred sitting ducks to nimble deer.[18]

Part of the problem was that so few colonists had experience as hunters. The game laws of 1603 and 1605—precisely when Puritanism became a force in England—had raised the steep property restrictions on hunting, excluding lesser gentry and others whose income did not come from land. In 1671 the qualification for hunting was raised still higher to an annual income of over 100 pounds from land or over 150 pounds from leasehold or copyhold, a figure that would not change for 160 years. Less than 1 percent of the English population could hunt legally during the seventeenth century.[19]

With such stringent laws in place, few Puritans—apart from the occasional poacher—had hunted before arriving in the New World. This inexperience, along with a scarcity of weapons, apparently contributed to chronic food shortages among early colonists. "Indescret men," lamented Phineas Pratt after joining the Plymouth Colony in the 1620s, "hoping to incoridg thayr friends to Come to ym, writ Letters Conserning ye great plenty of Fish fowle and deare, not considering yt ye wild savages weare many times hungrye, yt have a better scill to catch such things then Einglish men have."[20]

Freed from the game laws and the jealous scrutiny of the elite in their New World Canaan, Puritans could have become mighty hunters. Instead, the New World produced a dilemma. Without the corrupt gentry against whom to compare themselves, how would Puritans maintain their beliefs and social order? How could their society function without a demonized other?

Puritans resolved this problem by adopting Indians as their nemesis. They believed that Indians, like English aristocrats, were gamblers, fornicators, and ardent hunters, men who repudiated steady work habits and godliness. These traits were precisely the ones that Puritans sought to purge from themselves, whether in New World or Old.[21]

Promotional tracts might wax eloquent about a New World hunting paradise, yet Puritans had no intention of subsisting primarily on wild game. Colonists instead transformed themselves into exemplars of agrarian discipline. Puritans would do well, explained cleric John White, to recall that in Biblical times "men, being newly entered into their possessions, and entertained into a naked soile, and enforced thereby to labour, frugality, simplicity, and justice, had neither leisure, nor occasion, to decline into idlenesse, riot, wantonesse, fraud, and violence."[22]

If White had not conjured up the frontier thesis three centuries before Frederick Jackson Turner, he at least prefigured the doctrines of Thomas Jefferson and the Physiocrats. "Husbanding of unmanured grounds," White argued, "and shifting into empty Lands, enforceth men to frugalitie, and quickneth invention." The "setling of new States," he added, "requireth justice and affection to the common good."[23] The colonial enterprise was to be an exercise in virtue, piety, and discipline, all of which bloomed from agriculture. Some Puritans hunted, yet hunting figured as a marginal enterprise, not a touchstone of colonial identity.

Through clearing and plowing, colonists believed they took rightful possession of the land. Prospective settlers might wonder, wrote Pilgrim divine Robert Cushman, whether they had a right to settle in the land of the heathen, but America, he reasoned, was "a vast and empty chaos," whose native peoples "do but run over the grass, as do also the foxes and wild beasts," and who lacked art, science, and the capacity to use the land for anything other than hunting. Just as "the ancient patriarchs" of the Old Testament had moved from crowded areas to those less peopled, argued Cushman, "so is it lawful now to take a land which none useth."[24]

So emerged the doctrine of *vacuum domicilium* (vacant abode), the part-Biblical, part-Enlightenment doctrine that uncultivated lands become the property of those who cultivate them.[25] God had commanded humans in Genesis to subdue the earth and make it fruitful—and to obtain their bread "by the sweat of their brow"—not to live like savages from wild game. The farmer became the godly citizen because he obeyed this injunction; he claimed the land and made it fruitful by the sweat of his brow.

Such logic was hardly airtight. As Roger Williams argued, under the doctrine of *vacuum domicilium,* Puritans might claim the hunting parks of the English elite (which was precisely what commoners did during the English Civil War). Williams was not arguing that Puritans should lay claim to English hunting parks; he wished to show that Indian hunters owned their land just as the king owned his royal forests because both the king and the Indians improved their lands to produce greater quantities of game. The Massachusetts General Court recognized a variant of this doctrine when it awarded exclusive hunting privileges to Europeans who had improved ponds or islands by placing decoys and hunting nets on them.[26]

Puritans, however, were too closely wedded to their farms—and to the ideal of the farmer—to accept Williams's proposals. Though in practice colonists gained lands through conquest and treaty (albeit sometimes on the shady side), they justified possession under the doctrine of *vacuum domicilium*. Williams, for "his violent and tumultuous carriage against the patent," was banished to Rhode Island.[27]

The idea that wilderness was inhabited by godless hunters who had no rightful claim to the land worked in tandem with older objections to the English elite to prevent colonists from becoming a hunting people. Indeed, Puritans identified the wilderness itself as a demonized other, the reverse image of the civilization they cherished. Puritans did not always and everywhere fear wilderness, but—in the early decades of settlement—they imposed reproach and stiff penalties on settlers who ventured too far into the churchless woods.[28]

Because the wilderness represented a place where humans were beset with thorns and briars and vicious beasts, it reminded Puritans of Adam's fall and hence of their own depravity. Adam's sin had caused God to create wilderness to chasten his erring children, and for Puritans Adam—at least Adam after the fall—symbolized man in a state of nature, unreconstructed by community and church. In the eyes of Puritans, only by renouncing one's natural self—by renouncing pride, vanity, and licentiousness—could one do the work of God, and only by living in settled communities and attending church could one renounce the self. There would be no wilderness-loving, "half-horse, half-alligator" hunter-heroes among Puritans.

New Englanders, however, did not ignore faunal resources. Even as John Josselyn regretted that so few deer were slain by the English, he reported dozens of medicinal remedies derived from New England fauna. "The Fangs of a *Wolf* hung about childrens necks," he wrote, "keep them from frightning, and are very good to rub their gums with when they are breeding of teeth." Equally beneficial was "the grease of a *Beaver,*" which was "good for the Nerves, Convulsions, Epilepsies, Apoplexies, & c."[29] It is hard to say how often such remedies were employed, but certainly New Englanders—influenced by their own folk tradition and that of Algonquian peoples—were aware of the medicinal potential of wild animals.

New Englanders were also aware of the comestible potential of wild animals, so much so that turkeys had become rare by the 1670s. Moose had disappeared from parts of eastern Canada as early as the mid-seventeenth century and were largely extinct in Maine by the late eighteenth century, and white-tailed deer had become so scarce that in 1718 Massachusetts forbade deer hunting for three years. Rhode Island and Connecticut had likewise banned deer hunting out of season as early as the seventeenth century.[30]

These early game laws were primarily intended to restrict Indian hunters who traded meat and skins with the English. "For us to seek for deer it doth not boot [profit]," explained Plymouth governor William Bradford, because Indians could kill game more efficiently than colonists could. Despite taking the occasional duck or deer, Puritans retained their civility by slaughtering domestic animals—pigs, cows, sheep, goats, and chickens—rather than wild game. The colonists also retained civility by grafting familiar names, dwellings, and churches onto their new homeland and by transforming the wilderness into something recognizably English and pastoral.[31] By literally making their colony into a new England—destroying indigenous ecosystems and the game they supported—Puritans gained a foothold in North America.

Noting the scarcity of game in New England, Timothy Dwight, president of Yale College, remarked in the early nineteenth century that "hunting with us . . . exists chiefly in the tales of other times."[32] What Dwight might have said was that hunting had always existed "chiefly in the tales of other times" for New Englanders. Game populations were depleted by the time Dwight wrote, but New Englanders had never seen themselves as a hunting people. Far from being wilderness or genteel hunters, they were a people of the Bible, the plow, and the doctrines of moderation and industry.

What, then, of Israel Putnam? He was indeed a hunter-hero insofar as he slew the Pomfret wolf to make way for civilization, yet Putnam was far from being a Daniel Boone who ventured alone into the wilderness to live like an Indian. Nor did he resemble sportsmen of old England, who rode against the wily fox or tested their skill against the noble hart. Putnam, finally, was more a hero of the American Revolution than of colonial New England. His confrontation with the wolf, though known to members of the Pomfret community before the Revolution, seems to have attained legendary status only after biographers seized upon it as an omen of the great one's rise to fame.[33]

Unlike the heroes of nineteenth-century Americans, the heroes of the Puritans were—Putnam excepted—farmers, ministers, martyrs, and civil authorities, not hunters. Moreover, although we think of Puritans as religious radicals, their emphases on piety, industry, calling, temperance, and farming were common to Protestant peoples. "Let my children be Husbandmen, and housewives," inveighed Quaker William Penn upon founding his New World colony; "'tis industrious, healthy, honest, a good example like Abraham, and the holy Antients, that please God, and have obtained a good report." Even in the first decade of the nineteenth century, John James Audubon recalled that his father's Quaker agent in Philadelphia "could not bear me to carry a gun, or fishing-rod, and, indeed, condemned most of my amusements."[34]

In the eighteenth century, these Dissenters—Quakers, Baptists, Presbyterians, Methodists, Congregationalists, Mennonites, Moravians, Pietists—represented a majority of the white population of colonial America.[35] Thus the Puritan temperament, with its emphasis on innate depravity and renunciation of self, was but one variant of the Protestant—indeed, the colonial American—temperament.

It is hard to say to what degree the Protestant temperament militated against hunting. What is clear is that although many colonists took advantage of wild game, others—like eighteenth-century Moravian farmers on the Virginia frontier—sought to lift themselves above "the dregs of human society who spend their time in murdering wild beasts."[36] Thousands of Americans hunted, but not all aspired to be hunters.

3

Hunting as a Social Problem

 Venturing into the Virginia backwoods with a survey party in the 1720s, William Byrd of Westover—later a noted philanderer, friend of London's literati, and colonial gentleman—observed that his party's chaplain, when offered bear meat, "would growl like a wildcat over a squirrel." Eating bear meat, continued Byrd, "inclines the eater . . . strongly to the flesh, insomuch that whoever makes a supper of it will certainly dream of a woman or the devil, or both." It was bear meat that Byrd regarded as the secret of American Indian fertility, and he was not surprised when the married men in his party, and most of the bachelors, became fathers nine months after their return to civilization. The chaplain, however, despite his fondness for bear meat, "made a shift to cast out that importunate kind of devil by dint of fasting and prayer" and was exempted from scandal.[1]

Byrd's portrayal of his party's descent into savagery, though satirical, belied deeply held attitudes about the hunting life. Byrd believed, as did his Puritan counterparts in New England, that dependence on wild game made one slothful, even barbaric. "No Tartar ever loved horseflesh or Hottentot guts and garbage better than woodsmen do bear," avowed Byrd, adding pointedly that "the greater our plenty" of wild game, the "later we were" in decamping. Byrd wrote contemptuously of the only genuine woodsman encountered by his party, one "Epaphroditus Bainton," who "is said to make great havoc among the deer and other inhabitants of the forest not much wilder than himself."[2] Less than a century later, men like Bainton would become American heroes. In Byrd's estimation, however, Bainton's hunting made him an object of scorn.

Like Byrd, the French expatriot J. Hector St. John de Crèvecoeur, in his *Letters from an American Farmer* (published in 1782 but written mostly before the American Revolution), cast aside his high regard for Pennsylvania settlers to warn that the chase had made some of them "ferocious, gloomy, and unsocial." The settlers' diet of "wild meat," explained Crèvecoeur, "tends to alter their temper," producing a "lawless profligacy" in comparison with which Indians appeared respectable.[3]

For Byrd and Crèvecoeur, eating game made men not only barbaric but also assertive, independent, and antisocial—traits identified by most colonists as evils. To middling and elite colonists, frontier hunters resembled the wild men of medieval and early modern European folklore who resided alone in the woods; subsisted on raw meat, wild berries, and nuts; wore animal skins; and wielded clubs.

The wild man, like the backwoods hunter of the colonial imagination, was a man free of restraint. He was physically powerful, reckless, instinctual, erotic, and devoid of religious sensibility. Like the backwoods hunter, he was the foil of the chivalrous knight (or colonial gentleman) who was equally powerful but also Christian, civilized, and self-controlled.[4] To be civilized meant to bridle one's masculine passions, to subordinate one's will to that of the community, and to subsist from the civilized staples of grain, dairy products, and domesticated animals.

When the so-called manly qualities of political, social, and psychological autonomy became more widely valued in America, so did hunting. Throughout the eighteenth and early nineteenth centuries, however, frontier hunters were often viewed—as Byrd and Crèvecoeur illustrate—as little better than bandits who preyed on more established colonists who owned slaves and livestock and who grew crops. In part this attitude reflected a religious prejudice against backwoods hunters and wilderness generally, but it also reflected a division between respectable settlers and poor frontiersmen. Whereas in Europe class formed around the fault line between noble and peasant, or between bourgeois and worker, in America class formed around the fault line between propertied men in settled (and newly settled) regions and their poorer cousins on the frontier. Thus to pin on a man "the Epithet of Buckskins," recalled Reverend Devereux Jarratt of his eighteenth-century Virginia childhood, was "as great a Reproach as in England, to call a Man Oaf, or Clown, or Lubberkin."[5]

Throughout the colonial and early national era, sober, religious, propertied men considered it their duty to ameliorate the evils of backwoods society and to transform poor hunters into respectable farmers. Consider the South Carolina Regulators, a 1760s vigilante group composed of farmers and traders of the backcountry who feared the depredations of hunters. Although the Regulators sought equitable political representation in the South Carolina Assembly, their chief concern was to put down a vigorous, loosely organized frontier banditti.

The speaker of the South Carolina Assembly characterized these bandits in

1750 as "many hundred men whom we know little of and are little the better, for they kill deer and live like Indians." In 1769 Lt. Gov. William Bull, who sympathized with the Regulators, described the bandits as "back inhabitants who chuse to live rather by the wandering indolence of hunting than the more honest and domestic employment of planting." These wandering men were in some cases characterized as "Mulattoes" but were also said to include runaway slaves, Indians, and poor whites. They probably also included runaway indentured servants, who—invariably wearing homespun hunting shirts—sometimes absconded with their masters' guns.[6] On the frontier, possessing a gun could mean steady meals and income from hunting.

Charles Woodmason, an Anglican who preached to Carolina's frontier settlers in the 1760s, believed that the frontier had created a class of English savages who

> range the Country, with their Horse and Gun, without Home or Habitation. . . . For, they having no Sort of Education, naturally follow Hunting—Shooting—Racing—Drinking—Gaming, and ev'ry Species of Wickedness. Their Lives are only one continual Scene of Depravity of Manners, and Reproach to the Country; being more abandoned to Sensuality, and more Rude in Manners, than the Poor Savages around us.[7]

To combat these hunters, South Carolina broadened its vagrancy statute to include as an offense "possession of land but not cultivation," which was aimed specifically at those who subsisted through hunting rather than farming. The assembly also promulgated strict hunting laws in 1769, establishing deer seasons and forbidding night hunting (bandits were notorious for shooting settlers' cattle, pigs, and horses and then using darkness to elude detection). Meanwhile the Regulators meted out extralegal punishments to stop the depredations. Other colonists believed with Aedanus Burke that only free schools in the interior would spread "knowledge and learning thro' the land" and cause "the Youth in our Back Country" to "become valuable useful men, instead of being . . . brought up deer-hunters and horse thieves."[8]

In North Carolina, too, anxiety caused by "idle and disorderly Persons" who subsisted by hunting rather than "by Industry or honest Calling" gave rise to restrictions on hunting privileges as early as 1745. To stop the "many abuses committed by White Persons, under the pretense of hunting," the colony required hunters to certify that they had planted at least five thousand corn hills. In 1784 North Carolina, like its southern neighbor, also barred deer hunting at night.[9]

From Canada to Georgia, the frontiers of colonial and early national America were plagued periodically by "barbaric" and "indolent" white hunters. In New

Brunswick fellow settlers said that these hunters were "not a whit better than the real Indians"; in Pennsylvania (as far east as Bucks County) appeared "banditti" in hunting shirts and bearskin overcoats; in Georgia there were "*Crackers*, [men] who have no settled habitation, and live by hunting and plundering the industrious Settlers."[10]

What to do about the infestation? Without economic development, reasoned the New York City *Gazette* in 1771, western territories would be plagued by men who "remain still in their first State of Nature, and subsist by Hunting alone." If canals and roads were not established soon, western territories would forever remain "of all others the most thinly peopled."[11]

Here was a grave social problem, a problem akin to the anxiety over crime and poverty in the late twentieth century. These "roaming" and "rambling" men of the frontier—men who resembled nothing so much as wild beasts, men who were forever squatting on lands owned by "law-abiding" speculators—might join Indians in rebellions against constituted authority. In an alternate scenario, their incursions into Indian lands might force the colonies, or later the United States, to wage costly wars to protect errant settlers.[12]

Behind the fear of frontier hunters stood monumental dilemmas. Europeans had always justified the appropriation of American soil via the logic of *vacuum domicilium*. Civilized men—white men—were farmers, whereas uncivilized men—red men—were hunters. But what if these racial and moral distinctions broke down? What if a significant class of white settlers exchanged plows for guns? What if white settlers turned their backs on agrarian civilization? What if these white hunters refused to obey the authority of their betters?

Finally, if white men, not just red men, were hunters, on what basis could racial distinctions be made? Was it unjust for white farmers to take land from white hunters? If so, then surely it was unjust for white farmers to take land from red hunters. Racial distinctions, in that case, would dissolve, and the colonial edifice would crumble.

The greatest threat posed by white hunters of the frontier was that they seemed to constitute a counterculture whose ideals and aspirations inverted those held by respectable men; hunters' very existence called into question the justice of colonization. Hence established colonists often regarded hunting much as Americans of the 1950s regarded communism: as a contagion that threatened civilization.

Whether these dilemmas were conscious or unconscious, middling and elite colonists solved them by repudiating hunting as a way of life. Government, too, offered solutions, first with the British Proclamation Line of 1763, which restricted entry by whites into Indian lands west of the Appalachian Mountains, and later with a series of land ordinances passed by the U.S. Congress.

Though designed to allow for the survey and sale of frontier lands to repay war debts, the Land Ordinance of 1785—one of the most significant pieces of legislation passed under the Articles of Confederation—was intended to restructure frontier society. This restructuring would be accomplished indirectly, but the result would be the same: the survey and sale of lands provided for in the ordinance would be followed by growing populations of farmers, roads, and commerce with eastern markets. Order would replace chaos; industry would replace indolence; commerce would replace isolation. Once western lands were linked to eastern markets, hunters would put down their guns and pick up their plows.[13]

In framing this legislation (one wants to call it social engineering), Americans drew on the most brilliant luminaries of the age. The eighteenth-century was a pre-Marxian universe, yet with the clash of New and Old Worlds, the rise of the European bourgeoisie, and the fluidity of colonial and early national American society, savants were forced to devote a great deal of thought to the problem of social development and class. In doing so, they characterized frontier societies, both Indian and white, as representative of all that civilization was not.

While the basis for such thought surfaced in the works of Thomas Hobbes and John Locke in the seventeenth century, this philosophy attained its fullest expression in the eighteenth-century works of the four-stages theorists. Appearing in the 1750s in the writings of Adam Smith in Scotland and Anne-Robert-Jacques Turgot, Baron de l'Aulne, in France, four-stages theory posited the existence of four developmental stages of society corresponding to modes of subsistence: hunting, pasturage, agriculture, and commerce.[14]

Four-stages theory took many shapes over the next several decades, but each shape shared an essential logic. In the first and most ancient stage, men lived solely from the chase and from the fruits of the wilderness. Because these hunters had no need for, and hence no concept of, property (beyond their immediate possessions), they had no need for or concept of government, whose purpose was to protect property. In this "state of nature," men secured their rights, as Hobbes had claimed, by "their own strength."[15]

As did his philosophical progeny of the eighteenth century, Hobbes explained that in a state of nature there could be no industry "because the fruit thereof is uncertain." Consequently, there could be

> no Culture of the Earth, no Navigation, nor use of the commodities that may be imported by Sea; no commodious Building; no Instruments of moving, and removing

such things as require much force; no Knowledge of the face of the Earth; no account of Time; no Arts; no Letters; no Society; and which is worst of all, continuall feare, and danger of violent death.

Under these conditions, man was an "arrant wolf" whose life was "solitary, poore, nasty, brutish, and short."[16]

In Hobbes's view this state of nature gave way to civilization and government once men, tiring of brutality, consented to the rule of king or lord. In the view of later four-stages theorists, hunting gave way to a more advanced stage because it provided a meager and uncertain existence. Hence men learned to domesticate the beasts of the chase, transforming themselves into pastoralists.

In this second pastoral stage, private property—herds, pastures, water—assumed greater import, as did the institution that protected property, government. However, only in the third stage—the agricultural stage—did men fully value private property and the necessity of government in protecting it. In the third stage the advancements of modern society also became possible. Literature, music, drama, navigation, architecture, science, manufacturing—the benefices spoken of by Hobbes—were byproducts of an agricultural economy. Finally, after the firm establishment of agriculture and the arts came the fourth and final stage of social development, the commercial stage. Agriculture and commerce were conceived of as synergistic, acting like blades of a propeller to pull society upward.[17]

When commerce took precedence over agriculture, however, the result was thought to be luxury and dissipation for a wealthy few, impoverishment and degradation for the many, and ultimately tyranny for all. For many four-stages theorists, whether American, French, or British, the third stage, or a mixture of the third and fourth stages, was ideal; farming formed the true basis for prosperity and virtue. Commerce and manufactures might be signs of prosperity, but underlying these enterprises was agriculture, that "most ancient and noble of employments," in the words of the French political economist François Quesnay.[18]

Adding his voice to the four-stages chorus was Emmerich de Vattel, a Swiss philosopher who published in 1758 a treatise on international law, *Le Droit des gens* (The law of nations). In that work Vattel—echoing propositions that had been put forth by Protestants for more than a century—affirmed that cultivating peoples had every right to lay claim to the fallow lands of hunting peoples (ignoring the fact that most Indians were farmers). Though Vattel took aim at the land tenure of Indians, his arrow hit white hunters too. Widely read in Europe and America, Vattel's treatise gave Enlightenment sanction to the old trope of *vacuum domicilium*.[19]

Alongside the Protestant celebration of work and disavowal of luxury, Enlightenment theory made farmers paragons of virtue, while relegating frontier hunters to the level of savages. "It appears," explained Benjamin Rush, the first American surgeon general and a signer of the Declaration of Independence,

> that there are certain regular stages which mark the progress from the savage to civilized life. The first settler is nearly related to an Indian in his manners—In the second, the Indian manners are more diluted: It is in the third species of settlers only, that we behold civilization completed.[20]

Imbued, like Rush, with the principles of four-stages theory, educated travelers of the eighteenth and early nineteenth centuries routinely condemned, rather than praised, backwoods hunters. Upon departing from long-settled regions, travelers first observed civilized agriculturalists of whom they ardently approved. Farther west the intelligent visage of the farmer gave way to that of the half-civilized pastoralist, who lived without labor and instead turned loose hogs and cattle to roam the countryside. When hunger called, the lazy pastoralist located a handy pig or goat for slaughter. Even this modus operandi was superior to that of people inhabiting the most distant frontiers, where travelers found what cultural conditioning had led them to expect: rude and violent white and Indian hunters who ranged through the woods with no thought of laying up a store of food for the morrow.[21]

"Hunting wild beasts is the first and most indolent life in every new country," explained a correspondent of the *American Museum* monthly in 1791, "and always previous to the shepherd's life, as that also is to the proper cultivation of the earth." The first white settlers of frontier America, agreed an English traveler in 1822–23, were pure hunters, who were in turn replaced by men who farmed and hunted both, and finally by men who supported themselves by farming alone. Though the Englishman found backwoods hunters to be invariably "open hearted and very hospitable," he noted that "it has been much the fashion in the United States to speak ill" of such men.[22]

The American Revolution to some extent contradicted this censure by invoking hunters in buckskins as martial heroes, men who would stand up to the arrogant redcoats. The political questions posed by the Revolution, however—who should govern, who should vote, and who was the virtuous citizen—were answered with paeans to agrarian republicanism.

Spawned by the civic humanism of the Renaissance and the heated admonitions of England's so-called Real Whigs, republican ideology posited two supreme evils: a corrupt government, with its powers of patronage and taxation, and an ambitious, decadent, and decidedly urban elite that manipulated government to favor its commercial interests. If unchecked by virtuous citizens, these forces—a corrupt Parliament and a corrupt elite—would destroy English liberty.

According to England's Real Whigs, who espoused republican doctrines long before Americans did, the rural squire—ever a foe to urban iniquity and a friend to country virtue (including hunting)—was the moral beacon of society. Because he lived on fixed rents from tenants rather than manufactures and trade, the squire remained disinterested; he did not need to manipulate government to obtain protection or favors. Neither dissipated by great wealth nor dependent on those who produced it, the squire was the happy median. He alone could bring virtue to government; he alone could prevent government from depriving the people of rights and liberties.

American men—the vast majority of whom were freeholders and small producers of middling rank—translated republicanism differently. With their Protestant, evangelical emphasis on work and calling, they were not so willing to accept the country squire, or his American equivalent, as the natural leader of republican society; Americans conceived of the yeoman freeholder as the backbone of republicanism. Small farmers were the self-sufficient, liberty-loving, disinterested men capable of guaranteeing good government and virtue.

Republicanism, like four-stages theory, appeared in multiple idioms, but in each (even in the Federalist version) the freeholder found a distinguished place. Farming was thought to bring happiness, dignity, health, and long life; it was the occupation intended for Americans by the Creator. Farming, moreover, justified racial distinctions and American claims to the lands of hunting peoples. Thomas Jefferson—who also touted four-stages theory—expressed the sentiment of his Revolutionary countrymen when he wrote that

> those who labour in the earth are the chosen people of God, if ever he had a chosen people, whose breasts he has made his peculiar deposit for substantial and genuine virtue. It is the focus in which he keeps alive that sacred fire, which otherwise might escape from the face of the earth. Corruption of morals in the mass of cultivators is a phænomenon of which no age nor nation has furnished an example.

Jefferson (and presidents after him) applied this same logic when asking Indians to give up the chase and take up the plow. Farming produced republican civilization and virtue; hunting produced savagery. The sooner the game of forest and prairie was depleted, the better. "Hunting," as Crèvecoeur wrote, "is but a licentious idle life"; it was the farmer who became the ideal natural citizen of America, the man in harmony with nature, society, and republican government.[23]

Neither republicanism, nor four-stages theory, nor Puritanism, however, kept men from feeding their families with game. That so many farmers were hunters on occasion enabled Americans of later generations to seize upon hunting as the source of American greatness. Both farming and hunting were rural occupations; both brought men closer to the land; both seemed traditional. Moreover, backwoods farmers of the colonial era regarded hunting not as a privilege but as a right; to be American was to take game without the hindrance of aristocratic game laws.

When the moment was ripe, Americans would transfer the virtues of the farmer to the hunter. In the colonial and early national eras, however, the right to hunt did not constitute a celebration of hunting. Only insofar as farmers hunted for their larder or to kill pests and predators was hunting deemed morally acceptable.

When not subordinated to agriculture, hunting was the bane of civilization. "Once hunters," warned Crèvecoeur, "farewell to the plough." He urged fellow settlers to "keep ourselves busy tilling" to avoid dissolution, but frontiersmen—despite Congress's efforts to promote commerce in the West—ignored his advice. By 1785 the backcountry of Kentucky had become "thickly inhabited, by all sorts of indolent ignorant people, who raise a little corn, but depend chiefly on hunting for their support," wrote a settler who had moved there. As hunters, according to the author of a 1793 account of Kentucky, such settlers became "unqualified for any other kind of life."[24]

In 1803 botanist François-André Michaux observed that Ohio Valley frontiersmen made a business of shooting bear and deer for profit, an enterprise that Michaux found "prejudicial to their lands." A decade later Quaker entrepreneur George W. Ogden found the same Ohio Valley to be inhabited by industrious farmers but noted that settlers of western Virginia were yet degraded by hunting. "The great abundance of wild game allures them to the forest . . . [and] in consequence of this, they neglect the cultivation of their land . . . [and] are not far removed, in point of civilization, from the savages." So, too, in 1807–1808, English observer Edward Augustus Kendall reported while traveling in Maine that wherever "the fishery or the chase is present to the poor, the poor cannot be induced to submit themselves to daily labour" (though Kendall was more concerned with another form of barbaric indolence, lumbering, to which settlers resorted after depleting wild game).[25]

Alexis de Tocqueville summed up the conventional American (and European) wisdom that the gun was the nemesis of the plow when he wrote in the 1830s that those "who have once abandoned themselves to the restless and adventurous life of the hunter feel an insurmountable disgust for the constant and regular labor that tillage requires." Throughout the eighteenth century and well into the nineteenth, Americans insisted that "it is the order of events, that the hunter should give place to the husbandman."[26]

Far beyond the boundaries of Puritan New England, the doctrine of *vacuum domicilium*—the part-Biblical, part-Enlightenment notion that uncultivated land became the property of cultivators—profoundly influenced American thinking. From the outset of colonization, the farmer had qualified himself as heir to the continent by mingling his sweat with the soil. The farmer was the happy median, the industrious man who neither sought entry into the corrupt gentry nor fell to the level of the savage. The backwoods hunter, by contrast, was a fallen man: lawless, ignorant, cruel, and profligate. Only by reforming him could American society hope to thrive.

Hunting as a Way of Life

The year is 1757. In the forests of western New York, three men in hunting shirts and moccasins are running. Holding long rifles in their right hands, they move effortlessly through undergrowth and trees, down hills and across a rocky stream. Two of the men are Indians. The other is European, though his long black hair is dressed in Indian fashion, with a braided scalp lock in back. The European strips off his hunting shirt and ties it around his waist as he runs. Suddenly he stops. Crashing through the underbrush appears a bull elk, its antlers in velvet. The white hunter raises his rifle, fires, and watches the elk fall, killed with a single shot. Now the three men converge on the elk. "We're sorry to kill you brother," says a middle-aged Indian, speaking in Algonquian. "We do honor to your courage and speed, your strength." Finally, all three—the white man, Hawkeye, and his Indian companions, Chingachgook and Uncas—gently rub the elk, bidding its spirit farewell.

This scene opens director Michael Mann's 1992 film version of *The Last of the Mohicans*. The scene was not transcribed from James Fenimore Cooper's 1826 novel, but he might have approved it. Cooper made his Hawkeye (whose European name was Natty Bumppo) in the image of the noble savage, an uncorrupted man of the forest who loved animals even as he killed them for subsistence. Moreover, Cooper's Hawkeye—like Mann's—appeared as a rugged individualist who rejected the hubris of civilization. "I don't call myself subject to much at all," Mann's Hawkeye retorts in Cooperian style when a British officer questions his patriotism.

At the same time, Mann's Hawkeye is a product of the twentieth century. He seems to revere not only animals but also the animistic customs of his Indian companions. Unlike real backwoodsmen of the eighteenth century, he would probably be an environmentalist were he alive today. More important, Mann's Hawkeye kisses the heroine at film's end, whereas Cooper's Hawkeye returned to the forests alone. Cooper's Hawkeye, as Henry Nash Smith pointed out in 1950, lacked social graces and could not—in keeping with literary propriety—wed any proper lady.[1]

Insofar as Hawkeye could not wed a lady, eighteenth-century Americans would have found him believable. Yet in other respects, neither Mann's nor Cooper's Hawkeye would have conformed to the sensibilities of most American colonists of 1757. Hawkeye was a figment of the modern imagination, an ancestral American who became truly American by loving the wilderness rather than transforming it with an axe.

Before 1763 the majority of colonists were loyal to agrarianism, the British Crown, and a chain of hierarchy that stretched from king to gentleman to artisan and farmer. Though colonial America offered more social mobility than England, colonists expected one another to know their places and respect their betters. As a man who defied constituted authority and lived like an Indian, Hawkeye would have appeared to most eighteenth-century Americans as an absurd and dangerous figure, a representative of disorder and ignorance. As a pure hunter, rather than as a farmer who happened to hunt, Hawkeye would have stood at the bottom of the American social hierarchy.

Between the mid-eighteenth century and the mid-nineteenth, backwoods hunters metamorphosed from repulsive savages to hardy individualists. Neither image faithfully represents real backwoods hunters. Who, then, were the backwoods hunters of colonial and early national America? Were they Indian-like figures who paid homage to animals after slaying them? Were they demisavages, men without respect for property or law? Were they rebels against monarchical society and hence progenitors of the American character?

Ubiquitous complaints about the hunter banditti in the late eighteenth and early nineteenth centuries suggest that for some men hunting truly was an alternative way of life. Hunting seems to have offered the hope of a free and easy existence far beyond the toils and cares of the farming life. But no hunter could escape civilization. Powder, shot, guns, salt, axes, and knives, not to mention luxury goods like blankets and iron cookware, had to be purchased. To obtain these goods, white hunters—no less than Indians—participated in the market.[2] Though it is tempting to see subsistence hunters as pre-industrial heroes, men who repudiated market capitalism, few lived in perfect isolation.

Most backwoods hunters were doing what others were doing throughout the colonies—seeking opportunity. Backwoods hunters were often men who sought land on the frontier, usually with the intention of farming, but also with the intention of petty speculation. If they neglected to cultivate land, that was because they did not need to cultivate it to profit from it; they simply waited until new settlers arrived and land values rose. Then the hunter sold his parcel and moved his family to another frontier where he would repeat the process. This easy profit, as much as any desire for solitude, was the reason why backwoodsmen sought elbow room.

Though most nineteenth-century artists romanticized backwoods hunters, James Henry Beard offered a more realistic portrait. The flimsy lean-to, shabby clothes, and deep lines on the faces of this hunter and his wife show a family that is rich in game but poor in all else. James Henry Beard (1811–93), *Westward Ho!,* ca. 1850 (oil, 62 × 80 inches). DePauw University Permanent Art Collection, Greencastle, Indiana. Gift from John P. Kinsey. 968.3.1.

Some hunters also refused to cultivate land because they could not own it;
they were squatters. In cases where preemption laws did not permit squatters to
purchase land, or where purchase prices were too high, it made no sense to gir-
dle trees, clear stumps, plow fields, and build fences. It was easier to hunt for subsistence than to carve out farms, just as it was more lucrative to sell skins and furs
than to sell produce, at least where agricultural markets and transportation net-
works had not caught up with settlement.

Market hunting, indeed, could be extremely profitable. One pair of New York
market hunters made $300 in a single hunting season in 1790–91, while others in
the early national era reportedly made as much as $1,000 a year. In addition to
profiting from hides, skins, and furs, hunters (and their wives) sold or traded meat
to soldiers and settlers; used tallow to manufacture soap, candles, and lye; cured
leather from deer or elk; and made yarn from buffalo wool. To earn $1,000 from
hunting in the early national era was extraordinary, but hunting had its benefits.
Few got rich from it, yet few got rich from farming either.[3]

Finally, some backwoodsmen hunted to escape the tedium of everyday life. In
his 1824 encomium to backwoodsmen, Rev. Joseph Doddridge, an Episcopal minister and Freemason, wrote that after the first snowfall the hunter became restless at home and "disagreeable"; he found his house too warm, his bed too soft,
and his wife "not . . . for the time a proper companion." Under these circum-
stances, wrote Doddridge,

> I have often seen them get up early in the morning . . . walk hastily out, and look
> anxiously to the woods and snuff the autumnal winds with the highest rapture, then
> return into the house and cast a quick and attentive look at the rifle, which was al-
> ways suspended to a joist by a couple of buck horns, or little forks.

Loading a packhorse with flour, cornmeal, blankets, and hunting supplies, and
accompanied by an eager dog, the hunter lit out for the forests.[4]

Most of these hunters were more interested in the long run in growing crops
than in killing game. For a few, however, hunting was all that mattered. When
farmers put his beloved hunting grounds to the axe, Benjamin Patterson, the great
hunter of Steuben County, New York, moved to "a land as yet unmolested by
plowmen and wood-choppers."[5] The most noteworthy hunter of them all, Daniel
Boone, likewise moved on when farmers took possession of his hunting grounds
in Kentucky. Moving to greener hunting pastures was not necessarily a romantic decision; for men skilled in hunting (or in speculating on frontier lands), moving on often made economic sense.

By the mid-nineteenth century, these frontier hunters had metamorphosed from detestable savages into celebrated heroes in the mold of Hawkeye and Boone. Regional histories of the nineteenth century often relate tales of "courageous and energetic" hunters who had explored the area, naming creeks, springs, meadows, and mountains and killing hundreds, even thousands, of deer and bear in the process. Such a hunter, wrote one nineteenth-century chronicler, was a *"Knight-Errant* of the primitive and chivalrous days" of old.[6] How this transition came about—how the hunter turned into a prince when kissed by the American public—is the subject of later chapters.

Long before backwoods hunters became American idols, they were respected in backwoods communities. "A great hunter," wrote an antebellum historian of frontier life, was the backwoodsman's "beau ideal of a man." Among backwoodsmen, explained ethnographer Henry Rowe Schoolcraft in 1818, "to excel in the chace [*sic*] procures fame, and a man's reputation is measured by his skill as a marksman, his agility and strength, his boldness and dexterity in killing game, and his patient endurance and contempt of the hardships of the hunter's life." "Feats of daring," noted another historian of early hunters, "such as climbing bold precipices, following for days the trail of some particularly mammoth Hart, coming out victorious in conflicts with hoof and horn of a wounded quarry, [or] the slaughter of thousands of deer by certain individuals, raised the prestige of deer hunters to an extravagant degree."[7]

Because nineteenth-century authors often sought to manufacture heroes as well as to record the past, however, it is hard to say just how celebrated backwoods hunters were in their own time and place. Certainly Samuel Edwards, the "Great Bear and Deer Hunter" of early nineteenth-century Ohio, found that his reputation was not enough to win over the father of his chosen bride. Despite the young woman's love for Edwards, her father refused to let her marry "one who with a dog and gun could spend half his time in the woods."[8] Cooper's Hawkeye might have appreciated Edwards's disappointment.

That hunters did not always receive permission to marry their beloved may have had something to do with their Indian-like appearance. The standard hunting outfit consisted of a linen or buckskin shirt (a hip-length frock, open at the front and often fringed), a breechcloth tied around the waist, and deerskin leggings extending up over the thigh. The outfit was completed by deerskin or elkskin moccasins that could be stuffed with deer hair, buffalo wool, or leaves for warmth in colder months. Some hunters also wore fur caps, whereas others, like Daniel Boone, preferred the more civilized hat. To their belts hunters affixed tomahawks, shot pouches, and knives (often in beaded sheaths of Indian manufacture), and from their necks they slung plain or engraved powder horns. Finally, across their shoulders or in their hands they carried the Kentucky or long rifle, a relatively light, small-bore (generally .45 caliber or less), blackpowder rifle designed by German gunsmiths who had settled in western Pennsylvania. Outfitted thus, backwoods hunters seemed to become hardy survivors in a Hobbesian universe. They "expect no mercy, and they shew no fear," wrote an Englishman on a tour of the frontier in 1817–18; "'every man's hand is raised against them, and their hand is against every other man's.'"[9]

It is tempting to think of these frontier hunters as Hawkeyes all, true children of the forest. Nineteenth-century writers depicted them that way. "Every true backwoodsman was a hunter," proclaimed Theodore Roosevelt in *The Winning of the West*, a multivolume history published in 1889, and all backwoods hunters were "emphatically products native to the soil." Long before the Revolution, these men had "lost all remembrance of Europe and all sympathy with things European"; they had "become Americans, one in speech, thought, and character."[10]

Some historians of our own day, though critical of the pioneers' racism, nonetheless portray them as Indian-like figures, authentic products of the American soil. Insofar as Indians and European backwoodsmen borrowed one another's customs and busied themselves in "hunting and gathering, cutting and burning," asserts Elliott West in *The Oxford History of the American West*, the two groups were "more similar than not."[11]

There is truth here. Like Indians, backwoodsmen learned to roll a piece of birch bark into a funnel and blow into it to mimic the sound of the moose and to hold branches in front of themselves as they stalked caribou. Like Indians, backwoodsmen also subsisted on berries, plums, grapes, and nuts and became profoundly knowledgeable in woodcraft and geography. According to West, backwoods settlers even "concocted tales of all-powerful bears of mysterious properties; living in the Indians' world, these people embraced stories that spoke of the same view of life."[12]

Tempting as it is to accept this proposition, few backwoodsmen—Hawkeye excepted—shared the Indian view of life. Backwoodsmen sought to exterminate bears and other predators, not to honor their spirits. Though backwoodsmen— impelled partly by nineteenth-century writers—came to regard bears, particularly grizzlies of the Far West, as noble foes, this sentiment entailed fear and respect rather than awe.[13] Unlike Indians, backwoodsmen did not worship the natural world or its faunal denizens.

Nor did backwoods hunters exemplify Enlightenment rationality. Backwoodsmen carried with them the folk wisdom of their European forebears and sometimes invented their own. Thus a hunter who survived an attack by a wounded stag, according to Henry Shoemaker, an early twentieth-century historian of frontier hunters, was thought to be invulnerable to the bullets of enemies. Shoemaker also reported that hunters believed that looking at a dying stag brought bad luck and that albino stags were ghosts of those who had committed incest. When killed, the flesh of these stags was said to turn black and to putrefy immediately.[14]

Though Shoemaker's veracity as an ethnographer has been questioned, other sources confirm that hunters were a superstitious lot. Some believed that a deer that survived three shots and having its throat cut was a witch (not a poor guess) and that shooting on the Sabbath invited bad luck for the rest of the week. Frontier hunters also put faith in omens. "The croaking of a raven, the howling of a dog, and the screech of an owl," wrote Doddridge, "were as prophetic of misfortunes among the first adventurers into this country, as they were amongst the ancient pagans." When such signs proved insufficient guides, backwoodsmen might divine the future through dreams, all the while keeping up their guard against spells cast by witches.[15]

Such beliefs, although marking backwoodsmen as heirs to a folk tradition predating Christianity, did not make them animists. Apart from the occasional "white Indian" (someone who had been taken captive and acculturated among Indian peoples), no white hunter chanted to prey or observed fastidious rules of butchering. White hunters might be superstitious, but they did not fear offending either animal spirits or "game bosses," mythical beings said by Indians to be responsible for the abundance or scarcity of game.

Backwoodsmen nonetheless developed folkways to govern their enterprise. The most important of these customs was the sharing of the kill. In group hunts of the nineteenth century, the man who drew the first blood of a deer (even if he did not kill the deer) got to keep the skin and half the meat. The other half of the meat was divided among his fellows. This custom probably varied somewhat with time and place but seems to have been an old tradition.[16]

Hunters also formulated rules governing the hunt itself. Philip Tome reported in his memoir of the early national era, *Thirty Years a Hunter,* that a man who failed to reload his gun immediately after firing (hence risking the loss of wounded game) was forced to sit on a stool while his friends circled round, pulling his hair and sometimes plucking out a few strands. This mild torture, called "randeling," was customary punishment "for any neglect of duty."[17]

Though evidence is sketchy, some backwoodsmen also seem to have claimed local lands as private hunting territories (much like Algonquian families of the fur trade era). Those who poached on these territories could expect to be tarred and feathered and their dogs to be shot.[18]

Shooting matches were commonplace in eighteenth- and early nineteenth-century America.
George Caleb Bingham (1811–79), *Shooting for the Beef*, 1850 (oil on canvas, 33⅝ × 49⅜ inches).
The Brooklyn Museum of Art, Dick S. Ramsay Fund, 40.342.

Frontier hunters also popularized shooting matches, which were held throughout the United States in the late eighteenth and early nineteenth centuries, even in the vicinity of Boston. In most matches living animals were tied to posts or trees and shot at from a variable distance, often one hundred paces. Each entrant paid a fee to shoot, but only the winner—the man who killed the hostage animal—got to keep the carcass. Afterward the local publican—frequently the sponsor of such matches—served drinks or dinner to contestants, while politicians might harangue them with speeches. In other shooting contests, men "barked" squirrels (shooting at the bark to which a squirrel clung and killing it with concussion rather than ball) or shot at targets (often the head of a nail).

European travelers—not to mention Americans—expressed astonishment at the shooting abilities displayed in these contests.[19]

Travelers likewise expressed astonishment at the skills displayed by Americans in hunting. It was reckoned "very unsportsmanslike," observed William Newnham Blane after his excursion to the frontier in 1822–23, for a backwoodsman (even a boy) "to bring home a squirrel or a turkey, that has been shot anywhere, except in the head," since body shots damaged the meat. Backwoodsmen of Indiana and Illinois, wrote another English traveler in 1817–18, "are the best marksmen in the world, and such is their dexterity that they will shoot an apple off the head of a companion." Likewise on the Alabama frontier of the 1830s, testified English naturalist Philip Gosse, "the long rifle is familiar to every hand; skill in the use of it is the highest accomplishment which a southern gentleman glories in; even the children acquire an astonishing expertness in handling this deadly weapon at a very early age." All backwoods peoples, testified Fortescue Cuming in 1810, "are wonderfully expert in the use of [the rifle]: thinking it a bad shot if they miss the very head of a squirrel, or a wild turkey, on the top of the highest forest tree with a single ball."[20]

Given their skill in shooting, it is hardly surprising that hunters left their mark on the English language. In addition to the term "buck" for a dollar, Americans used, and still use, such expressions as "the whole shooting match," "flash in the pan" (when gunpowder would flash in the pan of a musket or rifle without firing the ball), "spitball" (a ball lubricated with saliva before being rammed down the barrel of a gun), "ramrod" (the rod used to ram the ball down the barrel), "sitting duck" (a duck on the water rather than in the air), "stool pigeon" (a tame pigeon used to lure wild birds), and "dead in the water" or "dead in its tracks" (a helpless animal or one killed instantly). In the nineteenth century, Americans also used the phrase "take the shoot," which meant to set forth boldly on a course of action. "Pot shot" also qualifies as a hunter's phrase but was adopted by nineteenth-century sportsmen to deride those who hunted for the pot.

Even if hunting influenced American idiomatic speech, one wonders whether a true hunting culture formed on the American frontier. If such a culture did evolve, moreover, did it spawn an American hunting tradition? Thousands of latter-day hunters, not to mention writers and scholars, have answered in the affirmative on both counts, yet to make such judgments without qualification is to oversimplify the historical record.

When backwoodsmen of colonial and early national America hunted, they generally did so to make a profit, to fill the larder, or to clear land of pests and predators. Because most backwoodsmen wed themselves to agrarian civilization, they thought of hunting as a short-term pursuit—despite the rituals and adages of the chase. In fact, hunting big game and fur-bearing animals (though not squirrels and birds) was almost by definition a short-term pursuit; hunting and habitat reduction made it almost impossible for such animals to replace their numbers. William Cooper, the proprietor of vast frontier tracts in New York State in the late eighteenth century, estimated that settlers on his lands would hunt out native game within a decade; steep declines in the number of furs and skins traded at Cooper's store indicate that the process occurred more quickly. Even hunters who ventured into game-rich regions of the interior, moreover, employed their geographical knowledge in the service of additional surveys and land sales that undermined hunting as a way of life.[21]

Backwoodsmen, because of their attachment to agrarian civilization, held in contempt Indians, whose cultures did revolve around hunting. With little concern for the hunting rights or subsistence cycles of Indians, backwoodsmen grabbed as much land as they could and held it by force, all the while driving off or exterminating game. When settlers moved on or near Indian hunting grounds, it was said, game animals rapidly disappeared, and the Indians were forced to move farther into the wilderness. Once the old hunting grounds had been rendered worthless, Indians were forced to sell them to the government for pennies an acre. As a consequence, when Indians and backwoodsmen met on the trail—Hawkeye and Chingachgook aside—they were more likely to be mortal enemies than friends.[22]

Unlike whites, Indians hunted not to make way for civilization but because their cosmography instructed them to hunt, because their ancestors had hunted, and because they expected their children to hunt. Admittedly, there was a contradiction within Indian attitudes toward hunting: how could a people for whom game was sacred engage in the fur trade? Postcontact Indians, by killing so much game, jeopardized their way of life.

Some scholars contend that Indians hunted for market only after they had renounced or neglected animistic religions that put men and animals on the same spiritual plane. Yet Indians did not necessarily see a contradiction between animism and market hunting. In some cases animism—by positing that abundance came not from the procreation of game but from the goodwill of spirits—may have worked against conservation.[23]

Other scholars contend that Indians hunted for market because they recognized the superiority of European goods. According to James Axtell, Indians were eager participants in the eighteenth-century consumer revolution, trading skins and furs for mirrors, combs, jewelry, and cloth, as well as guns.[24] This paradigm, however, underestimates the necessity of market participation.

Indians hunted for market not solely (or even primarily) because they had apostatized, or because they sought luxury goods, but because trade became imperative in a world wrenched by epidemics, forced migrations, and imperial and local rivalries. By trading furs and skins for guns, powder, lead, and manufactured goods, Indians bolstered their ability to fight off enemies and to forge alliances (with other tribes and with Europeans) through trade and the exchange of gifts. Indians hunted for market, in short, for the same reasons that the United States and the Soviet Union engaged in an arms race. To fall behind in the production of furs and the acquisition of guns (or other goods) was to risk irrelevancy or, worse, annihilation.

In this quest for security lay the seeds of destruction. Furs and skins were often traded for whiskey, whose corrosive impact on Indian societies is well documented. When Indian hunters exterminated game within their own territories, moreover, or when settlers intruded on their lands, Indians were forced to seek new hunting grounds. This movement brought tribes into perpetual conflict in some areas (the most famous example being the seventeenth-century beaver wars of the Iroquois and Algonquians), catapulting them toward subjugation at the hands of whites.[25]

Rather than hunt, Indians could have intensified their farming to gain needed goods, but to do so would have meant giving up a way of life. Even in the late eighteenth and early nineteenth centuries, when the fur trade was in decline east of the Mississippi River, missionaries and government agents found it difficult to persuade Indians to stop hunting and become full-time farmers. Meanwhile, Indian spiritual leaders from time to time called on followers to forswear trade with whites and to return to the conservative hunting practices of old.[26]

Anglo-Americans also called on hunters to rein in the slaughter. In the 1770s Transylvania, a shadow colony carved out by speculators, passed legislation introduced by Daniel Boone to halt the wanton killing of game, particularly "wild cattle" (buffalo). In doing so, Transylvania followed the precedent of colonies that had promulgated deer seasons as early as the seventeenth century. These laws, however, were seldom enforced.

The Transylvania law was designed to protect meat supplies until settlers could carve out farms and introduce livestock. It was not intended to save buffalo or other animals as species or to perpetuate hunting as a way of life. Without any real effort to save them, buffalo disappeared from Kentucky by 1820 and from every other state east of the Mississippi River by 1832.[27] Elk disappeared at about the same time, while deer, bear, and turkeys, with their higher reproductive capacities, were exterminated in some areas but not others.

Despite the occasional admonition against waste, Anglo-American hunters gave little heed to the fate of game. It was common for market hunters to take four hundred to five hundred deer in a season, not to mention the skins of beavers, otters, minks, and other fur-bearing animals that fell victim to traps. Daniel Boone, with one partner, took some seven hundred beaver pelts in a single season from Missouri hunting grounds. At $2.50 a pelt, Boone's income from beavers that year would have amounted to almost $1,000.[28]

Smaller game, too, came in for persecution. Pens were used to trap as many as a hundred turkeys a winter, while communal circle hunts, or "surrounds," claimed the lives of thousands of animals. One such hunt on December 24, 1818, in Medina County, Ohio, resulted in the deaths of seventeen wolves, twenty-one bears, and three hundred deer, "besides *turkeys, coons* and *foxes* not counted." Men also hunted for the thrill of competition. In 1845 two men in Ohio took a total of 164 deer during a sixty-day contest; the winner killed 99.[29]

For Protestants, that which was sacred lay in the Bible rather than in the natural world. In Genesis God had given men dominion over the natural world, and hunting was a way of exercising that dominion. Unrestrained by either animism or a Christian ethic of stewardship, backwoodsmen "did destroy [game animals] and waste them then, at a mighty rate," recalled one old hunter.[30]

The backwoodsmen who supposedly gave America its hunting tradition showed little concern about preserving their way of life for future generations. It is not destructiveness, however, that leads one to conclude that backwoodsmen formed no true hunting culture—Indians were also wasteful—but rather the reasons behind that destructiveness. Whereas for Indians hunting deer and beaver for market was a defense of tradition in the maelstrom of contact, for backwoodsmen killing game was a way station on the road to civilization. Indians failed to conserve game because hunting was their way of life; backwoodsmen failed to conserve game because hunting was not their way of life.

Yet not every backwoodsman wasted game "at a mighty rate"; full-time hunters composed a tiny minority of frontiersmen. Some settlers found themselves too busy improving lands to hunt; others, unskilled in the chase, preferred to buy game from experienced hunters. Indeed, it seems that a minority of eighteenth- and early nineteenth-century settlers owned guns.[31]

Before the era of mass production, muskets and rifles could be difficult to obtain. In the colonial era, Americans did not build a single gun manufactory, in part because Parliament made it illegal for colonists to manufacture iron goods.

Americans who wanted guns often had to import them even in the early nine-teenth century. Though firearms were handmade by gunsmiths, such craftsmen were relatively scarce everywhere except Lancaster County, Pennsylvania, where the Kentucky rifle originated in the eighteenth century.[32]

When guns could be purchased, they were expensive. Michael Bellesiles notes that an unused eighteenth-century musket would have cost the average Ameri-can laborer about two months' worth of earnings at a time when the same laborer would have spent half his income on food. Even the inexpensive rifles produced by a Hagerstown, Maryland, "factory" in the 1790s cost twenty dollars, making the cost of a good rifle comparable to the cost of a computer—or even a car—in modern America. Some men no doubt bartered for guns, yet guns appear irreg-ularly in colonial and early national probate records.[33]

Because of the cost and scarcity of arms, backwoodsmen might borrow guns from acquaintances or relatives before hunts, resort to bows and arrows, or do without weapons altogether. "One of my greatest privations was the want of a gun," testified William Cooper Howells, recalling his youth in frontier Ohio; "as father did not think he could afford to buy one, or was not very deeply impressed with the importance of having one, I had to wait a long time for the consumma-tion of a powerful desire."[34]

Of those who did hunt, few considered themselves sportsmen. Among "back settlers," averred an English traveler in the 1790s, "shooting . . . is rather business than sport." Recalling his childhood in early nineteenth-century Ridgefield, Con-necticut (which, though not a backwoods locale, was far from the beaten track), Samuel Griswold Goodrich confirmed that "everybody was then a hunter, not of course a sportsman, for the chase was followed more for profit than pastime." A hunter of nineteenth-century western Pennsylvania similarly recalled that his father and grandfather "were not hunters in the modern meaning of the word, as game came up to their doors to be shot." Others set unsportsmanlike snares, traps, or deadfalls or, having little time or inclination to hunt, left the task of killing game to children.[35]

Aware of how few Americans concerned themselves with the protocols of sport, English emigré William Cobbett complained in 1818 that "the general taste" of Americans was to "*kill* things in order to have them to *eat*, which latter forms no part of the *real sportsman's* object." For their part, backwoodsmen disdained sport hunters. To backwoodsmen killing for sport meant killing for pleasure, wasting an animal's meat and skin.[36]

To determine whether a hunting culture developed in the American back-woods thus leads to ambiguity. Perhaps the question is too wooden, implying an either/or hypothesis rather than a continuum with a pure hunting culture on one end and a pure farming culture on the other. On such a continuum American backwoodsmen appear somewhere in the middle, albeit more toward the farming pole than toward the hunting pole. American backwoodsmen did not participate in a pure hunting culture (as did, say, the Naskapi of Labrador), yet hunting was sufficiently important to backwoodsmen to generate peculiar customs and folkways. Backwoodsmen participated in a hunting and a nonhunting culture simultaneously (never let it be said that a culture cannot contradict itself).

Yet between 1820 and the end of the nineteenth century (or earlier, if we count the literature of Daniel Boone), Americans began to recall their forebears primarily as a hunting people and secondarily as a farming people. Like eighteenth-century Britons who traced English liberty to the Saxon past, writers and artists traced the American love of hunting—and liberty—to a quasi-mystical pioneer past. In doing so, they sought to give American men a mythic standard to live up to, yet the creation of the myth required the obfuscation of the source. In truth, pioneers did not single-handedly sacralize hunting; it took educated men to do that.

Nor was this sacralization easily accomplished. Because of four-stages theory, republicanism, and the canonization of the farmer in American culture, it took decades for hunters to rise to the level of American culture hero. As late as 1827, complained Timothy Flint, a Harvard-trained minister turned chronicler of frontier life, urban Americans conceived of backwoodsmen as "a kind of humanized Ourang Outang, . . . recently divested of the unsightly appendage of a tail." According to Flint in his 1833 biography of Daniel Boone, backwoodsmen were widely perceived as "demi-savages," with "long beard, and a costume of skins, fierce, and repulsive."[37]

By Flint's estimate, reality differed drastically from image. Real backwoodsmen exhibited "noble, square, erect forms, . . . clear, bright, truth telling eyes, and vigorous intellects." Backwoods hunters, with their "simplicity of manners, manly hardihood, and Spartan energy and force of character," should serve as an example to the "shrinking and effeminate spirits, the men of soft hands and fashionable life" propagated by commerce.[38]

Backwoodsmen, agreed Rev. Joseph Doddridge, "have lived, and died for posterity," and "ought to be rewarded with imperishable fame, in the grateful remembrance of their descendants." For Doddridge, who had grown up in eighteenth-century western Pennsylvania, recording the history of backwoods hunters was "a sacred duty." In telling their story, Doddridge sought to inscribe the American land with a heroic lore comparable to that of the Greeks and the Romans.[39]

As a minister, however, Doddridge sought to do more than commemorate backwoods life; like Flint he made his book a statement on modernity. Doddridge observed that some affluent Americans cared nothing about the "names, or remains" of "noble" backwoodsmen, but for these cynics he had a reply. Backwoodsmen "lived, toiled and suffered for others; you on the contrary, live for yourself alone: their example ought to live, because it is worthy of imitation; yours on the contrary, as an example of sordid avarice, ought to perish forever."[40]

"To lie, to cheat, to desert a fellow hunter in distress," added Professor Mann Butler in his 1834 history of Kentucky, "were vices unknown to the brave and simple men who conquered Kentucky." Jacksonian moral codes, worried Butler, had become complex and ambiguous, yet the "gallant and magnanimous hunters of Kentucky will ever be sacred to the hearts of all lovers of brave and noble deeds."[41]

Another trumpet blast in this moral orchestra was sounded in Jeptha R. Simms's popular book *Trappers of New York*, first published in New York in 1850 and dedicated to the "Youth of our Nation." Buoyed by the rhetoric of predecessors, Simms, a clerk and teacher who had lived in the Mohawk Valley, sought "to connect [the] names and deeds" of pioneer hunters "forever, with the rifle-mimicking mountains, the awe-inspiring glens, the hill-encompassed lakes, and the zigzag-coursing rivulets." These "disciples of Nimrod," like saintly hermits, had made their "orderly," spartan camps in a "wilderness, womanless home." Here, explained Simms—obedient not only to the logic of Hobbes but also to the nascent logic of social Darwinism—"in the absence of any other tribunal, *might* made *right*."[42] This was not a state of nature and society for which to apologize, but one that Americans, by Simms's reckoning, should recall with pride. As avatars of nature, backwoods hunters would serve Americans as exemplars of what men should be, hardy individuals in a realm of noble strife.

Preeminent among these hunters were Daniel Boone and his fictive counterpart, Cooper's Natty Bumppo, called variously Leatherstocking, Deerslayer, Pathfinder, and Hawkeye. Boone and Bumppo were such profoundly important figures in American history that they merit closer attention in later chapters. Their example of heroic self-reliance amid wilderness perils would set a precedent for sport hunters of later decades.

The juxtaposition of modern corruption with backwoods virtue made hunters enormously popular in nineteenth-century America. Such tales, however, were not simple histories of a simple past. In the imaginations of nineteenth-century writers, men who hunted began to replace men who farmed as paragons of ancestral rectitude. But what sort of ancestral rectitude was this?

For Joseph Doddridge, who, as a Freemason and an Episcopal minister, was a member of an elite, backwoods hunters were men who favored self-sacrifice for the benefit of community and commonwealth over their own self-interest. This ideal of self-sacrifice harked back to the republican ideology of the American Revolution—or at least one important brand of republican ideology—that taught that the interest of the nation came before the interest of individuals. Self-interested men, it was said, injured the community and compromised good government. To those who subscribed to this ideal, the salvation of the United States lay in the willingness of its citizens to subordinate their interests to those of the national community; to do so was to display republican virtue. In Doddridge's view, the virtue of the founders had waned in the decades after the Revolution, whereas self-interest—the desire to make a profit—had waxed amid economic expansion.

For Jeptha Simms, on the other hand, backwoods hunters lived for no one but themselves. Far from being pillars of the community or commonwealth, backwoods hunters pursued their self-interest amid the liberty of the wilderness. Simms's hunters represented everything Doddridge preached against, yet Simms's rugged individualists, more than Doddridge's communitarians, were remembered as ancestral Americans whose manliness, courage, and enterprise were to be emulated. In the memories of nineteenth-century Americans, the agrarian virtues described by the founding generation became stretched and warped until they no longer fit old patterns.

Through the efforts of Simms, Doddridge, Butler, Flint, and dozens of others, hunters would triumph in the American imagination. They would become American Natives, men who seemed to be indigenous products of American nature, men who expressed many old virtues—and some new ones—once associated with farmers. By the late nineteenth century, Americans had forgotten that there had been a time when hunters had not been praised.

We should avoid making the same mistake. Although the trope of abundant game and good hunting figured prominently in colonial promotional literature, this auspicious beginning was dampened in the eighteenth century by the flow of Enlightenment social thought. Far from being a hunter's nation, the United States emerged from the intellectual ferment of Protestantism, four-stages theory, republican ideology, and the radical force of reason. In none of these ideologies did hunters figure as heroes or exemplars of civic virtue; instead they figured as civilization's antithesis. To educated men of the Enlightenment, the farmer was the moral backbone of the young republic; backwoods hunters represented everything Americans, and America, should not be. Yet the past is seldom straightforward; the Revolution, ironically, produced the first literary celebrations of backwoods hunters.

Backwoods hunters would climb to prominence in American culture—if on wobbly legs—because the evils they represented were reverse images of their virtues. In a sense, backwoods hunters were more American than farmers. The hunter lived closest to wild nature; through his roaming and rambling, he comprehended the geography and topography of North America; he understood the wilderness and its wild fauna. The backwoods hunter's resemblance to the Indian made him seem indigenous, a man whose character and conduct were products of his wilderness environment, a man whose tie to the land was more profound than that of any civilized individual. Between the Revolution and the Civil War, the hunter would become idolized as an American Native, the ideal man in harmony with nature and society. Before this new hunter could take his bows, however, America would undergo profound changes.

5

The Problem with Sport Hunting

In the Chesapeake colonies, sport hunting gained a following among planters eager to mimic the English elite, but even there hunting never freed itself from the taint of bad character. Francis Osborne, whose *Advice to a Son* circulated among planters in the seventeenth century, excluded hunting from the sports suitable for young gentlemen because it undermined the equanimity that he considered a mark of the gentry. The popular conduct books of Sir Thomas More and Philip Dormer Stanhope, fourth earl of Chesterfield, likewise counseled against "excessive indulgence" in hunting because of its cruelty, expense, and wastefulness.[1]

These authors were influenced not by Puritanism or four-stages theory but by Renaissance and Enlightenment ideas about the value of reason, rationality, and humanity. As early as the sixteenth century, sport hunting had been attacked in the writings of Montaigne and Erasmus, who complained that hunting made men cruel and savage. Hunters "drive at nothing more than to become beasts themselves," admonished Erasmus, "while yet they imagine they live the life of princes." A century later, Shakespeare employed hunting imagery not to praise a hero by comparing him with a hunter but to deride excessive machismo and to rouse sympathy for brave or innocent victims by likening them to the hunter's prey.[2]

This antipathy to blood sport would culminate in the Society for the Prevention of Cruelty to Animals, formed in Britain in 1824 and in the United States in 1866. A milestone in the lobby for animal rights, however, had come decades earlier. In 1776, along with the Declaration of Independence and Thomas Paine's *Common Sense,* appeared Rev. Dr. Humphrey Primatt's *Dissertation on the Duty of Mercy and Sin of Cruelty to Brute Animals.* Primatt's book mustered every argument of the past two centuries against the mistreatment of animals. He argued from the Bible, from science, and from philosophy, and he emerged with the simplest of principles: "Cruelty is ATHEISM."[3]

If Primatt's thoughts did not circulate widely in America, those of Soame Jenyns, a member of Parliament, did. Jenyns's "Disquisition on Cruelty to Inferior Animals" was reprinted in no less than five different American magazines between 1785 and 1797. "What name should we bestow on a superior Being," queried Jenyns, "whose whole endeavors were employed, and whose whole pleasure consisted, in terrifying, ensnaring, tormenting, and destroying mankind?" "Just such a Being," he concluded, would be called "a sportsman."[4]

What we need to know is how ubiquitous, or rare, such sentiments were in America. Common sense would tell us that few colonists opposed hunting; too many Americans were hunters themselves. Even animal rights advocates of the late nineteenth and early twentieth centuries seldom opposed hunting.

Far from being less apt to oppose hunting, however, Revolutionary and early-national-era Americans were more likely to oppose hunting than those of later generations. A survey of periodical literature from the second half of the eighteenth century reveals eleven unambiguous attacks on sport hunting (six tracts, including reprints of Jenyns's arguments, and five poems) in weekly and monthly magazines and only four unambiguous celebrations of hunting (two songs and two poems). Even the great American naturalist and wilderness traveler William Bartram, influenced by his Quaker heritage, spoke eloquently against sport hunting.[5]

The most meticulous statement against hunting by a Revolutionary era American appeared in 1790, written by no less a figure than Dr. Benjamin Rush, the nation's preeminent surgeon and a signer of the Declaration of Independence. Rush enumerated six reasons why young Americans should be discouraged from what he termed "gunning."

1. It hardens the heart, by inflicting unnecessary pain and death upon the animals.
2. It is unnecessary in a civilized society, where animal food may be obtained from domestic animals, with greater facility.
3. It consumes a great deal of time, and thus creates habits of idleness.
4. It frequently leads men into low, bad company.
5. By imposing long abstinence from food, it leads to intemperance in eating, which naturally leads to intemperance in drinking.
6. It exposes to fevers, and accidents. The news-papers are occasionally

filled with melancholy accounts of the latter, and every physician must have met with frequent and dangerous instances of the former, in the course of his practice.

While recognizing that "the early use of a gun is recommended in our country" to prepare men for war, Rush nonetheless wondered "why should we inspire our youth, by such exercises, with hostile ideas toward their fellow creatures?—Let us rather instill into their minds sentiments of universal benevolence to men of all nations and colours."[6]

At one level, Rush's strictures on gunning seem to reflect a Revolutionary condemnation of aristocratic indolence. The American Revolution began with a boycott of British luxury goods and a new call for spartan simplicity in dress and deportment. As part of this campaign, shooting (with cockfighting and gambling) was banned on Sundays, and both the U.S. Congress and the states called on hunters to save powder and shot for the war effort.[7]

Rush's comment that hunting "leads men into low, bad company," however, suggests that he—as an heir to four-stages theorists—objected to hunting because it smacked as much of barbarism as of aristocracy. Rush's ideal republican would be a citizen of the world, an individual guided by virtue, self-sacrifice, and duty to community, not an illiterate backwoodsman or a narrow-minded aristocrat wedded to the interests of caste. Moreover, this ideal republican would be a man of reason and moderation. Hunting—with its implicit celebration of passion, cruelty, licentiousness, and barbarism—had no place in Rush's America.

Does Rush's statement indicate a widespread movement against hunting? Certainly Benjamin Franklin—like other respectable men, no doubt—eschewed "shooting" lest his reputation for industry suffer.[8] Yet the sources are ambiguous; Rush's comments indicate that although some Americans opposed hunting, others had come to see it as the backbone of republicanism. To be a soldier-citizen required skill in the use of arms, a skill that could be attained through hunting. Rush, however, in company with others influenced by the Enlightenment, offered a more pacific prescription for curing the body politic and keeping it healthy.

Rush's strictures were part of a larger attempt to scrutinize every action, every behavior, for its compatibility with republicanism. What sort of men would republicans be, and how should young men be indoctrinated with republican precepts? If, in answering these questions, some theorists urged Americans to adopt hunting as a school of martial valor, others agreed with Rush. *The Hare; or, Hunting Incompatible with Humanity; Written as a Stimulus to Youth Towards a Proper Treatment of Animals*, published in Philadelphia in 1802, recounted the brutality of the hunt from the point of view of the hare, adding that "the beauties of the scene" should have a humanizing influence on the hunter yet "make no impression upon his heart." *A Peep into the Sport of Youth,* published in Philadelphia in 1809, similarly included a woodcut of the "huntsman" who "is just returned from what he terms fine sport, and holds the poor lifeless hare dangling in his hand, little thinking how many pangs his amusement has cost it" (the book contradicted itself, however, with a more flattering woodcut depicting the "sportsman").[9]

This emergent concern for animals sprang from an emergent concern for humans. The English latitudinarians of the seventeenth and eighteenth centuries had embraced benevolence—the milk of human kindness—in their attempt to win back the people from the zealotry of Puritanism. The well-to-do were henceforth expected to help the unfortunate wherever possible. The rewards were the riches of self-congratulation. In time, as James Turner argues, this sentiment was applied to "brute animals," too, particularly after anatomical studies showed remarkable similarities in the nervous systems of humans and animals. As Jeremy Bentham wrote in 1789, the question was not whether animals could reason, or whether they could talk, but whether they could suffer.[10]

The concern for animal rights—and the opposition to hunting that accompanied it—represented the fullest flower of the Enlightenment, with its codes of pacifism, rationality, and sobriety, together with the Protestant renunciation of the passions. When reason triumphed over passion, humanity would thrive; wars would cease; men would become citizens of the world; and both individuals and nations would come to see themselves as interdependent.[11] There might be no all-out assault on hunting in the eighteenth and nineteenth centuries, but neither was hunting—with its celebration of passion, cruelty, and savagery—accorded a privileged place in Enlightenment thought.

Lurking in the new strictures against hunting was an ideology of domesticity. Society, in this view, would not be a place of unfettered competition and self-interest but rather a place of rational deliberation and goodwill. The public sphere would imitate the private sphere, where individuals treated one another with respect and courtesy. By learning to treat animals well, humans would learn to treat one another well. Seldom, however, did this idea dominate American thinking.

Like the good and evil twins of American Indian creation stories, domesticity—the attempt to domesticate humans and society—perpetually wrestled with its evil twin, self-interest and individualism, an ideology that would soon be embodied in the image of the American hunter-hero. The struggle seemed Manichaean; the two forces existed in a kind of perpetual balance, each as a complement to its opposite, neither fully able to prevail. This dualism does not mean that the popularity of hunting remained static; the popularity of hunting as a sport skyrocketed in nineteenth-century America. Yet Americans of the colonial and early national eras had not fixed upon hunting as a source of American greatness.

Had there been no sport hunting in eighteenth-century America, however, there would have been no opposition to it. From the outset of colonization, sport hunting appealed to elite colonists who read British literature, who were often educated in England, and who sought to build personae and estates comparable to those of the English gentry.

In South Carolina, the woods "abound with deer," recalled the English traveler John Davis in 1803, "the hunting of which forms the chief diversion of the Planters." These planters—some of whom might have belonged to the St. Thomas Hunting Club, which was formed in Charleston in 1785—seemed to have had more loyalty to the idea of sport than Virginians, who, as Robert Beverley had reported a century earlier, trapped, netted, or treed game animals more often than they killed them in fair chase. The South Carolina planters mentioned by Davis ordered slaves and servants to chase deer into the open where they could be shot in a sporting way.[12]

Hunting was also popular among certain elite colonists of the middle and northern colonies. The first American hunting and fishing club, the "Colony in Schuylkill," appeared in Philadelphia in 1732. This organization survived into the nineteenth century as the "Schuylkill Fishing Company" (interestingly, members left the word "hunting" out of their club's name altogether). One need not have belonged to a club, however, to hunt for sport, since land for rent in New Jersey in the 1770s abounded "with gentlemens game" according to a newspaper ad. The ad's author promised "good shooting and fishing at this seat," adding that it "would suit any gentleman's family extremely well, for a rural retreat during the summer season." In Boston, too, men sometimes hunted for sport; the patriot and silversmith Paul Revere liked to ride and shoot on occasion.[13]

As early as 1753, a richly dressed, fourteen-year-old Thomas Mifflin, Pennsylvania's future governor, appears in a portrait by American painter Benjamin West. Young Mifflin stands with his fowling piece; several ducks he has shot lie on the ground behind him, and his retriever fetches yet another duck from the water. A similar scene by William Dering depicts a son of the Virginia elite, George Booth, in genteel garb, holding bow and arrow, and accompanied by a dog with a bird in its mouth.[14]

What is noteworthy about such portraits is their rarity. While English painters manufactured dozens, perhaps hundreds, of hunter portraits for elite patrons in the seventeenth and eighteenth centuries, only a few appeared in colonial American art.[15] The fact that the portraits of Mifflin and Booth depict children, moreover, suggests that although colonists might deem hunting an acceptable childhood pastime, they did not necessarily commend it for adults.

The most surprising thing about sport hunting in colonial and early national America is not that elite Americans would mimic their British counterparts in their enthusiasm for the chase but that sport hunters would remain so quiescent in America. Even in the literature of the colonial South, one finds only fleeting references to sport hunting. Perhaps the fact that hunting was open to every man in the New World tarnished its gentility. Members of the American elite sometimes found that they could no more claim a monopoly on game than they could on social authority; if the two were no longer bound together, why hunt for sport at all?

When references to sport hunting appeared in American literature, they tended to be copied from British originals. In 1774, amid the first huzzahs for Revolution, appeared "The Hill Tops, A New Hunting Song" in Isaiah Thomas's *Royal American Magazine,* together with an engraving showing mounted gentlemen observing their hounds attack a distinctly un-American species of stag. The song concluded with "toasts to our Lasses our Country & King." Because Thomas was a patriot, the song's Tory sensibility seems incongruous. To some, it must have appeared like a warning that King George would soon attempt to bring the rebel stag to bay.[16]

In 1783, soon after the English regulars themselves had been brought to bay, appeared the first American hunting book—*The Sportsman's Companion, or, An Essay on Shooting, . . . by a gentleman who has made shooting his favorite amusement upwards of twenty-six years in Great Britain, Ireland, and North-America.* Though published in New York City, this book seems to have been an English production. It borrowed heavily from English hunting literature and was almost certainly written by a British officer. While agonizing over the character of his hounds, the author, who described shooting heath hens (pinnated grouse) on Long Island, displayed a rather un-American self-assurance about his sport. One finds here no discussion of the morality of hunting, a topic that often appeared in American hunting literature of the nineteenth century. The author did discuss, however, the morality of stealing dogs, arguing that dog thieves should go to the gallows.[17]

A second issue of the *Sportsman's Companion* appeared in Burlington, New Jersey, in 1791, but no additional hunting title was published in America until 1827. That book, *The American Shooter's Manual, by a Gentleman of Philadelphia County,*

"The Hill Tops, A New Hunting Song," from the *Royal American Magazine*, 1774. Courtesy of the Beinecke Rare Book and Manuscript Library, Yale University, New Haven, Connecticut.

which was published in Philadelphia, was little more than a plagiarization of the English *Shooter's Companion* and Alexander Wilson's *American Ornithology*. The Boston painter John Ritto Penniman likewise presented Americans with several bird hunting scenes between 1805 and 1820, but these paintings were copies of English works.[18]

In the same years, British presses poured forth a barrage of hunting art and literature. As a sport, however, hunting appears to have captivated a small fraction of the American populace. Sport hunting seemed too elitist and indolent to appeal to the majority of American freeholders. Far from becoming a recommendation, hunting's association with the gentry brought it into contempt.

On January 25, 1770, one "JERSEY FARMER" appealed to the public via a letter in the Pennsylvania *Gazette* to stop the abuses of would-be American aristocrats. The letter decried those who pursued the "great cause of liberty" by crying out against English taxation yet all the while indulged in dissipation at home. And who were these "haughty gentry" who played the hypocrite? They were "fox hunters," men whose pastime had become so popular "that it is become dangerous, in some Places, for a Man to think himself so much Master of his own Land, as to attempt to hinder those Freebooters from ravaging every Part of it at their pleasure."[19]

The particular fox hunters to whom the JERSEY FARMER objected were probably members of the Gloucester Fox Hunting Club of Philadelphia, organized in 1766 with 125 members and a slave named Natty serving as huntsman, or keeper of the hounds. Most of the Gloucester Club's hunting was done in New Jersey, although, by the time of the Revolution, fox hunters and subscription packs (trained hounds) could be found in New York, Virginia, the Carolinas, and, after the Revolution, in Washington, D.C.[20]

As opulent displays of horsemanship, valor, and social distinction, fox hunting appeared in the colonies at roughly the time that it gained popularity in England. Alexander Hamilton rode in fox hunts, as did Thomas Jefferson in his youth, and George Washington made a near fetish of the sport, judging by the number of times the topic occurs in his journals. Southern gentlemen like Washington went so far as to import riding frocks, waistcoats of fine scarlet cloth and gold lace, and handsome buckskin breeches from England. Even the English red fox, considered superior to the American grey fox, was imported in 1730 and was said to range up and down the seaboard, interbreeding with natives.[21]

Yet fox hunting did not square with republicanism. What the JERSEY FARMER recognized was that as fox hunters spurred their horses over ditches and fences, they leaped over social boundaries that common men were bound to respect. Incensed by the pretensions of this elite, the JERSEY FARMER urged his fellow freeholders not to fear "the Sneers of them who are galloping merrily on the Highway to Destruction" but rather to press charges against them for trespass. Farmers had only "our own Inattention and Supineness," he wrote, "for suffering our Laws to be thus publicly, and daily, insulted and trampled upon, and ourselves treated like Vassals by—Fox Hunters."[22]

In the egalitarian climate of the early Republic, fox hunters did not prevail against those who opposed them. "Hail noble lads!" wrote the American author of a 1798 poem that mocked fox hunters,

> Ye heroes of the chase,
> That love upon your horses' backs to run
> In search of blood, and think it glorious fun;
> Hail! noble jockies of Neronian race!

Haltingly and grudgingly, the banner of aristocratic fox hunting was furled. It was too tangled in the web of the English aristocracy to become republican sport. Fox hunting demanded formality in costume and protocol; it called for expensive horses and more expensive dogs; and it was better suited to the open acreages of large plantations than to the small, fenced tracts and rocky, hilly terrain of New England and the middle states.[23]

As the common man gained political ascendancy in the decades after the Revolution, there appeared "a growing suspicion" that fox hunting "was a questionable if not demoralizing diversion." This suspicion led to the dissolution of the Gloucester Fox Hunting Club in 1818. While fox hunting continued to be popular among gentlemen planters of the South, in much of the North it became a neglected art in the Jacksonian and antebellum eras and remained so until a new elite rediscovered it in the Gilded Age. "Fox hunting," remarked the author of *Schreiner's Sporting Manual* in 1841, "is but little practiced of late in the northern and middle states, and viewing it as a species of sport, cruel, and somewhat demoralizing in its tendency, . . . I shall purposely withhold any further remarks upon the subject."[24]

With all the moral and social stigma attached to hunting, it would have been difficult to have surveyed colonial or even early national America and predicted that by the time of the Civil War hunter-heroes would hold center stage in the American imagination. Nor would it have been easy to predict that hunting

Elite fox hunters came under a barrage of criticism in the early national era. This painting shows fox hunters trespassing on the fields of a common farmer. Anonymous, *The End of the Hunt,* ca. 1800 (canvas, 34½ × 53⅞ inches). National Gallery of Art, Gift of Edgar William and Bernice Chrysler Garbisch. Photograph © Board of Trustees, National Gallery of Art, Washington, D.C.

(alongside fishing) would become the most popular participatory sport of middle-class men.

Though thousands of Americans hunted in the seventeenth, eighteenth, and early nineteenth centuries, they were ambivalent about doing so. Hunting spanned the gamut of contradiction, epitomizing in many ways everything an American should not be: it seemed too Indian, too barbaric, and at the same time too English, too aristocratic. For many Americans it also seemed cruel, anti-agrarian, unhealthful, and irreligious. There was every reason to think that hunting, as a sport for respectable men, would disappear in the northern and middle states as they became more developed and urbanized. Yet sport hunting followed a paradoxical trajectory; its popularity grew at a dynamic rate until, by the time that Theodore Roosevelt assumed the presidency, hunting seemed to be the fount of American greatness.

6

Hunters Ascendant

In 1824 there appeared a fabulous tale with the improbable title *Life and Remarkable Adventures of Israel R. Potter, (a Native of Cranston, Rhode-Island,) Who Was a Soldier in the American Revolution . . . after which He Was Taken Prisoner by the British, Conveyed to England, Where for 30 Years He Obtained his Livelihood . . . by Crying "Old Chairs To Mend."* The title told most of the story, but what it did not tell was that Israel Potter portrayed himself as a frontier hunter who could compare his experience shooting British officers at Bunker Hill to his experience shooting deer in New Hampshire.[1]

Certainly Benjamin Rush would have taken equivocal satisfaction from Potter's claim; pride in gunning was what Rush preached against. No naysaying, however, could diminish the dramatic impact of the frontier hunter bringing to bear his powers against the English elite. Not surprisingly, Potter became a legendary figure after publication of his memoir, despite the fact that he probably never fired a shot in the Battle of Bunker Hill and may or may not have spent thirty years in England after being taken prisoner.[2]

Men like Potter—self-sufficient, spartan backwoods hunters clad in buckskin shirts and leggings—have been credited in popular histories and oral tradition with winning the American Revolution. George Washington Parke Custis, adopted son of George Washington, recalled in his *Recollections and Private Memoirs of Washington* that the buckskin hunting shirt became "the venerable emblem of the Revolution," having been the "uniform" not only of American militia men but also of such famous soldiers as George Rogers Clark, Daniel Morgan and his sharpshooters, and Ethan Allen and his Green Mountain Boys. The U.S. Congress had issued hunting shirts to noncommissioned officers, perhaps at the instigation of Washington, who, according to Custis, had recommended the buck-skin shirt as the uniform for the colonial militia as early as 1758.[3]

It was an odd turn of events, however, that saw backwoods hunters rush to the defense of an infant country. The founding fathers—among them land specula-tors like George Washington and Henry Knox, grandees like Alexander Hamil-ton and John Hancock, and wealthy planters like Thomas Jefferson and James Madison—must have been a trifle surprised that the buckskins had thrown in their lot with the patriots. That was not everywhere true, of course, as many back-woods locales, particularly in the South, were either hotbeds of Toryism or, more often, politically neutral.

Yet enough backwoodsmen joined the cause of the patriots to create a sensa-tion. "I have had the Happiness," reported a newspaper correspondent in 1775,

> of seeing Captain Michael Cressap, marching at the Head of a formidable Company, of upwards of 130 Men from the Mountains and back Woods, painted like Indians, armed with Tomahawks and rifles, dressed in hunting Shirts and Mockasons [some had marched eight hundred miles from the Ohio River Valley]. Health and Vigour, after what they had undergone, declared them to be intimate with Hardship and fa-miliar with Danger. . . . What would a regular Army, of considerable Strength in the Forest of America do with 1000 of these Men, who want nothing to preserve their Health and Courage, but Water from the Spring, with a little parches of Corn, and what they can easily procure in Hunting; and who, wrapped in their Blankets in the Damp of Night, would choose the Shade of a Tree for their Covering, and the Earth for their Bed?[4]

In Virginia these backwoods patriots were the "damn'd shirtmen," according to Tories, who described their "Virginia univorm" as "an Oznab[urg] Shirt over their Cloaths, a belt round them [and] a Tommyhawk or Scalping Knife." To pa-triots such men were "heroes in hunting shirts." Georgia went so far as to print the image of the buckskinned hunter on some of its earliest bills of exchange, making the backwoods hunter a symbol of the Revolution.[5] Thus the epithet "buckskins" was transformed by the Revolution into a title of honor. But how could this Hobbesian figure, this threat to agrarian civilization, symbolize the Revolution?

Great metamorphoses occur with subtle shifts of thought. The Hobbesian hunter—the brute who defied constituted authority and lived in antisocial iso-lation—became an ideal symbol for heroic defiance of the British Empire. Far from being a barbarian, the hunter was the jealous guardian of individual liber-ties against the tyranny of Great Britain. Like the backwoods hunter—indeed, like that other symbol of Revolutionary defiance, the American Indian—patriots saw themselves as indigenous men of America, proud, powerful, self-sufficient, hunting folk who would stop at nothing to escape the imperial yoke.

Dressed in homespun hunting frocks, American militiamen and army recruits must have looked to English officers suspiciously like the poachers of England. Here was a rebellion against the British elite, whose social privilege and authority had always been bound up with its exclusive right to hunt. Colonists seemed to say that in America every man was a hunter, and no man would brook the tyranny of an English master. The backwoods hunter—a powerful, masculine figure, even in his guise as wild man of the woods—was ensconced as an indigenous symbol of liberty and manliness.

The image of the buckskinned hunter as Revolutionary hero almost certainly appealed to small farmers and backwoodsmen—men who were themselves buckskinned hunters and riflemen—rather than genteel patriots of the Atlantic seaboard. Often these plebeians—the Green Mountain Boys of Vermont, the Liberty Men of Maine, the Shaysites of Massachusetts, the Regulators of the Carolinas—were the first to challenge the deferential order of colonial America. Although frontier farmers opposed the banditti who subsisted by hunting alone, many farmers were hunters themselves, particularly in the fall and winter when the harvest was in and game could be taken for sale at market.[6]

Whereas planters and traders of established regions feared that the Crown would enslave them through taxation, for backcountry men slavery had more palpable dimensions. For them slavery might mean the inability to pay the great proprietors for lands on which they squatted. Or it might mean paying taxes to support churches they did not attend (backcountry men—insofar as they were religious at all—were drawn not to state-sponsored religions like Congregationalism and Anglicanism but to the egalitarian and emotional appeal of Baptists, Methodists, and Pietists). Slavery might also mean political subordination to planters and other great men who believed it was their right and duty to serve in colonial legislatures. In some cases slavery meant indentured servitude, which for many poor folk was a necessity rather than a choice. In the South (and in the North before the nineteenth century), slavery even meant the ownership of human beings.

Freedom, on the other hand, meant the right to own land, to command one's affairs, and to seek opportunity on the frontier. The freest man—the antithesis of the slave—was the buckskinned hunter, who symbolized the right to independence, self-assertion, and self-governance. Plebeian Americans saw themselves as a simple, egalitarian people whose defense of individual liberty was embodied in the Kentucky rifles and tomahawks they carried, and whose rejection of luxury, effeminacy, and arrogance was expressed by their buckskin garb. The backwoods hunter was "fearless of every thing," noted an English observer in the early national era, "attacks everything that comes in his way, and thinks himself the happiest and noblest being in the world."[7]

The natural home of these plebeians was in the Anti-Federalist movement and, after the adoption of the Constitution, in the party of Jefferson, the Republican party (also called the Democratic Republican party). Small farmers and backwoodsmen did not compose a unified political movement, but in general they believed in limited government, states' rights, low taxation, debtor relief, paper money, free land, and internal improvements like roads and canals. They also opposed the Constitution (and the strong central authority it represented), standing armies in peacetime, and the national debt, which they saw as an instrument with which to redistribute wealth from hard-working taxpayers like themselves to parasitical holders of government securities.

Jeffersonian Republicans were upholders of individual liberties, and the America they hoped to build would be a libertarian realm in which every individual would be free, independent, and competent to participate in government. The new country would not be the hierarchical, deferential, monarchical world of colonial America, nor would it be a world ruled by a disinterested gentry (the sort attracted to the Federalist party) who felt it was their right and duty to govern lesser men. In the Jeffersonian view, republicanism translated into unfettered individualism and grassroots political participation. In this world every man would be a hunter insofar as every man could claim the rights, liberties, and privileges that only elite hunters held in England.[8]

Identities, however, can be borrowed and reconfigured by people they are intended to exclude. At least one patriot urged Virginia's elite burgesses to attend their session in shirtmen garb, "which best suits the times, as the cheapest, and the most martial."[9] How often the burgesses followed his suggestion is unclear, but certainly the patriot cause encouraged many a Virginia planter to adopt the spartan, simple demeanor of the common men who in earlier decades had opposed them.

Despite their tendency to mimic the style of the English elite, members of the Virginia gentry of the Revolutionary era found themselves, according to Rhys Isaac, "trapped between the nether millstone of popular disaffection and the upper millstone of imperial determination to keep the colonial ruling groups in a subordinate position." Threatened with losing the respect of Baptists, Methodists, and frontier buckskins, members of the elite cloaked themselves in the principles of spartan patriotism. Patrick Henry, with his "homespun pronunciation," his extemporaneous, evangelical political speeches, and his disdain for classical rules of rhetoric, epitomized the new style. Meanwhile, Henry—a member of the planter elite—donned buckskin clothes to tour the woods with his brother shirtmen.[10]

Even in the early national era, however, hunters often walked amid clouds of doubt rather than warm praise. Though the Revolution marked a turning point in American attitudes toward hunting, many Americans still saw hunters as men of independence and impudence. Hunters were not heroes to those who sought to shore up old patterns of deference and hierarchy in the wake of the Revolution. Nor were hunters heroes to those who sought to replace old patterns of deference and hierarchy with agrarian republicanism.

The hunter became the war chief of American society, but the farmer remained its peace chief. In 1804 Connecticut poet David Humphreys wrote,

Hail, model of free states! too little known,
Too lightly prized for rural arts alone:
Yet hence from savage, social life began,
Compacts were fram'd and man grew mild to man.
Thee, Agriculture! source of every joy,
Domestic sweets and bliss without alloy.

"The American system of agriculture and republicanism," added Samuel Williams in 1809, "have [*sic*] such an affinity to each other, that they will both flourish or decline together." Joel Barlow, the Connecticut-born diplomat, poet, and Jeffersonian Republican, meanwhile described an idyllic future when the American earth "by culture warms the genial skies," explaining in a note that "cultivation seems to have softened" the American climate.[11]

Jefferson—through his pro-agriculture and antimanufacturing policies—continued to pay tribute to yeoman farmers; hunters reeked too much of indolence and savagery to dominate the iconography of his Republican party. How could Jefferson and his followers fly the banner of the hunter at the same time that they urged Indians to give up the chase and take up the plow? Yet Jefferson himself helped tailor a hunter-hero for the new nation.

7

The Hunter's Empire

 In the first years of the nineteenth century, a small party of American explorers, christened the Corps of Discovery by Thomas Jefferson, labored up the Missouri River, en route to the Rocky Mountains and the Pacific Ocean. In the Far West, much of which had come under American dominion with the Louisiana Purchase in 1803, members of this expedition found adventure, excitement, and landscapes "beatifull in the extreme." More often, however, the men, led by captains Meriwether Lewis and William Clark, found hard work, privation, and monotony. The trials and tedium of the journey made the occasional respite in hunting all the more satisfying. Thus Meriwether Lewis, having been confined to his boat for several days, resolved on September 17, 1804, "to devote this day to amuse myself on shore with my gun and view the interior of the country."[1] The day would reward Lewis with more than amusement.

Setting out with six of his best hunters in what is today South Dakota, Lewis found a countryside composed of "irregular hills of 100 to 200 feet high," at the top of which "the country breakes of[f] as usual into a fine leavel plain extending as far as the eye can reach." Atop this plain grew lush grass, the result of a burn that had occurred, Lewis figured, a month earlier, while to the west stretched "a high range of hills" from north to south. "This scenery already rich pleasing and beatiful," wrote Lewis, "was still farther hightened by the immence herds of Buffaloe deer Elk and Antelopes which we saw in every direction feeding on the hills and plains."[2]

The object of the day's excursion was not to appreciate scenery but to kill a female pronghorn antelope as a scientific specimen, a male having been taken earlier. Observing "several herds," the hunters walked eight miles from camp to pursue them but found the pronghorns "extremely shye and watchfull insomuch that we had been unable to get a shot at them." The pronghorns "seelect the most elivated point in the neighbourhood," reported Lewis, "and as they are watchfull and extreemly quick of sight and their sense of smelling very accute it is almost impossible to approach them within gunshot; ... they will frequently discover and flee from you at the distance of three miles."[3]

Having singled out a herd of seven, Lewis followed his quarry as they ran up a low hill that gave them visual command of three directions. The one direction that they could not see, noted Lewis, was the direction from which the wind blew. The pronghorns would smell him even if they did not see him. Eager to obtain a specimen for President Jefferson, Lewis continued to stalk the animals, hiding behind a shallow ridge as he moved uphill.

The sole male in the group, Lewis observed, "frequently incircled the summit of the hill on which the females stood in a group, as if to look out for the approach of danger." When Lewis came to within two hundred paces of the animals, they fled, and Lewis proceeded to the top of the hill where they had stood. The prong-horns, having run into a ravine, reemerged some three miles away. "I doubted at ferst," wrote Lewis, "that they were the same that I had just surprised,"

> but my doubts soon vanished when I beheld the rapidity of their flight along the ridge before me[.] [I]t appeared reather the rappid flight of birds than the motion of quadrupeds. I think I can safely venture to ascertion that the speed of this animal is equal if not superior to that of the finest blooded courser.[4]

Even without taking a female pronghorn, Lewis had made an important discovery: he had observed the fastest quadruped in North America.

That was not the only discovery of the day. When Lewis returned to camp, he brought buffalo meat for his men and a black-billed magpie for science, the first of its species known to Americans. The party's other hunters had killed what Clark described as a "Curious kind of Deer, a Darker grey than Common," with "hair longer & finer, the ears verry large & long ... its tail round and white to near the end which is black & like a Cow." In other respects, wrote Clark, it was "like a Deer, except it runs like a goat." "Large," he added. This animal was a mule deer, another species new to American science. Finally, wrote Clark, the party had seen "a Small wolf with a large bushey tail," an animal Americans would soon know as the coyote.[5]

On September 17, 1804, three new species—the black-billed magpie, the mule deer, and the coyote—were either collected or described by Lewis and Clark, while another, the pronghorn antelope, was observed in the exercise of its greatest talent, running from danger. The scope of what was American was permanently changed by the observation of these creatures. Though the public would be made aware of these discoveries only months or even years later, they became part of the legacy bequeathed to the nation by its "pioneering naturalists," as Paul Russell Cutright calls Lewis and Clark.[6]

The discoveries of Lewis and Clark also became part of the legacy bequeathed to the nation by another pioneering naturalist, Thomas Jefferson. Through his Corps of Discovery, and through Meriwether Lewis in particular, Jefferson sought to complete the catalog of the nation's fauna, flora, and geography that he had begun in *Notes on the State of Virginia.* Accordingly, before the expedition, Jefferson enlisted the nation's most eminent scholars to refine Lewis's knowledge of botany, zoology, and ethnology, the infant sciences that would enable him to comprehend the continent.[7]

Even as Americans lionized farmers as guarantors of republican virtue and heirs to the land they cultivated, Lewis, as a naturalist, was more than an agrarian agent of civilization. Though Lewis's mission was a step toward the agrarian settlement of the Far West, it represented an attempt to tie together the continent in a unified, scientific whole long before it could be appropriated by men with plows. Lewis took possession of the continent not through planting but through science.

Lewis also took possession of the land by hunting. "We eat an emensity of meat," wrote Lewis on July 13, 1805. "It requires 4 deer, an Elk and a deer, or one buffaloe, to supply us plentifully for 24 hours." Though this was a large order, it was one the hunters could usually fill. Like the earliest American colonists, Lewis and Clark found a hunter's paradise in the West. On the banks of the Missouri River, the explorers could "kill whatever we wish," wrote Lewis, enabling them to dine on "fine veal and fat beef" from buffalo, as well as "venison and beaver tails." So numerous and tame were buffalo and elk in May 1805 that "the men frequently throw sticks and stones at them in order to drive them out of the way."[8]

At other times, game was scarce, yet few Americans remember the privations endured by the explorers; Americans instead remember the bounty. As Richard White reminds us, Lewis and Clark were (and are) portrayed as the "first white men" to enter the "untouched paradise" of the Far West.[9] That this paradise was not untouched and that Lewis and Clark were not the first to enter it are beside the point. Americans look upon Lewis and Clark as the first Americans in the Far West because they, not Indians or Métis, represent a chosen people come to claim the promised land beyond the Mississippi. Lewis and Clark are remembered as the first Americans, moreover, because they entered the wilderness without despoiling it. In the American imagination, Lewis and Clark remain innocents in a state of natural virtue, men who delivered a message of goodwill to Indians while absorbing the austere beauty of the landscape.

As heroic hunters Lewis and Clark were something new in American history. Whereas backwoodsmen of the colonial imagination were, to quote Crèvecoeur, "ferocious, gloomy, and unsocial" because of their dependence on game, Lewis and Clark remained virtuous. At no time did they descend into a Hobbesian state of nature, becoming forces and empires unto themselves. Though hunters, they remained representatives of republican civilization and Enlightenment science. Insofar as Lewis and Clark entered any state of nature, it seemed more akin to that described by Rousseau than Hobbes.[10]

Though no ordinary four-stages theorist, Rousseau, in his *Discourse on the Origins of Inequality,* posited four stages of prepolitical society, the third of which—that of the hunting societies of American Indians—was the ideal. In this stage, contended Rousseau, men were not smitten by self-love and pride (*"amour-propre"*); they had not learned to elevate themselves over others, which was the disease of developed societies. In this earlier ideal stage, men retained an instinctual empathy for one another, a hatred for suffering and cruelty, and an egalitarian camaraderie.[11]

Coupled with Rousseau's concept of ideal hunting societies—preceding it, in fact—was the logic of the Deists. Having done away with the idea of original sin, Deists envisioned humans in a state of nature as virtuous and pure, uncontaminated by civilization. Jefferson, himself a Deist, jested that he was "savage enough to prefer the woods, the wilds and independence of Monticello, to all the brilliant pleasures" of a European metropolis. For Deists, knowledge and virtue were to be gleaned not from the Bible but from a different holy text, nature.[12]

Though Jefferson did not consciously mold Lewis and Clark to any Rousseauian or Deist standard, he did not envision them as arrogant conquerors either. In Jefferson's view, American Indians were to be won over to farming and civilization by reason and goodwill. With this purpose in mind, Jefferson equipped the expedition with medallions bearing the legend "peace and friendship" for distribution among Indian leaders, as well as sundry trade goods and a quantity of smallpox vaccine with which to innoculate Indians. Brute conquest of the Far West was beyond the power of the American government, but it was also contrary to Jefferson's ethical vision.

Following Jefferson's lead, Americans recalled the explorers' innocence—their friendship and goodwill toward Indian peoples—rather than the uneasy peace (or active hostility) that often prevailed during the expedition. The first statue of Lewis, a wax figure sculpted in 1807 by Charles Willson Peale for display in his American Museum in Philadelphia, thus showed a buckskin-clad Lewis holding a calumet (peace pipe). Over Lewis's shoulder was draped an ermine-skin tippet (a long scarf) given him by the Shoshone chief Cameahwait when the explorers were encamped at the headwaters of the Salmon River in 1805. A placard emphasized the benevolence of the expedition; Lewis had supposedly accepted the tippet with a speech about his people's desire to bring peace and to teach the Indians the arts of civilization. When Indian delegations visited Philadelphia, as they often did in the early national years, Peale conducted them to his waxen Lewis, hoping to show them the peaceful nature of American expansion.[13]

For much of the nineteenth century, artists ignored Lewis and Clark as subjects. Perhaps because of the ignominy attached to Lewis's suicide, artists found other explorers and hunters to glorify. When Lewis and Clark did reappear in late nineteenth-century and early twentieth-century painting, sculpture, and coinage (triggered partly by centennial commemorations of the expedition in St. Louis and Portland), they appeared in scenes of amity and goodwill. In paintings by Charles M. Russell and Edward Samuel Paxson, the buckskin-clad explorers shake hands, sit in councils, and trade with Indian peoples, often accompanied by their Shoshone interpreter, Sacajawea. The idea of white hunters as vicious and corrupt had been exchanged for a Rousseauian idea of hunters as humane and virtuous. When sport hunters of the antebellum and postbellum decades sought out nature, they sought to reenter a state of natural virtue like that of Lewis and Clark.

That trope was not the only one that could be gleaned from the Corps of Discovery. Elsewhere, sport hunters pressed into service a view of themselves as strong-armed winners of a heroic battle with wild beasts, much like Lewis and Clark in their triumphs over grizzly and buffalo. Although these two ideas—one Rousseauian, the other proto-Darwinian—ran on separate ideological tracks, both became conduits for the popularization of sport hunting.

In dressing men of science in Indian costume, American artists cast Lewis and Clark as American Natives, representatives of a race destined to replace the Indian as heir to the continent. The friendly interactions portrayed between explorers and Indians disguised the bitter contest that followed, making it seem almost as if Indians approved Lewis and Clark as worthy successors.

The American fascination with Lewis and Clark had begun almost as soon as the explorers departed. "Never did a similar event excite more joy thro' the United States," wrote Jefferson in 1813 as he recalled the expedition. "The hum-

In the late nineteenth and early twentieth centuries, Americans recalled the amity between Lewis and Clark and the Indians they had encountered during the famous 1804–1806 expedition to the Pacific Ocean. Charles M. Russell, *Captain William Clark of the Lewis and Clark Expedition Meeting with the Indians of the Northwest,* 1897 (oil on canvas, 29½ × 41½ inches). Sid Richardson Collection of Western Art, Fort Worth, Texas.

blest of it's [*sic*] citizens had taken a lively interest in the issue of this journey, and looked forward with impatience for the information it would furnish."[14]

Upon their return from the West, Lewis and Clark were congratulated and feted in Washington and in Virginia for having "extended the knowledge of the Geography of your country," enriching science, and opening the West for commercial development. Lewis, speaking to citizens of Charlottesville who had gathered to honor him, spoke of "the merit of having added to the world of science, and of liberty, a large portion of the immense unknown wilds of North America." Quibbling Federalists might argue that the explorers had discovered a "great waste" suitable for game, not farmers, but most Americans regarded Lewis and Clark as heroes who had linked a burgeoning people with a great realm.[15]

The fate of Meriwether Lewis, however, was not what Jefferson had hoped. Appointed governor of Louisiana Territory in 1807, Lewis found that he possessed few of the skills necessary to succeed as an administrator and a politician. Nor could he succeed as an author. Though he hoped to fulfill Jefferson's expectation that he produce the most thorough compendium of American geography and natural history yet published, Lewis found himself unable to put pen to paper. Here, at last, was an expedition too arduous. Depressed and drinking heavily, Lewis committed suicide in 1809 as he returned to Washington, D.C., to respond to criticism of his actions as governor.

The official report of the Lewis and Clark expedition would not appear until five years after Lewis's death. When it did appear in 1814—written by lawyer Nicholas Biddle rather than Lewis—the public found in its first pages a letter from Thomas Jefferson giving an account of the life of Capt. Meriwether Lewis. Addressing a nation that mourned Lewis's suicide, Jefferson discussed Lewis's distinguished ancestry, his father's death in the Revolutionary War, and his early life in Virginia's Albemarle County. When he spoke of Lewis's youth, Jefferson noted that although Lewis's "talent for observation" and "accurate knolege of the plants & animals of his own country, would have distinguished him as a farmer," he had elected to join the army instead.[16]

For Jefferson, who had spent a lifetime lauding the farmer as guarantor of republican virtue, the assertion that his protégé would have made an excellent farmer was obligatory. Yet Jefferson's words called attention to the fact that Lewis, although he had managed his family's plantation as a young man, had elected not to remain a farmer nor to become a producer of any sort. Lewis became a soldier, a private secretary, an explorer, and a bureaucrat. He did not occupy a neat place in the ideal republic of small farmers, yet Jefferson had mentored Lewis, and Jefferson still endorsed him.

In identifying the germ of Lewis's greatness, Jefferson emphasized the naturalist, frontiersman, and hunter in Lewis rather than the farmer. "When only 8. years of age," wrote Jefferson, Lewis

> habitually went out in the dead of night alone with his dogs, into the forest to hunt the raccoon & opossum, which, seeking their food in the night, can then only be

taken. In this exercise no season or circumstance could obstruct his purpose, plunging thro' the winter's snows and frozen streams in pursuit of his object.

In what appears to have been an earlier draft, Jefferson had displayed an even greater flourish of melodrama, writing that young Lewis "might be tracked through the snow to his traps by the blood which trickled from his bare feet."[17]

Continuing in this vein, Jefferson appended to the litany of good character (courage, perseverance, leadership) the fact that Lewis was "intimate with the Indian character, customs & principles, habituated to the hunting life, [and] guarded by exact observations of the vegetables & animals of his own country, against losing time in the description of objects already possessed." Together with scrupulous honesty, these qualities made Lewis's reports "as certain as if seen by ourselves" and appeared to Jefferson to have been "implanted by nature in one body" for the "express purpose" of the transcontinental expedition.[18]

Jefferson had supplanted the sturdy farmer with the adventurous hunter and naturalist as the instrument of empire. Lewis was anointed by nature to take charge of the Louisiana wilderness not by cultivating it with a plow, like Jefferson's farmer-hero, but by cultivating it with his scientific reports, his aboriginal persona, and his acumen as a hunter. In his eulogy Jefferson reiterated the idea of Lewis as an American Native, a man who was as virtuous as the farmer, but whose claim to the continent and whose worth as a citizen were not based on planting.

After Lewis's death in 1809, his place in the American imagination lost its luster. Even if Lewis was neglected for a time, however, the trophies he had obtained were remembered, at least until the grander collections of later explorers replaced them. Jefferson kept many of the expedition's specimens, displaying them in his Indian Hall, the entrance hall at Monticello. Upon entering, visitors could gaze at a fascinating collection of Indian bows and arrows, peace pipes, weapons, clothing, wampum belts, and paintings on buffalo hides (one depicted a battle between the Osage and Pawnee, and another diagrammed the Missouri River and its tributaries). Across the hall from these ethnographic artifacts appeared crystals, shells, fossils, preserved reptiles, mammoth bones, a bear claw, the antlers of deer, elk, and moose, and what must have been the crown gem of the collection, the head of an American bighorn sheep.[19]

The lesson taught by Jefferson's Indian Hall was that hunting and scientific collecting were not such different enterprises; both were means of taking possession of the continent. As the century progressed, they would become more closely related. Drawing on the legacy of Jefferson and Lewis, American hunters of the nineteenth century would define themselves not merely as sportsmen but as hunter-naturalists. They, like Lewis, would take possession of the continent by hunting, collecting, and displaying their trophies in cabinets of natural history.

The greatest trophy of all, however, a living American mammoth, eluded Jefferson. Since the discovery of fossil mammoth bones in America in the eighteenth century, Jefferson had believed that the mammoth—a creature he took to be a massive carnivore—must survive in the dim mists of the West. The Creator would hardly have contrived a species only to extinguish it; the Creator did not make mistakes in the Great Chain of Being, an immutable chain composed of a hierarchy of beings from the simplest organism to the most complex and intelligent.[20]

Jefferson employed the mammoth in his famous refutation of the French naturalist George Louis Leclerc, comte de Buffon, who had claimed that the New World produced smaller, less vigorous fauna than the Old. The mammoth, wrote Jefferson, "should have sufficed to have rescued the earth it inhabited, and the atmosphere it breathed, from the imputation of impotence in the conception and nourishment of animal life." Indeed, after Charles Willson Peale displayed a virtually complete skeleton of a mammoth in his musuem in 1801, the word "mammoth" became an adjective for any American natural production of enormous proportion.[21]

Jefferson was so fascinated by the mammoth that in *Notes on the State of Virginia* he had related an Indian belief that the mammoth still survived. During the Revolution, recalled Jefferson, the governor of Virginia had entertained a delegation of Delaware Indians who recounted an ancient story of a herd of "big buffalo" (Jefferson took these to be mammoths) that congregated at the Big-Bone Licks in Kentucky, where fossil mammalian bones were continuously turning up. This herd devoured bear, deer, and buffalo until the Delaware Indians' culture hero, "Great Man," perched himself atop a mountain and killed the mammoths with lightning bolts. Only one animal, a gargantuan male, escaped to the West and there lived to the present day.[22] According to the Delawares, the Great Man's footprints could still be seen on the mountain, making this one of the myths that explicated the Delawares' tribal landscape.

Like the Delaware Indians, Jefferson was eager to find evidence of titanic creatures and epic struggles in his own tribal landscape. In 1793 Jefferson instructed the French botanist François-André Michaux to hunt for the living mammoth as well as the megalonyx (literally, great claw), a giant, extinct sloth that Jefferson took to be a monstrous lion, based on fossil claws he had seen. Michaux's transcontinental expedition did not materialize (he reached Kentucky before being recalled after his implication in a French plot to wrest Louisiana from

Spain), but Jefferson got a second chance with Meriwether Lewis.[23]

Jefferson did not explicitly tell Lewis to hunt the mammoth, yet to claim an animal for science, one had to take a specimen. But what would Lewis have done had he come upon a mammoth? One imagines Lewis gathering his men for a joint assault yet retreating in the face of the mammoth's overwhelming superiority. The grizzly—which sometimes absorbed ten balls before giving up a fight—was foe enough for the party's rifles. "I do not like the gentleman," wrote Lewis, "and had reather fight two Indians than one bear."[24] If the party had trouble dispatching the grizzly, how could it—short of employing a cannon—take a mammoth?

Lewis's search for the mammoth proved fruitless, much to the pleasure of Federalists. In a poem lampooning the expedition, young John Quincy Adams wrote of Lewis:

> He never with a Mammoth met, However you may wonder;
> Nor even with a Mammoth's bone, Above the ground or under.[25]

Instead of a mammoth, Jefferson employed other trophies to refute Buffon, requisitioning for him, at great expense, the horns, skeleton, and skin of a Vermont moose. This animal, Jefferson claimed, could accommodate the Lapland deer (the animal Buffon took to be the European analog of the moose) under its belly. More interesting is the memory of this event in folk culture. According to Rev. E. P. Wild's 1871 history of Brookfield, Vermont, it was Vermont settlers (not Jefferson) who, having heard that the English (not the French) spoke contemptuously of America, "stuffed the skin of an elk [not a moose] of gigantic dimensions and sent it to England as a specimen of what Vermont could produce, with an intimation that her men, also, were hard to beat."[26] The story had become confused over many generations, yet the legend and the actual event were not so different. The potency of American fauna illustrated the potency of American people.

Most of the faunal trophies collected by Jefferson's explorers ended up not in Europe, nor in Jefferson's Indian Hall, but in Charles Willson Peale's American Museum (also called Peale's Museum), the Republic's preeminent natural history museum. Insisting that Americans must comprehend the natural productions of their own country "to distinguish the peculiarities of other countries," Peale set about in 1786 to collect and to display "every thing that is curious to this Country, but particularly its 'natural forms.'" "Natural history is not only interesting to the individual," Peale would proclaim in 1799, "it ought to become a NATIONAL CONCERN, since it is a NATIONAL GOOD."[27]

Through the scientific display of American fauna and flora, Peale—artist,

Revolutionary War veteran, pacifist, Deist, and member of Jefferson's Republican party—transformed the disorderly wilderness of the colonial imagination into a school of republican reason. Just as the diverse constituents of the natural world displayed in his museum seemed to compose a harmonious, purposeful whole, so Americans separated by politics and religion could find "concordance of sentiment in admiring the wonderful works of creation," wrote Peale. "Political squabbles cease," he maintained, "in the divine admiration of the infinite wisdom, and wonderful order of the *Creator*!" Peale made his "Great School of Nature" into a source of American identity, substituting a temple of reason for a state-sponsored church.[28]

After Lewis and Clark and Zebulon Pike had forwarded their specimens to Peale (via Jefferson)—including the American bighorn, grizzly, and pronghorn—Peale's Great School of Nature extended its scientific empire to the Rockies. Praising "Capt. Lewis for his endeavors to increase our knowledge of the Animals of that new acquired Territory," Peale wrote in 1805 that "every thing" from the Louisiana Territory "must now become interesting to the Public." Peale even volunteered to make drawings for the engravings that would appear in Lewis's account of the expedition.[29] Like Meriwether Lewis, those who visited Peale's Museum became American Natives; their ties to the Creator, to republican virtue, to science, and to nature were commensurate with their ties to the continent.

In displaying the wax figure of Lewis alongside the stuffed and mounted animals he had captured on his expedition, Peale discarded the Rushian opposition between hunting and republican rationality. For Peale, the hunter—as epitomized in Lewis—was rational and republican. The hunter killed animals not for sport but for knowledge and progress. In fact, Peale actively sought out American hunters to provide him specimens for his museum. In later decades Peale's own son Titian Ramsay Peale would hunt and paint big game in the Far West while serving as naturalist for Maj. Stephen Long's scientific expedition to the Rocky Mountains in 1819–20.[30]

Peale's other sons, encouraged by their father's success, opened museums in Baltimore in 1814, New York City in 1825, and Utica in 1828, each of which combined natural history with less didactic forms of entertainment. William Clark, as governor of Missouri Territory, also established a museum of natural history in St. Louis in 1816. There he displayed hunting trophies alongside ethnographic artifacts, petrified wood, crystals, agates, and portraits of Indian chiefs. The explorer and ethnographer Henry Rowe Schoolcraft, one of many travelers to visit the museum, commented that Clark had arranged his exhibits "with great taste and effect."[31]

Peale and his sons, with Jefferson and Clark, cloaked hunters in the robes of republican dignity, pointing the way toward the nineteenth-century celebration of the hunter-naturalist. These men also pointed the way toward the great faunal and ethnographic collections assembled in the mid-nineteenth century by the National Institution and its successor, the United States National Museum of the Smithsonian Institution. Through these institutions, hunter-naturalists—and thousands of ordinary Americans who viewed the specimens they had collected—became American Natives.

We tend to think of Jefferson, Peale, and the hunters who assisted them as heirs of the Enlightenment, men engaged in a scientific effort to know the world, and that is what they were. Yet having placed these men within the Western scientific tradition, we should consider other ramifications of their work. Their project was not solely scientific; it was an attempt to link Americans to a tribal landscape. How

The conspicuous antlers in the interior of the Smithsonian Institution Building (ca. 1860s) seem to testify to the chivalrous conquest of the North American continent. Neg. 2000-1312, Smithsonian Institution Archives, Record Unit 95, Photograph Collection, 1850s–, Box 41, Folder 3, Smithsonian Institution, Washington, D.C.

different were the antlers, heads, and hides displayed by Jefferson from the faunal totems, icons, and costumes displayed by Indians?

For American Indians, antler headdresses and hundreds of other faunal totems were pieces of a larger body of myth, legend, and folktale, an entire cosmography. This cosmography defined the history of each animal, its usefulness and relationship to humans, and the place of humans in the universe. Together with myths that inscribed tribal geography, faunal totems affirmed tribal cosmography, identified tribal members as a group, and attached them to specific lands. In this process, the hunter was instrumental; he took possession of the land and its faunal spirits, guaranteeing the tribe's survival.

The faunal specimens collected by another sort of hunter, Meriwether Lewis, affirmed not mythology but the seemingly superior discourse of science, rationality, and utility. Yet the specimens taken by Lewis and displayed by Jefferson and Peale were no less symbolic of a sacred wisdom than were the totems of American Indians. For Lewis, Jefferson, and Peale, natural history was the surest way humans had to discern the logic of the Creator; nature was a perfect school of republicanism; and to study nature was to follow the path toward the fulfillment of the Creator's plan for the perfection of America through the utilization of its natural resources.

In a sense, Lewis, Jefferson, and Peale made their countrymen more truly American Natives than the aboriginal peoples who have come to be called Native Americans. American Indians tended to see themselves as native to particular tribal realms rather than to the continent as a whole. They did not conceive of geography in continental units before the arrival of Europeans, and they did not choose to have themselves and the lands they inhabited named for Amerigo Vespucci.

Ironic though it may seem, to call Lewis, Jefferson, Peale, and their post-Revolutionary countrymen American Natives is justified. Their progenitors had given the name of an Italian navigator to the continent; they comprehended America as a zoological, geological, and geographical entity, and they called themselves American to identify themselves with the continent they inhabited. Finally, they associated their cultural and political values with American nature and, through natural history, scientific exploration, agriculture, art, and hunting, came to see themselves as divinely appointed custodians of the continent. These lessons would not be lost on later generations of hunters.

8

Daniel Boone

 Had he lived longer, Meriwether Lewis might have become America's preeminent hunter-hero. Lewis, however, was in some respects a hero imposed from above; he was as much the intellectual child of Thomas Jefferson as the grassroots choice of Americans.

George Washington also might have qualified as the first American hunter-hero. In his youth Washington donned buckskins to survey land west of the Blue Ridge Mountains and to fight the French, and in later life he became an avid fox hunter. Although Washington was certainly the first American celebrity to transcend regional loyalties, he was really a surrogate aristocrat, a natural leader for a country not ready to dispense with traditional notions of deference and hierarchy. A different sort of hunter—not a fox hunter, nor a scientific explorer, but a market hunter named Daniel Boone—appeared on the cultural horizon in the early national era and went on to become one of America's most revered common man heroes.[1]

As emblematically American as he came to seem, Daniel Boone was an unlikely champion for a society that had once identified backwoods hunters with savagery. Had he lived a generation earlier, Boone might have seemed more rogue than hero. Boone was literate, but barely, and he refused the settled, predictable life of farming, preferring to live like an American Indian, hunting and exploring the continent's interior. Boone even looked like an Indian; he dressed his hair with bear grease and wore it "plaited and clubbed up" and cloaked himself in black deerskins.[2]

Boone also moved in circles that, by colonial standards, were given to insolence, irreligion, and debauchery. Adultery was not unusual among wives of long hunters like Boone whose frontier rambles lasted weeks or months. According to oral testimony, Boone's wife and daughter—not to mention Boone himself—fell short in the pursuit of chastity. Nor did long hunters commit themselves to the canons of Protestantism; they placed faith in dreams and oracles instead. Though Boone was born a Quaker, he maintained no affiliation with organized religion and seldom read the Bible. Long hunters, moreover, were egalitarian men who shared game in times of shortage, called one another brother, and expressed distaste for planter society.[3]

Boone might have made up for these shortcomings with his courage in fighting Indians and redcoats, but although he fought bravely in the Indian campaign known as Lord Dunmore's War in 1774, he remembered killing only three Indians in his lifetime and held no animus toward them. He also fought in the Revolution, but his patriotism was suspect, and he was court-martialed for treason (he was acquitted).[4] Boone's role in the Revolution was primarily the defense of kin and community against Indian attack. He did serve briefly in Virginia's legislature but did not esteem himself a great patriot.

As a man of enterprise, moreover, Boone was a perennial ne'er-do-well. He lost his land when Virginia absorbed the Transylvania region after the Revolution, and he lost thousands more acres by failing to comply with preemption requirements. By the end of the eighteenth century, Boone was landless and deeply in debt to men who sued him because his poor surveying had left their properties open to counterclaims.[5]

Boone proved how tenuous was his allegiance to the United States when in 1799 he moved to Spanish Missouri to escape creditors. Glad to attract a well-known settler, Spain gave Boone ten thousand arpents (eighty-five hundred acres), but he lost this land too after the Louisiana Purchase because he had failed to fulfill his obligation to cultivate it. In 1814 the U.S. Congress, at the behest of Kentucky's senators, stepped in to grant the aging Boone a tenth of his original holdings.[6] It was ironic that America's hero of expansion lost every acre he had claimed until Congress awarded him a special grant, yet it was America's thirst for a culture hero—not Boone's successes or failures—that propelled his celebrity.

The first Boone biography—a so-called autobiography ghostwritten by an ex-schoolmaster turned land speculator named John Filson and appended to his *Discovery, Settlement, and Present State of Kentucke*—appeared in 1784, immediately after the Revolution. Though the book caused a stir in Europe, it aroused little comment in the United States. Only after Connecticut printer John Trumbull boiled down the Filson narrative into a tale of action and intrigue—eliminating much of Boone's philosophizing—did the tale become well known in America.[7]

It was Filson's philosophical hero of the woods, however, who became the model for popular biographies of the Jacksonian and antebellum eras.

Unlike woodsmen described by William Byrd of Westover and J. Hector St. John de Crèvecoeur, Filson's Boone did not fall to the level of savage; Boone was ennobled by hunting. When captured by the Shawnee, Boone—although careful not to outshine his captors—earned respect by showing his prowess with a rifle and was befriended by the "Shawanese King."[8]

This affinity for the Indian became a standard trope as subsequent writers made Boone a white indigene. Timothy Flint, a Harvard-trained minister who wrote a Boone biography in 1833, went so far as to suggest that Boone worshiped the Great Spirit ("the woods were his books and his temple; and the creed of the red man naturally became his") but added that Boone would have accepted Christ had he studied the Bible. Boone, however, was said to be superior to the Indian in withstanding pain, in athletic ability, and in hunting expertise.[9] As dozens of writers and thousands of readers made Boone an American Native—the civilized man who was as skilled in woodcraft, tracking, and hunting as the Indian—they transmuted their hero into an exemplary figure, the authentic progeny of American nature.

Indeed, though Indians had long been demonized in American culture, there had always been a latent appreciation for them as hunters. Both New England and Chesapeake colonists, despite their devotion to agriculture, praised Indians for the skill and athleticism they showed in hunting. Though Thomas Jefferson urged Indians to become farmers, he noted that the Indian's "vivacity and activity of mind is equal to ours in the same situation; hence his eagerness for hunting, and for games of chance." William Guthrie, the British author of a world atlas that went through numerous reprints in the late eighteenth century, added that hunting gave Indians strength and agility and made their bodies "uncommonly strong and wel proportioned."[10] Even as Europeans condemned Indians for hunting, such testimony shows that Europeans envied Indians, too. Hunting seemed to make Indians healthy and lithe, revealed their intelligence, and marked them as genuine Americans. These ideas about hunting and Indians—not the idea of savagery—were channeled into the worship of Daniel Boone.

The celebration of Boone as heir to the Indian signaled a growing middle-class fascination for athleticism and the body, a fascination that would burgeon after the Civil War. More important, the Boone tale served as a jeremiad chastening an ascendant middle class for falling away from republican virtues. Taking cues from Filson (whose Boone observes that "felicity, the companion of content, is rather found in our own breasts than in the enjoyment of external things"), biographers speculated that Boone had moved to Kentucky to escape the luxury and ostentation of wealthy Scots traders and officials of the Crown. John Mason Peck, a Baptist minister and promoter of frontier development whose Boone biography appeared in Jared Sparks's *Library of American Biography* in 1847, added that Boone had left North Carolina in disgust at "luxury and effeminacy."[11] Boone symbolized the sturdy republican who rejected the spiraling vanity brought by early national prosperity.

One might ask why such pious sentiments no longer resounded from the mouth of a farmer? How had a backwoods hunter become the voice of virtue and republican simplicity? In colonial and Revolutionary America, the censure of luxury and effeminacy often prefaced a celebration of farming, yet the Boone literature did not call on readers to return to the agrarian fold. If Boone sought to escape luxury and effeminacy, he likewise sought to escape "the empire of the cultivator's axe and plough," in the words of Flint.[12] Despite occasional efforts to farm, Boone was neither a model yeoman nor a worthy member of the elite like Jefferson, champion of the small farmer, or Washington, the Cincinnatus who returned to the plow after serving his country.

Boone's rise in popularity can be attributed partly to the Revolutionary War, which encouraged Americans to pride themselves on woodcraft and marksmanship and to identify backwoods hunters as symbols of liberty. Yet judging from the quantity of art and literature celebrating him, Boone's popularity peaked not after the Revolution but in the Jacksonian and antebellum eras and remained buoyant for the rest of the century.

Illustrating Boone's rise to hero status are a host of images produced by Jacksonian and antebellum artists, ranging from Enrico Causici's 1826 sandstone relief of Boone battling an Indian to George Caleb Bingham's 1851 painting of a Mosaic Boone leading his people to the promised land. Both Causici's relief and Horatio Greenough's sculpture of a figure modeled on Boone (in combat with an Indian), carved in the early 1850s, were commissioned for display at the U.S. Capitol, as was Emanuel Leutze's 1860 painting *Westward the Course of Empire Takes Its Way [Westward Ho!]*, a version of which included a Boone portrait. The American people testified to their reverence for such images not only by buying mass-produced Boone portraits but also by chiseling talismanic pebbles from the fifteen-foot stone monument erected over Boone's grave in 1860.[13]

As artists created shrines to Boone, writers helped to define him. Some half dozen biographies of Boone—each outdoing the other in praise—appeared before the Civil War. The most influential of those was Flint's *Biographical Memoir of Daniel Boone, the First Settler of Kentucky.* Under various titles, Flint's book saw fourteen printings between 1833 and 1868, making it, according to John Mack Faragher, the most widely read American biography of the century.[14]

In the romantic grasp of Flint, Boone became an Achilles wanting only his Homer "worthily to celebrate his exploits." Flint considered Boone as important as William Penn or Benjamin Franklin. Like Flint, most of Boone's Jacksonian and antebellum chroniclers were so eager to extol the virtuous, heroic hunter and pathfinder that their works amount to hagiographies. "Out of the long and brilliant list of patriots—whether orators, or warriors, or statesmen, or divines," wrote George Canning Hill in his 1859 Boone hagiography, "no name shines with a purer lustre than that of Daniel Boone."[15]

But among whom did Boone's image shine so brightly? What sort of Americans would worship a frontier hunter? Certainly hunters themselves adored Boone. Backwoodsmen, according to an Englishman who toured the Ohio Valley in 1822–23, "look upon [Boone] as one of the greatest heroes that ever lived." Boone is also said to have maintained an important place in the folk tradition of rural Tennessee, where a good hunter became known in the nineteenth century as a "Boone."[16] As a species, farmer-hunters of European descent rapidly expanded their range in the years that Boone became a culture hero (displacing indigenous species in their wake). With Boone, they marched across the Appalachian Mountains into Kentucky, then into Missouri, Ohio, Indiana, and Illinois. They spread southward, too, into Tennessee, Alabama, Louisiana, Mississippi, Arkansas, and Texas, and northward into Iowa and Michigan.

Pioneers also expanded their political range in the early nineteenth century. In state after state, property qualifications for voting were jettisoned as the movement for manhood suffrage carried the day. Millions of ordinary men became politically active. Some joined the Democratic party of Andrew Jackson (successor to the Democratic Republican party of Thomas Jefferson); others joined the Whig party of Henry Clay (successor to the Federalist party). On election day the rough-and-tumble men of the West crowded together at the polls, shouting, jostling, drinking, and fighting. The common man had emerged into the sunlight of full citizenship.

Insofar as Boone represented the confidence, assertion, and freedom of common men, he personified thousands of pioneers who were opening new geographical and political frontiers. Not surprisingly, pioneers embraced Boone as their hero. But pioneers alone could not have absorbed the Boone hagiographies that flowed from eastern presses. Americans from more established regions also contributed to Boone's fame.

The urban publishing industry of the Atlantic seaboard played every bit as important a role in boosting Boone to hero status as did frontiersmen themselves. Before John Filson's *Kentucke,* there is no evidence that Boone was legendary among frontiersmen. Boone was respected by his peers, even envied, but that hardly made him legendary or mythical. Filson wrote about Boone not because he learned the Boone legend on the frontier but because he heard tales of adventure from Boone and his friends, who served as Filson's guides in Kentucky. Once Filson made Boone a literary hero, however, the Boone legend percolated downward from an urban publishing industry and a middle-class readership as well as upward from the frontier.[17]

It is important to note that literacy levels and print consumption—and presumably sales of Boone hagiographies—were highest in regions penetrated by the market. Publishers could distribute wares only along existing transportation routes, which restricted pioneers' access to books. Backwoods folk, moreover, tended to read intensively; they carefully read the Bible (often aloud) and perhaps newspapers and almanacs, but little else. Middle-class men and women, by contrast, could afford the relatively high cost of books and thus read extensively, and it was they who had access to the bookstores and libraries that appeared in cities and towns. The image of Boone shone brightly among pioneers, yet it shone equally brightly among the middle class.[18]

If Boone was a hero to thousands of Americans who battled wild beasts and braved trackless wilds, he was likewise a hero to many more thousands—even millions—who did neither. How do we explain this contradiction? To evaluate this question, we need to know who read the Boone literature. We need to know how readers perceived Boone and how they related his deeds to their lives. The sources, however, are all but silent; no records disclose precisely who read the Boone literature or what readers gleaned from it. In lieu of such records, we are left with educated speculation, but educated speculation tells us much.

Boone served as a bridge between two Americas, the America of the Jeffersonian Republicans and the America of the Jacksonian and antebellum middle class. Indeed, as politicians, presidents Thomas Jefferson and Andrew Jackson, for all their differences, were extremely similar. Both were wealthy planters who promoted, at least rhetorically, liberalism, grassroots democracy, weak central authority, and agrarian free enterprise. Whereas Jefferson presided over a society of small freeholders, however, Jackson presided over a society undergoing rapid urbanization, industrialization, and expansion. Jacksonian America was a nation in transition, a nation in which the authority of community, family, and church was being undercut by the market revolution.

There was never a time in American history when eager merchants and investors had not sought profit. The market revolution, however, integrated millions of Americans—many of whose parents and grandparents had participated in what was essentially a barter economy—into the universe of high-stakes capitalism. What produced this market revolution were advances in transportation, communication, and manufacturing.

Between the War of 1812 and the Civil War, the nation was bound together by turnpikes and canals and, beginning in the 1830s, by railroads. The power generated by the steam engine—used first in boats and then in locomotives—began to replace the power generated by wind and water. As a consequence, transportation costs fell dramatically. The 363-mile-long Erie Canal, for instance, completed in 1825, cut freight rates between Buffalo, New York, and Albany, New York, by tenfold. At the same time, inventors and entrepreneurs introduced the idea of interchangeable parts, revolutionizing the manufacture of iron tools, built efficient power looms that allowed Americans to compete with the English in textile production, and created faster printing presses that made newspapers and books cheaper and more numerous than ever before. Then, in the 1840s, came the invention of the telegraph, permitting almost instantaneous communications between cities.[19]

The outcome of these innovations was the market revolution. Farmers prospered by selling crops to urban markets, while urban manufacturers prospered by selling wares to farmers. Beef, pork, wheat, and cotton exports climbed steeply, as did the value of urban real estate. Coal mines, iron mines, and machine shops employed thousands of Americans, while thousands more immigrated to newly opened farm lands in the West and South. Americans everywhere were making money; their motto, in the idiom of Davy Crockett, was "Go Ahead!" To go ahead, however, required vast cultural and psychological changes.[20]

In a curious sense, Jacksonian America was fulfilling the Jeffersonian promise as individuals were cut loose from the vestiges of hierarchical and communal authority and freed to pursue self-interest. Self-interest, ambition, and self-aggrandizement, which in the idiom of classical republicanism represented forces destructive to the commonweal, were now conceived of as wheels of progress. If every man was free to pursue self-interest, unhampered by the exigencies of birth or duty to the greater good, the gargantuan powers of enterprise would be unleashed, and Americans would find themselves afloat on a rising tide of wealth and happiness. The whole society stood to benefit.[21]

On the other hand, these forces would create the world that the founders had warned against. America, like Europe, would become an urban, industrial, money-grabbing society, the sort of society that produced luxury and effeminacy among the wealthy, depravity among the masses, and dissolution for all. What must follow, according to classical republican doctrine, was tyranny, riot, mayhem, and destruction.

This fear of decline underscored a nostalgia for a simpler, republican past when men like Boone had lived in harmony with nature. The artist Thomas Cole, despite the apocalyptic message of his series of paintings called *The Course of Empire*, proposed in his sketchbook of 1827 to paint another series in which "Morning may be an American scene—Evening an Italian one. The morning—all freshness newness + youthful vigor—The Evening—Decay + Ruin—The Morning may be a wild scene with a Hunter's cabin." Cole painted this morning scene in *The Hunter's Return*, which showed two frontier hunters making their way home, carrying on a long pole the carcass of a deer. As they approach their cabin, the hunters see a small boy playing with a toy gun, while the boy's mother watches from outside the cabin door. The lead hunter—despite the full head of hair—appears to be a self-portrait of Cole.[22]

The lesson taught by *The Hunter's Return* was taken to heart by Americans, who realized that the world they lived in—the world created by the market revolution—differed from that of the founders. To prosper in this world—and to avoid social dissolution—men would have to recapture the youth and vigor of their republican ancestors. At the same time, the fiercely competitive, laissez-faire, middle-class society in which they found themselves demanded that they become rugged individualists, men whose fate would be determined by their own enterprise. Here, too, Boone led the way.

Even as Boone symbolized the spartan, manly republicanism of the Revolution—the American dawn—his chivalry, composure, and ceaseless migrations made him the prototype for an atomistic, commercial, mobile society. As a new sort of American Native, Boone resembled the Jeffersonian man with his liberal impulse and his zealous defense of natural rights, but Boone raised this logic to new heights. Boone would not be merely a libertarian; he would be a fortress unto himself. Unlike the Jeffersonian man, the enterprising and restless Boone refused to bind himself to farm or community. His loyalties were to unfettered autonomy, geographical mobility, and "steady perseverance and resolution," traits that defined the middle-class male.[23]

Despite the fact that he was a lonely hunter and wanderer—indeed, because he was a lonely hunter and wanderer—Boone could become the cultural pathfinder both for thousands of young men who migrated west in search of new farms and, oddly enough, for those who moved to cities and towns. Both sets of men became

Jacksonian Americans lamented the loss of spartan, republican virtues of frontier hunters like those depicted here. Thomas Cole, *The Hunter's Return*, 1845 (oil on canvas, 40⅛ × 60½ inches). Courtesy of the Amon Carter Museum, Fort Worth, Texas.

increasingly middle class and market oriented in the Jacksonian and antebellum eras, yet the growth of cities most visibly undermined republican tradition, and the city—as well as the frontier—set in motion the Boone literature.

Together with overseas immigration, the migration of young men from the countryside (and lesser numbers of women) caused cities and towns of over ten thousand to grow by 797 percent between 1820 and 1860, a faster rate than at any other time in U.S. history. Statistics, however, underrate the impact of cities, for they were more than locales with dense populations; they were symbols of a changed and intensified set of social and market relations that appeared—at different times and rates—across the United States. Cities generated anxiety not because of their otherness but because they symbolized forces unleashed throughout the nation—even in the countryside—by the market revolution.

As thousands of young men ventured into the anomic and isolate world of the city, they left behind the patriarchal and religious authority of the agrarian past. In their new milieu, they found themselves free to rise according to their abilities but likewise free to drink and carouse, to indulge sexual appetites, and to gamble. Fearing chaos, ministers and moral guardians produced hundreds of advice books as substitutes for the strictures of father, community, and church. Such books prescribed internalized codes of conduct for middle-class men who barricaded themselves within what Joseph Kett describes as a "fortress of character."[24]

Interestingly, Boone's Jacksonian and antebellum hagiographers came from the same ranks as advice writers. John Filson was a schoolteacher; James Hall was a jurist and banker; John Mason Peck, John McClung, and Francis Lister Hawks were ministers; Timothy Flint was a former minister. Even filibusterer and Boone celebrant Charles Wilkins Webber had attended Princeton Theological Seminary.

Though only one of Boone's hagiographers, Cecil B. Hartley, had actually written an etiquette manual, all of them wove into their Boone tales the concept of character, which Boone was said to display in abundance. Indeed, the virtues and aphorisms of Boone served as oblique commentaries on life in the city. Flint employed Boone as an example to those who lived in the "midst of the rivalry, competition, and scramble of populous cities," while W. H. Bogart noted in his 1854 hagiography that "the heavens above [Boone] seemed nearer than to *us*, who are forever attracted by the *crowd* around us [emphasis added]."[25]

Even more pointed were lectures delivered to New York City audiences by William Henry Milburn, former chaplain to the U.S. Congress. Boone's sterling character, proclaimed Milburn, had made him "the one white man who dares to trust himself alone with nature." Other frontiersmen might sink to the level of savage but not Boone. Not only the wilderness, however, but also the city tempted men to fall from grace. Boone, argued Milburn, was an example to urban youth who lived in a time when

> the sexes seem undergoing a transmigration, at least when the distinctions of their apparrel are destroyed; when the women are doing in public what they have been so long accustomed to in private—wearing pantaloons; and the stronger sex, by way of retaliation, have stolen their shawls—you may note upon Broadway, or the promenade of any of our principal cities, a dapper, diminutive thing, which seems to pos-

sess some features of both sexes, and yet the distinctions of neither. Its legs remind you of pipe-stems, its arms of oaten straws. It ogles every woman that it meets—staring with brazen-faced impudence, till she, from very shame, must drop her eyelids, to shut out this apparition—half brute, half baby. It talks magniloquently of first circles, and old families, until you fancy that its lineage dates from Doomsday Book; yet its father—excellent and worthy man—began life as an obscure tailor, shoemaker, or brick-layer, and by . . . his industry, economy, and enterprise, has achieved fortune and social position, and is now enjoying as he should the fruits of his labor. He is a notable man, but unfortunately does not know how to raise boys.[26]

The Philadelphia-born Milburn, who had fulfilled the obligations of manhood by working as a clerk and minister in the West before taking up residence in New York City, portrayed a society in the throes of dissolution. Republican virtues were dying. Manly women were breaking the chains of patriarchy, and womanly men were abdicating moral authority. Only the example of Boone—along with temperance and universal education—could save the nation.[27]

Boone held hope for America's youth not only because he—as a wilderness hero—was so different from them but also because he was the same. Whether they lived in towns or on farms or moved back and forth, American men were hunters insofar as they had to be self-reliant individualists. Unlike youths of earlier generations who often learned their fathers' vocations, young men of Jacksonian and antebellum America tended to be nomadic in their careers; their ties to specific individuals and enterprises could change rapidly. They lived, moreover, in a world mediated by self-interest, a world characterized by a paradigm of predator and prey rather than kinship and community.

This new breed of restless youth, like Flint's Boone, sought to cultivate "peculiar self-possession," or to quote Alexis de Tocqueville, American men were forced to learn "the habit of always considering themselves as standing alone," imagining "that their whole destiny is in their own hands." American society "separates [each man's] contemporaries from him," explained Tocqueville, "and threatens in the end to confine him entirely within the solitude of his own heart."[28]

Even Boone's pecuniary failures did not dull his aura of self-reliant virtue. Boone's financial embarrassments allowed middle-class hagiographers to preach against the excesses of law and litigation. Neither poor backwoodsmen nor wealthy merchants could evade a widening net of legal entanglements, foreclosures, and bankruptcies—especially during the panics of 1819 and 1837—and Boone represented a martyr to their cause. Boone had been robbed of everything by "the chicanery of the law," as one hagiographer expressed it. Peck made his

"Daniel Boone," according to the text accompanying this engraving, "was preeminently the architect of his own character and fortunes." James B. Longacre (after Chester Harding), *Daniel Boone,* 1835 (line and stipple engraving). *National Portrait Gallery of Distinguished Americans,* vol. 2 (Philadelphia, 1854).

Boone a virtual libertarian; Boone had "a natural sense of justice and equity," wrote Peck, and felt "repugnance to the technical forms of law, and the conventional regulations of society and of government, unless they were in strict accordance with his sense of right."[29]

The colonial notion of a Hobbesian wilderness in which individual hunters savagely battled both nature and civilization, observing no law or authority but their own, metamorphosed into the notion of wilderness as libertarian arena. In this new equation, wilderness became the domain of hardy individuals like Boone who rose according to their merits, without the impositions of inheritance, law, or government. Boone was a new type, wrote Flint, "author and artificer of his own fortunes." At about the time that Flint's hagiography appeared, advice literature began to praise self-made men in business as well; Boone himself appeared among Charles C. B. Seymour's exemplars in *Self-Made Men,* published in 1858.[30]

From a modern perspective it may seem strange that a backwoodsman could exemplify good conduct, yet this contradiction seldom troubled nineteenth-century writers. Even as Boone tested his wits in a wilderness realm of libertarian strife, among civilized folk he was "gentle," "conciliating," and "far from possessing a ferocious temper." Boone might retreat into the wilderness to protest society's ills, yet he was no enemy to society. "When poverty and distress held him fast," recalled one of Boone's Transylvania associates, he remained "a noble and generous soul, despising everything mean." Boone's hagiographers added that he had hunted and trapped as an old man to pay off creditors. After settling his debts, Boone supposedly announced that he was ready to die, since no one could call him dishonest.[31]

"Simple commercial honesty," writes Anthony F. C. Wallace, was "the moral axis around which all . . . human relationships were formed" among the American middle class. Thus Boone—despite the lawsuits—was never portrayed as a confidence man, charlatan, or fool but always as a model of integrity. Boone, wrote W. H. Bogart, stood "immeasurably above" the "wretched class of men" endemic to frontiers. Peck's Boone even repudiated tobacco and liquor.[32]

Boone attained his lofty moral position not through application of the plow but through dedication to the chase. Peck described Boone's hunting as "mental discipline," a habit rarely attributed to colonial farmers and mechanics. Hunting promoted the internalization of virtue demanded by middle-class life; hunting taught "self-possession, self-control, and promptness in execution," "patience," "perseverance," "sagacity," and "knowledge of human nature." This last

Boone embraces his wife, Rebecca, before leaving on a long hunt, illustrating the affection that bound middle-class families. Engraving from William H. Bogart, *Daniel Boone, and the Hunters of Kentucky* (Buffalo, 1854).

Boone as child prodigy, coolly firing on a panther as other boys flee. "It was a striking instance," wrote Timothy Flint, "of that peculiar self-possession, which constituted the most striking trait in his character in afterlife." Timothy Flint, *The First White Man of the West, or the Exploits of Col. Daniel Boone, The First Settler of Kentucky* (Cincinnati, 1847).

skill might seem odd for a hunter, yet it obsessed advice writers and phrenologists, who perceived the import of judging character in the urban world of confidence men, gamblers, and other shadowy characters.[33]

Boone required mental discipline not to elude urban tricksters but to elude red-skinned tricksters of the wilderness, who constantly set ambushes for the unwary. Boone's mental discipline permitted him to survive in a treacherous realm of combat and killing, a realm no woman could safely enter.[34] If Boone's hagiographers made the wilderness an idealized image of libertarian society, they also made it an arena of manly struggle, a place fit for those with quick wits and trigger fingers. And if Boone became a larger-than-life reflection of the middle-class individualist, Boone's backwoods milieu became a larger-than-life reflection of a public sphere increasingly portrayed not as emasculating but as competitive and dangerous. The hunter-hero—like the successful businessman—became the nascent voice of social Darwinism, the strong-armed, male victor of a grand, yet vicious, contest for survival.

The actual public sphere of the self-made man was more ambiguous than the symbolic realm of Boone. In the real world, rules were vague; success was fleeting; and rugged individualists linked themselves to partners, employees, employers, banks, credit agencies, and voluntary organizations. The contradiction between the ideal of self-made success and the actuality of dependence must have generated anxiety among men who feared they did not control their destinies. Self-possession is the desire of those in turmoil. As Carroll Smith-Rosenberg has observed, "individuals, experiencing themselves as powerless in the face of massive and unremitting social transformation, respond by attempting to capture and encapsulate such change within a new and ordered symbolic universe."[35] The wilderness of Boone became such a universe, a place where the self-possessed hero triumphed over adversity without and anxiety within.

The traits exhibited by the hunter-hero did not correspond to the psychological imperatives of colonial farmers, nor do they correspond to the imperatives of the consumption mentality of today. The traits of the hunter-hero were the traits of the nineteenth-century self-made man. Accordingly, they defined

Boone glorying in wilderness solitude (one presumes that the gun on which he rests is unloaded). Timothy Flint, *The First White Man of the West, or the Exploits of Col. Daniel Boone, The First Settler of Kentucky* (Cincinnati, 1847).

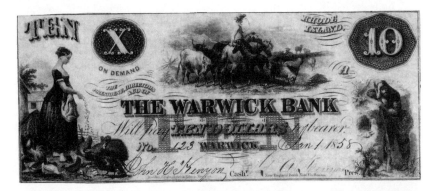

Antebellum banknotes with vignettes of backwoods hunters. The two dollar note of the City Bank of Georgia equates Daniel Boone with Saint George slaying the dragon. Note the cross formed by Boone's gun and knife. Courtesy of the National Numismatic Collection, Smithsonian Institution, Washington, D.C.

middle-class manliness in the Age of Jackson. "Middle-class masculinity," explains Charles Sellers, "pushed egotism to extremes of aggression, calculation, self-control, and unremitting effort," all characteristics displayed by the Boone of literature.[36]

Though Boone protested late in life that "many heroic actions and chivalrous adventures are related of me which exist only in the regions of fancy," he had also become a modern crusader, a knight errant venturing afar to battle the infidel. Boone was a secular rather than a religious crusader, yet like the heroes of Sir Walter Scott's historical romances, he participated in a medieval fantasy that stood in stark contrast to the tawdriness of modern society. Not surprisingly, Boone's forest chivalry seemed to belong to a time gone, a time when men were nobler, purer, better.[37]

But it is too simplistic to view Boone as courtly foil to an ignoble present. If Boone symbolized courage, composure, and chivalry, that was because middle-class men identified such traits with themselves. As a common man rather than a dandified aristocrat, moreover, Boone tempered his forest chivalry with the republican formula of sincerity and simplicity in character and dress. The hunter-hero—popularized by an urban, middle-class publishing industry—combined old codes of behavior with new, rooting middle-class manliness in the sanctity of nature.

It would be facile to argue that Boone's popularity came solely from urban writers and readers. Farmers and southern planters likewise joined in the chorus of middle-class sensibilities; they too were embroiled in the market revolution, and their concern with redefining self differed from that of urbanites only in degree. Indeed, insofar as Boone was neither city dweller nor farmer, he could be revered by both. Francis Lister Hawks appealed to urban and rural youth alike when he explained in his 1844 hagiography that while some chose to live in "crowded cities" and others chose the "peaceful quiet of a country farm," Boone belonged to a separate—and exemplary—class of men who "roam through wild forests, and make their homes in the wilderness."[38]

No doubt Hawks's youthful readers imagined Boone as a refugee from middle-class society, not a celebrant of it. Boone constantly sought elbow room; he was an omnipotent being who ventured into the wilderness alone (or with a few hunting partners), free from family, church, and society. But escapes into fantasy correlate with real world desires. Young men dreamed of Boone-like omnipotence because society demanded that they become like Boone; fantasy and reality were opposite sides of a single coin.

The very name Boone suggested the optimism and exuberance of a time when Americans were proving the success of the republican experiment. Part of that optimism and exuberance came with the market revolution, but another part came with a different sort of boon: Manifest Destiny.

The drive for empire in the Jacksonian and antebellum eras was the culmination of centuries-old expansionism, yet it differed from what had come before. The old logic of *vacuum domicilium*—the right of farmers to appropriate so-called vacant lands—proved a clumsy cover for the blitzkrieg appropriation of vast arid and semiarid domains in the nineteenth century. *Vacuum domicilium* also proved to be a clumsy explication for the genius of a chivalrous, individualistic, middle-class people. Thousands of emigrants continued to move west with the ambition of farming, yet the idea of *vacuum domicilium* as a justification for empire was increasingly overshadowed by a drama enacted by hunters.

This new drama had appeared as early as 1813 in Daniel Bryan's epic poem about Daniel Boone, *The Mountain Muse*, which garnered 1,350 subscribers from ten states and every section of the country. Bryan, a nephew of Boone, considered his poem an American *Aeneid* and wrote of angels choosing the hunter Boone to open a western sanctuary from civilization's vices. Oddly, when Bryan's Boone gazes at the Mississippi River, he sees "Mercantile Kingdoms," "FREEDOM's Cities," and "brilliant diadems of COMMERCE crown'd."[39] Such regal imagery might have conjured up images of regal luxury, the very thing Boone fled, yet it made sense that a middle-class hero would establish commerce and cities wherever he ventured.

Boone disliked the poem and wished he could sue his nephew for slander, but the theme of hunter as instrument of empire was taken up again by Jacksonian and antebellum writers. W. H. Bogart wrote his life of Boone specifically to show that Boone's skills in hunting and woodsmanship—not farming—allowed him to lead "the march for a nation to the seat of empire." To Flint, Boone was simply the "First White Man of the West." Through the Boone literature, expansion was transformed into a grand jousting match, a chivalrous contest in which the white hunter gained his kingdom by defeating buffalo, bear, and Indian.[40]

What might have appeared odd about all this to colonial Americans was not so much that the nation had found a hero of expansion but that this hero was a hunter. According to the logic of *vacuum domicilium*, the hunter was an enemy to empire; he could make no claim to lands he refused to clear and plant. The hunter, in fact, was the barbaric antagonist of civilization. Yet even as Americans continued to cite the indolence and savagery of Indian hunters as justification

Boone poses in Byronic fashion, a chivalrous figure alone (but for his faithful dog) in the wilderness. William C. Allan, *Daniel Boone*, 1839 (oil on canvas, 103 × 64½ inches). Special Collections and Archives, Kentucky Historical Society, Frankfort, Kentucky.

This family portrait shows the middle-class man (Andrew Jackson Grayson) in the guise of hunter-hero. Note Grayson's cravat and white shirt below his buckskin hunting jacket. The boy—heir to the realm conquered by his father—wears the ermine robes of a prince. After making his fortune in business, Grayson—inspired by Audubon's *Birds of America*—studied ornithology and became an accomplished painter of birds in his own right. William S. Jewett (1821–73), *The Promised Land—The Grayson Family*, 1850 (oil on canvas, 50¾ × 64 inches). Terra Foundation for the Arts, Daniel J. Terra Collection, 1999.79; photograph courtesy of Terra Museum of American Art, Chicago.

for taking Indian lands, they began to celebrate white hunters as the vanguard of civilization.

William Jewett captured this theme in *The Promised Land,* his 1850 painting that depicts Andrew Jackson Grayson—an 1846 emigrant to California who made a fortune in real estate—stationed on a mountain, leaning on his hunting rifle, a slain buck in the background. Grayson, who commissioned the painting, appears to be Boone himself, yet his partly opened buckskin jacket reveals the white shirt and black cravat of the middle-class man. At his side reclines his stylishly garbed wife, while his son—heir to the realm—wears the ermine robe of a prince.[41]

In envisioning himself as knight errant in frontier buckskins—a man who in killing a buck has conquered an empire—Grayson reflected the attitudes of middle-class emigrants. California, whose population was concentrated in the urban San Francisco Bay area and goldfield mining camps when it entered the Union in 1850, was rapidly settled by middle-class men: bankers, lawyers, and merchants. Even forty-niners and sodbusters tended to come from middle-class backgrounds, since only men with a dash of capital could afford passage to California or Oregon. It made sense for such men to conjoin the chivalrous individualism of the hunter with the trope of *vacuum domicilium* in their rhetoric of Manifest Destiny and social success.

To comprehend the Boone of nineteenth-century art and literature is to comprehend a middle-class hero and a middle-class manliness. Yet Boone became the symbol for new cultural fashions precisely because he seemed to express frontier tradition. This versatility allowed Boone to unite disparate forces. He united an old republicanism associated with the American Revolution and the era of Jefferson with the new republicanism of Jackson and the burgeoning middle class; he united frontiersman, farmer, and town dweller behind a single myth of Americanness; and he united the fantasy of escape from society with the formula for success within it.

With the example of Boone to guide them, Americans soon made hunting—with angling—the most popular participatory sport in America. Boone, however, was not the sole captain of this crusade.

9

A Pantheon of Hunter-Heroes

 As if to validate the Boone myth for future generations, several newspapers reported in 1818 that Boone had passed away at eighty-four, his rifle cocked and aimed at a deer. Boone surely laughed at the liberties taken with the facts of his life; he lived until 1820. More important, his image resonated in American culture as writers and politicians struggled to assume the mantle of the hunter. The poem *Hunters of Kentucky* ("We are a hardy, free-born race / Each man to fear a stranger; / Whate'er the game, we join in chase, / Despising toil and danger") not only celebrated the American victory at the Battle of New Orleans but also became Andrew Jackson's unofficial theme song in 1824 and 1828. Although the poem (first published as a broadside in Boston in about 1815) praises backwoods hunters, it is addressed to "Ye gentlemen and ladies fair / Who grace this famous city." Noah Ludlow, who sang *Hunters of Kentucky* in 1822 in New Orleans dressed in buckskins and moccasins, recalled that his audiences would ask him to repeat the song wherever he performed.[1]

George Bancroft's depiction of Andrew Jackson as "nursling of the wilds" likewise owed much to the Boone of literature, yet it was Congressman Davy Crockett—the Jacksonite turned Whig—who most convincingly adopted Boone's mantle. When Crockett stopped in Philadelphia on his Down East campaign trip in 1834, New England Whigs, aware of the symbolic import of the chase, presented him an ornate hunting rifle. Whig or no, Crockett never became a figure of middle-class propriety. As Carroll Smith-Rosenberg has noted, the dialect-speaking, clownish Crockett and his folksy almanacs seemed to commend drinking, carousing, cursing, and other so-called immoral practices.[2]

The real Crockett was a backwoods Tennessee politician with a gift for homespun wit and ready speech. He was elected twice to the Tennessee legislature and twice to the U.S. Congress, where he made a name for himself as a satirist. In rebutting an opponent in the Tennessee legislature who had referred to him as the "Gentleman from the Cane," Crockett pinned to the sleeve of his coarse shirt the same cambric ruffles that his opponent wore. The effect was ridiculous, and Crockett won the duel, at least insofar as the chagrined opponent retired from the floor amid a chorus of laughter. On another occasion, Crockett memorized the campaign speech of his opponent, Dr. William E. Butler, and then gave it verbatim at an event at which Butler was scheduled to speak next.[3]

Crockett's modus operandi was to pitch himself as a simple backwoodsman, a hunter who had smitten 105 bears in a single season, and who would smite the wicked bears in Congress as well. There is much to admire in the man, from his cleverness as a politician, to his support for the Tennessee Vacant Land Bill (which would have allowed squatters to acquire lands cheaply), and his opposition to Andrew Jackson's Indian removal policies. But his Down East speaking tour and his speeches against Jackson got him in trouble, causing him to lose his bid for reelection to the U.S. House of Representatives in 1835. Humiliated, Crockett marched off to Texas, not to join the rebellion against Mexican rule, but to recoup his fortune. There, he became embroiled in the Texan struggle, was captured—not killed—at the Alamo, and was executed on the orders of General Santa Anna.[4]

Though Crockett was well known before the Alamo, he was by no means on a par with Daniel Boone. Before the Alamo, Crockett was merely a politician with a sense of humor; after the Alamo, he was a martyr to democracy and a symbol of Anglo-American expansion.

Even Crockett—ever the self-promoter—could not have conceived how his image would be contorted and stretched by those who promoted him after his death. From being a congressman with a serious political message and a rich fund of folkish humor, the Davy Crockett who appeared in dozens of almanacs (rather like comic books of our day) became a tall tale.

The first of these almanacs, titled *Go ahead, or Davy Crockett's Almanac of Wild Sports of the West and Life in the Backwoods,* appeared in 1834, two years before Crockett's death, although it was neither written by Crockett nor copyrighted in his name. In the late 1830s and 1840s, Davy Crockett's almanacs continued to pour forth from the presses of eastern cities. Everyone knew Crockett was dead, yet he continued to speak through the medium of big-city hack writers, declaring that he could "walk like an ox, swim like an eel, yell like an Indian, fight like a devil, and spout like an earthquake, make love like a mad bull, and swallow a nigger whole without choking if you butter his head and pin his ears back."[5]

This fulminating, Indian-hating, racist Crockett was no more a creature of backwoods folklore than Daniel Boone. Like Boone, he was the creature of a dialectical relationship between urban writers and young male readers.

As a cultural figure, Crockett—with boatman and hunter Mike Fink and the fictitious Roaring Ralph Stackpole of Robert Montgomery Bird's *Nick of the Woods*—represented the older, savage image of the frontier hunter. Such figures were said to be half-horse, half-alligator men who enjoyed their freedom with reckless abandon. By contrast, the humorless Boone of literature seldom deviated from his code of conduct. While the noble Boone was "of the wilderness," explained Crockett's first biographer, James Strange French, Crockett was "of the frontier," a "less attractive state."[6] Crockett inverted the codes of middle-class manliness that Boone had sanctioned, providing a safety valve for a surplus of self-control.

The third great hunter of the Jacksonian era—James Fenimore Cooper's fictive Natty Bumppo—was, like Boone, of the wilderness rather than of the frontier. Making his debut in *The Pioneers* in 1823, Bumppo, or Leatherstocking, was said to have been "in his youth . . . an Indian warrior, or, what is the same thing, a white man leagued with the savages."[7] Modeled on Boone, Bumppo was a simple, natural man victimized by lawyers, speculators, and more recent settlers. The very name "Nathaniel Bumppo" seems to have been intended by Cooper to remind readers of Daniel Boone.

Sentenced to the stocks by Judge Marmaduke Temple for having menaced the man sent to arrest him for killing a deer out of season, the noble Leatherstocking finds that civilization and its restraints are fast closing in. It is not primarily Judge Temple's laws, however, that Natty fears. Natty's real enemies are settlers who chop down trees and drive out deer to make room for farms. "You've driven God's creaters from the wilderness," exclaims Natty upon being arrested, "and you've brought in the troubles and diviltries of the law, where no man was ever known to disturb another." Told that the land is for Christians, not deer, Natty comes to realize that the farmer's triumph is the hunter's defeat, and he, like Boone, must flee to the West.[8]

Though historians have classed hunter-heroes like Leatherstocking as representative of the farmer-hunters of the real frontier, the heroes of literature seldom fit this description. Cooper cast hunters and farmers as competitors rather than allies. Neither Bumppo, Boone, Kit Carson, nor Buffalo Bill Cody—the nation's premier nineteenth-century hunter-heroes—were portrayed as farmers.

Hunting, exploring, and Indian fighting made such men seem glorious. Perhaps Crockett—who was a backwoods farmer—stands as an exception, yet Crockett achieved national fame via his hunting exploits, not his farm labors.

Before the nineteenth century, hunters stood for savagism and farmers stood for civilization. Hunters and farmers remained opposites in nineteenth-century literature, but the new hunter-heroes were no longer the savages described in four-stages theory. Leatherstocking, like Boone, is a model of republican self-restraint. When he sees villagers festively slaughtering the passenger pigeons that sometimes darkened the skies of New York, Leatherstocking decries the hunters' wantonness. "It's much better to kill only such as you want," he remonstrates, "without wasting your powder and lead, than to be firing into God's creaters in this wicked manner. . . . I don't relish these wasty ways that you are all practysing, as if the least thing was not made for use, and not to destroy."[9]

It is hard to say whether Leatherstocking's criticism of these profligates represented Cooper's genteel sensibilities or those of real frontiersmen. Certainly colonists had sought periodically to protect deer from wanton slaughter; Daniel Boone himself had presented a bill to protect game to the Transylvania assembly. Conservation meant to preserve one's supply of meat, however, differs from conservation meant to stamp out sin. The latter concerned Cooper; Leatherstocking decries wickedness, not mere waste. In arguing against slaughter, Leatherstocking became the voice of republican self-restraint—even the voice of gentility—preaching with the authority of a saintly hermit against the wicked rabble.

Elite sportsmen of the 1820s employed the same ministerial tone to argue for game seasons and restraints on market hunting and would continue to do so throughout the century. Leatherstocking, however, while voicing the ethic of conservation, opposed the game laws of the elite. "There's them living," insists Leatherstocking, "who say Nathaniel Bumppo's right to shoot on these hills is of older date than Marmaduke Temple's right to forbid him." Before Bumppo departs for the West so that he may remain a pure man of the wilderness, however, he finds that he and Temple are on the same side. Both reveal themselves to be secret representatives of the true lord of the land, Major Effingham, the British officer whose son, Oliver, has reappeared to lay claim to his deceased father's estate.[10]

If Leatherstocking was the secret servant of Major Effingham, surely he was even more the secret servant of Cooper and his readers, who made Leatherstocking the courier of their unconscious wishes and sentiments. As a pure hunter of the wilderness (as opposed to impure farmer-hunters of the real frontier), Leatherstocking existed in a realm of fantasy and play where new cultural fashions were modeled, tested, and finally accepted or discarded.

Hunter-heroes were a cultural vanguard, pathfinders for a new age. And they became tremendously popular. Bumppo might speak in a realistic frontier dialect, as opposed to Boone's genteel eloquence, yet his appeal to readers affluent enough to pay two dollars a book helped make Cooper the first American to earn a living from fiction.[11] Sport hunters of later decades would recall Cooper's Leatherstocking tales, along with the literature of Boone and the hunting tales of Mayne Reid, as their boyhood reading.

Natty Bumppo, noted a contributor to *Forest and Stream* in 1889, had taught Americans that "nobility is inborn" and not bestowed by a king or a kaiser. Bumppo's "sterling qualities of truth, courage, self-reliance, and all the attributes of the true hero," he declared, "stamped him with the impress of nobility." One of the popularizers of field sports in America, he concluded, had been Natty Bumppo, who had inspired American boys and men to prove their own nobility in the woods.[12]

Even if some young men could not fully identify with the rustic Leatherstocking, they could identify with Leatherstocking's dark-haired, dark-eyed sidekick. Though educated and well spoken, young Oliver Edwards is rumored to be of mixed ancestry, part Indian and part English. When Oliver declines to become Judge Temple's assistant, Temple's friends speculate that he is expressing "the natural reluctance of a half-breed to leave the savage state," his "attachment to a wandering life" being "unconquerable."[13]

At the end of *The Pioneers,* Oliver refutes the rumor that he is part Indian but adds that his father had been adopted into the Delaware tribe and given the name "Eagle" after saving the life of Chingachgook. The name "Eagle," or "Young Eagle," descended to the son upon the father's demise, along with the enormous tract of Otsego County land granted to the father by the grateful Delawares. Thus the genteel Oliver Effingham—not Edwards, as he at last discloses—could claim title to both the land and to an honorary Indianness without admitting any biological relation to Indians.[14]

In giving themselves Indian pen names and in learning the skills of tracking, hunting, and woodcraft, sport hunters managed the same sleight of hand. They too were genteel men who laid claim to Indianness without having any biological relation to Indians. If all sport hunters were Natty Bumppos, they were also Oliver Effinghams. More important, they—like Bumppo and Effingham both—were American Natives.

Subsequent hunter-heroes more often claimed the integrity of Boone and Leatherstocking than the comic qualities of Crockett and Fink. In the 1840s, mild, soft-spoken Kit Carson—said to be Boone's grandson—became the "modern Nimrod" whose "deeds of coolness, daring, energy, and perseverance" served as an example to the "rising generation." Despite his "wild and romantic" appearance, Charles Deas's imaginary *Long Jakes,* one of many western hunters in bright red shirts and buckskin leggings painted in the 1840s, likewise showed "traits of former gentleness and refinement in his countenance," according to a New York reviewer. From this mold also came Buffalo Bill, who had slaughtered thousands of buffalo to feed railroad crews and, later, to please tourists. Buffalo Bill was as much a showman as a hunter, yet he remained a gentleman rather than a "ring-tailed roarer."[15]

The degree to which these heroes reshaped the self-image of American men is revealed in innumerable nineteenth-century portraits of men wearing hunting garb and carrying guns. Until the Revolution, no artist painted his patron in hunting shirt or buckskins; to do so would have been insulting. Portrait artists and photographers of the nineteenth century, however, presented the nation with a pantheon of heroic figures in buckskins that included not just Boone, Crockett, Carson, and Buffalo Bill but also more ordinary men. As a youth, Theodore Roosevelt posed for photographers dressed in buckskins and later pronounced the buckskin hunting outfit "the most picturesque and distinctively national dress ever worn in America."[16]

Buoyed to respectability by such rhetoric were rank-and-file backwoodsmen, many of whom metamorphosed from crude, threatening, marginal men into nature's noblemen. In his 1840s adventure on the Oregon Trail, Francis Parkman described his party's French hunter, Henry Chatillon, as having "a natural refinement ... such as is rare even in women." Chatillon's face, wrote Parkman, expressed "uprightness, simplicity, and kindness of heart" that belied the courage of a man who had killed thirty grizzlies. Regardless of his character, Chatillon was illiterate, yet he displayed intelligence and reverence for nature by studying game "as a scholar studies his books." Charles Lanman, an artist who journeyed to the Adirondacks in the 1850s, likewise expected his guide to be a "huge, powerful, and hairy Nimrod" yet instead found a man "small in stature, ... modest and thoughtful, ... gentle in his manners, ... a devoted lover of nature and solitude."[17]

In glorifying frontier hunters, middle-class writers, when they did not portray their subjects as alligator horses in the mold of Crockett, bestowed on them a middle-class patina of character and grace. It should have come as no surprise to Cooper's readers when Oliver Edwards revealed himself as heir to a genteel tradition. Like an antebellum Superman—or like Andrew Jackson Grayson in William Jewett's painting *The Promised Land,* or Daniel Boone, or John James Audubon—Edwards seemed able to transform himself at will from masculine hero to mild-mannered gentleman.

Parkman, Lanman, Jewett, and others not only wrote about and painted frontier hunters but also traveled west to play out their own chivalrous roles on the vast stage of the western territories. Middle-class writers who worshiped Boone and Leatherstocking helped make the western travel narrative a standard genre—and a powerful tool of expansion—for the rest of the century. As early as 1819, Estwick Evans, a young Boston lawyer, published an account of a western pilgrimage that he undertook in 1818 to "acquire the simplicity, native feelings, and virtues of savage life" in the manner of Boone. Evans, who left New England wearing clothes made of deer, bear, and buffalo skins and carrying a small arsenal of weaponry, wandered four thousand miles on the frontier, hunting and fishing as he went. Washington Irving—who celebrated the hunter in the figure of Captain Bonneville—likewise made a hunting pilgrimage to the Far West in the 1830s, explaining that a "tour on the Prairies" produced "that manliness, simplicity, and self-dependence, most in unison with our political institutions."[18]

By the 1840s such pilgrimages were no longer exceptional. As Robert Johannsen argues, American men of all regions—stirred by the romances of Sir Walter Scott and the no less romantic military histories of the 1830s (not to mention the Boone literature)—made the Mexican War into a masculine crusade for "chivalry" and "honor."[19] (No doubt the same processes were at work in the Civil War.) Johannsen attributes such fantasies to an uneasiness over antebellum materialism; Americans sought to identify themselves with some loftier purpose than greed.

Yet behind this anxiety lurked the rapid growth of cities and the gradual erosion of agrarian patriarchy, along with the middle-class man's need to cultivate self-possession and to balance the claims of gentility with older definitions of republican simplicity. Thus pushed and shunted, American men remade themselves in the image of the chivalrous, self-possessed hunter, and they cast the public sphere—like the wilderness—as a decidedly male realm of strife and danger. These conditions fueled the popularity of hunter-heroes and, through them, the popularity of Manifest Destiny (fittingly, members of the northern secret societies of the 1840s that sought to annex Canada to the Union were called patriot hunters).

With the examples of these hunter-heroes, sport hunting, too, became popular as a ritual of republican austerity. Hunter-heroes adhered to an ascetic code that required them to turn their backs on society, yet most middle-class men were more compromising; they entered the wilderness as hunters only for brief interludes to cleanse themselves of sin and to reinvigorate themselves for business. Even in "cities and populous places," Timothy Flint reported in his Boone biography of 1833, Americans had become "so fond" of hunting "that they ransack the cultivated fields and enclosures of the farmer" in search of small game. "What, then," wondered Flint, "must have been the feelings of Boone, to find himself in the grand theatre of the hunter—filled with buffaloes, deer, bears, wild turkeys, and other noble game?"[20]

As historians have long noted, Americans of the early national period feared that cities and wealth would weaken their civilization, their patriotism, and even their bodies and minds.[21] The agrarian ethos remained powerful into the Gilded Age, when it boiled over in the Populist movement of the late 1800s. But decades earlier the image of the hunter-hero had begun to reveal an alternative brand of patriotism and virtue that no longer focused on farming.

By the Mexican War, tales of hunters had so colored the American imagination that Charles Wilkins Webber could write that hunting had always been "the chief occupation of the American people."

> All the impulsion of our national character—all of the hardy, stern, resolute and generous that may be native, we take through the noble blood of our hunter ancestors. That terrible soldiery which devastated Mexico, was composed of hunters almost to a man; the eagle they carried before them was a hunting bird—the fierce-eyed king of the winged hunters![22]

Webber revealed how much the nation had come to see itself as predatory imperialist, a hunting nation eager for conquest rather than the peaceful expansion of the yeoman society imagined by Jefferson. Indeed, by the time Webber wrote, middle-class men had proceeded beyond the manufacture and the worship of hunter-heroes. To reclaim republican virtue and to recodify expansion and empire in their image, middle-class men were becoming hunters—and American Natives—themselves.

10

The Sport Hunter's Awakening

In the sparsely settled woods of Otsego County, New York (home to James Fenimore Cooper's fictive Natty Bumppo), members of a rare American fraternity—the hunting club—convened in 1821. Each morning during what was to become an annual four-day event, a bugle signaled breakfast, after which members of the Unadilla Hunt fanned out in pursuit of deer.

Positioning themselves alongside "runways," paths used by deer for escape, the hunters waited for hired men and hounds to drive game out of the forest. "The cry of the dogs is enchanting," recalled club member Levi Beardsley, "as they pass from hill to hill; now swelling into full chorus, and then receding till entirely lost; again returning, and their cheerful notes reverberating among the hills." When a large buck was shot, "one continued shout went round, and echo answered, 'this day a stag must die!'"[1]

Here, seemingly, were bold hunters who did honor to Natty Bumppo, hero of James Fenimore Cooper's Leatherstocking tales. One wonders, however, what Natty would have thought.

Thirty members strong by 1822, the club took twenty-one deer with assistance from thirty-one "drivers" and fifty-two hounds. After enjoying their sport, the hunters filled their evenings with wine and song (leaving out women) and dinners that "would have done honour to the most splendid drawing-room in the Union." More important, the Unadilla hunters—whose wealth and high station belied often humble origins—formed friendships that gave them a sense of themselves as a fraternity, even as a class. "By day," writes Alan Taylor, club members "in ritualized deer-killing ... affirmed their enduring manhood; at night in equally ritualized dining and toasting they manifested their new gentility; by both day and night they hoped to become brothers."[2]

Their celebrations were marred, however, by men like Natty Bumppo, subsistence hunters who had no fondness for gentlemen. Time and again, recalled Unadilla members, poachers would appear to shoot the deer. "A large buck with antlers erect," reported one of the Unadilla Hunt members, "is seen on the opposite side making his way directly to you.... You are certain of a shot, and a moment more you have him. Pop goes a smooth bore, and Spikerman, the poacher, has killed him."[3]

These subsistence hunters were not poachers in the eyes of the law. In New York State (as elsewhere in the United States), the Supreme Court had ruled that game became the property of the man who had killed it, whether or not another man had been in pursuit of the animal when it was killed. One justice dissented from an 1805 ruling on this question, fearing that a "saucy intruder" might too often kill game pursued by another hunter.[4] To rule that game belonged to pursuer rather than killer, however, was tantamount to awarding elite sportsmen, with their dogs, horses, and drivers, privileges comparable to those of English aristocrats. Moreover, a decision favoring pursuer would cause endless wrangling among hunters, genteel or plebeian, who inadvertently crossed paths and killed one another's game. Who was the legitimate pursuer and who was the interloper?

Without the law to back them, and without ownership of their hunting grounds, Unadilla members were forced to put up with "pirates" who killed deer as they were chased from cover. To control the problem, members kept the dates of their rendezvous secret, even if that compromised their desire to publicize themselves as an elite fraternity. They also hired brawny locals to pummel deference into interlopers. "One of those lawless intruders who ... was disposed to be troublesome and impertinent," wrote a member of the Unadilla Hunt, "received from one of the drivers ... his pay in undepreciated Kentucky currency, producing a total obscurity of his day-lights and a most copious effusion of 'claret.'"[5] That would not be the last time that elite hunters would hire toughs to vanquish challengers.

That members were willing to go to such extremes to hunt reveals how eager they were to develop rituals suitable to their class. These men sought a rural pastime that would reflect the status, virtues, and ethics of those whose lives revolved around commerce and courts rather than farms. In hunting gentlemen found a way to invigorate mind and body while ritually defining a manliness that harked back to monarchical America. What they did not find—nor seek—was friendship with the Natty Bumppos of the region.

In some respects, the Unadilla Hunt represented a force that would transform the American cultural landscape. Similar clubs—not necessarily modeled on the Unadilla, but popular for the same reasons—soon appeared throughout the country. In the 1830s in Cincinnati, reported Charles Fenno Hoffman, "a literary soirée and a sporting-club dinner would . . . be two of the most characteristic circles into which I could carry you." Hoffman, a leading literary light of antebellum society, added that he felt more at ease among sportsmen than litterateurs.[6]

Hoffman's sporting club may have been the Cincinnati Shooting Club, which claimed twenty-five members in 1833, held biannual competitive hunts (to which friends were invited), and served up yearly dinners of fresh game. That this club was composed of city men and not farmers is clear from a report in a sporting journal by a member who wanted to prove that Westerners had more interesting amusements than "cutting down timber and cultivating the land." A St. Louis club made its membership more explicit, bragging in 1851 that "but a few years since" its rolls had included a congressman, a Supreme Court justice, and an army general. Another midwestern club boasted in later years that it was "well represented by the honorable callings—merchants of dry goods, manufacturers, and real estate dealers, bankers, and gentlemen of leisure."[7]

Before the Civil War, sporting journals reported on hunting clubs in New York, Boston, Philadelphia, Chicago, Rhode Island, Washington, D.C., Maryland, Georgia, Mississippi, Arkansas, St. Louis, and Ft. Gibson, Indian Territory (the latter club was composed of army officers). Hunting clubs, like hunting literature, appealed to men of the North, South, and West alike.[8]

In addition to hunting clubs were rifle and military clubs, which promoted regional rivalries by competing against one another in shooting matches.[9] Hunting clubs were different from rifle and military clubs, however, having been established partly to lobby for stricter game laws and to prosecute those who killed or sold game out of season.

If the Unadilla experiment was a harbinger of hunting clubs to come, in other respects it was a failure. The gentlemen were forced to disband their club in 1827 upon passage of an act—apparently sought by backwoodsmen and their allies in the state legislature—forbidding the driving of deer with dogs (this law was repealed only in 1844). By 1827, moreover, much of the Unadilla River valley had been cleared for farms, greatly reducing the deer population.[10] Gentlemen had to look elsewhere for game.

The principal reason for the failure of the Unadilla Hunt was the fact that backwoods settlers did not view gentlemen as representatives of a superior class with a special right to kill game or, for that matter, to hold the reins of government. Nor would backwoodsmen stand by while dozens of deer—deer that might sustain backwoods families during the hard months of winter—were sacrificed for gentlemen's pleasure.

Perhaps backwoodsmen of English and Scottish extraction recalled struggles between elite hunters and poachers in their homelands, where hunting had long been a locus of symbolic warfare over class and power. At least one settler in the area, notes Alan Taylor, had been charged in England with a poaching offense; surely other settlers in America had fled British soil after similar brushes with the law.[11] The gentlemen who intruded on the domain of the backwoodsmen probably shared such cultural memories, if from a different perspective. In Europe, to be a member of the elite meant to hold monopoly rights on hunting; why not, well-to-do Americans seemed to ask themselves, in the United States, too?

The Unadilla conflict was about who would exclude whom from the hunt: would gentlemen exclude common men, or would common men exclude gentlemen? By extension, the conflict was about who would exclude whom from the definition of manliness and citizenship. Who would control American society?

These issues were not resolved by the collapse of the Unadilla Hunt. Backwoodsmen (as market and subsistence hunters) would go on contesting elite hunters into the twentieth century. What the fate of the Unadilla Hunt did resolve was whether elite hunters who mimicked English precedent in republican America would go unchallenged: they would not.

When sport hunting emerged as a favorite pastime of middle-class Americans in later decades, it flavored the English tradition of genteel sport with the American tradition of frontier self-reliance. There is "something peculiarly attractive about stories of border life and wilderness experience," wrote the author of an antebellum article about sport hunting in the Adirondacks, "something heroic in depending upon one's rifle and right arm, miles and miles beyond the sound of human voices, or the aid of human hands, in the fresh and silent forest." The Lewis and Clark expedition, he added, had "more romance than the Arabian Nights."[12]

Rather than setting apart practitioners as members of an elite, hunting allowed middle-class men to recapture—not reject—spartan virtues of legendary backwoodsmen like Natty Bumppo. This outcome was not incompatible with middle-class fraternity; the ethic of individualism would become the rallying cry of Jacksonian men on the make even as it obscured the bonds of class.

Meanwhile, sport hunters met resistance from a different direction. Despite the brief success of the Unadilla Hunt, Jacksonian era sport hunters found antihunting biases still alive, forming a dense thicket between hunters and the moral high ground they sought. Far from being revered in early national America, sport hunting was either ignored in the press or ridiculed as a waste of time and money. Even in the 1830s, recalled Henry William Herbert, the antebellum champion of hunting, American sport hunters were "tabooed, as a species of moral and social pariah." Young men who admitted to hunting could not expect promotions from merchant employers, while lawyers dared not tell clients of their love of shooting for fear of losing business. According to Herbert, William Post Hawes, a New York City attorney and author of antebellum hunting literature, lived in "fear and trembling" lest others see his name in print and was forced to use a pseudonym.[13]

In 1885 hunter and conservationist George Bird Grinnell averred that "a man who went 'gunnin or fishin' in the early nineteenth century lost caste among respectable people just about in the same way that one did who got drunk." Sport hunters, Grinnell explained, had been "looked upon as idlers and ne'er-do-wells, for it was thought that these pursuits were mere excuses for laziness—the avoidance of work." According to the author of a 1900 editorial in *Outdoor Life*, hunting was in Washington's time, and to a degree in Lincoln's, "considered only fit for the poor and labouring classes" (and by no means universally approved in them).[14]

Sport hunting had not disappeared in early national America, yet surviving alongside it were vestiges of the Puritan (or Protestant) objection to idleness, the Enlightenment objection to cruelty, and the four-stages theorists' objection to savagery. All three attitudes had coalesced into a widespread northern disdain for sport hunting, a disdain that would take decades to overcome.

Consider "A Discourse Against Laziness in Sportsmen," a text that appears to have been a sermon. Published in New York City in 1835, the essay concluded with a plea for hunters to share game with the author, whose spiritual duties prevented him from hunting. Yet the sermon began with a strident attack on sport hunting reminiscent of Puritan jeremiads. "To what purpose do *you* hunt?" the author asked his audience.

> Is it to obtain the means of living? No. Is it to increase your influence among your fellows for any useful purpose? No. Is it to conquer mankind, and to found empires, kingdoms, colonies, or even towns? No. For what then do you take the trouble to break dogs; to hire carriages; to consume time; in order that you may shoot a few harmless snipe, woodcock, or quail? . . . It is with most of you from *foolish vanity*, or from *idle habit*.

Citing Solomon's censure that "the slothful man roasteth not that which he took in hunting," the author termed sport hunters "degenerate sons" of Nimrod and called them to task for "cruelty and hard-heartedness."[15]

Conspicuous here was the suggestion that hunting was inhumane and extravagant and, more important, that it in no way benefited community or commonwealth. Unlike Israel Putnam, who had killed the Pomfret wolf to clear the way for agrarian civilization, and unlike Daniel Boone, who had hunted to found an empire, sport hunting seemed to be an individual pursuit and thus foolish vanity or idle habit. What the author of the discourse failed to understand—or understood too well—was that sport hunters, as they wandered the fields and woods of eastern America, were reformulating American manliness.[16]

Unlike their grandfathers, who attached themselves to what Gordon Wood terms "monarchical" society, or their fathers, who might have subscribed to the republican ideal of sacrifice for the sake of the community or commonwealth, sport hunters revered individualism. They abandoned, if temporarily, ties to community as they searched the countryside for game, sometimes alone or, more

Sport hunters measured success on the amount of game they could bag on a given day. "Hunter's Journal" from the *American Turf Register and Sporting Magazine*, 1829. Courtesy of the Beinecke Rare Book and Manuscript Library, Yale University, New Haven, Connecticut.

Where killed.	When.	Partridge.	Pheasant.	Woodcock.	Snipe.	Ducks or wild fowl.	Hare.		Total each day.	Shots mis'd	Remarks.
	Mond.										
	Tuesd.										
	Wed'y										
	Thurs.										
	Frid'y										
	Satur.										
	Total.										

GENERAL OBSERVATIONS.

The Sportsman may add columns at pleasure for other game.

often, with a couple of partners. And despite making an occasional gift of game to friends and family, they measured success not on their provision for others but on their personal success. "This day [I] saw four coveys of partridges," bragged a hunter in the pages of the *American Turf Register and Sporting Magazine* in 1829, "and bagged twenty-four of them."[17] To hunt for sport was to enact the atomistic codes of a libertarian, middle-class America.

Perhaps recognizing that hunting would be a permanent part of the cultural landscape, the author of "A Discourse" stepped reluctantly into the Jacksonian present by condoning sport hunting as long as it partook of the discipline of a calling. Contrasting the "true sportsman" with the "idle, careless, procrastinating . . . hunter," the author urged hunters to exercise "judgement," "diligence," and punctuality in their sport.[18]

The author seemed to realize that no Puritan jibe would slow the momentum of sport hunting. Yet the discourse also indicated that as hunters reformulated American manliness, they would be required to reformulate their sport. If sport hunting was cruel and hard-hearted, it would have to be made genteel and compassionate through a code of sportsmanship. If sport hunting was foolish vanity or idle habit, it would have to be rededicated to a vision of national greatness. And if the hunter was careless and procrastinating, he would have to refashion himself into a man of integrity, industry, science, and health.

Evidence of the growing fascination with sport hunting came not only in sermons and tales of border life but also in a new sporting press. As early as 1820, John Stuart Skinner's *American Farmer,* a weekly devoted to technical advice on agriculture, began printing small accounts of English bird hunts and shooting matches lifted from English journals. In 1825 one of Skinner's subscribers petulantly insisted that Americans could shoot as well as Englishmen and lamented that "amongst us, for want of a suitable medium, sporting events are not recorded."[19]

As if to gratify the correspondent, Skinner, a dog and horse breeder, a fox hunter, and a foe of such city sports as cockfighting, ratting, and gambling, began running a regular column on American field sports called "Sporting Olio." Then in 1829, without subscribers and without advertising, he launched a new monthly— a gamble by American standards—devoted to field sports: *The American Turf Register and Sporting Magazine.* Skinner was no neophyte at this sort of project; he had begun the *American Farmer* (which he sold for the princely sum of $20,000 to concentrate on his new project) the same way, and he was well connected, numbering among his friends Andrew Jackson, John Quincy Adams, and William Henry Har-

Vignettes on the 1831 masthead of the *American Turf Register and Sporting Magazine* suggest the growing popularity of sport hunting. Courtesy of the Beinecke Rare Book and Manuscript Library, Yale University, New Haven, Connecticut.

rison. Skinner also had a handy second job for an editor of a journal with ambitions for national circulation: he had been appointed postmaster of Baltimore by James Madison in 1816 and served in the post for twenty-three years.[20]

As a Southerner and a fox hunter, Skinner had few reservations about the semiaristocratic tone of his magazine; hence he modeled the *American Turf Register* on the *Sporting Magazine* of London, which had been in existence since 1792. The *American Turf Register*, as its name implied, was primarily a registry of thoroughbred horses, but Skinner also wished to give his journal "an *American* cast, conveying . . . amusement and instruction, in regard to our own country, its animals, birds, fishes & c." To this end, Skinner would include regular material on "SHOOTING, HUNTING, FISHING,& C."[21]

On the heels of Skinner's *American Turf Register* appeared John and Thomas Doughty's *Cabinet of Natural History and American Rural Sport*, a more impressive journal that more explicitly linked hunting with natural history. The Doughtys' publication was not as successful as Skinner's; the total output ran to three volumes, with installments appearing in a desultory fashion after 1830 and selling for the steep subscription price of eight dollars a year (Skinner's journal sold for five dollars). But the *Cabinet of Natural History* gave readers not only innumerable accounts of hunting and fishing but also fifty-three elegant, hand-colored lithographs of American fauna situated in handsome landscapes drawn by Thomas Doughty.[22] True to its name, the *Cabinet of Natural History* was as much a popular natural history as a sporting work.

Though lacking the journalistic experience and connections of John Skinner, the Doughtys had the artistic skills of Thomas, whose reputation peaked at roughly the time of the *Cabinet*'s debut. Born into a Presbyterian family in Philadelphia in 1793, Thomas Doughty was apprenticed at sixteen to a leather currier, yet through some beneficent twist of fate, he became at twenty-four the first American to be listed as landscape painter in a city directory. Like other American painters of his time, he had only a dash of formal training and relied instead on his own wits, educating himself by copying the old Dutch masters and the French painter Claude Lorrain.[23]

Initially Doughty's success came from painting stately commercial buildings and country estates, works that found a ready market among Americans who hoped to glorify their own civilization by mimicking a conventional English genre. Later Doughty was among the first Americans to paint landscapes devoid of man-made edifices, capitalizing on, and helping to create, a growing American tendency to see in the country's native forests a cultural heritage equal to the monuments and crumbling ruins of Europe. By 1840 writer Nathaniel Parker

Willis had pronounced Doughty the best landscape artist in America and perhaps the superior of any English artist, and the *Knickerbocker* magazine spoke of
Doughty as the "Painter of Nature."[24]

Doughty might also be called a father of American hunting art. A hunter and
fisherman himself, Doughty traveled and sketched in the Adirondack and the
Catskill Mountains of New York and the forests of Maine, Massachusetts, and
New Hampshire, everywhere making a close study of nature (an artist's success,
he reasoned, comes not from "imagination" alone but from "a knowledge of Natural History"). Unlike Arthur Fitzwilliam Tait, who entered the American scene
a generation later, Doughty never made the hunter the dominant focus of his can-
vases. In fact, he was criticized for his inability to paint human figures, yet he often
added to his landscapes tiny figures of gentlemen hunters scouring the countryside for game or anglers in the act of casting.[25]

Though this sort of painting had British precedents, Doughty was among the
first Americans to depict his countrymen interacting with American nature without placing them in scenes of cultivation and industry. Like Thomas Jefferson
and Charles Willson Peale, Doughty made nature a source and monument of
American identity. The hunters and anglers in his later paintings move through
a natural world free of the man-made edifices that had appeared in his earlier
work and free of the technological intrusions that sometimes figure in paintings
of the Hudson River school.

The flagship of the antebellum sporting press was neither the Doughtys' *Cabinet of Natural History and American Rural Sport* nor Skinner's *American Turf Register* but William Trotter Porter's *Spirit of the Times.* Porter, a tall, genial man with
an education in Greek, Latin, and *The Compleat Angler, or the Contemplative Man's
Recreation* by Izaak Walton, launched the *Spirit of the Times* in 1831 after leaving his
native Vermont for the publishing pastures of New York City.[26]

Modeled, as was the *American Turf Register,* on an English sporting paper (in
this case *Bell's Life of London*), the *Spirit of the Times* succeeded where other up-
starts failed by providing a goodly dose of humor and timely information on
horse racing and other sporting events (the *Spirit of the Times* came out weekly;
the *American Turf Register* monthly). Unlike the gentlemanly *American Turf Register,* the *Spirit of the Times* encouraged entrepreneurs to advertise in its pages guns
and ammunition, fishing tackle, horses and equestrian paraphernalia, and resorts.
Porter further advanced his cause by assembling a corps of highly talented correspondents, including humorist Thomas Bangs Thorpe and English exile and
hunting writer Henry William Herbert.

Initially the *Spirit of the Times* paid more attention to horse racing than hunting, but by 1840 the balance began to equalize as correspondents from through-out the country sent in narratives of the chase. Stories of hunting buffalo, bear, panther, and deer came from the Deep South, from Louisville and Cincinnati, from New York, from Boston, and from army officers and travelers in the Far West. Soon the *Spirit of the Times* could boast of having readers and correspon-dents throughout the nation, making it one of the first American weeklies to tran-scend the sectional jealousies of the time.[27]

Without lists of subscribers, it is impossible to determine the exact distribu-tion of the *Spirit of the Times* or the identities of its readers, but its content indi-cates that it appealed to middle-class urbanites, gentlemen farmers, southern planters, and officers of the army and navy ("we are not aware of a single Mili-tary or Naval station of the United States, in any clime," bragged Porter in 1853, "where the 'Spirit of the Times' is not to be found").[28] In addition to sporting ma-terial and regular reports from officers on the frontiers, the *Spirit of the Times* in-cluded a literary department, a theatrical department, and a column titled "Salmagundi—Sayings and Doings About Town."

This sort of entertainment failed to garner the *Spirit of the Times* the 100,000-plus circulation attained by *Frank Leslie's Illustrated Newspaper* and *Harper's New Monthly Magazine* in the 1850s and 1860s. As one army officer stationed in Missouri wrote to Porter, the rough frontiersmen around him would consider subscribing to the *Spirit of the Times* about the same as subscribing to a paper from the moon. Yet the *Spirit of the Times* (and the *American Turf Register* before it) attained a cir-culation of forty thousand—unusual for any periodical of the time—thus cre-ating and holding together a national fraternity of sportsmen.[29]

Sport hunting's popularity also rose on a tide of books. Before 1827 only one American book had focused on sport hunting, but the number of hunting books climbed exponentially in subsequent decades. Led by Henry William Herbert (whose pseudonym was Frank Forester), authors of antebellum hunting narra-tives and how-to books included William Post Hawes (whose pseudonym was J. Cypress, Jr.), Joel Tyler Headley, Alfred Billings Street, Samuel H. Hammond, John Krider, Elisha Jarrett Lewis, Charles Wilkins Webber, Charles Edward Whitehead, and William Elliott. In addition authors of travel narratives—Est-wick Evans, Charles Fenno Hoffman, Washington Irving, Francis Parkman, and Charles Lanman among them—offered lengthy accounts of hunting experi-ences.

What is singular about these authors is their youth and sectional origins. Though we tend to think of sport hunting as a southern pastime, only one of these authors, Elliott, lived permanently in the South (Webber grew up in Kentucky but lived in New Jersey and New York as an adult before venturing west). And all, with the exception of Elliott, Irving, and Krider (whose birth date is not recorded), were under fifty at the time their first hunting or travel book appeared. Most were in their thirties. These men represented what was often called "the rising generation."

Hunting literature burgeoned as part of an antebellum print revolution made possible by cheap paper, fast presses, and better communications and transportation. Technology alone, however, cannot explain why hunting—judging by evidence from the sporting press—became as popular among urban professionals and businessmen as it was among southern planters.

When partridge season opened in 1834, commented the *American Turf Register,* "two or three coveys are to be contended for by half the lawyers, doctors, schoolmasters, sporting persons, and tradesmen in the place." In 1854 Samuel H. Hammond's book *Hills, Lakes, and Forest Streams: or, A Tramp in the Chateaugay Woods* urged urban hunters to "throw down your book or your pen, close your ponderous ledger, cast away your briefs . . . and turn your back upon the glare and heat of the city, its eternal jostlings and monotonous noises." A similar strain of romantic primitivism suffused the report of another urbanite who reported in the *Spirit of the Times* "how glorious" he felt in fustian coat and breeches, with moccasins on his feet and a rifle on his shoulder. "God," he wrote, "never intended that man should live in brick walls, walk on pavement, and use his nose for no other purpose than to smell the perfume of city gutters."[30]

The old judgment of Benjamin Rush—that hunting endangered health and made men susceptible to binges of eating and drinking after the abstinences of the chase—was reversed; hunting was deemed to be healing. In 1829 one correspondent of the *American Turf Register* went so far as to suggest that the inactivity of urban men produced "numbness and stupor" and argued that any healthy young man who failed to appreciate field sports must have a "sickened intellect and a disordered sensibility." A correspondent of the *Cabinet of Natural History and American Rural Sport* added in 1830 (without conscious irony) that "astonishing cures have been made by the most effective of all surgical instruments, the gun," citing instances in which city men were cured of illness by taking up the shooting of partridges (ruffed grouse). By the 1850s hunting authors argued that urban men would physically degenerate if they failed to commune with nature.[31]

Urban men desperately needed to recall the chivalry, health, and manliness of the hunt because among them republican definitions of masculinity seemed to break down. *Hunt's Merchants' Magazine* pointed out rather too cheerily in 1855

that the clerk (a designation that might refer to all young men in nonmanual occupations) "is to business what the wife is to the order and success of the home—
the genius that gives form and fashion to the materials for prosperity . . . furnished
by another." Surely few clerks were pleased with such a comparison, yet fewer
still could return to the familiar role of producer and head of household on a
family farm.[32]

Aware that they had lost the old moorings of masculinity, young men like
Oliver Wendell Holmes worried that cities produced "black-coated, stiff-
jointed, soft-muscled, paste-complexioned youth" who did no credit to the
Anglo-Saxon race. Horace Mann likewise complained of a "general effeminacy," noting that the "old hearts of oak are gone" and that "society is suffering
under a curvature of the spine." Another author put the issue in stark terms:
cities and mercantile classes, he wrote in 1855, had wrought "the effemination of
a whole race of men."[33]

Young men might have looked to the church to orient their manliness, yet the-
ologian Henry James Sr. complained in the mid-nineteenth century that "religion in the old virile sense has disappeared, and been replaced by a feeble Uni-
tarian sentimentality." America's religious and literary culture, according to Ann
Douglas, became "feminized" as ministers and writers composed sentimental
sermons and novels for middle-class women freed from domestic chores by the
commercial revolution.[34]

While men reconstituted the masculine God of Calvinism in the secret rituals of fraternal organizations, these rituals highlighted how outmoded the old
masculinity based on a man's role on the farm and in the church had become.
Boyhood itself was "feminized" as women came to dominate child rearing, teaching their sons the Christian selflessness and polite behavior of the domestic
sphere rather than the selfishness and competition of the public sphere.[35]

Confronted with the disjuncture between the values they had learned from
their mothers and those required for success in the marketplace, young men
adopted new values as they entered manhood. In the dispensation created by the
market revolution, observed Ralph Waldo Emerson, success would no longer be
"measured by the exact law of reciprocity; much less by the sentiments of love
and heroism" (those were but the old Christian virtues). Instead, what had come
into being was "a system of distrust, of concealment, of superior keenness, not
of giving but of taking advantage."[36] If any logic was epitomized in hunting, it was
that.

Perhaps, as Mark Carnes argues, the secret rituals of fraternal organizations
provided the "dark" crossing from the sentimental realm of boyhood to the stark

realm of manhood, yet surely hunting helped point the way.[37] In the crusade to remasculinize American culture, sport hunters—inspired by the literature of Boone—marched in the vanguard. One hunter offered a poem in the *Spirit of the Times* that contrasted his stern sport with the decadent fashion of the time:

> Let some impale the sunny skies,
>   An offering to the muses,
> While others rave o'er ladies' eyes,
>   Twin obsolete abuses,
> And bore you with their prosy rhymes,
>   On sun, moon, stars, and flowers,
> Of gnarled oaks and knotted vines,
>   Boudoirs and shady bowers.
> I sing a strain of loftier note,
>   A nobler, manlier lesson,
> Come, with me to the woodlands float,
>   We'll expiate transgression
> And there, in lieu of 'beauty's queen,'
>   We'll sing, unsung to fame,
> But fame deserving well, I ween,
>   Our trueborn, native game.[38]

By offering "a nobler, manlier lesson," hunting ritually "expiated" the "transgressions" of men who lived in a changing society. America had long been a nation of farmers, a nation in which political, moral, and manly virtues bloomed from cultivated fields. That America was giving way to something else, something nebulous in the early national era, but whose outlines could be distinguished. The new America would be more commercial, more urban, and more affluent. It would be an America that no longer fit the founders' prescriptions for social health. "No instance has yet occurred," insisted minister Lyman Beecher in 1829, "in which national voluptuousness has not trod hard upon the footsteps of national opulence, destroying moral principle and patriotism, debasing the mind and enervating the body, and preparing men to become, like the descendants of the Romans, effeminate slaves."[39]

"Will you tell me," John Adams had written to Thomas Jefferson as early as 1819, "how to prevent riches from producing luxury? Will you tell me how to prevent luxury from producing effeminacy intoxication extravagance Vice and folly?"[40] By entering the sacred, spartan woods in sober sincerity, gun in hand, American sport hunters answered Adams's question.

Hunting could become a ritual of American identity because—unlike horse racing, pugilism, ratting, and billiards—it seemed pure. It did not involve gambling, nor—despite the hunters' indulgence in the occasional flask of brandy—did it revolve around the saloon. Young men of the "rising generation," insisted a correspondent of the *American Turf Register* in 1829, should "spend their leisure time in the *open field*, and in *manly exercises*—instead of seeking to kill time in an oyster cellar, or village stores, drinking still-burnt whiskey, and in other and more pernicious haunts of dissipation." "I rejoice," he continued, "that we have at last an elegant repository which will beget a fondness for healthy rural sports, and where no gentleman will be ashamed to see his feats and his name."[41]

Repent "your vanities and follies, and shameless waste of God's good gifts," added F. S. Stallknecht in 1860, uttering a sentiment that had become a cliché. Come to the Adirondacks, he advised the gamblers who patronized Saratoga horse races, to find the "contentment and health" that "[you] vainly strive for in your selfish, aimless existence."[42]

Through sport hunting, American men achieved more than "contentment and health"; they reenacted the chivalrous dramas of old, discovering an antidote to the "utilitarian jargon" of those who wished to "eradicate from men's souls the love of the chivalric, the heroic, the independent deeds of great men."[43] The cumulative effect was to make the literature of hunting, like the literature of Boone, a jeremiad against the corruptions and effeminacy of urban (or plantation) life. This attack on modernity, however, was camouflage. The nineteenth-century fascination with chivalry revealed not so much a nostalgia for Sir Walter Scott's knights and castles, or for the frontier of Boone, as a burgeoning cult of individualism. To be chivalrous was to be a brave knight in the armor of character, the hero of one's fate in a libertarian realm of noble strife.

Gentlemen hunters might don moccasins or buckskins to go into the woods, but nothing better reveals their chivalrous gentility than Elisha Jarrett Lewis's caution in his 1851 *Hints to Sportsmen* to those

> whose occupation or profession makes it desirable that they have white and smooth hands, and there are but few gentlemen whose employments do not require this, they ought . . . to wear gloves when shooting, as nothing to our eyes looks more *outré*, if not vulgar, than a coarse, scratched and scarred hand.[44]

Americans who took up sport hunting lived most of their lives amid all the luxury they could afford, picking up their rifles (and gloves) each autumn to invigorate themselves with frontier (and aristocratic) virtues. During the rest of the year, they obtained chivalry, health, and moral vigor by reading sporting literature in the comfort of home or office. "I have enjoyed sporting excessively in *books*," admitted a New York City greenhorn upon embarking on his first deer hunt in 1846, "but, as I never was in the field, I cannot say whether the practice is as agreeable as the theory."[45]

One could seek sanctuary in ways other than hunting. In the early national years, Boston's commercial elite—lawyers, statesmen, merchants, physicians—purchased country estates where they sought to regain the moral health of agrarian life. Recalling the prescriptions of Virgil and Horace, as well as Whig essayists Joseph Addison, Richard Steele, and Alexander Pope, urban, commercial men transformed themselves into gentlemen planters. In doing so, they sought to cultivate in themselves "moderation, virtuous habits, and piety" instead of luxury, dissipation, and venality.[46]

In making this transition, members of the Boston elite took pains to establish themselves as mentors to smaller farmers nearby, establishing the Massachusetts Society for Promoting Agriculture in 1792. Over the next several decades, the Boston elite, through this society, disseminated among supposedly lesser men the latest scientific methods of agriculture. Members of the society sought to buttress their credentials as virtuous farmers while buttressing their credentials as natural leaders of agrarian society.[47]

In casting themselves as gentlemen farmers, members of the Boston elite, in good Federalist style, made themselves anachronisms. The agrarian values they promoted were at odds with those of the newer, more socially fluid America. The idea of rural retirement harked back to republican logic, with its emphasis on the disinterested squire who existed outside the marketplace, living a life of calm contemplation. As the American economy evolved in the nineteenth century, however, few men of commerce found themselves able to return to agrarian bliss, nor did they wish to do so. They wished to celebrate the individualistic drive that made them—and the nation, as they saw it—successful.

Insofar as hunting served as an alternative form of rural retirement, it allowed men of commerce and cities to return to nature and natural virtue yet sanctified self-reliance and hardy enterprise. In a sense, hunting recapitulated classical liberalism, with its exaltation of the self-made man and the power of will. Whereas the old republican codes valued restraint, calm deliberation, and duty to community and commonwealth, Jacksonian hunters expressed what E. Anthony Rotundo terms the "passion" and "aggression" so integral to the bold articulation of self.[48]

Passion and aggression had to be modulated by self-restraint; middle-class men were expected to bridle their passion to spend, to gamble, or to give way to sexual desire outside the marriage bed. They were also expected to bridle their aggression by treating one another with tact, respect, and good etiquette. Yet in the interstices of self-restraint emerged the powerful need to glorify the self by demonstrating one's superiority over life's other contestants. This desire for superiority led middle-class men to exhibit passion and aggression both in the killing of game and the game of free enterprise.

It may seem odd that a sport that exemplified American individualism could also exemplify English aristocracy. English aristocrats bragged of how many pheasants they had killed on a given day just as eagerly as did Americans, yet that did not make these aristocrats into middle-class men on the make. Aristocrats tended to remain loyal to an agrarian, hierarchical vision of society and to resist the growing power of traders and manufacturers (whose American counterparts began to call themselves "middle class" during the Age of Jackson) even in the nineteenth century.

How then could sport hunting in England suggest a worldview of aristocrats yet in America suggest a worldview of the middle class? The answer to that question lies in the eagerness with which middle-class Americans adopted the cultural forms of the aristocracy and gentry. As Americans grew affluent and able to afford luxury goods and leisure, they remade themselves, as John Kasson and Richard Bushman argue, in the image of their social betters. Middle-class Americans built lavish estates, bought elegant china and silverware, drank fine wines, rode in expensive carriages, learned good manners, and in all things strove to make themselves genteel. Whereas only members of the royal courts of Europe had been able to afford such luxuries in past centuries, the market revolution made these luxuries available to great numbers of Americans.[49]

For American men, to hunt for sport was another way to claim the status of gentlemen. Not only was sport hunting intrinsically genteel, but it also was a ritualistic means of demonstrating self-assertion and social authority, rights once available to members of the aristocracy and gentry alone. Thus sport hunting could express middle-class and aristocratic values simultaneously. When Americans became sport hunters, however, they did not renounce other middle-class sensibilities—thrift, diligence, frugality, and temperance—that aristocrats tended to neglect. American sport hunters reconciled their social status with their Calvinistic heritage by developing a rigid code of sportsmanship. This new code of sportsmanship, with its attention to self-restraint and humanitarianism rather than arcane terminology and mystical rites, differed profoundly from that of the English gentry and aristocracy of earlier centuries.

An American code of sportsmanship would mature after the Civil War. Old prejudices against hunters and hunting, however, had begun to fall by the wayside in the antebellum years. Some Americans might still complain like their

The fashionable jacket and cravat worn by this gentleman hunter set him apart from his plebeian guide. Note the gentleman hunter's fringed knife sheath and half-stock Kentucky rifle, which identify him as kin to border heroes like Boone. Arthur Fitzwilliam Tait, *Going Out: Deer Hunting in the Adirondacks,* 1862 (oil on canvas). Courtesy of the Adirondack Museum, Blue Mountain Lake, New York.

Puritan ancestors that sport hunting was for the vain and indolent, but others argued the point.

Far from signifying indolence, depravity, or savagery, sport hunting—as seen by hunters—was a way to recapture the health, piety, and moral vigor that once belonged to farmers. Hence, sporting journals referred to hunting and fishing as rural sports, setting them apart from less virtuous urban sports, and subtly associating them with both American farmers and English gentry. "It is truly gratifying," wrote a correspondent in the first issue of the *American Turf Register,* "to see that a fondness for field exercises and rural sports . . . is taking place of groaning, and sighing, and lamenting the immorality of the age and the hardness of the time."[50]

Even the Indian, who had epitomized the old fears of hunting as a school of barbarism, seemed to benefit from new attitudes about sport hunting. Judging from an article in the *Cabinet of Natural History and American Rural Sport,* a good hunter among the Indians might almost take rank with the middle-class sportsman by showing himself to be "more wise and less depraved" than those around him, forgetting "quarrelling, gaming . . . and even his ferocity" while engaged in a hunt.[51]

II

Manliness and Its Constraints

On the day before Christmas, 1853, a young man of New York City picked up his gun and gear and boarded the Erie Railroad, westbound for the forests of Addison, New York. A few decades earlier, the Addison area had been hunting grounds of the Iroquois and, after that, of Benjamin Patterson, the Daniel Boone of Steuben County. The young man from New York, however, had never hunted a deer in his life.[1]

Elbowing his way through crowds of pedestrians as he stepped through the ice and muck of city streets, he made his way to the railroad station. There he stepped smartly in front of "sundry corpulent and gouty gentlemen" to snatch a comfortable high-backed chair, one of the last seats on the train.

Puffing its way through a fierce winter storm, the train wound westward through New York. A day and a night later, the hunter exited in Addison and headed toward the Eagle, an inn that served as a rendezvous for old friends and fellow hunters. Among them were

> Ned F., . . . a true sportsman and as free-hearted, jolly good fellow, as ever swung a rifle, or drew a bead upon a buck—mine host, B., one of the b'hoys, yet a fine, whole-souled companion; and, my friend of kin, facetious Jack H., frequently styled "Old Hall," from his common propensity to "argue" matters, and draw his logical conclusions in a manner perfectly satisfactory, particularly to himself.

After breakfast, this foursome, together with several gentlemen unknown to the young hunter, boarded a sleigh. Three or four miles later, they emerged and waded through snow to the hunting grounds. The author and his friend Jack, being neophytes, took "good care to keep well in the rear." With Ned leading the way like a "greyhound," they "found it difficult to keep anywhere else!"

While dogs roamed the woods to scare up deer, the men hid beside runways, "not a sound arising to disturb the quiet that 'reigned supreme.'" Several times, reported the young hunter, "I fancied I heard the deer approaching." With "true hunter spirit my rifle was cocked and as quickly brought to my shoulder, and my mouth twisted in the manner Ned had taught me to sing out to stop the game, but alas! 'twas my imagination." His patience worn thin, the young man "was half resolved to shoot a poor little mouse." Hoping for bigger quarry, he refrained.

Deprived of glory, the men capitulated to hunger. Coming upon a settler's cabin amid the snowy woods, smoke from its fireplace curling into the sky, the foursome decided to "petition for 'fodder.'" Inside they found themselves welcomed to venison pies and plates of cakes "such as country dames only know how to make." Then they tramped back to the Eagle to meet the derision of "Col. P.," a haughty local "familiarly surnamed 'Old Pres.'"

"'A pretty set of hunters,'" laughed Old Pres, "'a pretty set of hunters, I declare! Hunt all day, and return deerless.'" Deerless or not, the hunters had found humor, camaraderie, and good cheer.

Like thousands of brother sportsmen, these men were not members of a hunting club. Arriving in small numbers in the backwoods, the men were less threatening to locals than Unadilla members had been and less intent on proving themselves to be members of an elite. Their narratives contain reservoirs of the bonhommie so often lacking in antebellum America. To go a-hunting was to escape the cares and toils of the workaday world and enter a realm of play. Hunting was fun.

At the same time, hunting was serious. In the backwoods, sport hunters sought to regain not only self-respect but also the respect of "sturdy, honest patriots, [rural] men who less belie their character of republicans than any other class."[2] To return deerless was, as the young New York hunter found, to defeat this purpose, inviting ridicule rather than respect.

After resting on the Sabbath, the Addison hunters embarked again on Monday, intent on success. This time another neophyte, "young Ned F." (son of the elder Ned), joined them, bringing to three the number of hunters who had never before "'shot a buck nor skinned a doe.'"[3]

For five days the hunters plied their skill without success. The situation had become desperate—the young man from New York was scheduled to return soon—and the party decided to change its tactics by hunting to the west of town.

With a bright sun rising in a clear sky, Saturday "bid fair to be an excellent day to put up the deer." Stationed at their stands, the hunters heard the song of the dogs rounding up the deer. As the author moved quietly uphill for a better position, he saw a doe emerge from a cluster of bushes.

"Now then for my first deer!" he thought to himself. The excitement, however, proved too great.

> Never did mortal *shake* so furiously. My teeth chattered, and the tops of my high India-rubber boots rattled against my legs like a dislocated guide-board in a strong nor'wester. I had previously boasted of my coolness and my utter contempt for anything like excitement, if I should see a deer, but alas! for human frailty, I had forgotten that the dictionary had ever contained such a word. I forgot that I had a rifle, and even if I hadn't, in my excited state, as well might I have aimed at the Flying Dutchman as at the deer, with any prospect of hitting my mark. . . . I was really suffering under a severe attack of the *buck fever.*

Rousing himself at last to fire, the hunter pulled the trigger of his twin-barreled gun (the upper barrel, containing a single ball, was rifled, while the lower, containing ten buckshot, was smoothbore). The gun misfired. Again he pulled the trigger—bang! Springing "forward to seize my deer, and throwing down my rifle, [I] jerked out my jack-knife to cut its throat, but lo! not a trace of the animal was to be found." Raising his gaze, he saw the doe "flying down the ravine, her flag waving as though in defiance of my skill as a marksman."

"It is not necessary to assure the reader but once," wrote the young hunter, "that I had then sold my reputation as a *deer slayer* for not a very exorbitant price." But luck was with him. He soon locked eyes on a second doe. This time he held the gun steady, but again it misfired. The deer, stopping to reconnoiter, remained motionless long enough for the hunter to adjust his trigger, and bang! "Away went deer No. 2 as usual, waving her white flag." This time the hunter "noticed several times ere she disappeared, that she had some difficulty in travelling."

The afternoon was late, and the three neophytes—still without a kill—decided to return to the inn. Before surrendering, they resolved to search for the wounded doe. "'Cuss 'em,'" said Jack, referring to the experienced hunters in the party, "'those old fogies think that because we're green 'uns, they'll leave us behind, but we'll show 'em we're game, right out and out. What say you boys? Let's follow the track.'"

Like bloodhounds, the neophytes—the author, Jack, and young Ned—followed the scarlet trail of their prey toward a river. Crossing a tree trunk that lay along the path, Jack slipped and found himself upside down in snow, "his heels . . . playing all sorts of antics in the air." Jack was jester of the moment, but his resolve held fast.

At last the men came upon the deer, fallen from loss of blood. Dispatching her quickly, they dressed the carcass and loaded it on a sleigh that was en route to town and fortuitously approached at the proper moment. At eight in the evening, the three were back at the Eagle to find themselves heroes of the day. "Three times three were given for the 'three blood-hounds,' as we were surnamed when we entered. Old Ned declared that we were 'trumps, and there's no putter about that,' in his usual comical style. 'Old Pres,' too, stood by to give us a grip."

In many ways, one could not find a more representative hunting tale than this. The story of the first deer hunt was a regular staple of antebellum sporting journals. Authors of such tales invariably began in high spirits and concluded with success. Back at camp (where guides built lean-tos for gentlemen who dared to rough it), or back at the inn, successful hunters claimed the respect of local Natty Bumppos and gentlemen sportsmen alike. Meanwhile, the hunters regained the camaraderie that so often eluded men in cities, who were wont to pass on the street without so much as a greeting.

Camp scenes like this one from the Gilded Age were common even before the Civil War. Courtesy of the Adirondack Museum, Blue Mountain Lake, New York.

Hunting was sport. Men loved to hunt because they loved adventure, exercise, and friendship. But was there more to it? To define hunting as sport is to state the obvious. More important, such a definition places hunting outside the scope of important affairs like politics, economics, and law. For most of us, sport denotes leisure, a realm of life that—until recent decades—fell outside the historian's purview. Leisure was banal, simple, and timeless. How different was the hunting of nineteenth-century Americans from that of ancient Greeks or eighteenth-century Englishmen? Doesn't sport hunting always and everywhere entail the pleasure of pursuit, the celebration of the kill, and the fellowship of brother hunters?

The answers to these questions are yes and no. Nineteenth-century Americans often hunted for the reasons that men of other centuries and other nations have hunted. Yet American sport hunting had its own raison d'être. It was not banal, simple, or timeless, nor was it solely a ritual of fraternity and bonhommie. Hunting became both a venue for pleasure and—as the greenhorns of Addison, New York, proved—a testing ground of manly skill, fortitude, courage, and Americanness.

To become the favored sport of middle-class Americans, however, hunting had to test something more than these qualities. Hunting had to test the fortress of character that protected middle-class men from sloth and sin. Hence, to ennoble their sport, hunters were required to adopt a code of ethics known as sportsmanship. They also had to ensure that hunting remained a suitable venue for manly jousts of pride. If sport hunting was to be a theater for middle-class displays of character and fraternity, it would also be a theater for individualistic competition.

The principal axis around which competition revolved was the gun. As early as 1830, sport hunters quarreled in the pages of the *Cabinet of Natural History and American Rural Sport* over how far to lead a bird in flight when firing a smoothbore weapon. After an acrimonious exchange of letters, complete with scientific drawings and exegeses, it became clear that neither party would emerge the victor. If the parties could not agree on methods, however, at least they could agree that Americans were bringing "the science of shooting to its greatest perfection."[4]

Perfection is a relative term; advances in weaponry would continue throughout the century, as percussion caps replaced flintlocks, cartridges replaced percussion caps, and bullets replaced balls. In the twentieth century, many hunters have become fascinated by archaic weapons, but nineteenth-century hunters took pride in employing the latest and best technologies. To be a sport hunter was to be a perfectionist, and to attain perfection demanded the best ordnance. More important, to attain perfection demanded contests that measured success.

Consider an 1848 letter to the *Spirit of the Times* by the Boon Club of Harrodsburg, Kentucky. "As you have brought rifle-shooting to greater perfection in New York [City]," wrote the Kentuckians, "than it has attained to in any other part of the Union, or perhaps in the world, we ask for the result of your experience upon a few points."

> What length of barrel, what calibre, and what weight of gun do you prefer? Do you use the half-globe, full-globe, or open-notched sight? Do you hold that propping or resting the elbow upon the hip, which we call a half-rest—a clean and fair off-hand, or shoulder-shooting? And above all, for we are itching to hear, what do you call a good offhand shot?[5]

After this technical talk, the Kentuckians arrived at the real point, which was to challenge New York City marksmen to a shooting contest. Taught that "our rifles and our liberties are synonymous" by the sporting press, marksmen had identified firearms as symbols of Americanness.[6]

Colonists had fired guns centuries earlier to impress American Indians and had carried guns in public to guard against attack. Still later, eighteenth-century backwoodsmen made shooting matches popular, and Revolutionaries conceived of rifles as symbols of liberty. Yet the fascination with the gun was largely a nineteenth-century phenomenon.

Throughout the colonial and early national eras, a minority of Americans owned firearms (perhaps less than 25 percent of adult white males). Because they were handmade by artisans, guns were expensive and at times scarce, even on the frontier. So few Americans owned guns that when members of militia companies drilled in the early nineteenth century, they sometimes practiced with rusty or broken muskets or even walking canes.[7]

As the fires of industry burned hotter in the antebellum decades, per capita gun ownership began to rise sharply, then boomed after the Civil War.[8] Two factors catalyzed this jump in gun sales: the number of guns coming from factories geared up for wartime production and the number of men trained to use guns during the Civil War (and, to a lesser degree, the Mexican War before it). With ad campaigns and salesmanship lubricating the engine of consumerism, guns of every description became household items. Programmed by manufacturers to think of guns and hunting as sources of national greatness, Americans forgot that there had been a time when owning a gun was not universal.

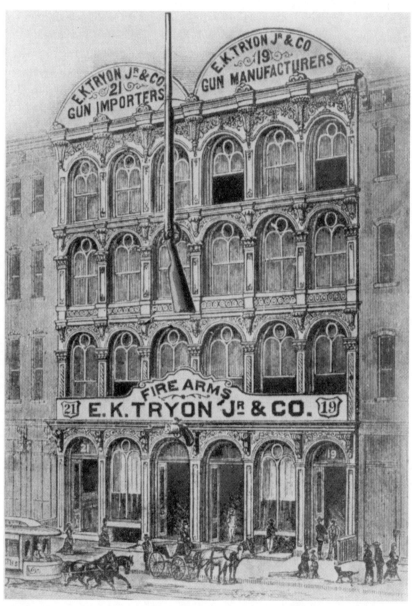

The gun stood tall in advertising and American consciousness alike. Facade of Edward K. Tryon's store, Philadelphia, 1868–86, from Charles Zimmerling, *History of a Business Established 100 Years Ago* (Philadelphia, 1911). An antebellum store at another locale had a similar prop. Courtesy of the Hagley Museum and Library, Wilmington, Delaware.

That is the economic explanation for how America became a gun culture. Yet behind the popularity of guns was more than mass production and advertising.

Guns appealed to American men because they were scepters of self-reliance. A man with a gun was a man who, in theory, could sustain himself with wild game and who need brook no tyranny from any would-be despot. Fittingly, the allegorical center of the drama of Daniel Boone was the rifle, symbol of a society based on assertive individualism and social mobility rather than static hierarchy and rank. Boone's "peculiar habits of character," waxed Timothy Flint, "were fortified by his long cherished habit of wandering for days together with no other companionship than his rifle and his own thoughts."[9]

Young men embroiled in the market revolution also wandered into the woods with no other companionship than their rifles and their own thoughts. To possess a gun for the first time and to use it in hunting were to separate oneself from family and community. As ritual, entering the wilderness with gun in hand prefigured the independence of young men in the atomistic world of market capitalism. As fantasy, entering the wilderness with gun in hand allowed men to imagine that they truly were self-reliant, aloof from social ties and obligations.

As one sport hunter wrote in 1851,

> The youth never tastes the enjoyment of absolute independence, just as he does when standing on the mountain's brow, conscious of strength and exhilarated by strenuous exercise, grasping in his hand a rifle that he can trust, and knows how to use. Let some worthy game lie dead at his feet, and his proud feeling of self-reliance is complete.[10]

Finally, Americans cherished guns because, like the machinery of the industrial revolution, guns were "manifestations of the sublime," to borrow the words of John Kasson. Sporting rifles—even those that were mass produced—became folk art, often decorated with engraved hunting motifs, American eagles, intricate scrolling, and gold and silver inlay. To own "that most beautiful of weapons, the rifle," was to own a powerful icon of independence, manliness, nationalism, and technology. For hunting purposes, contended one sportsman in the pages of the *Spirit of the Times*, the American rifle "has no competitor."[11] As artifacts of technology, indeed, guns stood in a category of their own.

Learned Americans, noted Leo Marx in 1964, had welcomed the technological innovations of the nineteenth century. Writers and artists thought that trains, steamboats, and even textile mills would complement nature; technology would bring an American millennium. As the century wore on, it became clear that technology was a mixed blessing. Far from complementing the garden, machines threatened to destroy the garden.[12] Machines threatened to destroy individualism itself by reducing humans to operatives, caretakers for the mechanical behemoths they had created. But in the gun was a different dialectic.

In the minds of Americans there was no contradiction between gun and garden or between gun and wilderness. To enter the wilds with one's gun was to become a perfect atom (or Adam), a free man, fearless, bold, and in harmony with nature. Gun and wilderness were bound together like ship and sea, or like airplane and sky.

Because they brought men into contact with wilderness virtue, guns and hunting became perfect vehicles for nationalism. The game animals described in sporting journals became simultaneously a sort of national noble foe, and to hunt these animals was to define an indigenous manliness suited to Northerner, Southerner, and Westerner alike.

By encouraging men to vie with one another in martial courage and prowess with firearms, however, hunting—far from cementing feelings of nationalism—contributed in the short term to sectional discord. When conflict came to a head in 1861, one southern correspondent, expressing what appears to have been a common sentiment, declared in the final issue of the *Spirit of the Times* that the South's hunting tradition would make it invulnerable to invasion. The *Spirit of the Times* attempted to avoid the issues of the Civil War—it even criticized northern agitators—but the loss of southern subscribers made it one of the war's first casualties.[13]

In reality the South's hunting tradition—like its vaunted traditions of chivalry and martial prowess—was not so different from that of the North. Men of both regions read Sir Walter Scott's novels, participated in the cult of Boone, and joined hunting clubs (in equally small numbers). Both regions published military periodicals, established military academies, sent men to West Point (493 northern cadets to 330 southern cadets in 1860), and contributed officers to the army (620 Northerners to 460 Southerners in 1860). Finally, in 1861 men from both regions rushed to join their respective armies. Yet in both the North and the South, the sport hunting tradition (like the military tradition) was ascendant before the Civil War rather than fully developed.[14]

Judging from the frequency of hunting as a topic in periodicals and books, one might argue that hunting was flowering in the North and the South simultaneously. One can find as much hunting, or martial, literature in antebellum southern journals as one wishes to find, but the same can be said of northern journals. Moreover, the majority of antebellum hunting authors (those who wrote books) were from the North, as were the majority of sporting editors and journals. The

South, because it was more rural, probably had a higher proportion of hunters—especially if one includes slaves and other subsistence hunters—than the North. The South also had an older tradition of hunting for sport. Yet in neither section does it appear that the majority of adult white males embraced sport hunting between the American Revolution and the Civil War.

When all is said and done, the rising popularity of sport hunting probably had little direct impact on the Civil War. Yet sport hunting put a premium on chivalry, honor, and martial prowess, each of which contributed to the drift toward war. Though the stream of hunting did not flow directly into the river of war, both issued from a common spring.

After the Civil War, sport hunting again became a force for unity. *Turf, Field, and Farm,* taking over where the *Spirit of the Times* had left off, reunified the "Old Family" of field sport enthusiasts, barred politics from its pages, and commented that "the want of a Journal devoted to the best interests of the whole country was never so severely felt as now." The Old Family was not only reunited but also greatly expanded. Between 1865 and 1900 appeared thirty-nine periodicals devoted to field sports, the most popular of which attained a circulation of nearly 100,000. Among the most successful of these journals was *Forest and Stream,* which in 1893, its twenty-first year of publication, bragged that it had "never appealed to sectional pride nor sought to batten on sectional prejudices.... Our ambition has been to make this in the widest, truest, most liberal sense ... an American journal for American readers."[15]

In the decades before the Civil War, other forces had appeared on the cultural horizon, forces that were not necessarily favorable to hunters. If middle-class hunters, northern and southern, took guns in hand to define themselves as hardy individualists, all around their beachhead of insurgent manliness rose a tide of domesticity. The idea of a society of unregulated individualism—a society of gun-toting hunters giving free rein to their passions—was not altogether welcomed in nineteenth-century America, just as it had not been welcomed in colonial and Revolutionary America.

Eager to promote, rather than to reject, community and commonwealth, thousands of Jacksonian and antebellum Americans engaged in a campaign to domesticate their society. They did so in the religious sphere by emphasizing the compassionate, redeeming Christ rather than the vengeful, arbitrary Jehovah of Calvinism. They did so in the private sphere by cultivating manners, morals, and Christian selflessness. They did so in the social sphere by creating utopian communities that rejected the idea of personal property and selfish competition.

They did so in the educational sphere by pressing for universal schooling to moderate the passions of American children and to develop their virtues. They did so in the public sphere by attending the recitals of Jenny Lind, whose music was said to tame men's savage propensities (the *Spirit of the Times* reported weekly on the "Jenny Lind mania" at mid-century). And they did so in the political sphere by campaigning for peace, against slavery, and on behalf of children, workers, women, and animals (even game animals).[16]

This hash of reform arose for different reasons and from somewhat different constituencies, most centered in the North. Taken as a whole, reform represented an attempt to tame or to domesticate society, to rein in the forces of passion and self-interest. Reform's analog in art and in ideas about nature was the *Peaceable Kingdom*, the title of several dozen works that Quaker artist Edward Hicks painted between 1820 and 1849. In accord with Isaiah 11:6 ("and the wolf shall dwell with the lamb, and the leopard shall lie down with the kid, and the calf and the young lion and the fatling together; and a little child shall lead them"), the *Peaceable Kingdom* depicted human and beast in harmony. The message was millennial, domestic, and implicitly antihunting. The nation, its people, even its fauna, suggested Hicks, would be made docile by Christ.

Astride this cultural fault line stood a now reverend figure in American culture, Henry David Thoreau. In retreating to Walden Pond, Thoreau became, like the sport hunter (or like Daniel Boone), a perfect atom, a saintly figure who sought out nature to cleanse himself of worldly sin. There he fished and farmed enough to support himself, supplementing his spartan regime with the occasional meal cooked by his mother or Mrs. Emerson. But what of hunting? Was not hunting, as well as fishing and farming, an ideal way to sustain oneself in the woods? Thoreau wrestled with this question throughout his adult life.

In "Higher Laws," a chapter from *Walden; or, Life in the Woods,* Thoreau professed that he was tempted at times to seize a woodchuck and eat the animal alive for the "wildness he represented." "No morsel," declared Thoreau, "could have been too savage for me." Thoreau did not reject the belief that eating game made one savage; he made savagery a condition to be valued. To friends who asked whether they should allow their sons to take up hunting, Thoreau responded yes. When he was a youth, recalled Thoreau, almost every boy had "shouldered a fowling-piece between the ages of ten and fourteen." Hunting had been one of the best parts of his education and had given him his "closest acquaintance with Nature."[17]

Despite this sanction for hunting, Thoreau made clear in the rest of "Higher Laws" that he believed a diet of flesh to be unclean. Hunting was a stage in mankind's development, he insisted; the hunter must graduate to the rank of poet or naturalist; he must even become a vegetarian. "I have no doubt," wrote Thoreau, "that it is ... the destiny of the human race, in its gradual improvement, to leave off eating animals, as surely as the savage tribes have left off eating each other when they came in contact with the more civilized."[18]

Manifest in Thoreau were traces of four-stages theory, with its emphasis on hunting as a social stage, intermingled with the Puritan disdain for hunting. Also apparent was the peculiar dilemma of nineteenth-century America. Although thousands of Americans saw nobility in hunters, a significant few objected to the hunter's brutishness.

Stung by such charges, William Elliott, in his *Carolina Sports by Land and Water* of 1846, felt compelled to defend hunting as "innocent and manly," whatever the objections of "our ascetic innovators, who would make ... all amusements ... as a waste of time unworthy of immortal beings!" According to Elliott, the man who habitually applied himself to hunting would "become more *considerate*, as well as more prompt, more full of resource, more resolute," and a better soldier. In support of his assertions, Elliott noted that not a single "serious" hunter known to him had been "touched by the vice of gaming," revealing the degree to which hunting had become identified with middle-class values rather than with the traditional values of the southern gentry.[19]

Who Elliott's ascetic innovators were is hard to know. We do know that a small but vocal number of Americans (Sylvester Graham among them) suggested that to refrain from eating flesh was to create a higher society and a healthier, more refined, more spiritual individual. Behind these radicals stood those of more moderate temperament who adhered to Enlightenment concepts of reason and rationality and the Protestant disdain for passion and play. These were the domesticators with whom Thoreau at last sided in "Higher Laws," despite finding chivalry in hunters and despite romanticizing them as men who comprehended nature.[20]

Like a dogcatcher after a runaway hound, those who sought to domesticate American society would chase its wild hunters down the long trail of history. In the twentieth century the domesticators have closed in, but in the nineteenth century they lagged far behind. Hunters formed the cultural vanguard of the nineteenth century; their social vision of struggle, strife, and individual effort captured the nation's imagination. Sport hunters, however, were not immune to the domesticators' campaign. From the flood of antebellum hunting literature came a new reformer—and reformee—in American culture, the true sportsman.

Far from being savage, idle, or cruel, the true sportsman was scientific, industrious, and humane. More important, the true hunter controlled his passions. A man with a gun he might be, but he understood the proper balance between self-assertion and good etiquette.

In keeping with the republican self-restraint of his forebears, the true sportsman was "satisfied with a moderate quantity of game," insisted Thomas Doughty in the first issue of the *Cabinet of Natural History and American Rural Sport*, "and is not ambitious to destroy life, for the sake of making a parade of his success." The true sportsman, moreover, would forebear to curse at his dogs or treat them cruelly.[21]

To treat dogs well, rather than prey, testified to the hunter's humanitarian sympathies. Yet game animals, too, seemed to benefit. The true sportsman, wrote Philadelphia physician and hunting author Elisha Jarrett Lewis in 1851, never took satisfaction in wounding game; kills were to be made cleanly and quickly to prevent suffering. Sport hunters, moreover—though at ease with killing individual animals—integrated into their cause the Enlightenment objection to cruelty by campaigning for game laws that protected animals as species. The antebellum campaign for game conservation prompted Henry David Thoreau to acknowledge in *Walden* that the hunter had become "the best friend of the animal he hunts."[22]

Another 1830s commentary, "Sportsmen," defined the ideal hunter more explicitly by contrasting him with two other types: the "vagabond sportsman," who represented a "numerous class of men . . . in the purlieus of large towns and cities," and who was a braggart, a drunk, a brawler, and a poacher; and the "dandy sportsman," a "gentleman *par excellence*," who owned the finest silver-trimmed gun, the fanciest shooting jacket, and the best imported dogs, which, like his clothes, were "of the most fashionable colour." The dandy, however, knew little of the habits of his quarry and filled his bag with birds purchased from farm boys.[23]

Ranked against these extremes was the true sportsman, who was "temperate, cool, calculating and observing" and punctual in rousing himself for the hunt, and who displayed an "ardent love of healthful exercise." The true sportsman also displayed a thorough knowledge of his sport by providing a ready explanation for why he hunted in one locale and not another and demonstrated his affinity for natural history by studying and admiring the plumage of the birds he had killed. Even the true sportsman's dogs were well trained and would not deign to raid the kitchens of unsuspecting neighbors.[24]

One may assume that the true sportsman was a middle-class man because, despite the author's assurance that the true sportsman was drawn from all ranks, he was expected to buy a hunting wagon big enough to hold his dogs.[25] Equally clear was that the true sportsman was not an American version of the English aristocrat. His tastes were simple, his values republican. Yet neither was he a common man. He might claim kinship with the Boone-like backwoodsman, but the true sportsman was a middle-class man with a code of conduct as strict in the hunt as in professional life.

The foil of the true sportsman was the "pot hunter," who, according to Elisha Jarrett Lewis, was "disgusting," "unmanly," and "heartless." The pot hunter, claimed Lewis, would

> lay waste all animated nature . . . without regard to etiquette, humanity, law, or even the common decencies of life. . . . His boasted motto, *Fill the bag, and damn the means,* should be chalked upon his craven back in well-defined characters, as a warning to all young Sportsmen to shun his company, and detest his vices.[26]

The pot hunter became the repository of all the traits—cruelty, depravity, savagery—that had defined hunters in the colonial imagination. The pot hunter epitomized everything a middle-class American was not supposed to be. Yet the pot hunter was the most common hunter of all, the man who hunted for larder or market.

As pot hunters became pariahs, hunting methods employed by backwoodsmen for centuries suddenly seemed contemptible to sport hunters, despite their hero worship of border men like Daniel Boone. "Crusting," or hunting on the frosting-like layer of ice that forms on snow that has partially melted, then refrozen (the crust supports men but not large quadrupeds, which sink into the snow), came in for especially heavy rebuke. Charles Fenno Hoffman, the one-legged editor of the *Knickerbocker* magazine who resigned to roam the frontier in the 1830s, found that whole villages turned out to shoot deer disabled by the crust. This sort of hunting, inveighed Hoffman, "all true sportsmen hold in contempt." Samuel H. Hammond, an Albany, New York, journalist and author of one of the first books on sport hunting in the Adirondacks, reported that his guide once beat a "half-breed" for taking deer "on the crust." This manner of taking game, wrote Hammond, "every true hunter holds in profound abhorrence."[27]

Another ignoble technique was the imitation of a fawn's bleat to attract the doe. Edmund Flagg, who toured the West in 1836, called this a "diabolical *modus operandi*," while the German sport hunter and frontier traveler Friedrich Gerstaecker asserted that it was "base and cruel to lure the mother to her destruction by imitating the cry of her young." The only thing as abhorrent as bleating like a fawn was killing the doe while it was pregnant, which, according to an Englishman who had hunted in Texas, would be "as much disliked by American hunters as . . . by English game-preservers."[28]

Another practice that came into disrepute was "jacklighting," also known as "jacking," or "torch-hunting." Typically the hunter would ignite a hot fire in a broad iron pan fixed to the end of a wooden pole. One man would sling the pole over his shoulder, with the glaring pan (called a "jack") on the end, while his fellow hunters would shoulder their guns. Entering the woods at night, the hunters watched for the reflection of the fire in the eyes of dazzled game. Much the same procedure (often called "floating") was used by hunters in canoes and rowboats, who fixed lanterns on prows to blind deer that came to water's edge to feed or to drink at night.[29]

South Carolina hunting author William Elliott, who pursued his prey from the back of a horse, characterized torch-hunting as a practice of surly overseers jealous of the prerogatives of plantation owners. Elliott spoke of a class of hunters who employed the torch-hunt to supply restaurants and hotels with venison, wiping out deer populations in the process. Plantation owners made superior hunters, thought Elliott, because they were men of caution and moderation who appreciated the intrinsic merits of the chase.[30]

If Elliott wished secretly for the exclusive hunting rights of the English elite, he was not alone in his disdain for ignoble methods. In 1858 *Harper's New Monthly Magazine* reported that conscientious sportsmen seldom practiced the torch-hunt, and the consummate arbiter of sportsmanship, Henry William Herbert, called torch-hunting "a dirty advantage of the stupidity of animals."[31]

Even as sport hunters identified Boone-like backwoodsmen as fellow American Natives, they eschewed the vulgarity, cruelty, and depravity associated with backwoods hunters. By creating an etiquette of hunting and a code of sportsmanship, sport hunters distinguished themselves from those who hunted for subsistence or market. Yet the distinction between the true sportsman's honorable, humane killing and the pot hunter's dishonorable, cruel killing required a degree of hypocrisy.

Sportsmen, wrote Charles Dudley Warner in 1878, always conducted their deer hunts in "the most manly fashion," adding that "there are several methods, and in none of them is a fair chance to the deer considered." Gentlemen hunters in the Adirondacks often resorted to the torch-hunt until it was outlawed in the late nineteenth century, while at other times guides and dogs chased deer into lakes where hunters fired at them from boats. Guides would even grab hold of the deer's tail to give the sportsman a certain shot. Many hunters described this as murder yet admitted that they had resorted to it on occasion.[32]

Conflict also raged between those who favored the still hunt, in which hunters stalked deer on foot, and those who favored driving, in which dogs, mounted men, or men on foot would pursue deer toward hunters who hid beside game trails. Charles Fenno Hoffman noted in 1839 that Adirondack hunters would argue for one or the other of these methods so vehemently that they "only want their poet, or historian, to make their interminable bickerings . . . as celebrated as those of the Guelphs and Ghibbelines." Still-hunters in the Adirondacks and in Pennsylvania were known even to kill drivers' dogs because they were thought to scare away game.[33]

In antebellum America, however, driving had the aura of nobility. John Cheney, the celebrated Adirondack guide, considered driving with horse and dogs the only "manly" way to take deer. Fire-hunting and still hunting, he insisted, were "beastly," while others called them "skulking" and "murderous."[34]

Henry William Herbert similarly lauded southern horsemen who, following their keen hounds, pursued deer in the English fashion. Herbert, grandson of an English earl, contrasted such sport with deer hunting in the North, which he found "idle and contemptible" because it seldom involved skilled horsemanship or the use of trained dogs. At the same time, Herbert (who tended to contradict himself) pronounced still hunting "by far the most legitimate and exciting" means of taking deer, demanding, as it did, "both skill in woodcraft, and endurance."[35]

The argument between drivers and still-hunters reflected a larger split in American sport hunting between those who favored the aristocratic traditions of England and those who favored the egalitarian tradition of their own country. Driving was an exercise in elitism, whereas the still hunt had been perfected by Indians and frontiersmen (Audubon referred to practitioners of the still hunt as "true hunters"). The still hunt, however, required so much patience and skill—a Gilded Age author called it a "sportsman's game of chess"—that it could seldom guarantee a good hunt in the short time that the sportsman could leave his professional duties. Even an "apt and observant scholar" of still hunting, noted Henry William Herbert, "shall require many seasons of apprenticeship to a wise woodman, ere he may hope for the least success in attempting it unaided."[36]

In the late nineteenth century, the controversy subsided when New York and other northern states abolished "hounding" (driving with dogs) and jacklighting. These prohibitions were intended not so much to restrict sportsmen as to restrict market hunters, who had begun to use such methods to deadly effect. Hounding and jacklighting continued in the South and, covertly, in the North but had become rare in much of the country by the twentieth century. To underscore the gravity of the matter, the Boone and Crockett Club, the preeminent sportsmen's association of the late nineteenth and early twentieth centuries, refused membership to any hunter who employed dogs to take deer.[37]

What emerged from the bickering over unfair methods was a gentlemanly sport that could not be labeled mere aggression (which translated into cruelty) but instead became an exercise in punctuality, self-restraint, scientific knowledge, and artistry. "I imagine," wrote Minnesota politician and sportsman Henry Hastings Sibley in 1856, that the animals taken by gentlemen hunters "pass out of existence with a feeling of consolation that they have been dealt with scientifically and artistically, and not been subjected to the tender mercies of the mere pot-hunter."[38]

It is hard to believe that a deer or grouse preferred to be killed by a true sportsman rather than a pot hunter. Yet the etiquette of sportsmanship held profound significance for middle-class hunters. By killing mercifully, as well as scientifically and artistically, hunters balanced the passion and aggression of their sport with the republican virtue of self-restraint. In preaching the ethic of sportsmanship, hunters aligned themselves with reformers, men who would curb the baser traits within themselves and their society.

In conforming to a code of sportsmanship, moreover, sportsmen echoed the rituals of respect and apology performed by Indian hunters over their slain prey, affirming the sacred bond between themselves and their game. Those who did not observe such rituals, in the view of sportsmen, did not deserve to hunt. True sportsmen sometimes bagged more game than propriety allowed or missed their shot, causing a deer or bird to suffer needlessly, but these acts were the sins of believers, who were forgiven.

This code of sportsmanship and the celebration of technology made sport hunting different from such forms of blood sport as ratting, cockfighting, and prizefighting. On its surface, hunting had a great deal in common with these seemingly vicious sports, especially prizefighting. There was something primal about hunting and boxing; both suggested a struggle for territory and status. In boxing, contestants fought gloveless, round after bloody round, often until the loser could no longer stand. In hunting, men challenged not fellow men but animals to a supposedly fair fight that usually ended in the animal's death. If boxing was a way of proving dominion over other humans, hunting was a way of proving dominion over the natural world. Why, then, did so many middle-class sporting journals—including *Spirit of the Times* and *Forest and Stream*—castigate boxing yet praise hunting?[39]

The short answer is class. Prizefighting celebrated, in the words of Elliot Gorn, "personal toughness, local honor, drunken conviviality, violent display—every bout upheld these powerfully antibourgeois values." Boxing appealed most to the underclass in American cities, especially the Irish, who flocked to see their men do battle with English and American fighters. The prizefight—or even the street match—upheld a working-class code of honor rather than a middle-class code of gentility.[40]

Sport hunting, like boxing, served as an escape from the effeminacy of civilization, but hunting was a courtly escape, not an attack on bourgeois propriety. Hunters, unlike pugilists, escaped the class and ethnic divisions of urban America. In the wilderness, gentlemen and frontiersmen seemed to stand as equals, their status determined by skill alone and not by birth or occupation. The real world of the cities might be marred by social conflict (a conflict epitomized in the prizefight), but the ideal world of the wilderness seemed true to the republican vision, or at least the Jacksonian version of it. To sport hunters, wilderness was a bastion of spartan virtues and rough equality.

The violence of hunting was further mediated by the gun, which promised to make killing clean, humane, and scientific. The bare fist with which pugilists struck one another, by contrast, seemed primitive and crude. Hunting was a violent sport, but its violence was made sophisticated and humane by technology, civilized by sportsmanship, glorified by nationalism, and sanctified by its association with rural retirement and wilderness bliss.

To be a true sportsman was to be a respectable, even a model, American. The old conception of the hunter as idle, cruel, or savage bore no relation to the true sportsman. His triumph was not in killing but in "the vigor, science, and manhood displayed—in the difficulties to be overcome . . . and lastly in the true spirit, the style, the dash, the handsome way of doing what is to be done, and above all, in the unalterable love of fair play."[41]

Through their devotion to sportsmanship, hunters escaped the sanctions placed on their sport by the republicans of eighteenth-century America and the domesticators of nineteenth-century America. Never cruel, never licentious, always scientific and high minded, true sportsmen vied with farmers as ideal men who lived in harmony with nature. Far from being the indolent, luxury-loving, effeminate men so feared by the founding generation, antebellum and postbellum sport hunters claimed to stand at the summit of society.

Sport hunters had made the climb as self-reliant, hardy, disciplined individuals. Upon reaching the summit, they embraced one another as fellow sportsmen and brothers in class. Below, the agrarian America of the founding generation was still visible. To see it, sport hunters had to look down.

12

American Natives

As men with a highly developed code of sportsmanship, sport hunters associated themselves with chivalry, humanity, gentility, and reform. As men with a highly developed appreciation for the country's fauna, geography, and sublime scenery, hunters defined themselves as American Natives. Charles Lanman's narratives of "scenery and sport" in *Adventures in the Wilds of the United States and British American Provinces,* explained Washington Irving in 1856,

> carry us into the fastnesses of our mountains, the depths of our forests, the watery wilderness of our lakes and rivers, giving us pictures of savage life and savage tribes, Indian legends, fishing and hunting anecdotes, the adventures of trappers and backwoodsmen; our whole arcanum, in short, of indigenous poetry and romance: to use a favorite phrase of the old discoverers, "they lay open the secrets of the country to us."[1]

William Post Hawes's *Sporting Scenes and Sundry Sketches* was likewise "an American book in the strictest sense," according to one reviewer, "a work so indigenous, so native to the soil, . . . we can hardly conceive that any but an American could possibly have been its author." Charles Wilkins Webber's book *The Hunter- Naturalist* was also "peculiarly American in design and execution," wrote another reviewer, who added that Webber had "sought nature where she is only to be found, in the wilderness and the prairie."[2]

Critical to this new Americanness, according to the sporting press, was a knowledge of natural history. The *American Turf Register and Sporting Magazine,* as John Skinner reported in the first issue, would contain not only hunting and fishing anecdotes but also "original sketches of the *natural history and habits of American game.*" These sketches alone, Skinner advised, justified the cost of subscription.[3]

Similarly, the "great aim" of the *Cabinet of Natural History and American Rural Sport,* proclaimed the Doughtys in the first issue of their magazine, was "to present such a history of our different native animals, as may amuse whilst it instructs." To this end, the Doughtys derived material for articles (as well as specimens for lithographs) from Peale's American Museum and the publications of Philadelphia naturalists Alexander Wilson, Thomas Say, and Titian R. Peale. They avoided, however, a slavish attention to taxonomy, which they considered mere nomenclature. Though the Doughtys gave attention to "scientific description," they attempted to explain the "characters" of American animals—including such western exotics as the pronghorn antelope and the bighorn sheep—with a simple "elegance of expression."[4]

In bringing natural history to the fore, sporting periodicals made hunting into rational recreation. To be a hunter would henceforth mean to know the secrets of science; indeed, to be a hunter was to unlock the puzzle of nature itself, at least insofar as that could be accomplished by knowing the haunts, habits, and physical characteristics of game animals.

Standing just off this new historical stage were Thomas Jefferson and Charles Willson Peale, who decades earlier had outfitted the hunter in the costume of science. In doing so, they, along with the sporting periodicals that followed, consecrated hunters to a nationalistic mission.

Hunting of old—the sort done by the English elite—had no rational purpose apart from preparing practitioners for war. Hunting in the old style was ritualistic; it reinforced the idea of hierarchy but added little to the intellectual treasures of humanity. In its nineteenth-century American incarnation, however, hunting seemed eminently useful. It was a form of leisure, yet it lent itself to the great enterprise of the era: the inscription of the world with science. In doing so, hunting transformed hunters into American Natives.

Although in the early 1800s the population of the United States was concentrated to the east of the Appalachian Mountains, the sporting press—through natural history, ethnography, and tales of adventure—escorted readers into the romantic regions of the West. The *Cabinet of Natural History* initiated the adventure in 1830 by abstracting material from Timothy Flint's *History and Geography of the Mississippi Valley* and William Darby's *Geographical Description of the State of Louisiana.* "The hydrographical basin of the Mississippi," declared the *Cabinet,* "displays on the grandest scale, the action of running waters on the surface of a continent." The *American Turf Register* added letters from the Great Plains by George Catlin and tales of wild horse roundups and buffalo hunts alongside more staid reports of English hunts.[5]

Forest and Stream masthead, 1873. Courtesy of the University of California at Berkeley.

For its part, the *Spirit of the Times* in 1845–46 published weekly installments of "Occidental Reminiscences. Farther West; or Rough Notes of the Dragoon Campaign to the Rocky Mountains in 1845." Ten years later (after many other tales of science and adventure in the Far West), the *Spirit of the Times* gave readers "New-Mexico—Its Animals and Game." The author of this piece complained that although government surveys had reported on the mineralogy and geology of the newly acquired territory, they had not described its fauna. The *Spirit of the Times* remedied this oversight with detailed entries on a variety of mammals, supplying readers with Latin binomials for each, as well as information on the animals' haunts and habits and the methods of hunting them.[6]

Though antebellum sporting journals became moribund before or during the Civil War, postbellum journals carried on the mission they had begun. *American Sportsman,* launched in 1871, devoted itself "Exclusively to Shooting, Fishing and Natural History," suggesting that sportsmen were superior to professional naturalists who did not study animals in the wild. "Science and pleasure," concluded the *American Sportsman,* "go hand in hand in this age."[7]

The epitome of this sort of entertainment came in 1873 with the launching of the hugely successful sporting periodical *Forest and Stream.* Like its predecessors, *Forest and Stream* suggested that a "knowledge of natural history" was of paramount import to any "thorough sportsman." To educate readers, *Forest and Stream* included a column written by a naturalist who had been approved by the Smithsonian Institution. In addition, it printed frequent reports from Lt. George M. Wheeler's U.S. Geographical Surveys West of the 100th Meridian and Dr. Ferdinand V. Hayden's U.S. Geographical and Geological Survey of the Territories.[8]

Forest and Stream (like the *American Sportsman*) also offered stereoscopic studies of natural history for schools and parlor entertainment and advertised an array of natural history and hunting works sold through Forest and Stream Publishing Company. Ads might list Elliott Coues's *Key to North American Birds* and Joseph Leidy's *Extinct Mammalian Fauna of Dakota and Nebraska* alongside Meschach Browning's *Forty-four Years of a Hunter's Life*. Not surprisingly, *Forest and Stream* did not hesitate to publish accolades bestowed on it by naturalists like Spencer Baird, second secretary of the Smithsonian Institution, and ornithologist Elliott Coues.[9]

In the nation's centennial year, the journal's fourth year of publication, *Forest and Stream* was able to report that it had provided more information on the "geography and natural history of the newly settled and wilderness districts of North America" than any other single volume. This encyclopedic array of knowledge covered

> the prairies of the west, the southwest, and the far west. It includes the mountain ranges of the whole country—the Laurentian chain, the White and Green Mountains, the Adirondacks, the Alleghanies and Blue Ridge, the Unaka and Clinch range, the Sierra and the Rocky Mountains. It embraces the everglades of Florida, the interior great lakes, the Dismal Swamp of Virginia, and the prominent points along the entire coast from Labrador to Mexico. In a valuable series of papers it covers the zoology and ichthyc fauna of the entire Northwest, and the writers on these various sections and topics are among the most intelligent of our frontier officers, and of the Canadian and United States Boundary Commissions and Government surveys.[10]

Forest and Stream, like Peale's Museum, and like the *American Turf Register*, the *Cabinet of Natural History*, and the *Spirit of the Times*, transported readers to places they would in all likelihood never see, yet gave them a sense that these places were American. Middle-class men who read the sporting press could see themselves not as residents of this or that town in this or that state but as American Natives, chivalrous sportsmen with a scientific mastery and a romantic appreciation for the continent. They could identify themselves with the whole of North America, and they could identify the whole of North America with themselves. Despite its attempt to steer clear of politics to woo a national audience (indeed, because it aimed at a national audience), the sporting press became an expression of the Manifest Destiny that extended the boundaries of the United States to the Pacific Ocean in the 1840s.

The sporting journals popularized the romantic project of cataloging American nature initiated by Jefferson and Peale. They were not alone in this endeavor; the country and its fauna had been mapped and described by fur traders and mountain men, naturalists, travelers, army explorers, and later by a trio of government agencies incorporated finally into the U.S. Geological Survey. But, with the exception of John C. Frémont's reports, which benefited from the artful prose style of his wife, Jessie Benton Frémont, government publications had few readers; they were printed in small numbers and distributed to government officials, libraries, and institutions. The sporting press culled information from these musty reports to give readers a condensed portrait of the continent that was scientific and romantic. Even an occasional hoax—like the discovery by the bogus Dr. Herman Ellenbogen of two supposedly new animals, the Prock and Gyasticutus, in the Rocky Mountains—was thrown into the bargain free of charge.[11]

If hunters portrayed themselves as men of science, it was only fitting that men of science be portrayed—or portray themselves—as hunters. "When we think of the ornithologist," wrote the biographer of Alexander Wilson, the nation's premier early nineteenth-century naturalist,

> the imagination does not present him to us in the safety and repose of a study; we think of him, as leaving the abodes of civilized man, launching his canoe on unbroken waters, depending on his rifle for subsistence, keeping on his solitary march till the bird has sung its evening hymn, and then lying down to rest, with no society but the sound of his fire, and no shelter but the star-lighted skies.

Wilson, he added, had combined the "self-complacent skill of the sportsman, and the wild romance of an adventurer."[12] Wilson, however, did not become the prince of American naturalists; that honor would belong to John James Audubon.

As early as 1833, the *American Turf Register* announced that every student of natural history "ought to have read the work of the simple, indefatigable, the virtuous, and the instructive Audubon." Five years later the *American Turf Register* noted that the great artist and ornithologist was still but little known due to the expense and scarcity of his works but pronounced his *Birds of America* "the greatest book ever published." Audubon's plates, claimed the *American Turf Register,* were "the best representations of life we ever saw." For its part, the *Spirit of the Times* consulted Audubon regarding the identification or behavior of birds, and one correspondent went so far as to suggest that the works of Audubon be substituted for calculus in the nation's colleges. "We are proud," said a review published in the *Spirit of the Times,* "to claim [Audubon's] noble work as a *native* in every sense."[13]

What made Audubon so attractive to the sporting press was his image as intrepid hunter and outdoorsman. Audubon had "combined in himself the best qualities of sportsman and naturalist," explained George Bird Grinnell, who, as editor of *Forest and Stream*, sought to collect funds in 1888 for a monument commemorating the great ornithologist (Audubon had died in 1851). Audubon, averred Grinnell, had done "more than . . . any other man to popularize the study of ornithology, and to instill into the hearts of his countrymen a love for nature and her creatures."[14]

Grinnell's observations accorded well with Audubon's moniker "the American Woodsman," a title that Audubon had tirelessly promoted. In *Ornithological Biography*, the prose counterpart to *Birds of America*, Audubon proffered a number of literary sketches dealing with hunting, and in *The Viviparous Quadrupeds of North America* he included a plate showing a mule deer with a bullet hole in its side. The hunter—apparently Audubon himself—appeared in the distant background. "In *my universe* of America," Audubon wrote in 1827,

> the deer runs free, and the Hunter as free forever. . . . America will always be my land. I never close my eyes without travelling thousands of miles along our noble streams; and traversing our noble forests. The voice of the thrush and the rumbling noise of the Alligator are still equally agreeable to my sense of recollection.[15]

If in his bird paintings Audubon glorified raptors by depicting them in the act of predation, in his prose he glorified Americans themselves as predators. In art and prose, Audubon appealed to the masculine and martial strain of American culture, whereas elsewhere—through depictions of nesting doves and delicate songbirds—he appealed to the sentimental and domestic. This versatility (indeed, this unresolvable contradiction) made Audubon the ideal figurehead for sentimentalists, scientists, and sport hunters who enlisted in the Audubon Society, a national organization founded in 1886 by *Forest and Stream* editor George Bird Grinnell.[16]

Audubon, however, wished to be remembered primarily as a hunter. He even linked himself with the most manly of American icons, Daniel Boone, recounting in *Ornithological Biography* a hunting excursion he had taken with Boone in Kentucky. Boone appeared "gigantic," recalled Audubon, his chest "broad and prominent," "his muscular powers displayed [in] every limb." It stretches the bounds of credulity to believe that such a meeting occurred, Boone having visited Kentucky just once after his move to Missouri in 1799, when in 1810 he had returned to pay off creditors. At the time Audubon would have met Boone, the old hunter would have been seventy-six and would have appeared more frail than gigantic. It is true, however, that in 1813 Audubon sent word to Boone that he wished to hunt with him, but Boone declined, citing age and poor eyesight.[17]

In portraits John James Audubon appeared as a wilderness hunter with middle-class sensibilities. John Woodhouse and Victor Audubon, *Audubon the Naturalist*, 1842. Neg. 335471. Courtesy of the Department of Library Services, American Museum of Natural History, New York.

This rebuff did not deter Audubon from adopting the style and demeanor of Boone. In a self-portrait, Audubon sketched himself wearing moccasins and a leather hunting shirt and carrying a tomahawk. Like Boone, Audubon dressed his shoulder-length hair in bear grease and posed for portrait artists in an open-collared hunting shirt or fur-collared coats, almost always carrying a hunting rifle. Audubon even had the look of a backwoods hunter; his step, according to an admirer, was "light as that of a deer," and his deep-set eyes and aquiline nose gave

American naturalists like Samuel W. Woodhouse, who accompanied government surveys of the Far West in the 1850s, portrayed themselves as backwoods hunters. Edward Bowers (1822–70), *Samuel Washington Woodhouse (1821–1904)*, 1857 (oil on canvas, 24 × 20 inches). NPG.72.28. Courtesy of the National Portrait Gallery, Smithsonian Institution, Washington, D.C.

him the appearance of "an imperial eagle." Despite all that, Audubon's sensibilities, like Boone's, seemed middle class; his "sympathies were always the most delicate, and his manners soft, gentle and refined."[18]

By combining masculine prowess with an intimate, experiential comprehension of nature, field naturalists like Audubon remained heroes to American hunters long after closet naturalists (with their institutional collections) had taken command of the discipline. As late as 1874, *Forest and Stream* praised naturalist Elliott Coues for "throwing off his scientific robes and leaving his technicalities in the desk" and studying "ornithology in a shooting jacket." Theodore Roosevelt would recall that when he entered Harvard in the 1870s, he was "devoted to out-of-doors natural history," and his "ambition was to be a scientific man of the Audubon, or Wilson, or Baird, or Coues type."[19]

Through the study of natural history and the admiration of naturalists, American sport hunters made themselves American Natives. In hunters' homes and clubs, meanwhile, appeared startling testimony to their sporting prowess and scientific mastery. Bears lunged, wolves howled, quail flapped, and deer and elk gazed majestically from above the hearth. "Perhaps you think a wild animal has no soul," wrote William Temple Hornaday, chief taxidermist of the Smithsonian Institution, in 1888, "but let me tell you it has. Its skin is its soul, and when mounted by skillful hands, it becomes comparatively immortal."[20]

While rudimentary technologies for preserving dead animals in lifelike form were old indeed, only a select few naturalists and aristocrats understood these secrets. In the nineteenth-century, however, taxidermy underwent a revolution in technology and popularity, passing at last "into the realm of art." Critical to success in the new medium was scientific verisimilitude. As early as 1847, one John Norval advertised his taxidermy in the *Spirit of the Times,* offering not only to clean and rearrange "Gentlemen's cabinets" but also to preserve any animal "with taste and accuracy, and a regard to symmetry, proportion and character, obtained only from an intimate knowledge of them in their natural state."[21]

The headquarters of the *Spirit of the Times* became a museum of natural history and sporting art, "the Mecca of every Western pilgrim visiting the Atlantic metropolis." So many sporting trophies and natural curiosities were contributed by army and navy officers that the *Spirit*'s collections were said to resemble the witches' caldron in Macbeth:

> Eye of newt, toe of frog,
> Wood of bat, and tongue of dog,
> Adder's fork, and blind-worm's sting,
> Lizard's leg, and owlet's wing.[22]

In displaying trophies, Americans followed the example of English sportsmen who commemorated hunting triumphs (often in colonized, or soon to be colonized, realms) by mounting heads, tails, and other anatomical selections. Americans proved equally ingenious in making use of deer feet for pegs to support hats, rods, and guns and antlers for furniture.[23] Though such exhibitions did not conform to the standards of scientific collecting, they served as shrines of manliness, chivalry, and knowledge of natural history.

The "spear and . . . bow, or rather rifle," attested Samuel Irenaeus Prime in 1874, "got [sportsmen] the trophies that now adorn their halls; the branching antlers of a noble buck are stuck upon the wall of their dining-room, and perhaps the skin has been made into an elegant mat that stretches itself before the fire."[24] Though most Americans were not inclined to see it thus, sportsmen's trophies were, as Prime suggested, not so different from the costumes and faunal totems of American Indians. Although Indian regalia made from deer, bear, or buffalo signified the status, character, and prowess of individual bearers, these emblems carried a mythological significance that whites labeled superstition. The sport hunter's faunal icons likewise symbolized the status, character, and manly prowess of their owners, but sporting cabinets could boast a scientific purpose and arrangement. By paying tribute to science over superstition and civilization over savagery, sporting cabinets seemed to make sport hunters cultural proprietors of the continent.

If hunters hitched their wagons to the star of science, they also hitched them to the star of romanticism. In entering the woods to hunt, American men followed the instruction of poets like William Wordsworth or, closer to home, William Cullen Bryant, who wrote

> Go forth, under the open sky,and list
> To Nature's teachings, while from all around—
> Earth and her waters, and the depths of air—
> Comes a still voice.

Ralph Waldo Emerson similarly insisted that "reason and faith" came from contact with "these plantations of God," the woods. There he found "perfect exhilaration" and "perpetual youth"; he had become a "particle of God."[25] The Deist, Rousseauist, and later transcendentalist notion of man in nature as man divine finally trumped the Puritan notion of innate depravity, encouraging hunters to seek God in nature.

Sport hunters did not believe, as did American Indians, in the anthropomorphic powers of animals, plants, rocks, winds, waters, and places. Sport hunters believed instead in the powers of the Christian God, or "Nature's God" in the language of Deists. This God exhibited awesome powers in the sublime features of wilderness landscapes—places like Niagara Falls and the Potomac Gorge—that became destinations for tourists and hunters alike. "The wilderness," testified

Taxidermy became a middle-class form of folk art in nineteenth-century America. Displays like this one testified to the hunter's courage, chivalry, and Americanness. Brandreth Preserve, ca. 1890s. Courtesy of the Adirondack Museum, Blue Mountain Lake, New York.

hunting author Alfred B. Street in 1860, "is one great tongue, speaking constantly to our hearts; inciting to love of the Supreme Maker, Benefactor, Father. . . . Here, with the grand forest for our worshipping temple, our hearts expanding, our thoughts rising unfettered, we behold Him, face to face."[26]

Because of lack of leisure, money, safety, and adequate transportation, tourism to sites of sublime natural beauty developed slowly in America. Though tourism blossomed in Europe in the second quarter of the eighteenth century, according to John Sears, it would not blossom in America for another hundred years. When it did blossom, tourism—one form of which was sport hunting—became a secular religion. Nature, wrote Perry Miller, "by her unremitting influence, . . . would guide aright the faltering steps of a young republic." As the symbol of American innocence and virtue, nature, whether as the wilderness or the sublime, would shield the nation from the decadence and corruption of Europe.[27]

While painters and poets expressed this reverence for nature, a hunter stood as the archetypal hero of wilderness virtue. Daniel Boone, wrote Kentucky-born naturalist and sport hunter Charles Wilkins Webber in 1851, was the "Romulus of Saxon blood" who, in founding a new order, "was fed, not upon the 'wolf's milk'—but upon the abundance of wild and serene nature—upon the delicious esculence of her forest game, and fruits of her wild luxuriant vines."[28]

The Boone literature made the wilderness a transcendent female America— the inverse of the masculine wilderness of combat and killing—and wilderness would fashion the man rather than vice versa. Colonial farmers had not framed their identity thus; for them nature was a nursery of virtue only insofar as it was tamed, plowed, and planted. But as Americans became increasingly urban and middle class in the nineteenth century, they began to revere Boone as scion of a wilderness that no longer required subjection to the plow. Rather than symbolizing danger and disorder, wilderness symbolized the self-reliant virtue of middle-class Americans.

Through the Boone literature, landscape painting, and tourism, America became, to quote Perry Miller, "nature's nation." Its mountains, rivers, and chasms were its churches; the hunter was its model citizen. Although Boone was the first of the breed, sport hunters soon followed. Thus Willard Barrows, president of a midwestern hunting club and subject of his brother's 1869 eulogistic biography *The General; or, Twelve Nights in the Hunter's Camp. A Narrative of Real Life*, had as a youth "thrilled to read of [nature's] 'mysteries locked up'" in the West. Later, he assisted in government surveys of the West, and by the time of his death in 1868, he, like a true middle-class man, had helped to found cities and the humane and religious organizations that went with them.[29] Barrows's great loves, however, were geography and travel.

Barrows received his nickname, "the General," by leading a wagon train to California, but his greatest mission in life was to search out the sublime treasures of the continent. Although he had been to the Holy Land, "never before had he seen antiquities, vastness, and glories" like the Rocky Mountains. "It must be mortifying," he would preach, for Americans "to say to the wandering Jew, or any other foreigner in those stinted ancient lands, that you have not seen Niagara Falls or Minnehaha, the mouths of the Missouri or a prairie."[30]

To protect part of this legacy, Barrows—following the precedent of artist and hunter George Catlin, who had preceded him on the Great Plains—pleaded for the creation of a national park. For Barrows the ideal park would be a six hundred square mile preserve between the Rockies and the upper Missouri River "on which any improvement beyond tent pins should be forever prohibited." Another sport hunter, Samuel H. Hammond, had already suggested in 1857 that the government "mark out a circle" in the Adirondacks "of a hundred miles in diameter and throw around it the protecting aegis of the constitution." Within this line, no logging or settlement would be permitted; it would be "forest forever."[31]

Forest and Stream editor Charles Hallock also campaigned in the 1870s for an Adirondack national park devoted to "sports of forest, lake and field." "Let the disciples of the rod and gun go up and possess the land," urged Hallock, turning inside out the logic of *vacuum domicilium.* Though Hallock's dream of an Adirondack national park never came to fruition, the state of New York did create the Adirondack State Park in part due to the efforts of sportsmen. In 1885 New York State amended its constitution to declare that the Adirondack forests should remain "forever wild."[32]

By hunting in the country's forests and prairies, by glorifying its naturalists, and by venerating its sublime scenery, hunters transformed themselves into American Natives. Their new identity was individualistic yet national. Natural history, wilderness, and the sublime transcended political and sectional differences; hunting added to these elements the power of fraternity. After the Civil War, these forces formed a robust alliance that reshaped ideas about manliness, dominion, nature, and civilization.

In identifying themselves as hunters and woodsmen, American men made themselves into American Natives. At times, indeed, sport hunters seemed intent on making themselves into American Indians. "We would teach you those secrets which necessity compelled the savages to learn," promised *Forest and Stream* in its first issue in 1873. *Forest and Stream* might brag that its subscribers were among the wealthiest men in the nation, yet these men needed to know how to make fire with sticks, to live off the land, to find their way in the forest, and to understand the habits of game. An apocalypse might come, warned *Forest and Stream*, that would deprive men of technological wizardry; even affluent men needed to learn how to live like Indians.[33]

Meanwhile, Indians themselves were systematically barred from subsistence activities on national parks, monuments, and game refuges throughout the country, even where treaties guaranteed them hunting rights.[34] Native Americans, it seemed, had no sacred tie with native game or wilderness, which were to be saved for American Natives.

The elimination of Indians from lands deemed sacred by sport hunters and tourists signaled a vast transformation in Americans' concept of nature and civilization. Whereas Indian peoples spoke of their emergence from a pond, lake, or cave within their tribal territory, white Americans spoke of their own culture's emergence from the wilderness (or the frontier). The wilderness, as white Americans conceived of it, was not only a place of struggle and strife but also a place of edenic perfection. In both these guises, wilderness was the birthplace of American civilization. To the degree, therefore, that wilderness was to be preserved, it was to be preserved in pristine form, without the troubling presence of dark-skinned peoples who claimed to be indigenous Americans but whose values differed from those of whites. In inscribing wilderness with their god, their science, and their cultural origins, white hunters and tourists displaced Indians as heirs to the continent.

Indians, however, were not the primary targets of sport hunters. With painters and poets like Thomas Cole, Asher Brown Durand, Albert Bierstadt, William Cullen Bryant, and Ralph Waldo Emerson, sport hunters crusaded against "the ravages of the axe," as Cole put it, that followed from Americans' barbarous utilitarianism. In saving game animals and wilderness habitats, sport hunters wished to hold on to something sacred, something more meaningful than gain. Yet their's was an ambiguous crusade, since hunters were themselves dynamos of free enterprise. The irony that escaped them was that in the very nature they deemed sacred they inscribed their apotheosis of self-reliant individualism.[35] To set aside hunting preserves and national parks as sites for secular worship was to set aside arenas for the celebration of laissez-faire values that elsewhere led to the destruction of nature. Preservation and destruction were bound together in the hunter's imagination like yin and yang. The task of disentangling the two, if they can be disentangled, is still unfinished.

13

Disciples of Sport Hunting

 The man who, more than any other, made sport hunting respectable before the Civil War and yet epitomized its contradictions was Henry William Herbert, a square-jawed, mustachioed English exile known by his pseudonym, Frank Forester. By 1850 Herbert had become the nation's preeminent hunting author and arbiter of sportsmanship. Before Herbert, commented his friend and biographer, Thomas Picton, the term "sportsman" savored of card playing and horse racing; after Herbert, the term "sportsman" applied to respectable professionals and businessmen who practiced "the wholesome, exhilarating excitements" of hunting and fishing.[1] Yet as his sport rose to respectability, Herbert declined into penury and, ultimately, tragedy. More than any other man, Herbert defined hunting as a virtuous sport of middle-class Americans, yet he never found acceptance in America and never could see himself as an American Native.

Having run up gambling debts while enrolled at Cambridge, Herbert, a grandson of the earl of Carnarvon, immigrated to the United States in 1831 as one of the so-called remittance men whose families had unofficially banished them from England. Taking up residence in an elite boarding house in New York City, Herbert soon found himself adopted into a circle of wealthy sportsmen who appreciated his breeding and talents and were eager to emulate him. His coterie included editors, lawyers, turfmen, and professional gentlemen who found Herbert to be punctilious in manners and dress, accomplished in field sports and athletics, fluent in French, and able to read and write Greek and Latin.[2]

Despite the wealth of his friends, Herbert had a modest income and was forced to take a job as the preceptor at Huddart's Classical Institute, where he taught Greek, Latin, and gymnastics. Not surprisingly, Herbert found the job at Huddart's beneath his dignity, and after some success in publishing articles in local newspapers, he embarked on a literary career.[3]

Herbert made rapid strides as a magazine editor and later as a translator of classical and European works, but his fondest wish was to be recognized as the equal of Washington Irving and James Fenimore Cooper in the romance genre and of Edgar Allan Poe and Henry Wadsworth Longfellow in poetry. As a novelist, Herbert worked assiduously, writing some half dozen historical novels of a serious nature in the 1830s and 1840s. His books sold poorly and received mediocre reviews, however, and penury forced him to churn out pseudonymous "penny-a-liners." Poe would remark that Herbert, despite his capacity to write in a "clear, neat, forceful" style, had "written more trash than any man living, with the exception of [Theodore S.] Fay."[4]

Despite his frequent hunting excursions with his well-heeled friends, Herbert never imagined himself becoming a sporting writer. Nor is it likely he would have, given the tenuous nature of the American sporting press, had not William Graham, brother of the publisher of *Graham's Magazine,* convinced Herbert that his future lay in sporting journalism. William Trotter Porter seconded the suggestion, asking Herbert to contribute hunting sketches to the *American Turf Register and Sporting Magazine,* which he had purchased from John Skinner in 1839.

Under the pseudonym Frank Forester, a name suggested to Herbert for its consonance with "modern notions of woodcraft," Herbert's hunting narratives were collected as *The Warwick Woodlands, Or Things As They Were Ten Years Ago,* published in 1845. Despite Herbert's suspicion that the book would fail, it gained immediate popularity. One success followed another, as Herbert's sketches were collected in novel-like narratives in *My Shooting Box, American Game in Its Seasons,* and *The Deerstalkers.* The crowning success was *Frank Forester's Field Sports of the United States and British Provinces of North America,* a two-volume nonfiction work on the habits and natural history of game, the mechanics of shooting, and the methods of the chase, illustrated with Herbert's own woodcuts.[5]

"No one abler, or elder, seemed willing to stand forth," wrote Herbert in *Frank Forester's Field Sports,* ignoring the influence of Graham and Porter in his destiny, "so . . . I have ventured myself as the champion of American Sport and Sportsmanship." Though others had initiated the struggle for respectability, Herbert—like his fellow Englishman Henry Chadwick, who became the great promoter of baseball—launched a moral offensive on behalf of hunting that reverberated for the rest of the century. Ascribing the vigor of the English aristocracy to its passion for blood sport, Herbert argued that hunting would "prevent the demoralization of luxury" and "the growth of effeminacy and sloth" and ensure "the maintenance of a little manhood in an age, the leading characteristics of which are fanaticism, cant, and hypocrisy."[6]

The argument followed the lines of the earliest defenses of hunting in the pages of the *American Turf Register* and the *Cabinet of Natural History and American Rural Sport,* but with a distinction: hunting was no longer on the defensive. Herbert censured his own peers—the wealthy classes of the eastern cities—for their decline into effeminacy and indolence, and he made hunting appear to be the last defense against the dissolution that Thomas Jefferson had foreseen fifty years earlier. Hunting alone could save the "the rich citizen, the man of wealth and luxury, and leisure . . . from drivelling down into a mere gluttonous sensualist, or yet worse, a mere effeminate man-milliner."[7]

To hunt, indeed, was to return to the ancient virtues of northern Europe's "warrior and hunter races," claimed Herbert. "To this day," he wrote in his *Complete Manual for Young Sportsmen,* "wherever a drop is to be found of that fierce Northern blood surviving in people's veins, there you will find, and in no other land, the passion for the chase alive and dominant."[8] To be a hunter was to be a member of a racial elite that was annexing the globe, an elite that American expansionists longed to join. Hunting was becoming an expression of ethnic identity.

Like others before him, Herbert also reaffirmed the importance of natural history for the sport hunter. Among Herbert's chief concerns was the American hunter's "vulgar, ignorant, slipshod habit" of referring to game animals by vernacular names and his lack of scientific interest in the habits of the prey. In Herbert's view, scientific knowledge separated sportsmen from pot hunters; he insisted that the habit of referring to the ruffed grouse as a "partridge" or a "pheasant" was "unsportsmanlike and unscientific" and even a "stupid barbarism."[9]

Herbert spoke of the "immortal celebrity" of naturalists like Alexander Wilson, John James Audubon, Georges Cuvier, and Louis Agassiz. Herbert even corresponded with Agassiz, the first professor of zoology and geology at Harvard's Lawrence Scientific School, and sent him specimens of smelt taken on the Passaic River. Herbert also applauded the growing popularity of natural history among "thousands of votaries, in the field, in the forest, in the arid desert." A friend recalled that Herbert's knowledge of his environment was so great that a stone "picked up in his wayside ramble . . . became a text from which he would read you an entertaining and instructive lecture on geology or mineralogy."[10]

Even if Herbert could never become an American Native, he was admired for a mastery of natural history that enabled him to read and to explicate the American land to his followers. Natural history allowed Herbert to give American sport hunters a sense of themselves as men in harmony with and in control of American nature. At a more utilitarian level, Herbert was in the vanguard of a campaign for game laws based on scientific knowledge rather than the hearsay of opponents, preparing his followers for highly charged conservation campaigns in decades to come.

Herbert did not, however, represent hunting as solely the pastime of wealthy, urban men. In an 1846 issue of the *New York Illustrated Magazine of Literature and Art* appeared Herbert's fictive biography of "Long Jakes, the Prairie Man," accompanied by an engraving derived from an 1844 painting by Charles Deas of a fur trapper. Here, Herbert imitated his literary hero, James Fenimore Cooper, by describing the frontier hunter as a model of manliness. Long Jakes, like Boone, was a man whose "untrammeled sense of individual will and independent power" stood against the corruption of civilization (about half of "Long Jakes" is given over to an exegesis on the failures of modern men). Yet Long Jakes was also a voice for Herbert's brand of antidemocratic elitism. Like Herbert, Long Jakes refused to give up the chase to work at a desk or to stoop to "the trickeries of trade," and Herbert contrasted his sense of honor with the rising power of the ill-mannered masses.[11]

Herbert molded Long Jakes into an incarnation of the English aristocrat, or perhaps the New York aristocrat, merely replacing shooting jacket with buckskins and the Queen's English with frontier vernacular. Yet in a perverse way, Long Jakes represented the man who did work at a desk or stoop to a trade. Such men bought Herbert's books and became devotees of sport hunting, and they would have seen in Long Jakes a spiritual counterpart who refused to bow to the meaninglessness and effeminacy of the world in which they lived.

Elsewhere, Herbert celebrated the gentleman hunter more directly. In *The Deerstalkers,* one of his most famous works of fiction, Herbert ventured outside the boundaries of the simple hunting narrative, transforming a deer hunting excursion into a murder mystery similar to the new urban novels of crime and suspense, but with a gentleman hunter as hero.

In this novel Harry Archer relies on his skill in woodcraft to bring to justice Black Ned, who has killed Archer's old friend Barhyte. Black Ned, whose race is never identified, is a barefoot backwoods hunter with a menacing visage—a figure straight out of melodrama—who represents the old, dark image of the savage frontier hunter. He is both cruel and debauched, having seduced the wife of the man he kills, and he must be vanquished by the gentleman hunter.

Harry Archer, a gentleman hunter of great honor, loyalty, and good conduct, defeats Black Ned by learning his own code—woodcraft—more thoroughly than

Henry William Herbert at his New Jersey home, the Cedars. Frontis engraving from David
W. Judd (ed.), *Life and Writings of Frank Forester. (Henry William Herbert.),* 2 vols. (New York,
1882). Courtesy of the Beinecke Rare Book and Manuscript Library, Yale University, New
Haven, Connecticut.

Ned himself. Coming upon the murdered Barhyte while hunting, Archer is able to determine the direction from which the killer fired by studying the entry and exit points of the bullet. He then locates the footprints that barefoot Ned, like an Indian, has attempted to cover with leaves and debris and is able to make plaster casts of them. With this evidence, Archer has Ned arrested and brought to trial, with Archer himself acting as prosecutor. After Ned is sentenced, the local coroner is left wondering whether Archer is a lawyer. The response comes not from Harry Archer but from Dolph, a Boone-like hunter and guide who has befriended Archer: "No he ain't . . . but he's a darned sight better thing, he's the very best and 'cutest woodsman I iver did see."[12]

In *The Deerstalkers*, Herbert gave the gentleman hunter his resounding triumph over the savage hunter and his claim to the mantle of American nature. The bad frontier hunter, Black Ned, is vanquished, and the good frontier hunter, Dolph, pronounces Archer the best woodsman he has ever encountered, a statement tantamount to admitting that Archer is as worthy an heir of nature—and as truly an American Native—as Dolph himself. Herbert tied together gentleman hunter and Boone-like guide in such a way that both appeared as indigenous species of the virtuous man. In the conclusion of the story, Archer offers the moral that his triumph over Ned proves "that there is not only much practical, but much moral utility, in the GENTLE SCIENCE OF WOODCRAFT."[13]

This sort of moral tale—in which the urban man gains virtue and identity from the American backwoods—would crop up again in the Boy Scouts, the Boone and Crockett Club, the Sierra Club, the Appalachian Mountain Club, and virtually the entire Back to Nature movement of the late nineteenth century. Although he would not live to see the popularity of his sport reach its apogee later in the century, Herbert had made hunting and woodsmanship not just respectable but redemptive. Indeed, Herbert appeared intent on redeeming himself through his hunting. The more famous he became as Frank Forester, the more completely he strove to resemble the persona he had created, substituting for his dapper suits a "full rural or hunting costume," and appearing on the streets of Newark, New Jersey, and New York City with a dog at his heels and a fur cap on his head.[14]

In 1845 Herbert removed himself from the corruptions of urban life by building a cottage, called the Cedars, on the Passaic River outside Newark. Although its interior boasted a fireplace and a manorial staircase, from the outside the Cedars looked like a Swiss chalet. On closer inspection, a dog kennel at the front (the dogs served as doorbells) and a deer skull over the entry hall, together with the array of hunting trophies inside, made the Cedars resemble an elegant yet monastic hunting lodge in the European tradition. In fact, Herbert had chosen the location partly for the good shooting at the adjacent cemetery. Despite Herbert's increasing reclusiveness, the Cedars became well known as the home of the country's preeminent sportsman. Apart from the home of Washington Irving, remarked Herbert's biographer in 1882, "no author's dwelling had grown more familiar by name to the world of literature . . . than was 'The Cedars.'"[15]

Herbert had always wanted to be a country gentleman rather than a city rake, and he had built his cottage a goodly distance from New York City to avoid becoming a "libertine, a profligate, or debauchee." But the Cedars proved to be no shelter from dissolution. After a decade of mental and financial decline, the final blow to Herbert came when he met, married, and was abandoned by a woman who claimed to be an heiress but was in fact an actress who had already left her first husband. Morose over his wife's departure, Herbert shot himself in a New York City hotel in May 1858. In a letter he had left for the press, Herbert wrote that in his twenty-six years in the United States "every hope has broken down under my foot as soon as it has touched it; every spark of happiness quenched as soon as it has been kindled."[16]

In truth, every hope had not broken down; Herbert had made himself the most popular sporting author in America. He had helped to fashion the middle-class man into a vigorous, manly hunter whose shooting prowess and knowledge of natural history gave him not only a kinship with the frontiersman but also an air of superiority. In short, Herbert had tailored a new identity for an urban, male public that could no longer identify its virtues with farming. Though by the end of his life he had alienated his elite friends, he had become a hero to an ever-growing middle-class readership. Despite all this success, Herbert could never quite see himself as an American Native.

Like his fictive hero, Harry Archer, who simultaneously wore the cap of an English huntsman and the buckskin shirt of a frontier hunter, Herbert was torn between his native land and his adopted land. He had never planned to become a permanent resident of the United States, and he maintained a staunch allegiance to the British Crown throughout his life. Even after he became famous as a hunting writer, Herbert continued to get into trouble with Americans who resented his English chauvinism. He was taken to task by American sportsmen for disparaging American fox hunting, for arguing that the American trout was smaller than its British counterpart, and for recommending English rifles over American makes for deer hunting.[17]

Such criticisms were elicited in part by Herbert's tendency to belittle the well-to-do men who were taking up sport hunting due in no small part to Herbert's influence. Long Island, wrote Herbert, had become "the suburban cockney sporting grounds of New York merchant princes [and] the verdant and impudent abortions known as the rising generation of Young New York and Progress." In another article, Herbert insisted that only the "Broadway dandy" would make a Long Island hotel his hunting headquarters, calling such vacations "high living by day, high play at night, soft pillows in the morning, with just enough sporting to serve as an excuse."[18] Herbert, as an English aristocrat and as a friend of New York's older gentry, refused to bow to the very men who read his books.

Not surprisingly, Herbert found himself on the receiving end of criticism. One hunter chastened Herbert for wronging his fellow sporting writer, the recently deceased William Post Hawes, by publishing "articles too sensuous." This critic claimed that Hawes, unlike Herbert, would never have furnished his hunting cabin with "Brussels carpets and curtains, and comforts, and varied wines." Hawes's "shooting-box" on Long Island had been, by contrast, a "temple" to republican masculinity, "simple, erect, severe, austere, sublime." It was the American, Hawes, not the Englishman, Herbert, who had "divided the lover of nature and nature's God, from the brute hunter who pursues his game without thoughts of aught around him."[19] Ultimately, however, none of this criticism detracted from Herbert's fame or the popularity of his sport; not even Herbert's suicide could slow sport hunting's momentum.

Herbert's unmarked grave had few visitors for the first few years after his burial (without ceremony) in the cemetery next to the Cedars. After the Civil War, a new generation of sportsmen, having discovered Herbert's writings, began to make pilgrimages to the Cedars, which had decayed into a peculiarly American sort of ruin. After it burned to the ground, the site was finally incorporated, as was Herbert himself, into the cemetery.[20]

In the centennial year, 1876, a group of Newark citizens formed the Newark Herbert Association, which held a ceremony for Herbert and placed on his grave a headstone with the inscription he had wanted: Infelicissimus (most unhappy one). The ceremony, attended by Newark's elite citizenry, was held in part to obviate efforts by the Frank Forester Memorial Fund Association of New York City to reinter Herbert at Greenwood Cemetery on Mount Pleasant. Herbert's headstone was veiled with a curious flag that interwove the English Banner of St. George with the American Stars and Stripes. Though the American half of the flag expressly commemorated the centennial, it also seemed to commemorate the impact Herbert had had on American middle-class men, while the English half of the flag recalled "that home he never for a moment forgot."[21] Even in death, even to his warmest admirers, Herbert remained the Englishman who had made hunting a respectable American sport.

Yet Herbert was no more elitist than the sportsmen who made him famous. If anything, Herbert, caught between his British and his American identity, was an exaggerated emblem of the divided loyalties of American sportsmen. Hunting appealed to middle-class Americans precisely because it was elitist—because it was the sport of British aristocrats like Herbert—and because it was the egalitarian pastime of the American frontiersman, the indigenous product of American nature. Like a cultural pendulum, American sport hunting swung back and forth between these extremes, one elitist and foreign, the other democratic and native. The American sport hunter became a Janus-faced man, now claiming social superiority through natural history and sportsmanship, and now claiming affinity with the common man, the frontier hunter.

As a genuine aristocrat who felt superior to his American followers, Herbert could not manage the same change of face. The problem was not that Herbert was chauvinistic while his readers were not but that Herbert's chauvinism displayed the wrong colors. For Herbert hunting was a way to retain an aristocratic identity in a democratic nation, whereas his followers—despite their elitism—hunted to reclaim republican virtue and to define themselves as Americans. Their chauvinism shone as patriotism, Herbert's as arrogance.

Even as Herbert made sport hunting commendable, he left others to make sport hunting eminently American, including some of the country's most celebrated politicians and writers. Among those was the Whig orator and statesman Daniel Webster, whom William Trotter Porter pronounced "one of the best shots in the United States" and "as destructive to the woodcock, as to his adversaries in debate." Each morning that he awoke at his estate in Marshfield, Massachusetts, Webster's first interview was with Seth Peterson, his hunting and fishing partner.[22]

Echoing the arguments of Herbert and the sporting press, Webster testified that his "manly taste" for field sports had given him a robust constitution, despite his sickly childhood.[23] By attaching a redemptive, masculine virtue to hunting and fishing, Webster, who was known for his towering intellect rather than his physical strength, betrayed the fear of effeminacy that plagued so many middle-class men.

Webster made a direct connection between his hardy sport and his politics by naming one of his hunting rifles "Wilmot Proviso," the name of the 1846 legislative provision that sought to ban slavery in the territories acquired in the Mexican War. Before the Compromise of 1850, Webster supported the proviso, and his attempt to associate it with his hunting weapon must have given southern politicians pause. Two other rifles were given more inscrutable names, "Learned Seldon" and "Mrs. Patrick," while a fishing rod was named "Killall."[24]

Webster further affirmed his manly prowess by competing in shooting contests. He was said to have once engaged in a turkey shoot in Ohio, which he won, only then revealing himself as the great politician (no doubt Webster was less proud of the time he shot and possibly lamed a hunting partner). Henry Clay, also a hunter and a fancier of guns and dogs, participated in a similar contest with militiamen in Kentucky after claiming to be the "best shot" in the country.[25] By participating in these frontier contests—or claiming to have done so—politicians established their spiritual affinity with genuine backwoodsmen. Such demonstrations were particularly important for men like Webster and Clay who had ambitions to be president.

Like his sporting contemporaries, Webster also immersed himself in natural history. Though Webster once sent John James Audubon a wagon load of birds killed on Webster's Marshfield, Massachusetts, estate, Webster himself planned to write a natural history of the Marshfield area. This fascination for natural history and field sports in turn made Webster a conservationist. The only bill he wrote and saw through to passage during his brief tenure in the Massachusetts legislature was a plan to protect trout and other game fish during the spawning season, and he later vowed to protect game birds as well.[26] Although Webster did not live to carry out his promise, thousands of other sport hunters enlisted in a fledgling conservation movement both before and after the Civil War. In their efforts to protect game, sport hunters sought to protect the rituals that defined them as American Natives.

By 1880 dozens of congressmen and senators hunted for sport, and at least three had won prizes in shooting contests. Presidents, too, let it be known that they were hunters. The outstanding hunter-politician would be Theodore Roosevelt, but James Garfield, Grover Cleveland (who wrote a book on hunting and fishing), Benjamin Harrison, and William McKinley had preceded him in the field, proving that hunting appealed to those on both sides of the partisan divide. Another presidential contender, Governor Horatio Seymour of New York (Ulysses S. Grant's Democratic opponent in 1868), had the honor, or dishonor, of taking what was thought to be the last elk in the Adirondacks in 1859.[27]

An equally profound connection between hunting and patriotism was forged by the novelist and demagogue Ned Buntline, who, through hunting and politics, cast himself as the most American of Americans. Though his parents made the mistake of giving their son the bloodless name Edward Zane Carroll Judson, he assumed the pseudonym Ned Buntline while serving in the navy during the Seminole War in Florida (a buntline was a rope attached to the bottom of a ship's square sail). In this war Buntline often went ashore with small groups of marines to engage in what today would be called counterinsurgency.

Buntline would later claim to have fought in the Mexican War (although he probably got nowhere near Mexican territory) and to have been breveted by the United States to the rank of colonel and chief of scouts in the Civil War (this rise in rank, too, was fictitious, although Buntline served in an undistinguished capacity). Whatever glory he later accrued, he saw no Seminoles in Florida in 1839–40 but did bag a stupendous number of ducks. He also sent the first of his innumerable hunting and fishing narratives to sporting magazines.[28]

Like Henry William Herbert, Buntline nursed a great ambition to write serious literature, but his next highest ambition was to be a sporting writer. Although he attended the informal gatherings of sportsmen at the offices of the *Spirit of the Times*—where he nearly got himself into a duel with Herbert by questioning the bravery of English sailors—he found his talents beneath the standards set by William Porter's other correspondents.[29] This failure was probably a blessing; Buntline went on to become perhaps the most popular and widely read American novelist of the nineteenth century. His total production of novels ran to something on the order of four hundred.

Buntline's initial rise to fame came chiefly through *Ned Buntline's Own*, a magazine that "scourged the lawless element" of New York City in the 1840s and 1850s, particularly those who were foreign born.[30] By 1848 Buntline had become perhaps the leading nativist in the United States, having worked as an active campaigner for the Know-Nothing movement (whose Buntlinian slogan was "America for Americans"), and having been sentenced to a year in jail for his role in fomenting the 1849 Astor Place riot in New York City. The riot was essentially a nativist outburst directed against English tragedian William Macready, who was performing *Macbeth*.

Little of Buntline's political life was directly related to hunting or sportsmanship, yet as he involved himself in patriotic organizations and nativist muckraking, Buntline began to see hunting as the distillation of American virtue. The proudest day in his life, recalled Buntline, had been his eighth birthday when his father gave him his first gun. Having impressed his father with his marksmanship, Buntline wanted to follow the "illustrious example of Daniel Boone" by becoming a professional hunter but was discouraged from this goal by the family's move to Philadelphia.[31] Buntline, however, did find a way to participate vicariously, and to allow others to participate vicariously, in the chivalrous hunting life.

Ned Buntline's fondest childhood wish was to become a hunter like Daniel Boone. "Ned Buntline. Ready for Game." Ca. 1880. Courtesy of the Adirondack Museum, Blue Mountain Lake, New York.

Thanks in part to the fictional hunter-heroes of his dime novels, Buntline became one of the best-paid writers in postbellum America, with an annual income of some $20,000.[32] Of all his literary efforts, perhaps the most important was a magazine piece on a hunter whom Buntline called Buffalo Bill. Buntline had met this man purely by accident, having traveled to Nebraska to write a story about the North brothers, two army officers who had rescued a white woman from Indian captivity. Frank North wanted no part of literary notoriety, however, and recommended that Buntline write about William Cody, a handsome, genial man who had worked as a teamster and hunter for railroad crews.

Buntline emphasized Cody's hunting exploits by awarding him the appellation "Buffalo Bill" (a common name among frontier hunters) and published "Buffalo Bill: The King of Border Men—The Wildest and Truest Story I Ever Wrote" in *Smith's New York Weekly* in 1869.[33] The story was soon made into a stage show in which Cody appeared alongside his fellow frontier hero Texas Jack Omohondro, both of whom played themselves. Despite his stage fright, Cody gradually mastered the Buntlinian art of self-promotion that culminated in his launching of Buffalo Bill's Wild West Show in 1883. But it was Buntline who had set the Wild West Show in motion by casting Buffalo Bill as the most recent link in a chain of chivalrous, courageous American Natives stretching back to Boone.

Buntline was not, like Henry William Herbert, a great popularizer of sport hunting, although his example could not have retarded the cause. He forged a connection, however, not only between hunting and virtue but also between hunting and nativism. After the Civil War, he and his hunter-hero, Buffalo Bill, toured the country together, organizing chapters of the Patriotic Order Sons of America, which sought to inculcate "pure American principles," to oppose "foreign interference" in the United States' affairs, and to promote "fraternal love," the preservation of the Constitution, and free education. Buntline had been one of the original founders of the order in 1847 and had since been elected "master of forms and ceremonies, and Custodian of the Red, White, and Blue Degrees."[34]

In the 1850s, Buntline built a cabin (or "shooting-box") in the Adirondacks that he called the Eagle's Nest because of its location on a lake where eagles came to roost. In this cabin, Buntline took refuge from the evils of New York City and Philadelphia. His fellow sportsman Fred E. Pond ("Will Wildwood") wrote that Buntline was a "modern knight errant" battling the evils of the metropolis but that he, like Boone, "preferred the solitude of the wilderness to the social forms of the cities." Buntline probably expressed it better in a poem in which he described the Eagle's Nest as a place

> Where the world's foul scum can never come;
> Where friends are so few that all are true—
> There is my home—my wildwood home.[35]

Actually, friends were few because Buntline preferred to make enemies. Buntline was jealous of any intrusion on his hunting grounds and was said to dress like an Indian and to perform war dances outside his cabin to scare other sportsmen

William "Buffalo Bill" Cody, the Boone of the Gilded Age, was discovered by Ned Buntline. This painting depicts Buffalo Bill as cousin to the Indian. Unknown, *Buffalo Hunt in 1870 with Scout William Cody (Buffalo Bill) and a Pawnee Indian* (oil on canvas, 40¾ × 68⅞). Courtesy of the R. W. Norton Art Gallery, Shreveport, Louisiana.

away. On one occasion he refused to entertain two gregarious (and apparently wealthy) sportsmen who had wandered by the Eagle's Nest to see him, subjecting them instead to a stern reproach for having bagged a fawn and a doe.[36]

In 1861 the Eagle's Nest burned, and Buntline refused to rebuild. As the Adirondacks became hugely popular as a vacation spot for urban sportsmen in later years, Buntline would write that it made him "sick" to revisit the site of his old cabin, adding that "a lover of Nature and Nature's gifts shudders at the advance of—dudes and their fancy accessories." In 1870, however, he did build a second Eagle's Nest in Delaware County, New York, where he enclosed a twenty-acre game preserve and gathered a large collection of sporting artifacts and tro-phies. At this Eagle's Nest Buntline ran up the American flag each day until his death in 1886.[37]

Through the efforts of Buntline, hunting was cleansed of its Englishness; dyed red, white, and blue; and worn anew as a uniform of Americanness. Although some postbellum hunters would remember the Englishman Henry William Her-bert as the father of their sport, others would remember him as a pathetic fig-ure, a pedant who, as one correspondent wrote in *Forest and Stream,* "cared little for really wild sports."[38] Other American champions of sport hunting—includ-ing Buntline, but, more significantly, Charles Hallock, George Bird Grinnell, and Theodore Roosevelt—would come forward to fill the void left by Herbert. Their legacy—their concept of hunting as an ancient and noble American tradition—echoes today.

14

Adirondacks and Aesthetics

 Even if Ned Buntline was the first to make hunting a sacred American rite, his decision to build a hunting retreat in the Adirondack Mountains had precedent. Like Long Island before them, the Adirondacks became an enormous resort for New York sportsmen who had discovered the mountains' steep, rocky, unpeopled promontories, myriad lakes and streams, and plentiful game as early as the 1830s. For every middle-class man who felt encumbered by urban life, the Adirondacks stood as a promise for the renewal of health, manliness, virtue, and Americanness. By 1862 answering "no" to the question "have you been to the Adirondacks?" was sure to be met with incredulity, wrote George William Curtis in *Harper's New Monthly Magazine*. "Not been to the Adirondacks!" would come the reply, "dear me!"[1]

Between the 1830s and 1870s, several dozen writers canvased the mountains, making them the locus of novels, poetry, and hunting narratives. Part of the popularity of the Adirondacks was the abundance of deer and trout within a two- to three-day ride by boat and wagon—or later train—from New York City. What also made the Adirondacks special was the chance for urban, middle-class men to interact with guides who, like Boone or Leatherstocking, were perceived as avatars of nature.

In the 1850s Samuel H. Hammond wrote that nature "preached" to his Adirondack guide, and the guide was in turn able to testify to the providential design revealed by nature to a Boston atheist who once had hired him. Another guide, John Cheney, became well known before the Civil War for a "silent, simple, deep love of the woods" befitting Cooper's Leatherstocking. Both Charles Fenno Hoffman and Charles Lanman noted in their Adirondack writings that Cheney, like a gentleman sportsman, refused to take deer by imitating the fawn's bleat or by blinding them with a torch in a fire-hunt.[2]

A more formal religious ethic was displayed by Mitchell Sabattis, an Abenaki Indian who worked as a guide until he was in his eighties. After giving up drinking, he began raising funds for the construction of a Methodist church and became a favorite guide for big city ministers from New York City, Boston, and Philadelphia. Joel Tyler Headley, a minister who gained fame for his popular biographies of famous Americans, recalled having shaken Sabattis's "honest hand" after an Adirondack trip in the 1840s "with as much regret as I ever did that of a white man."[3]

Guides like Sabattis and Cheney were not just servants who prepared meals and butchered game killed by gentlemen hunters; they were links between the American Native in the Boone tradition and the city sportsman. Guides, waxed

Adirondack guides pose for photographer Seneca Ray Stoddard in 1886. At the center, between two trees, stands Mitchell Sabattis, who had worked as a guide since the 1840s. Courtesy of the Adirondack Museum, Blue Mountain Lake, New York.

Hammond, displayed that "sturdy independence which enters so largely into the character of the border men of our country." In addition to ensuring a successful hunting or fishing expedition, the guide was a spiritual and cultural guide, an incarnate Boone or Leatherstocking who would guide the gentleman hunter to nature's secrets and manly virtues.[4] Yet the guide did not so much lead urban men into the unknown as lead them back to middle-class values. Guides were praised for religious zeal, temperance, and sportsmanship, attitudes that gentlemen hunters held sacrosanct. The guide made middle-class values appear to be fundamental facets of the American Native, traits rooted in nature.

By 1858 some of the nation's most eminent scientists, writers, and lawyers could be found in the Adirondacks, making sporting pilgrimages in search of moral and physical vigor. William Stillman, a landscape painter who had often recounted his Adirondack experiences to his intellectual circle in Cambridge, Massachusetts, organized an Adirondack vacation that included not only Ralph Waldo Emerson but also Louis Agassiz, the nation's premier naturalist and geologist, as well as author, poet, and diplomat James Russell Lowell and several prominent doctors and lawyers. Oliver Wendell Holmes, Charles Eliot Norton, and Henry Longfellow declined to go; Longfellow worried that Emerson would accidentally shoot another member of the party.[5]

The "Philosophers' Camp," as it became known, made manifest the spread of attitudes popularized by the cult of Boone and the literature of sport hunting. Emerson wrote of the camp, "Ten scholars, wonted to lie warm and soft / In well-hung chambers daintily bestowed, / Lie here in hemlock-boughs, like Sacs and Sioux / And greet unanimous the joyful change."[6]

The party also partook of the forest wisdom of its guides, nine of whom were hired to serve ten gentlemen, with Stillman serving as Agassiz's guide. This one-to-one ratio allowed each man to go his separate way, making the excursion a proper exercise in individualism. The multiple guides also served to give each man his private mentor in woodcraft. "Your rank is all reversed," Emerson announced, "Let men of cloth / Bow to the stalwart churls in overalls / [They] are the doctors of the wilderness, / And we the low-prized laymen."[7]

None of this celebration of the wild deterred the party from cheering when news reached the encampment that the first trans-Atlantic telegraph cable between Europe and America had been laid. The rejection of civilization was temporary, a protest for the sake of form. Emerson noted that the party might "praise the guide" but would never sacrifice "books and arts and trained experiment" for the life of a Sioux.[8]

The group also carried with it the scientific, civilized discipline of natural history, which allowed the men to glean nature's secrets more thoroughly than their rustic guides. Each morning Louis Agassiz, assisted by anatomist Jeffries Wyman, would lead the party in dissecting an animal or studying plant morphology. "Two Doctors in the camp," recalled Emerson, "Dissected the slain deer, / weighed the trout's brain, / Capture the lizard, salamander, shrew." Stillman stated simply that "no plant, no insect, no quadruped" could hide "its secret" from Agassiz.[9]

Finally, the group became hunters. Agassiz was said to be the best shot by virtue of his practice in sighting through a microscope, but Emerson also got into the act. Despite his Olympian detachment from the doings of his friends, Emerson, hearing the dogs on the trail of a deer, decided he must enter the fray. Day after day Emerson's guide took him into the woods to bag his deer, and day after day Emerson failed. In frustration, he resorted to unsportsmanlike methods, trying jacklighting, and even agreeing to let his guide hold the tail of a swimming deer for a point-blank shot. But there would be no trophy for Emerson, only the sensation of reverting to boyhood.[10]

This excursion would not be the last time the Philosophers' Camp held counsel. The group formed an Adirondack club, purchased 22,500 acres, and built a retreat on the site. The club fell into abeyance, however, after Stillman moved to Europe and the Civil War began.[11] The only memory of the Philosophers' Camp would be Stillman's painting, showing Agassiz and Wyman engaged in their dissections on one side, a party of hunters standing on the other, and Emerson leaning on a staff between the two groups. Although Stillman's painting portrayed the events of the camp, it also recapitulated the acts by which middle-class men annexed the wilderness through hunting and natural history.

More renowned than Stillman as an Adirondack artist was Arthur Fitzwilliam Tait, who painted hunting and fishing scenes from the 1850s to the 1870s. Tait, an obscure English lithographer who had immigrated to New York City in 1850, initially painted the same heroic frontiersmen in bright red shirts and buckskin trousers that had made Charles Deas and William Ranney famous. Tait himself appeared in a photograph aiming a rifle and wearing a fringed buckskin tunic that he had probably borrowed from Ranney; Tait liked this image of himself so well that he made it the central figure in his *On the Warpath,* a frontier scene painted in 1851. Critics, not surprisingly, felt that Tait's work lacked originality, and Tait found it expedient to switch from painting the clichéd frontier hunter to painting his middle-class cousin, the gentleman hunter, who had not been accorded his place in art.[12]

In addition to gentlemen hunters, Tait painted their quarry. Tait's depictions

Arthur Fitzwilliam Tait outfitted in buckskins, ca. 1860s. This print was probably made from a tintype. Courtesy of the Adirondack Museum, Blue Mountain Lake, New York.

of dead quail and partridges "have made his name famous in the land," noted an antebellum reviewer, while another commented that Tait's game bird illustrations "have become a kind of necessity to every well-ordered room." Part of Tait's success was his realism. His secret for obtaining the proper texture for feathers and fur was to wrap a piece of silk around his finger and roll it on the paint after it had become partly dry. Tait also prefigured trompe l'oeil by painting shadows on a neutral background in his dead-game still-life portraits.[13]

Tait's star rose quickly. In 1852 he was elected to the National Academy of Design, and although he was considered too commercial by some of his peers, he became a full member of the National Academy six years later. Currier and Ives also began reproducing Tait's dead-game still lifes. Between 1852 and 1864, forty-two of his paintings were made into lithographs (most of them hunting and fishing scenes or dead-game studies), making Tait the most prolific of Currier and Ives artists. Such reproductions sold for between twenty-five cents and three dollars apiece, offering a cheap, efficient way to market art to middle-class men who had begun to take up sport hunting.[14]

Tait was not alone as a hunting artist. In 1832 the Doughtys, in addition to their lithographs in the *Cabinet of Natural History and American Rural Sport,* issued prints depicting American game birds at $1.25 apiece. In the 1850s illustrated anthologies of American hunting and angling appeared in *Gleason's Pictorial Drawing-Room Companion* and in *Ballou's Sportsman's Portfolio of American Field Sports.* Currier and Ives produced some 140 prints devoted to American hunting, camping, trapping, wild animals, and dead-game studies, less than a third of which were derived from Tait's work.[15]

Tait, however, became the prince of hunting artists by gleaning for himself the secrets of nature. Tait lived the "real hunter's life," noted a critic in 1858, having ventured into the "primeval forests" of the Adirondack region to gather "spoils of deer antlers, heads and legs" to carry back to his studio. Despite his English birth, Tait painted "thoroughly American" scenes and "loves nature and hunts her out, with gun and brush in hand."[16]

It was ironic that an Englishman who would have been ineligible to hunt in his own land could become the outstanding painter of American hunting scenes. Unlike Henry William Herbert, for whom hunting reinforced an aristocratic identity, however, Tait, a commoner, had no reservations about befriending the American middle class, nor did middle-class Americans have reservations about befriending Tait. Through hunting, natural history, and art, Tait made himself as much an American Native as American hunters themselves.

It is nevertheless true that virtually no American sporting art—apart from depictions of frontier scenes—lacked an English pedigree. Tait was called "the American Landseer" because of his stylistic borrowing from Sir Edwin Henry Landseer, the great English animal painter. Tait's paintings, however, tended to depict animals in realistic postures and in natural settings, reflecting a more democratic, middle-class sentiment than the posed nobility of Landseer's animals.[17]

In another respect, too, American hunting art differed from that of England: American hunting art, including Tait's, tended to lack domestic and sexual imagery. English sporting art often depicted hunters bringing game home to their families or encountering nubile women in the field (thus merging the sexual and sporting connotations of *venerie*). As Ruth Irwin Weidner notes, such imagery was rare in American hunting art. American artists preferred to depict hunters in the act of tracking, shooting, or reposing in camp with their fellows.[18]

By depicting the hunter's separation from women, family, and community in the quest for game, American hunting art reflected the middle-class man's separation from women, family, and community in the quest for fortune. The feminine, however, was not absent in American hunting art. Given the ubiquitous portrayal of American nature as virgin female, American hunting art might be said to have represented the metaphorical wedding of hunter and nature. This union, seemingly holy and chaste, defined hunters as American Natives, every bit as wedded to nature as Indians or farmers (husbandmen) had been before them.

Tait bartered his last painting—an Adirondack scene with deer—for his gravestone (he died in 1905), but he was followed by a long line of American hunting and wildlife artists. Even Winslow Homer, perhaps the most outstanding American exponent of naturalism, took up the Adirondack theme, painting scenes that exhibited less joie de vivre than Tait's. Thomas Eakins, Albert Bierstadt, William de la Montagne Cary, and a host of others also painted hunting scenes, although Arthur Burdett Frost became America's best-known hunting artist in the late nineteenth and early twentieth centuries. His impressionistic forest scenes showing hunters in the act of shooting, together with the dead-game portraits of a new generation of still-life painters, kept alive the old themes of individualism, chivalry, and martial vigor.[19]

As in England, hunting scenes became common motifs in America's late nineteenth-century material culture as well, appearing on patent medicines, whiskey labels, musical scores, glass pitchers, pottery plates, powder horns, ammunition boxes, and guns.[20] Still grander displays of hunting motifs appeared on the regal dining room sideboards of the wealthy.

Intricately carved, sometimes more than nine feet tall, and as wide as seven feet, sideboards displayed dead game and hunting scenes with rococo flair. Although the style originated in Europe, immigrant artisans began carving Americanized versions in the mid-nineteenth century. Depicted on a sideboard's multiple panels might be hunting dogs, guns, powder horns, dead rabbits, partridges, quail, ducks, geese, pheasants, deer strung up by their hind legs, Indian hunters holding bows, and, atop those, the American eagle perched on the union shield.[21]

The sideboard, like the sporting cabinet, was a shrine to manliness and an aesthetic gender covenant. As Kenneth Ames argues, the sideboard suggested that man's role was to hunt (and to negotiate the world beyond the home) and woman's role was to cook (and to render domestic and edible that which had been wild and alien). By dominating the dining room—the only room in the house where the family routinely (and ritually) assembled—the sideboard attested to the image of men as robust hunters, bountiful providers, and liaisons with nature.[22]

Arbiters of taste might bespeak the ethic of domesticity, reminding Americans in 1878 that "the perpetual reminder of dead flesh and murderous propensities is not agreeable at table," but such critics did not hold the upper hand.[23] With or without sideboards, middle-class American men continued to surround themselves with images that recalled the moral vigor, chivalry, and manliness of the American Native.

After Tait and Stillman had made camping and hunting in the Adirondacks a suitable pastime for philosophers and professionals alike, it was but a short step for Rev. William H. H. Murray to make the Adirondacks into a religion. After publication in 1869 of Murray's travel guide, *Adventures in the Wilderness: or, Camp-life in the Adirondacks,* whole armies of hunters, anglers, and nature lovers descended on the Adirondacks to reclaim their bond with nature.

Murray, a burly, tall man who had graduated from Yale in 1862, established himself as one of the first sporting parsons in America, and the middle-class public adored him as if it had feverishly awaited a prophet to undo the Puritan strictures on field sports. Despite the fact that the sporting parson had been condemned by Puritan settlers, Murray became, according to his fellow hunter and biographer, Harry V. Radford, America's most distinguished sportsman (with the single exception of *Forest and Stream* editor Charles Hallock).[24]

Murray's *Adventures in the Wilderness* contained little about the Adirondacks that was novel yet went through ten printings before the year was out, including a waterproof edition with travel timetables. One of the book's strengths, as Warder Cadbury points out, was its practicality. It offered tips on what to take,

Giant sideboards with hunting motifs adorned the homes of wealthy hunters. American, sculptural elements possibly executed by Joseph Alexis Bailly, 1825–83. *Sideboard,* ca. 1855. Carved walnut and Groitte d'Italie marble, 114½ × 90½ × 27½ inches (290.5 × 229.7 × 70 centimeters). Courtesy of the Cleveland Museum of Art, 1999, purchase from the J. H. Wade Fund, 1985.72.

when to go, where to stay, and how to get there and avoided slang and graphic descriptions of the death of animals. And it caused a five-year rush to the Adirondacks by "Murray's Fools," as they were called, who swamped accommodations and created an insatiable demand for guides. One reviewer remembered that Murray's writings "brought out the aboriginal" in him by teaching him "what a wretched being a puny, sickly, scholarly" man is and directing him to the wilderness in search of vigor.[25]

The initial response to the sporting parson, however, had not been encouraging. During his first assignment as a clergyman at the Congregational Church of Washington, Connecticut, in 1862, Murray once became so preoccupied with his shooting that he had to skip supper and attend his service wearing his velveteen hunting breeches and shooting jacket and carrying his gun and game bag. He apologized to his flock but found no forgiveness; these rural New Englanders seem to have had little appreciation for sport hunting.[26]

This cold reception did not dampen Murray's ardor. He first visited the Adirondacks in 1866, accompanied by his wife and another couple, and soon began publishing articles on his experiences in the papers of Meriden, Connecticut, where he had assumed another parish. These articles were collected and published as *Adventures in the Wilderness* in 1869, only six months after Murray, at twenty-nine, had accepted the prestigious ministry of the Park Street Church in Boston, the leading Congregationalist church in New England.[27]

Within five years Murray had given up his ministry and engaged himself on the lyceum circuit, bringing home some $10,000 a year. His most popular lecture theme concerned the Adirondacks; Murray delivered a single Adirondack lecture to some five hundred audiences. He would later remark that this lecture was "the most influential utterance I ever made," a statement that agreed with his new popular appellation as "Adirondack" Murray.[28]

Not everyone responded so positively to Murray's crusade. Hunting writer and humorist Thomas Bangs Thorpe called *Adventures* "twaddle" and insisted that no sportsman could read such a book without indignation. Thorpe objected more to the sensation caused by the book than to the book itself. Only the "highly-cultivated mind" can appreciate nature, wrote Thorpe, whereas Murray's Fools—especially the women among them—had "neither skill as sportsmen, nor sentiment or piety enough in their composition, to understand Nature's solitudes."[29] Murray's Fools were unfit to be American Natives.

If Murray's Fools lacked sentiment, piety, and skill as sportsmen, they could glean these traits from John Norton, the fictive guide and hero of Murray's short stories. Murray created Norton in response to a conversation with Ralph Waldo Emerson in which Emerson had declared that all tales required a heroine to bring tears and laughter. Murray thought he could appeal to the full range of emotions in readers by using a male protagonist alone, and he created John Norton to prove his point.[30]

Murray's John Norton tales, claimed Harry Radford, showed a finer appreciation for nature than those of Cooper because Murray himself had

> never been equalled by any other sportsman, naturalist, or geographer. He has seen and studied every phase of forest and frontier life. . . . Among the mountains, on the

William H. H. "Adirondack" Murray in a poster for Saranac Gloves, ca. 1878. Courtesy of the Adirondack Museum, Blue Mountain Lake, New York.

plains, and in the recesses of that interminable forest of the north, he moves as easily from scene to scene . . . as Cooper upon the sea.[31]

As hunters, woodsmen, and naturalists, Murray and his character John Norton represented the most recent links in a chain of writers, artists, and sportsmen who cultivated a tribal proprietorship over the continent. Moreover, Murray and John Norton gave readers an insular wilderness, a realm where women were superfluous. Hunting would never be more manly.

Yet in 1876 Adirondack Murray found that his wilderness was not so idyllic as it had been before his sermonizing. To feed the hordes who had come to the Adirondacks—some as hunters, some as tourists, and some as female hunters and tourists—hotels and hired men were depleting the region's stocks of game and fish. Indeed, Murray's popularization of the Adirondacks—and the resulting crisis for sportsmen—was symptomatic of processes occurring throughout the United States. With Murray and his East Coast admirers to set the standard, hunting and angling had become by the Gilded Age the most popular middle-class participatory sports in America, far exceeding baseball, football, and boxing in popularity. Yet to celebrate Americanness through hunting, Americans had to have game, something that the popularity of hunting was making problematic.

15

The Far West

On a clear spring morning in 1848, George Rutledge Gibson, former editor of the *Santa Fe Republican,* was homeward bound for Missouri over the Santa Fe Trail. A few miles from camp, his party came to a sudden halt. "Girths were at once tight-ened," wrote Gibson, "guns and pistols examined, and every thing dispensed with that could encumber or impede in a long chase."[1] Aware that Comanches had be-come the scourge of travelers, the party was well armed. The mood, however, was far from grave; buffalo had been sighted.

Cantering away "with that awkward looking and rolling motion so peculiar to this animal," the buffalo attempted to escape four horsemen dispatched by the party. As the horsemen approached the buffalo, reported Gibson, "you hear a re-port of arms, see the flash, and the herd separate[s] before the horse and rider, you hear another and another, but in the meantime horsemen and buffalo are lost to your view." Then the hunters reemerged, chasing a few cows and calves to-ward the wagons, where riflemen waited. Fearful of shooting the pursuers, the ri-flemen watched the buffalo storm past and disappear in the distant sand hills. At last the horsemen returned, chasing a lone calf. Shot in the throat at the outset, the calf ran "probably 10 miles" before succumbing. "It is remarkable," wrote Gib-son, "how tenacious of life this animal is, nothing but the most deadly shot en-abling the hunter to get his game." Buffalo hunting, figured Gibson, in its "ex-citement and interest," ranked second to no other amusement in America.[2]

Much the same story was told countless times as argonauts, emigrants, and travelers journeyed overland to Oregon and California in the 1840s and 1850s. For these men and women, the West—particularly the Great Plains—represented a realm of freedom where Americans could revel in abundance and kill whatever they wished. To cross the Plains was the adventure of a lifetime; it was a chance to demonstrate stamina, heroism, and, for men at least, chivalry and skill in the chase. Recalling his hunting exploits in 1877, Lt. Col. Richard Irving Dodge compared the Great Plains with "an ocean in its vast extent, in its monotony, and in its danger," and "like the ocean in its romance, in its opportunities for heroism, and in the fascination it exerts on all those who come within its influence."[3]

Inspired by officers like Dodge, as well as by tales of Boone and border life, men on the trail seldom passed up a chance to pursue game. Two animals, however, stood above others as symbols of empire and as foils for manliness: the grizzly, "king of the game beasts of temperate North America," and the buffalo, "monarch of the Plains."[4]

"A vast country inhabited only by buffaloes, deer, and wolves," reflected Henry Marie Brackenridge as he prepared to hunt buffalo near the Missouri River in 1811, had more resemblance "to the fictions of the 'Arabian Nights Entertainment' than to reality." When later American hunters saw buffalo, they were equally amazed. In 1843 William Clark Kennerly, nephew of William Clark of the Lewis and Clark expedition, estimated a herd he had seen at a million head. "The pounding of their hoofs," he wrote, "sounded like the roar of a mighty ocean, surging over the land and sweeping everything before it."[5] The buffalo inspired awe; it represented American nature at its most sublime.

To vanquish the buffalo was not only to capture a piece of sublimity but also to make oneself an American Native, lord of a continent. Like Daniel Boone, or Kit Carson, or Jedediah Smith, immigrant hunters claimed the continent with guns before they claimed it with plows. Whereas farmers, through their laborious cultivation of the land, had gained the right to dispossess hunters in earlier times, in the nineteenth century hunters, too, became imperial claimants.

In their passion to do battle with the noble beast, chivalrous hunters of the Far West all but forgot the republican shibboleth of self-restraint. "Many of these fellows, who carry fire-arms," recalled Franklin Langworthy in his 1855 memoir of his journey to the Far West, "are so senseless or reckless, and withal so eager for sport, that, rather than lose a chance for a shot, they will discharge their pieces, no matter if they fire in the direction of the whole train." Often, reported Langworthy, he himself had been the hunter's game, bullets having "several times whistled past me, sent from the rifle of some straggling sportsman."[6]

In fact, hunting accidents were rampant on the trail. In the course of a buffalo hunt, reported the Quaker forty-niner Charles Edward Pancoast, "one man, in attempting to take his Rifle from the pommel, discharged it, the ball entering his shoulder; another put a ball through the neck of his Horse, a third was thrown, and

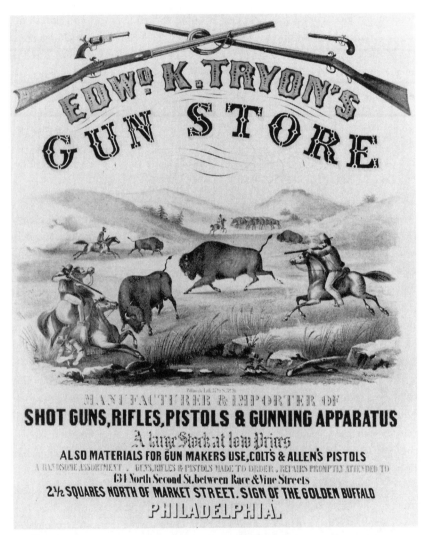

Eager sportsmen pursue buffalo in this antebellum poster for Edward K. Tryon's Gun Store.
From Charles Zimmerling, *History of a Business Established 100 Years Ago* (Philadelphia, 1911).
Courtesy of the Hagley Museum and Library, Wilmington, Delaware.

his Horse ran away with all his equipment and was never recovered." Pancoast's party succeeded, for all their troubles, in getting but two buffalo. No less embarrassed was the party of Heinrich Lienhard while on their way from St. Louis to Sutter's Fort in 1846. "Of the five men on horseback" engaged in a buffalo hunt,

> two had somersaulted, with one of them also being injured. Mr. Hoppe, who was so sure of his luck, got off worst of all. He lost his horse, reins, and saddle, as well as Hermann's pistol, and he himself was bruised from being dragged on the ground. It all turned out this way because we didn't know anything about this kind of hunting.[7]

Even those who avoided disaster did not necessarily cover themselves in glory. Armed with small-bore rifles and inexperienced at hunting big game, immigrants met more frustration than success. While en route to California in 1857, William Audley Maxwell reported that the men in his party scoured the countryside in search of game, but "our lack of experience and scarcity of proper equipment . . . were against the chance." Although the men fired repeatedly at a group of buffalo, "not one showed a sign of having been hit."[8]

Other immigrants were more successful, much to the surprise of wives. Seeing their men return from a hunt, Mary Stuart Bailey and the women of her party "thought they were making believe they had got meat." Observing blood on the hands of the men, the women realized their mistake. The men "had killed one & brought as much [meat] as they could," recorded Bailey. Eating buffalo that night, the men cracked jokes and told stories of the hunter's life. "I never saw men more excited," she wrote.[9]

Equally excited to engage buffalo were English sportsmen. Though for George Frederick Augustus Ruxton, a former English officer who ventured to the Great Plains in the 1830s, killing buffalo was "too wholesale a business to afford much sport," a fellow English sportsman, Sir St. George Gore, relished the buffalo hunt. Between 1854 and 1857, Gore roamed with fifty well-bred dogs through the wilds of Colorado, Wyoming, Montana, and the Dakotas, accompanied by a six-mule wagon full of English armaments and two wagons of fishing tackle. During his tour, Gore slaughtered two thousand buffalo, sixteen hundred elk and deer, and one hundred bears.[10]

When Plains Indians complained of Gore's slaughter, the regional Indian agent bitterly asked his superiors in St. Louis what he could "do against so large a number of men coming into a country like this so very remote from civilization?" The government toyed with the idea of confiscating Gore's trophy heads but took no action.[11]

For the English, to hunt buffalo was as much an act of imperialism as it was for Americans. English hunters did not necessarily have territorial designs on American soil, but they equated cultural and political mastery with accomplishment in the chase. In the carnage they wrought, Englishmen sought to prove themselves superior to lesser hunters throughout the world.

This pride made English hunters a target for ridicule by their American cousins, who contended that Americans were the greatest hunters in the world. Indicative of this conflict was the plight of Sir George C. G. F. Berkeley, a member of Parliament and sporting writer who toured the Far West in the 1850s with Capt. Randolph Barnes Marcy. Fairly or unfairly, Berkeley found himself pilloried in the *Spirit of the Times* for having demanded special railroad accommodations for his dogs and for expecting to find his buffalo in Westchester County, New York.[12]

A month later the *Spirit of the Times*, not satisfied with earlier barbs, belittled Berkeley for (supposedly) having pronounced himself the first man ever to shoot a charging buffalo. "When a positive misstatement is made regarding one of our noblest American sports," inveighed the *Spirit*'s editor, "we are contemptibly indifferent to our duty if we do not set matters right." The editor reckoned that shooting deer in English game parks while hiding in a cart pulled by donkeys— an experience Berkeley had written about—was Berkeley's forte.[13]

Even as American periodicals modeled themselves on the English sporting press, they demeaned British sportsmen whose "greatest exploits" were "killing a fox or a badger" and whose servants reloaded their guns and beat the bushes to scare up game. The English hunter, claimed a correspondent in the *Spirit of the Times*, "can have but a faint idea of the exciting and frequently perilous scenes in which the American hunters engage in pursuit of wild animals that inhabit the immense forests, or the boundless prairies of the far western world."[14] Whereas immigrant hunters of the Oregon Trail qualified as American Natives, elitist British hunters did not.

If killing buffalo made men American Natives, it also had a less fortuitous result: it made them wastrels. Dr. Edwin James, a naturalist who wrote the official report of Stephen Harriman Long's expedition to the Rockies in 1819–20, reported that hunters of his party slaughtered innumerable buffalo through "wantonness and love of the barbarous sport," leaving carcasses for wolves and vultures. William Clark Kennerly's 1843 hunting party, which included the Scottish baronet Sir William Drummond Stewart, also took more buffalo than necessary for its larder, "but what man would resist the temptation when the whole earth, it seemed, was a surging, tumbling, waving mass of these animals."[15]

These early parties were outdone by those who came after the Civil War. From Chicago, St. Louis, and Kansas City, well-to-do hunters of postbellum America embarked on railroad excursions to hunt the noble buffalo. Coming upon a herd, the engineer would slow the train so that passengers could blaze away from windows and rooftops, scattering hundreds of shells from breech-loading rifles. "Many of the poor animals fall," remembered one observer, "and more go off to die in the ravines."[16] Few were retrieved, leaving the area around the tracks dotted with decaying carcasses.

That buffalo came to the brink of extinction was not primarily the fault of sport hunters. Beset by drought, competition from horse herds, and diseases contracted from European cattle, buffalo numbers had begun to dwindle in the early nineteenth century. Exacerbating this decline was the commerce in buffalo robes between traders and Plains Indians, who, according to Josiah Gregg, killed between one hundred and one thousand buffalo for each one killed by whites in the 1830s. Frequently leaving carcasses to rot, Indian hunters exchanged robes at Bent's Fort in southeastern Colorado (and elsewhere) for as little as ten cups of sugar apiece in 1858.[17]

The death blow to buffalo came with the hide trade of the 1870s, which was made possible by tanning processes invented in Germany and adopted by New York factories. Once the transcontinental railroad had made hide shipments to eastern markets cheap and fast, hide hunters—generally white Americans, not Indians—descended on the buffalo. Hunting buffalo was a dirty, hard way to make a living, but it could be lucrative. Successful hunters killed as many as three hundred a day.[18]

Too heavy to carry to market, the meat from these animals moldered on the Great Plains, together with the notions of American chivalry and self-restraint. Where once the buffalo had symbolized all that was best in American culture, now it symbolized all that was worst about it. In the years following the great slaughter, bone pickers cleaned up the mess, sending millions of skulls, ribs, vertebrae, and leg bones to fertilizer factories.

Another animal could never mark the hunter as wastrel no matter how many one killed: the bear. Alongside the buffalo, the bear seemed to be the noblest of game. To hunting author William Post Hawes, the black bear was "Sir Bruin," who walked at a "thoughtful and philosophical" pace on his way to a rendezvous with "cold Diana." But it was the grizzly of the Far West—the biggest, strongest, bravest animal of the continent—that stood "ready to repel any invasion of his hereditary domain," wrote Josiah Gregg in the 1830s.[19] The ennoblement of the

If buffalo had come to symbolize all that was best about Americans, they had also come to symbolize all that was worst. L. W. Aldrich, *The Great and Cruel Slaughter of Buffaloes in the Years 1867 & 8 — from memory by L.W.A.*, n.d. (oil, 16 × 26 inches). Courtesy of the Joslyn Art Museum, Omaha, Nebraska; lent by the Omaha Public Library.

bear had proceeded so far by 1850 that the grizzly graced the state flag and state seal of California when it entered the Union.

"If you kill a bear," wrote a Californian (with tongue only partly in cheek) in 1861,

> it is a triumph worthy enjoying; if you get killed yourself, some of the newspapers will give you a friendly notice; if you get crippled for life, you carry about you a patent of courage which may be useful in case you go into politics. . . . Besides, it has its effect upon the ladies. A 'chawed up' man is very much admired all over the world.[20]

Great bear hunters were legion in nineteenth-century America: Davy Crockett, Samuel Edwards, Wilburn Waters, Wade Hampton, George Nidever, and George Yount (for whom Yountville, California, is named), to recall a few.[21] Perhaps the greatest of them in American memory was James Capen Adams, or "Grizzly" Adams, a New Englander who came to California during the gold rush.

Though a showman and a publicity seeker in his own right, Adams, like Boone, was enshrined in legend through the efforts of a biographer. Following the precedent of John Filson for Daniel Boone, Theodore Henry Hittell used the reminiscences of Adams to write a first-person narrative with the verisimilitude of autobiography.

Having left the California gold fields in the 1850s to begin life in the pristine Sierra Nevada, Adams had become a "misanthrope," according to Hittell's narrative, a Boone-like hunter who rejected the world of men. Yet this image bore too much resemblance to the antisocial hunters of the colonial imagination, an image never fully expunged from the American consciousness. Hence Adams came to recognize his "burden of responsibility" to society and began hunting not only for himself but also for others in need, particularly Indians.[22]

Americans perceived bear hunters as chivalrous knights of the frontier. William de la Montagne Cary, *A Bare Chance,* lithograph, ca. 1870. Courtesy of the author. Photograph by Terry Firman Jr.

In addition to making himself an altruist, Adams made himself an apostle of sportsmanship. Adams "never killed game in mere wantonness," having come to the woods "to live in peace, not to levy war upon the natives of the forest." Adams chided market hunters who made "great and inexcusable waste, giving too much cause for the reproach of indiscriminate slaughter," and upbraided himself for once killing a wounded deer that had no chance of escape. Even buffalo hunting, for Adams, suffered from a "monotonous sameness." Only the grizzly seemed challenging enough to make a suitable adversary, and although Adams at first avoided the bears, he came to "consider it a point of honor to give battle in every case."[23]

By battling the noblest of beasts, Adams could escape any accusation of savagery or licentiousness. The grizzly was so seemingly fierce that it had to be killed, although only the bravest of men could accomplish such a feat. No man could feel self-reproach for such killing, especially when the duel was equal, man against bear. Upon vanquishing his opponent, Adams could exult in feeling "like Alexander sated with victory, and wishing another foe to engage, worthy of my prowess."[24]

Adams did not always relish his killing, however, and began to take animals alive, collecting a menagerie of cougars, wolves, and grizzlies. This private zoo was a profitable enterprise: Adams exhibited animals throughout the United States and, near the end of his life, contracted with P. T. Barnum to display his menagerie with the circus. Beyond profit, Adams capitulated to the ethic of domesticity. While thousands of men became American Natives through hunting, Adams demonstrated the spiritual affinity between Americans and nature without killing. His menagerie of beasts resembled the *Peaceable Kingdom* of Edward Hicks, in which humans and animals lived in harmony. In exhibiting live animals, Adams pointed the way toward the zoological gardens of the Gilded Age, urban institutions that taught Americans a nonviolent way to interact with nature. Until the twentieth century, meanwhile, bear hunters remained American heroes, men who took possession of a new realm by triumphing over the noblest of foes.

If hunting bear and buffalo made American men into American Natives, it also led to the observation that an earlier, more skillful, and more indigenous hunter had preceded the white man. Although from one perspective the hunting life of the Indian continued to be understood as indolent and uncivilized, from another perspective the Indian was recognized as the great aboriginal nimrod.

In hunting, observed the author of a history of Illinois that appeared in 1844, the Indian excelled. "No device which the ingenuity of man ever discovered, for ensnaring and destroying wild beasts, escaped his attention. He discovered, as it were by instinct, the footsteps of animals, which escaped every eye but his own, and followed them with unerring certainty through pathless forests. When he attacked his game openly, his arrow seldom erred; and when he attempted to circumvent [game] by art, it was almost impossible to escape his toils."[25]

Only "'the hunters of Kentucky'" had surpassed Indians in hunting skill, according to the author. Kentucky backwoodsmen were "disgraced by drawing blood in the killing of game; perfection in the art among them consisting in shooting so near, as to stun and bring it to the earth without shedding its blood."[26] The perfection of the hunters of Kentucky, however, was not enough to secure a lasting triumph. As white Americans cast chivalrous hunters as symbols of empire, they felt compelled time and again to prove themselves superior to Indians.

On one occasion the officers of Fort Laramie held a competition between their Indian hunter and a white hunter named Houston who lived in Colorado. For what it was worth, Houston won, despite having to hunt on his opponent's ground. In 1883 Richard Irving Dodge (now a full colonel) provided a more reasoned, if biased, appraisal of the difference between Indians and whites as hunters in *Our Wild Indians: Thirty-Three Years' Personal Experience Among the Red Men of the Great West.* Dodge recognized that the "stealth, cunning, endurance, and knowledge of the habits of the animals" made Indians the best stalkers in the world, but he believed that bad marksmanship and excitability kept them from killing as much game as white hunters.[27]

Vignettes on antebellum banknotes like this one showed the great fascination white Americans had for Indian hunters. Courtesy of the National Numismatic Collection, Smithsonian Institution, Washington, D.C.

Henry Hastings Sibley, an American Fur Company factor and friend of Henry William Herbert, Randolph Barnes Marcy, and John C. Frémont, however, knew Indian hunters best. Sibley, a frequent contributor to the *Spirit of the Times* and the first governor of Minnesota, was one of many nineteenth-century politicians who took up sport hunting to cast themselves as masters of the continent. Unlike Daniel Webster or Theodore Roosevelt, Sibley came to power as an autocrat, an imperial administrator on the Roman or English model. As an American Fur Company partner, he had been judicial officer and lawgiver for a territory as large as France, an area later divided into the states of Minnesota, Iowa, and the Dakotas.[28]

Given that Sibley's domain was initially a realm of trade rather than farming, Sibley was a perfect candidate for the expression of an imperialism based on chivalry and woodcraft in the tradition of Boone. Sibley's contemporary biographer described him as "a frontiersman and vancourier by hereditary right, ... romantic, chivalrous, and self-reliant." Like Boone, Sibley worshiped nature as "a breathing, whispering, teacher of all things good, a source of the noblest and loftiest truths." Not surprisingly, Sibley became a "superlative Nimrod," a better hunter than the Indian.[29] These traits—chivalry, a reverence for nature, and skill as a hunter—seemed to make Sibley a fitting heir to the realm of the Dakota and Ojibwa.

Unlike other Americans, Sibley had to demonstrate his right to rule to the Indians themselves. Because his empire consisted of tribes with whom he had a business relationship, Sibley had to affirm his right to rule by means other than force. If Sibley was to earn the respect of Indians, he would have to measure up in an arena that he and they understood. That arena was hunting.

Sibley took great satisfaction in recalling one of his first contests with an Indian hunter, when he and a Dakota Sioux had fired simultaneously at a bevy of ducks. Sibley figured that he had killed at least six of the eight ducks that fell, but the Sioux fixed each one to his belt. Angered at this insult, Sibley, who was "double-armed," walked over to the Sioux and took away not six, but all eight ducks. Sibley later recalled how "dashed" the Indian was at his "cool presumption," as if Sibley had there and then established his authority as a hunter and as a white man.[30]

Sibley's pride as a hunter would undergo further buffeting when he attached himself to mobile Sioux hunting parties in the 1840s. These parties, numbering in the hundreds, appointed "soldiers" to patrol boundaries beyond which no hunting was permitted. The boundary system allowed hunting parties to move into new areas rich in game after the previous day's hunting ground had been de-

Henry Hastings Sibley matched his hunting skills with the Dakota Sioux before the Civil War. "Henry Hastings Sibley." Photograph by Zimmerman. Courtesy of the Minnesota Historical Society, St. Paul, Minnesota.

pleted. Sibley, however, attempted to shoot beyond the boundary and was reprimanded by an Indian soldier who threatened to break Sibley's gun (the standard penalty for such an offense). Refraining from that, however, the soldier chose to confiscate Sibley's fur cap. Sibley reported that he had "caught" the gun as the Indian swung it down to break it and that he had threatened the Indian with a baneful look.[31] The Sioux was probably deterred not for fear of Sibley personally but for fear of alienating the American Fur Company.

In another incident, Sibley's conflict with an Indian over ducks was repeated when an Indian killed a buck that Sibley had tracked with his dog. This time the Indian kept the kill, and Sibley reported in the *Spirit of the Times* that he walked back to camp "moody and disconcerted" while the Indian smoked his pipe. Sibley added that he had since taken revenge many times by using his powerful rifle to shoot elk and deer as Indians stalked them.[32]

In his attempt to express superiority to Indians through hunting, Sibley followed English precedent. Englishmen, too, hunted alongside natives in India and Africa, attempting to establish reputations as great hunters by killing man-eating predators or elephants. Superiority in hunting became for the English an imperial wedge, an expression of their quest for political dominion.[33]

Like English colonizers in India and Africa (whose hunting exploits Sibley probably read about in the *Spirit of the Times*), Sibley relied on superb weaponry and marksmanship to awe natives. But Sibley's hunting was problematic; the American Indian was a hunter from childhood, and even practiced sportsmen often found themselves inferior to Indians in the chase. Sibley's frustrations were symptomatic of the difficulties whites had in expressing racial superiority—and by extension the right to rule—through the ritual of hunting.

As governor of Minnesota, Sibley ultimately gained nearly absolute authority over Indians. In 1862 he led the militia that captured the Santee Sioux after the Minnesota uprising. But in one sense it was the Sioux who had co-opted Sibley. They had adopted him into their tribe, giving him the name "Wah-ze-o-man-zee," or "Walker-in-the-Pines," and he had for a time dressed as a Sioux and participated in their sports and customs. Perhaps because of his adoption, Sibley's many prose accounts of Indian life were surprisingly free of moral bias.[34]

Though accused of overcharging the Sioux for supplies while serving the American Fur Company, Sibley became a critic of federal Indian policy during his tenure in state and federal politics. Like other reformers of his generation, Sibley believed that the reservation system should be abolished but based this sentiment on the belief that Indians were "a noble race, gifted with a high order of intellect, and an aptitude for acquiring knowledge fully equal to that possessed by whites."[35]

Having defeated Indians in hunting and on the battlefield, Sibley appointed himself their liege protector. The measure of the victor's nobility was the nobility of his foe. There was, to say the least, a measure of pomposity in Sibley's attempts to "help" Indians by depriving them of their land and customs, yet Sibley was no worse than other reformers of the time.

Another campaign on behalf of sport hunting came from army officers of the Midwest and Far West. As lead actors in the drama of empire, and as frequent contributors to sporting journals, army officers were pivotal figures in buttressing the connection between hunting, natural history, and empire. By becoming the first whites to learn the geography and natural history of new territories, by conquering animals and aboriginal peoples, and by serving as models of manliness and chivalry, army officers fashioned themselves into American Natives.

The usual justification for officers' hunting excursions was to procure meat for enlisted men at no cost to the army, but sport was no secondary consideration. Maj. George A. McCall, stationed in Florida and Texas before the Civil War, commented that many days were "pleasantly passed" in deer hunting, "one day differing but little from another." As early as the 1830s, the officers at Fort Gibson, Indian Territory, formed a hunting club and sent reports of their activities to the *American Turf Register and Sporting Magazine*, while others sent hunting, travel, and battle narratives to the *Spirit of the Times*. Even officers not enrolled in hunting clubs sometimes chose sides for team hunting competitions, with losers providing winners a champagne dinner.[36]

Like the English, American officers saw their skill as hunters as emblematic of their right to possess the continent. Lt. Col. William H. Emory, on reconnaissance in New Mexico during the Mexican War, expressed astonishment that Mexicans left unmolested the flocks of sandhill cranes and geese within gunshot distance of their settlements. "No fact proves the indolence and incapacity of the Mexican[s] for sport or for war more glaringly," concluded Emory, than their failure to hunt these wildfowl.[37]

Meanwhile, Capt. Randolph Barnes Marcy, perhaps the most famous of the frontier Dragoons and pathfinders, drew up a utilitarian rationale for sport hunting among soldiers. The boredom of camp life, reasoned Marcy, was "detrimental" to the "physical and moral condition" of the men, who were to be encouraged to take up the chase as an antidote. Marcy's arguments bore originality in relation to the army itself, but he was reiterating notions about the effect of hunting on sedentary men that already pervaded the sporting press.[38]

While admitting that old-school drills and dress parades were beneficial, Marcy preached that hunting could teach Indian methods and tactics so necessary for success in the West. "The union of discipline with the individuality, self-reliance, and rapidity of locomotion of the savage is what we should aim at," he wrote, adding that an army "of well-disciplined hunters will be the most efficient of all others against the only enemy we have to encounter within . . . our vast possessions."[39] Unspoken was the fact that individuality, self-reliance, and mobility were not solely characteristics of Indians; they were traits of American Natives.

Those who hunted regularly on frontier outposts, however, were more often officers than enlisted men. Though Elizabeth Custer recalled that hunting broke down the unwritten rule against officers fraternizing with their men, officers often used enlisted men as hunting attendants, casting them in a role equivalent to English servants or beaters. Even when officers and enlisted men hunted together, officers brought down more game using expensive hunting rifles and fowling pieces than enlisted men using army-issue short-range carbines. Officers also distinguished themselves by keeping well-bred hunting dogs, including greyhounds for coursing antelope, wolves, and jackrabbits.[40]

The number of dogs kept by George Custer peaked at around forty in the

1860s. Elizabeth Custer remembered that the dogs howled as Custer blew his hunting horn "until they reached the same key." Custer, like other officers, used his dogs in wolf hunting, which offered a spectacle resembling English fox hunting when wives were brought out to observe the proceedings.[41] Like the English, Custer and his fellow officers made hunting a lesson in elitism, causing the image of the American Native to drift away from the egalitarianism of a Boone or Bumppo.

In July of 1874, while Custer led the Black Hills expedition, the *Chicago Inter-Ocean* praised his well-bred hounds and horses and claimed he had a reputation for being the best shot and best sportsman in the army. Of all forms of sport, Custer thought buffalo hunting the most "manly," presaging the buffalo's promotion to the rank of faunal emblem of American identity.[42]

On a mission to determine the whereabouts of the Cheyenne in the 1860s, Custer, eager as any emigrant to kill a buffalo, galloped off in pursuit of an old bull, accompanied by five dogs and an orderly lagging far behind. Upon reaching the bull, Custer's ecstasy was so great that he rode alongside without firing. When the bull turned to fight, Custer's horse leaped, and Custer discharged his pistol into the horse's brain. The buffalo turned away, apparently mollified, leaving Custer sprawled on the ground and disarmed. Custer was forced to walk with his dogs for several miles, searching for his men.[43]

Unbowed, Custer continued to cultivate his image as American Native by posing for photographs in a fringed buckskin hunting outfit and standing over freshly killed game. A pair of photographs by W. H. Illingworth from the Black Hills expedition of 1874 show a commanding Custer standing over a massive bear, accompanied by Bloody Knife (his favorite Indian scout), Capt. William Ludlow of the U.S. Army Corps of Engineers, and an enlisted man.[44]

The Illingworth photographs seem to testify that no army bureaucracy, no government chain of command, and no politician had awarded Custer his fame. Custer's buckskin costume suggested that his success was determined by his native abilities, which came from nature. The buckskin-clad hero of the Illingworth photographs is not only a chivalrous individualist in the Boone mold but also a man chosen by nature to rule the army, the Indian, and American nature.

Custer's men formed different opinions. George Bird Grinnell, naturalist of the Black Hills expedition, noted that the grizzly shot by Custer in the Black Hills (probably the bear in the Illingworth photographs) was a very old specimen, its teeth worn to stubs. A private wrote in his diary that the men believed it to be a cinnamon bear but agreed that it was a grizzly because Custer said so.[45]

Custer also took an interest in taxidermy, bragging that he had preserved the antlers, head, neck, skin, and hooves of an elk fifteen hands high so that it could be mounted in a pose "natural as life." The zoologists accompanying him, claimed Custer, appraised the elk as "the finest specimen . . . anywhere in the United States." Custer presented the trophy to his wife, but it proved too big to fit through the door and so was shipped to a hunting club in Detroit. Elizabeth received a buffalo head instead.[46]

Just as the Hobbesian hunter of the colonial imagination—the wild man in perpetual struggle with society and nature—had given way to the rugged individualist in the Boone mold, so the Boone figure had evolved into the grandiose Custer. If Boone was the Hobbesian man transformed into an ideal laissez-faire competitor, a perfect atom in a libertarian wilderness, Custer was the Hobbesian man become Darwinian. He—as his trophies seemed to prove—had triumphed over nature's adversity to become its fittest prince. Custer, like Theodore Roosevelt after him, was the dashing victor in the Darwinian struggle for survival, at least until the Little Bighorn.

Custer may be the best known army hunter because of his contributions to *Turf, Field, and Farm*—and because of the Little Bighorn—but just about all the top brass of the mid-to-late nineteenth century took up sport hunting. Army officers who became sport hunters included the most significant generals of the post–Civil War era: William Tecumseh Sherman, Philip Henry Sheridan, Nelson Appleton Miles, and George Crook.[47]

Crook was the most accomplished hunter among these men. After graduating from West Point in 1852 and assuming a post on the Pacific Coast, Crook, a tall, broad-shouldered man, spent his leisure time hunting. He was often accompanied by Indians, from whom he hoped to learn both Indian customs and the habits of game. Crook's aide and biographer, John Gregory Bourke, later observed that the taciturn general's "one great passion" was riding away with his dogs for a solitary hunt. Each year from 1878 to 1889, the year before his death, Crook journeyed into the Rockies in the fall to hunt big game. Crook had also gone hunting after the fight at Rosebud Creek in June 1876 (the only important defeat of his career), and he was hunting in the mountains, eighteen miles from his Goose Creek bivouac, when news arrived of Custer's defeat at the Little Bighorn.[48]

Crook learned tracking so well, wrote Bourke, that he became "conversant with all that is concealed in the great book of Nature" and "might readily take rank as being fully as much an Indian as the Indian himself." Bourke could not help but compare Crook with Daniel Boone in respect to his courage, his knowledge of the Indian, and his dislike of notoriety.[49] In Crook was the aura of the American Native, the man whose hunting skills and understanding of Indians made his conquests seem ordained by nature.

Crook's identification with the fauna of the West encouraged him toward the end of his life to campaign for game laws in Wyoming, although his last Wyoming hunt in 1889 was something of a slaughter. Crook's party took eighty-six antelope and thirty-eight deer, as well as an assortment of bears, coyotes, birds, and snakes, before a hunting accident that killed an enlisted man ended the binge.[50]

Crook had also become an avid naturalist, hunting butterflies and birds in the Bighorn Mountains, collecting eggs and nests, and, like Custer, learning taxidermy so that he could build his own collection of specimens. Crook studied natural history so assiduously, wrote Bourke, that he gained a "familiarity with the habits of wild animals possessed by but few naturalists."[51]

Custer, too, had become something of a naturalist, having shipped a porcupine and a cinnamon-coated black bear to the menagerie at Central Park in New York City. He also collected fossils and during the Black Hills expedition had used his best ambulance to transport his natural history collection (including reptiles, amphibians, prairie owls, a hawk, and a petrified tree trunk). Even brassy Philip Sheridan studied natural history early in his career, having taken up ornithology while stationed in Texas in the 1850s.[52]

Part of the army hunters' scientific interest in the continent can be ascribed to the efforts of the Smithsonian Institution, and its predecessor, the National Institution, to make the army into a corps of natural history collectors. But Crook and Custer were genuinely interested in their scientific studies. In collecting live and fossil "fishes, serpents, birds, crocodiles, lizards, turtles, bats, etc.," recalled Elizabeth Custer, army officers and their wives were overcome with the "strange sensation" of being "monarchs in a land which once was given up to all forms of vegetable and animal life."[53]

Through their love of hunting and natural history, army officers also cultivated a bond between themselves and elite eastern sportsmen. In the 1860s Capt. Randolph Marcy included in his memoirs, *Thirty Years of Army Life on the Border*, a section titled "Hints to Sportsmen" that gave explicit travel directions for gentlemen hunters venturing to the buffalo hunting grounds near Fort Kearney and Fort Riley. Marcy suggested that soldiers might serve as guides, a wise idea given the perils of the Great Plains. Col. Richard Irving Dodge had once come across a stalwart Sioux with a "magnificent buffalo gun" and two holstered, ivory-handled Colt revolvers; the Sioux had apparently dispatched a wealthy sportsman.[54]

Crook included in his hunting entourages congressmen, governors, and cabinet members, but Philip Sheridan put together the most spectacular assemblage of gentlemen hunters. In 1871 Sheridan organized a hunting party that included financiers Lawrence and Leonard Jerome, James Gordon Bennett Jr. of the *New York Herald* and New York Yacht Club, and an assortment of other magnates and officers. That "gallant sportsman of the plains," William "Buffalo Bill" Cody served as the group's Boone-like "guide, philosopher and friend." Buffalo Bill, however, was more fashion conscious than Boone had been, sporting a crimson shirt beneath his buckskins, and donning a sombrero.[55]

Armed like a small brigade, Sheridan's millionaires killed some six hundred buffalo in a matter of days. The sole mishap involved Buffalo Bill's horse, Buckskin Joe, who ran away after being loaned to Lawrence Jerome and ended up at Fort McPherson three days later. The following year Sheridan repeated the performance, this time with Russia's Grand Duke Alexis as guest of honor and Buffalo Bill, George Custer, and the Sioux chief Spotted Tail in attendance.[56]

What was clear from these expeditions was not just the existence of a bond between eastern and western hunters but the increasingly elitist tone of American sport hunting. The sort of hunt organized by Sheridan was neither a simple, republican pastime nor an exercise in frontier individualism. As robber barons like the Jeromes displaced Jacksonian entrepreneurs, they made sport hunting a spectacle of wealth, domination, and empire.

The connection between the gentleman sportsman and his frontier counterpart, the modest and self-reliant Boone, had become a parody of itself, if it had ever been anything else. Buffalo Bill, the new Boone, was a flashy showman whose signal hunting accomplishment was having slaughtered countless buffalo for the railroads. Neither Buffalo Bill's hunting skill, nor his code of chivalry, nor his republican virtue made him a bloodbrother to Gilded Age capitalists; his celebrity caught their attention, a celebrity hoisted high by Ned Buntline and Philip Sheridan.

16

Manly Men and Manly Women

Neither George Custer, nor Buffalo Bill, nor Phil Sheridan represented the American Native at his most majestic, imperial, and prescient; that distinction belonged to Theodore Roosevelt. Though Daniel Webster had been the first American hunter-politician and conservationist, Roosevelt became the most important hunter-politician and conservationist of the nineteenth and early twentieth centuries.

Roosevelt's love for nature, like Washington's love of truth, emerged during childhood. At age nine, he wrote "Natural History of Insects" (all insects discussed, wrote the young Roosevelt, "inhabbit [*sic*] North America"). Soon he had collected multifarious specimens and artifacts in his bedroom, calling the display the Roosevelt Museum of Natural History. As an adult Roosevelt continued his study of natural history at Harvard, planning to become a sporting naturalist of "the Audubon, or Wilson, or Baird, or Coues type" (his father had helped found the American Museum of Natural History in New York City). The dryness of academic natural history discouraged him from his ambition to become a professional naturalist, yet Roosevelt never lost his taste for the study of nature, explaining in 1918 that he could "no more explain why I like 'natural history' than why I like California canned peaches. . . . All I can say is that almost as soon as I began to read at all I began to read about the natural history of beasts and birds."[1]

To compensate for his childhood sickliness and to apply his talents in natural history—and to relive the adventures of Daniel Boone and Davy Crockett, whom he revered—Roosevelt took up sport hunting at a young age. He traveled to the Midwest to hunt with his brother upon graduation from Harvard in 1880, and in the next few years he would become a big game hunter and cattleman in the Dakota Territory. Upon his return to New York City in 1884 after a hunt for bighorn sheep, the *New York Times* reported that Roosevelt wore the fur cap and coonskin coat of a backwoodsman and carried a rifle and a shotgun.[2]

Hunting trips punctuated the greatest moments in Roosevelt's career. In 1900, after his election to the vice presidency, Roosevelt celebrated by taking a hunting trip to Colorado. Again in 1901, when notified of his ascension to the presidency after the death of William McKinley, Roosevelt was hunting in the Adirondacks.[3]

Like his uncle, Robert Barnwell Roosevelt, who had presided over the New York Society for the Protection of Game in the 1870s and helped create the U.S. Fisheries Commission, Roosevelt became an ardent conservationist. His founding in 1887 of the Boone and Crockett Club (named for the hunters he most admired) and his alliance with George Bird Grinnell, crusading editor of *Forest and Stream,* represented a breakthrough for those who wished to save wildlife. Though Roosevelt's views would turn more toward utility than preservation after his acquaintance with Gifford Pinchot, a prominent American forester, his utilitarianism was employed in the service of his love for nature and hunting.[4]

In the 1880s and 1890s, Roosevelt demonstrated his affinity for nature by writing a trilogy of hunting and natural history books (*Hunting Trips of a Ranchman, Ranch Life and the Hunting Trail,* and *The Wilderness Hunter*), and a multivolume history called *The Winning of the West.* True to the cult of Boone, Roosevelt made the chivalrous, self-reliant hunter the central hero of American history. Though noting, realistically, that backwoodsmen were farmers as well as hunters, he added that "a race of peaceful, unwarlike farmers would have been helpless before such foes as the red Indians." Hunting had made American backwoodsmen stern and strong: "no form of labor is harder than the chase, and none is so fascinating or so excellent as a training-school for war."[5]

"The virility, clear-sighted common sense and resourcefulness of the American people," Roosevelt proclaimed, "is due to the fact that we have been a nation of hunters and frequenters of the forest, plains, and waters." For Roosevelt, hunting embodied the essence of "the strenuous life," without which the nation would devolve into irrelevancy on the world stage. In Roosevelt's eyes, there were two types of men and two types of nation: strong, courageous hunters and weakly cowards. Those who opposed war with Spain in 1898 fell under the latter category; they were men "who fear the strenuous life, who fear the only national life which is really worth leading." Whether they suffered from timidity, laziness, ignorance, or overcivilization, argued Roosevelt, these weaklings would allow "bolder and stronger peoples" to "pass us by, and . . . win for themselves the domination of the world."[6]

"On the Trail. Mr. Roosevelt hunted in all parts of the country from southwestern Texas to British Columbia, killing every kind of big game common to the West." From Theodore Roosevelt, *Hunting the Grisly and Other Sketches. Homeward Bound Edition* (New York, 1910). Photograph by Terry Firman Jr.

Having absorbed the manly virtues and predatory imperialism that saturated the literature of Boone, Roosevelt—probably not by accident—began hunting in foreign lands not long after he supported expansion into Cuba and the Philippines. "Our greatest statesmen," Roosevelt once wrote, "have always been those who believed in the nation—who had faith in the power of our people to spread until they should become the mightiest among the peoples of the world." If George Armstrong Custer had himself photographed in his buckskins to show himself as a man chosen by nature to rule the army, the Indian, and American nature, Roosevelt in buckskins was the man who had designs on other parts of the world as well.[7]

Among the great adventures of Roosevelt's life was his expedition to Africa in 1909, a year after he had left the presidency. Roosevelt conceived of this expedition as a form of play, as he told his son Kermit, yet he also wished to serve science. Designated the Roosevelt-Smithsonian Expedition, the party's task was to collect specimens of African mammals for the Smithsonian Institution. In committing himself to science, Roosevelt rededicated his sport to the advancement of humanity.[8]

Inspired in part by Roosevelt's example, dozens of other hunters consecrated themselves to science by offering to collect specimens for the Smithsonian. At times the Smithsonian was bombarded by sport hunters who sent photographs of unusual animals they had killed or offered specimens that the institution did not want. On the whole, however, the alliance between sportsmen and the Smithsonian (and other scientific organizations) was beneficial to both sides. While hunters got to dress themselves in the cloak of science, the Smithsonian received valuable specimens and data on species variation from exotic locales. "I think it good policy," wrote an assistant secretary of the Smithsonian in a 1911 memorandum, "to encourage" collecting by "hunters who have become interested in the Museum."[9]

As the era of the great American buffalo hunt ended, the era of the great scientific safari began. Bearing papers attesting to their appointment as "Collaborator in Zoology" by the Smithsonian, wealthy hunter-naturalists gained entrée into exotic hunting grounds otherwise closed to foreigners. The American Museum of Natural History in New York City and Harvard's Museum of Comparative Zoology in Cambridge also worked closely with wealthy sportsmen eager to serve science.[10]

Despite the rhetoric of conservation, the slaughter wrought by sportsmen in foreign lands was often as immense as it had been on the Great Plains. "I have killed six Lions," bragged Roosevelt in 1909, "two Rhinos — both of which

charged viciously —, two Giraffes, one Hippo, together with various kinds of antelope, and Zebra, a Waterhog, *and so forth* [emphasis added]." "And so forth"
added up to two hundred animals by November 11, 1909. In defense of the slaughter, Roosevelt explained that "five-sixths" of these were to be preserved for the
Smithsonian and the rest were to be eaten.[11]

Unlike their English counterparts, Americans did not pave the way for colonization of lands they hunted, but they served the cause of empire in a different
way. Through far-flung expeditions that received coverage in books, magazines,
and newspapers, hunters like Roosevelt sought to demonstrate the scientific,
sporting, and racial superiority of Americans. The formula that had given Americans cultural propriety over North America now seemed to make them masters
of the globe. Americans were not political masters of the globe, yet in flying the
American flag over Africa, or in standing triumphant over a cape buffalo, Roosevelt and his fellow hunter-naturalists attested to the global superiority of white
Americans.[12]

Had Indians taken note of this American pride in hunting, they might have
choked on the irony in it. The very men who long ago had claimed the continent
from Indian hunters through farming—and who continued to urge Indians to
take up the plow—had come to see themselves as a hunting people. For Theodore
Roosevelt and thousands of others, hunting was the root of Americanness. Recall
that, according to Roosevelt, backwoods hunters were "emphatically products
native to the soil," men who had "lost all remembrance of Europe and all sympathy with things European." These men had been the first to "become Americans, one in speech, thought, and character." So far had Roosevelt reversed the
farmer-over-hunter dialectic that when "excess" Indian lands became available
under the terms of the Dawes Severalty Act of 1887, he seized upon them as potential game preserves.[13] Though animals were not to be hunted on these preserves, they were intended for the propagation of game species that, seemingly,
had made Americans a great people.

Lest we read these events exclusively through the lenses of hypocrisy or racism,
it is important to consider that excess Indian lands, under the terms of the Dawes
Act, would have been sold to private interests had they not become government
property. With the Great Plains gobbled up by farmers and ranchers, newly available Indian lands became prime candidates for preserves because they were cheap,
unspoiled, and potentially large, not simply because they were the lands of Indians. Nevertheless, irony permeated the events that saw the transformation of In-

As the era of the buffalo hunt ended, wealthy Americans sought big game in other parts of the globe. Col. E. A. McAlpin's Trophy Lodge at Brandreth Lake. Photograph by H. M. Beach, ca. 1912. Courtesy of the Adirondack Museum, Blue Mountain Lake, New York.

dian lands into game preserves, especially since Roosevelt believed that Indians had lost their claim to ancestral lands because they had been hunters.[14]

Conservationists missed the farce of making Indian lands into game preserves because they were blinded by romantic nationalism. Through Roosevelt and his fellows, hunting became more than the mystical source of American manliness; hunting became the mystical source of American national—and racial—identity. Now Roosevelt's noble, light-skinned race of American hunters spoke of world dominion.

For all his imperial bluster, the multifaceted Roosevelt remained a man of the people, a man who treated hunting guides not as servants but as equals. "I remember," wrote Kermit Roosevelt, "how amazed some were at the lack of formality in his relationship with the members of the [African] expedition." "Father," he added, "treated everyone with the same courtesy and simplicity, whether it was the governor of the Protectorate or the poorest Boer settler."[15]

While hunting cougars in Colorado, Roosevelt was equally democratic. There was no "stiffness and formality" in the president's demeanor, recalled guide John B. Goff. Goff's feelings for Roosevelt "grew warmer" every day until, at the trip's end, he felt he was parting with a "dear friend." Roosevelt's "demeanor, his manliness, his generosity, his big noble heart, his simplicity," reported Goff, "make him a companion in the flesh worthy the company of a king."[16]

This democratic bent, even if it made him "worthy the company of a king," made Roosevelt popular as a man and as a president. If he became at times a bully on the international stage, he remained a friend of the people, a man who would rein in the tyrannous reach of monopolists and robber barons. Although his willingness to regulate business may have fallen short of what others desired, he understood that runaway individualism had to be restrained by the state. "A great State," he explained, "can not rely on mere unrestricted individualism, any more than it can afford to crush out all individualism."[17] By restricting the individual rights of the powerful few, the individual rights of the many would be saved.

And saved these individual rights had to be, if America was to remain America. The crusade to preserve individualism seemed imperative in a nation transformed by corporations, monopolies, and bureaucracies. As late as 1870 the average American factory had eight employees. By 1890 the average factory had twenty employees, and factories with one hundred or more employees were common (some employed more than ten thousand). Such changes primarily affected working-class Americans, who were often consigned to unskilled manufacturing jobs throughout their lives, yet middle-class Americans were also affected. The individualism of the Age of Jackson was being swallowed up by corporate bureaucracies and urban anonymity. More and more middle-class men found themselves-working as clerks and salesmen, jobs that seemed to compromise one's manliness every bit as much as they had in earlier decades. Meanwhile the Civil War, which, after the Revolution, had been America's second great age of manliness, receded into the misty past. Even spirituality seemed to retreat in a society run on principles of efficiency, science, and bigness.[18]

As Henry Adams saw it, the "dynamo"—the huge Corliss engine that produced the electricity for machinery at the 1876 Centennial International Exhibition in Philadelphia—had become more powerful than the Virgin Mary, who long ago had inspired peasants to build cathedrals like Chartres. Machines and corporations had come to dominate the world, while humans had become impotent and God distant.[19]

In championing game laws and wildlife preserves, Theodore Roosevelt sought to save the vestiges of American individualism in the age of the dynamo. In doing so, he found himself enmeshed in irony. Only by restricting the individual's right to hunt could hunting be saved as a rite of individualism. And only by strengthening government could the individual's right to hunt be effectively restricted. Government, law, and bureaucracy were the tools with which hunting and wilderness were to be saved.

Having hunted in South Dakota and the Adirondacks, Roosevelt had come to believe that wilderness hunting demanded more "hardihood, self-reliance, and resolution" than hunting on a private game preserve, which was a "dismal parody." Private preserves were like monopolies, controlled by autocrats who took game at their pleasure. No amount of private preserves would sustain the character of the nation; public preserves were imperative. During his presidency, Roosevelt accordingly tripled the size of the National Forest System, set aside fifty-one wildlife refuges by executive order, and created corps of experts and agents to administer them.[20]

Roosevelt did not usher in a utopian era of wildlife and wildlands management, but he did establish a precedent for federal environmental oversight. It was this precedent—not the limited acreage that Roosevelt actually set aside—that would play a critical role in saving wildlife, habitat, and hunting on behalf of the democratic many, or at least the many who could afford hunting licenses and travel expenditures.

As naturalist, sport hunter, and devotee of the cult of Boone, Roosevelt was the supreme American Native, the indigenous man who seemed to incarnate the spartan, manly virtues of American nature. With his ascension to the presidency, the campaign to make America a nation of hunters reached its acme and gave way to a new campaign to ensure that America would remain a nation of hunters. What Roosevelt may not have realized was that, in the process, he had undermined the manliness of the sport he endorsed.

In October 1905 two hunters took a railroad from Utica, New York, to the Adirondack Mountains, then boarded a steamboat for the twelve-mile passage across Fourth Lake, and arrived at their lodgings in time for dinner. The following day, accompanied by guides, the hunters—their "packs laden with provisions and ammunition for a week's stay in the woods"—hiked eight miles through thick forest, then another three miles through mountains to Lime Kiln Lake. There the guides transferred the gear into boats and rowed it and the hunters across the lake, after which the party hiked another five miles "over steep mountains." When "it seemed as though [they] could possibly go no further," the hunters arrived at a "rude but comfortable log cabin" where the guides prepared flapjacks, bacon, and coffee.[21]

Early the next morning, the hunters embarked on a deer hunt. Coming upon a buck with a nine-point rack, one of the hunters fired, but the deer bounded away, and the hunter's "heart sank." But blood on the leaves where the deer had stood proved the shot to be true, and the deer's carcass was found a short distance away. The guide, who lugged the deer three miles back to the cabin, estimated its weight at 175 pounds. "To say I was overjoyed," remarked the successful hunter, "would draw it mildly.... My rifle had done its work well."[22]

This narrative, appearing in *Field and Stream* in 1906, was typical of the genre: first came the pilgrimage by rail and steamboat, then the long tramp in the woods, and finally the successful hunt. What made this story different was the fact that

Though women of the Gilded Age participated in hunting, they did not renounce their femininity. From *Outdoor Life*, July 1902. Courtesy of the Denver Public Library, Denver, Colorado. Photograph by Rhoda Pollack.

its author and her companion were women. Having listened to the hunting tales of the "sterner sex," Emma Preston had decided that she must bag a deer.

Like Preston, innumerable women of the late nineteenth and early twentieth centuries demanded that they be included in the society of hunters. Some accompanied their husbands into the woods, whereas others went alone or with female companions, but all seemed to agree that "there seems no reason why women should not enjoy [hunting] as much as men do; and derive lasting benefit from the carefree and health-giving experiences of camp life."[23]

The desire to hunt, claimed Mrs. Arthur F. Rice, was as instinctive in women as in men. "Two or three generations of hunting blood asserted themselves in my veins," she recalled, when she witnessed "a beautiful buck" swimming across an Adirondack lake. Though too far away for a good shot, Mrs. Rice "registered a vow then and there that I would at least shoot at a deer before leaving the mountains." Upon fulfilling her vow a few days later—and bagging her deer—she realized that she "had nerves, and that they were shaking a little" (men called this "buck fever"). Women, she added, "have a right to tremble, or even faint, after the excitement is all over."[24]

At the same time that these huntresses got their deer, others, inspired perhaps by Annie Oakley, the celebrated markswoman of Buffalo Bill's Wild West Show, joined trapshooting clubs. Women's trapshooting clubs, reported the *Illustrated Sunday Magazine* in 1914, had appeared in Wilmington, Philadelphia, White Plains, Minneapolis, Youngstown, Chicago, and Brunswick, Ontario, and more were forming. Members of the Chicago team claimed to be the best shots in the world, having broken 199 of 250 clay pigeons during a match with the Wilmington club.[25]

This claim was hardly a new one for Americans. Men's rifle teams engaged annually in matches with foreign marksmen at Creedmore, a rifle range on Long Island, to determine who was the best in the world, and thousands of male trapshooters likewise competed at American conventions and club meets. *Country Club Life* reported in 1914 that some two hundred thousand Americans had taken up trapshooting, enrolling in some three thousand clubs, thus satisfying (if vicariously) their innate urge to hunt. For women, however, to learn to shoot demonstrated "a complete reversal of the hereditary and instinctive antipathy to firearms" and offered "a spectacular illustration of woman's changed attitude toward her sphere in life."[26]

This observation was not entirely true. Frontier women had been hunting for generations. According to oral tradition, Rebecca Boone had hunted in Daniel's absence, having once bagged a deer in addition to her own horse. This male taunt belied the fact that frontier women could and did hunt just as successfully as men. Women of frontier Indiana, noted William C. Smith, "could handle the rifle with great skill, and bring down game in the absence of their husbands." Recalling her antebellum childhood in northern New York State, Livonia Stanton Emerson similarly testified that "it was not long after we moved into this wilderness before father brought mother a very nice rifle." Mother "took lots of game with that rifle," added Emerson, and even taught her ten-year-old son to hunt deer at night.[27]

For women of the backwoods, hunting was not so much a sport as a means of subsistence. Emerson's mother may have taken pleasure in the chase, yet like her male counterparts, she killed deer for the skillet. Her hunting differed dramatically from that of middle-class and elite women of the late nineteenth and early twentieth centuries, who hunted first for sport and second (if at all) for food.

It is hard to say how many middle-class and elite women gave up their "instinctive antipathy to firearms" to hunt deer or shoot clay pigeons. As sport hunting's popularity peaked among men, however, women—judging from their contributions to sporting periodicals—began to take interest. Women did so, as did men, because shooting was fun; hunting allowed women to engage in activities otherwise off-limits, and it seemed invigorating and healthy.

Thus Frances Roe, whose husband was an army officer stationed in the West after the Civil War, dismissed wives who complained about the monotony of the frontier as "stay-at-homes who sit by their own fires day after day and let cobwebs gather in brain and lungs." Mrs. Roe suggested that these "fault-finders" and "gossips" learn to ride and shoot and join their husbands in field sports, although she acknowledged that she preferred fishing to pursuing a "splendid animal running for his life."[28]

Mrs. Roe was eager to participate in field sports partly because she enjoyed them but also because, outfitted in the feminized tunic of a West Point cadet and riding sidesaddle, she did not give up her womanliness. Nor did other women. Women hunters did not cross-dress in the field; they wore silk sashes and ankle-length dresses and sometimes permitted themselves "to tremble, or even faint" after the kill. Yet in taking up hunting and shooting, women sought to break down the barriers of middle-class patriarchy.

Long before women joined trapshooting clubs and hired guides in the Adirondacks, they had rapped at the door of equality in other ways. As members of churches, tract societies, temperance societies, and abolition societies, and as readers, consumers, and schoolteachers, middle-class women had made themselves visible in Jacksonian and antebellum America. Meanwhile, agrarian patriarchy—in which the farmer-husband ruled with Biblical, even regal, authority—gave ground to a middle-class code of gender relations that made women the principal rearers of children and paragons of Christian virtue.[29]

Like other norms and traditions, middle-class gender roles oscillated in Jacksonian and antebellum America. While men expected wives to remain subordinate, no biological standard demanded submission, nor did middle-class women invariably oblige men by remaining in the home. In this new society, women seemed to ask themselves unconsciously (or consciously, in the case of women's rights advocates) what justified male authority. If women could appear in public as teachers and temperance advocates, could they not participate in other aspects of public life? What necessitated male supremacy in a world ruled by pen rather than plow?

As if to resolve these questions, men incorporated the frontier drama of hunter versus beast into a middle-class identity, asserting their manly vigor and the womanly weakness of their wives. "Women cannot conveniently become hunters or anglers," wrote popular essayist Wilson Flagg in 1871, "nor can they without some eccentricity of conduct follow birds and quadrupeds into the woods."[30] Flagg encouraged women who wished to participate in an outdoor hobby to take up botany. Because hunting was the fount and metaphor for the courage and manliness so necessary for success in politics, business, and professional life, women, who could not hunt, could hardly be expected to fend for themselves outside the home.

In the Gilded Age, women rapped more insistently on the door of equality. Middle- and upper-class women—called "new women"—increasingly insisted on going to college, working outside the home, voting, wearing less restrictive clothing, and practicing birth control.[31] Women—at least some women—would no longer be mere helpmeets and mothers, asexual creatures linked more closely to the realm of angels than that of humans. Hence, whereas men had entered the woods to bolster patriarchy (and continued to do so), women of the late nineteenth century entered the woods to challenge it.

That women could succeed in a Darwinian wilderness of strife and struggle was the lesson taught by Martha Maxwell, "the Colorado Huntress." Educated at Oberlin College, Maxwell moved to Colorado with her husband in 1860, where she developed her skills as a naturalist, hunter, and taxidermist. The climax of her career came in 1876, when she exhibited a prize-winning diorama of mounted game animals—specimens she had shot—at the Colorado-Kansas entry of the Centennial International Exhibition in Philadelphia. Above buffalo, elk, and mule deer, Maxwell—an ardent advocate of women's rights—placed a sign that read "Women's Work."[32]

Martha Maxwell, "the Colorado Huntress." Courtesy of the Colorado Historical Society, F41726, Denver, Colorado.

Martha Maxwell's Colorado diorama at the 1876 Philadelphia Centennial International Exhibition. From John Filmer and George C. Bell, *The Illustrated Catalogue of the Centennial Exhibition, Philadelphia, 1876*. Photograph by Terry Firman Jr.

How many huntresses joined Maxwell in the campaign for women's rights we do not know, but once women became hunters, suffrage was not far behind. If women were strong enough to hunt, surely they were strong enough to enter politics and business. Among women, the right to hunt could be as much a metaphor for the right to citizenship as it was among men.

Women's newfound interest in outdoor life, however, did not necessarily merit an invitation from men to join the wilderness club. When Kate Field, a journalist and lyceum lecturer, encouraged women to enter the Adirondacks in search of mental and physical vigor, Thomas Bangs Thorpe's response was bilious. Women, he argued, had nothing in their education "that makes such places appreciated, and no capability for physical exercise that causes that attempt to be pleasantly possible. . . . Let the ladies keep out of the woods."[33] Field's sin was that she had introduced the feminine into the forest bastions of middle-class manliness. Women could not be admitted to the sanctum of the American Native.

Insofar as men did permit women to accompany them on hunting expeditions, they often treated them with gentle condescension or drollery. When generals George Armstrong Custer and Nelson Appleton Miles took their wives on a buffalo hunt, the women were not permitted to ride or to shoot but were dragged around in a carriage to places where enlisted men were butchering animals already killed. On another occasion, Custer seated a fellow officer's wife on a freshly killed buffalo, then persuaded her, after she had stopped screaming, to cut a tuft of hair from the animal as a trophy (recalling an English practice in which a woman was chosen to deliver the coup de grace to a dying stag).[34]

In these cases, the wives' part in the hunt was to pay tribute to their husbands and to provide comic relief. Yet women were permitted, albeit reluctantly, to join the sporting fraternity in the Gilded Age and Progressive era. In doing so, they joined men in presenting a united front against the anxieties of the age.

In these years eastern and southern Europeans—swarthy Jews and Catholics—immigrated to America's cities, taking industrial jobs and joining labor unions. Fears of being swamped by foreigners were exacerbated by fears of race suicide. Though the term "race suicide" was first employed by psychologist Edward A. Ross in 1901, the concern over reproduction had emerged as early as 1880, when census data showed that Anglo-Saxon women were bearing fewer children than ever before. Psychologists meanwhile warned of the dangers of "neurasthenia," or "lack of nerve force," caused by too much brain work, and sociologists and historians worried over the closure of the frontier.[35] Without the challenge of settling new lands, how would Americans remain a strong and vigorous people? America seemed to suffer from a crisis of overcivilization.

Confronted with the problem of ethnicity and class and fearful of mental and physical decline, middle-class Americans embraced their racial identity as Anglo-Saxons and progeny of the frontier. "No nation facing the unhealthy softening and relaxation of fibre that tends to accompany civilization," announced Theodore Roosevelt, "can afford to neglect anything that will develop hardihood, resolution, and the scorn of discomfort and danger" once associated with the frontier. Moved by this logic, middle- and upper-class women, with tacit approval from men, took up hunting and shooting. These pastimes might not produce high birthrates, but they assuaged high anxieties.[36] Yet women's participation in hunting tended to undermine its promotion of manliness, the very trait that hunting was supposed to save.

Children too were to be brought into the hunting fold. Psychologist G. Stanley Hall updated four-stages theory by positing that humans, like societies, ex-

"The Gun an Important Factor in the Saving of the American Race," from *Outdoor Life*, January 1904. Photograph by Rhoda Pollack.

perience distinct stages of development. In one of these stages, wrote Hall, "the child revels in savagery." Only by encouraging their children's "tribal, predatory, hunting, fishing, fighting, roving, idle playing proclivities" could parents assure them of graduating to a higher stage and becoming happy and productive adults. Without these outlets for their youthful energies, children would lose interest in life, developing "weakness of character" and "slowness of intellect."[37]

To promote and to capitalize on the child's need to revel in savagery, Ernest Thompson Seton founded the Woodcraft Indians, and Dan Beard founded the Sons of Daniel Boone in the first decade of the twentieth century. In these organizations, along with the Boy Scouts, which soon subsumed both, American boys were taught the skills of tracking, trapping, and taxidermy. Elsewhere, boys learned the "elevating" ethic of sportsmanship, which had been "the training school of the greatest nations of ancient and modern times," according to the *American Field.* "The man who wishes his boy to get the most benefit from his boyhood, in the way of preparation for later life" wrote the *American Field*'s editor in 1904, "will ... give him an insight into its purest and most remunerative pleasures, by putting into his hands a gun, rifle, or rod."[38]

Throughout the Gilded Age and Progressive era, dozens of hunting novels for boys appeared in libraries and bookstores. Charles Austin Fosdick, or "Harry Castlemon," wrote the Sportsman's Club Series, the Rod and Gun Series, and the Boy Hunter Series, while Edward S. Ellis wrote the Deerfoot Series and the Boy Pioneer Series. Together with works by George Bird Grinnell, William Temple Hornaday, Emerson Hough, and Stewart Edward White, these books gave American boys a sense that hunting and pioneering set them apart from less vigorous boys of other countries. If the Boone literature had made boys into American Natives, the new literature made them nativists.

Typical of such books was Thomas W. Knox's *Young Nimrods in North America,* published in 1881, in which two city boys embark on adventures in a dangerous world filled with Irishmen, lumberjacks, and Indians. Hunting and fishing all the while, the boys—like Lewis and Clark—journey from the Atlantic to the Pacific, escorted by their chaperone, the Doctor, who gives them lessons in natural history.[39]

Like others of the genre, Knox's book was no dime novel; it was intended to "be unexceptionable in point of morals" so that it could "be freely placed in the hands of the youth all over the land."[40] With some 250 illustrations, in addition to a gilded cover and spine depicting moose, fish, hare, owl, fox, pronghorn, Indian with bow, and charging buffalo, the book was clearly meant for the children of parents with means.

The irony is that the men, women, and boys who were encouraged to reacquire the spartan, manly virtues of frontier life were products of an urban, middle-class society dating back several generations. Their memories of the frontier were more likely to be drawn from the novels of James Fenimore Cooper or Charles Austin Fosdick than from actual experience or oral tradition, and they were more likely to learn to hunt from peers or from guides than from fathers and grandfathers.[41] In identifying with the frontier experience, however, they conceived of their society as a realm of racial struggle and strife, a realm in which it was critical for all—men, women, and children—to learn the skills of hunting.

While native-born Americans were encouraged to hunt, state governments restricted the hunting rights of immigrants (partly as a conservationist measure and perhaps partly due to the fear of armed radicals). According to William Temple Hornaday, one of the nation's leading conservationists, the Italian immigrant would not only "root out the native American and take his place and income" but also would behave like a "human mongoose" in destroying native songbirds for food. Only strict game laws and strict enforcement would solve the problem. In keeping with this nativist philosophy, Hornaday wrote anti-union, anti-Bolshevik, and anti-German tracts during and after World War I, and his New York Zoological Park hosted a world conference on eugenics in the early 1920s.[42]

The whole Back to Nature movement of the late nineteenth and early twentieth centuries, in which men like Hornaday played such prominent roles, distinguished morally and physically healthy Americans from seemingly degraded aliens pouring into the country. The movement also distinguished Americans from aliens who remained outside the country, whether they be Filipino, Japanese, Indian, or African. "When the real crisis arrives," warned G. L. Lehle, a promoter of rifle clubs, in 1908, "when the newly-awakened and insolent hordes of another race must be reckoned with—then I hope to serve at the side of intelligent students of the art of rifle shooting, knowing that by reason of their superior ability and proven patriotism they will prevail over the enemy."[43]

This imperial identity was buttressed by the National Collection of Heads and Horns, a fantastic assemblage of the heads and horns of big game. In the National Collection, William Temple Hornaday, who served as director of the New York Zoological Park for some thirty years, sought to assemble examples of the world's big game species before they had disappeared entirely. This collection memorialized the chivalry, courage, and manliness of elite sport hunters yet preserved the democratic ideal by offering admission to anyone who cared to visit.

Unlike displays of American game at the Philadelphia Centennial International Exhibition and the World's Columbian Exposition, the National Collection was international rather than primarily American in scope. The collection's chief boast was the largest set of elephant tusks ever recorded, and horns and heads were arranged by taxonomy for comparison of species from throughout the world. "To know thoroughly the horn-bearing mammals of the world," wrote Hornaday in 1907, "is to know the world also."[44] As America became a world power, the American Native became a man (or woman) of the world.

Henceforth, however, there would be two sorts of knowledge of horn-bearing animals: that of those who hunted them and that of rank-and-file visitors to the collection. It was "natural," wrote Hornaday, for men "to desire a collection" of trophies but "not desirable that many men should be animated by the desire for large collections" as that would lead to the destruction of game. Most men would have to be content to visit the National Collection; hunting could no longer be a democratic way of fashioning American identity. The "personal trophies" collected by wealthy men with the wherewithal to navigate the globe were "quite another matter." By adding the names of wealthy donors to each display, Hornaday gave ample credit to the upper-class sportsmen who had parted with their personal trophies for the good of science and the public.[45]

The National Collection of Heads and Horns was the Peale's Museum of the Gilded Age. It rendered the exotic into the familiar but at the same time attempted to instill in urban Americans—including working-class immigrants—a reverence for the upper-crust, Anglo-Saxon hunters who conquered buffalo, elk, and grizzly and, ultimately, elephant, lion, and rhinoceros as well. If the conquest of nature through sport hunting and through the exhibition of game species was initially a way of taking possession of the American continent, in the early twentieth century it became a way of demonstrating world power. Oddly, however, the National Collection revealed not so much a sense of power as a sense of weakness. Unable to impose order on the "insolent hordes of another race," in the words of Lehle, Progressives like Hornaday imposed order on alien races of animals.

17

Conservation and Conflict

 The problem faced by hunters at the end of the nineteenth century and the beginning of the twentieth century was the decline of game. Shunted aside by farms, ranches, and cities, and hunted ruthlessly for market, America's big-game populations reached their nadir at about the turn of the century. The American frontier had disappeared, and it seemed that American game animals would disappear with it. How, thousands of Americans wondered, could game be preserved, together with the self-reliant, manly virtues that game animals had come to symbolize?

Art offered one solution. In 1884 a reviewer for the *Century Illustrated Monthly Magazine* praised sculptor Edward Kemeys for doing "incalculable" service for his country by commemorating its disappearing fauna with bronze statuettes. "The American bear and bison," queried the reviewer, "where will they be a generation hence? Nowhere, save in the possession of those persons who have to-day the opportunity and intelligence to decorate their rooms and parks with Mr. Kemeys's bronzes."[1]

Another solution appeared in the 1890s, when members of the Boone and Crockett Club, with the New York Zoological Society and the city of New York, helped establish "the most magnificent composition of land and water . . . ever dedicated to zoology," the New York Zoological Park, or Bronx Zoo. The zoo housed herds of bison and other American quadrupeds in so-called natural environments. With admission fees low enough for the masses to afford, and with grounds five times larger than any European counterpart, the Bronx Zoo became the nation's preeminent zoological repository. The Bronx Zoo, wrote Leonidas Hubbard Jr., in *Outing* magazine in 1904, offered "a chance to restock the native American forest with native animals, and to show us something of what our country was like in the days when our fathers . . . killed deer and fought Indians."[2]

In the era of Theodore Roosevelt, joining a hunting club that lobbied for conservation made rugged individualists into organization men. This late nineteenth- or early twentieth-century photograph shows the Grasse River Club of New York. Courtesy of the Adirondack Museum, Blue Mountain Lake, New York.

A more satisfying way of preserving America's game, along with the country's noble hunting tradition, was to join hunting clubs and to press for game laws. Whereas "a few years since a sportsmen's club was a thing unknown," wrote the editor of *American Sportsman* in 1874, "now they may be counted by scores, and exist in almost every important city in the Union." Over the next several decades, hunting and game protective clubs continued to proliferate, their numbers tripling to

308 (not including clubs devoted solely to trapshooting) between 1874 and 1878, according to *Forest and Stream*. By 1891 this total had tripled again. In *The Sportsman's Directory*, Fred E. Pond listed 968 "rod and gun clubs." Of these, 563 were in the Midwest, 265 in the Northeast, 103 in the West, and just 37 in the South.[3]

Despite their frequent camp-outs and game dinners, members did not join solely to fill their leisure hours. Club members, reported *Forest and Stream* editor Charles Hallock, were to "constitute a valuable detective and police force" for the prosecution of game law violators. Hallock was not announcing any new policy among hunting clubs. Club members had campaigned for game laws and prosecuted those who killed or sold game out of season since at least the 1840s.[4]

The postbellum increase of efforts to promote conservation and to prosecute game law violators revealed more clearly than before the deep cleavages in the hunting fraternity. Even as city sportsmen worshiped at the altar of Boone, the diminution of game in the late nineteenth century caused them to assail their fellow hunters whose livelihoods depended on hunting. Two populations of

The very popularity of hunting contributed to the scarcity of game. Hunters responded by endorsing conservation. "First Duck of the Season," *Forest and Stream* 7, no. 8 (September 28, 1876): 113. This illustration first appeared in *Scribner's Magazine*. Courtesy of the University of California at Berkeley.

FIRST DUCK OF THE SEASON.

hunters—one urban, middle class, and educated, and one largely rural and un-educated—could not be sustained by declining game populations. The result was a breach in the old alliance between the backwoods American Native and his middle-class cousin.

The campaign for game protection was not strictly a Gilded Age phenomenon. Deer seasons had existed in American colonies as early as the seventeenth century. In 1791 New York State had passed what was perhaps the first post-Revolutionary game law, prohibiting the killing of heath hens between April 1 and February 5. Massachusetts followed suit with laws protecting game birds in 1818, as did New Jersey in 1820. The majority of game laws, however, appeared after the 1840s as a result of lobbying by hunting clubs and game protective associations.[5]

Not until the late nineteenth century were these game laws strictly enforced. New Hampshire, for instance, appears not to have prosecuted a single deer poacher until 1878, when it created the Office of the State Game Commissioner.[6] But the campaign for game laws reached a crescendo in the Gilded Age when states appointed game wardens paid for by fees charged to sportsmen for hunting and fishing licenses.

Hunting clubs and game protective associations also became increasingly centralized and able to lobby more effectively over the course of the century. The New York State Sportsmen's Association invited delegates from all of the state's hunting clubs to its convention in Geneva in 1859, and the National Sportsmen's Association held its first convention at Niagara Falls in 1874 with eighty-six delegates representing sixteen states.[7]

The climactic moment of the game preservation movement came when the U.S. Congress passed the Lacey Game and Wild Birds Preservation and Disposition Act of 1900. This act forbade the interstate shipment of game killed out of season (or otherwise illegally) and allowed cooperation between states to bring violators to justice. As a result, market hunters who killed game illegally in one state, then shipped it to another for sale, were put out of business—if they were caught.

By the early 1900s, several national organizations sought to protect game. The League of American Sportsmen, the American Bison Society, the Camp Fire Club, the American Game Protective Association, the Permanent Wild Life Protection Fund, and the Boone and Crockett Club were foremost among them; each boasted a distinguished membership. The rolls of the Boone and Crockett Club included Theodore Roosevelt, Owen Wister, Albert Bierstadt, Henry Cabot Lodge, Elihu Root, and George Bird Grinnell.[8]

Founded by Theodore Roosevelt in 1887 to promote the "energy, resolution, manliness, self-reliance" and "capacity for self-help" that had been associated with hunting since the cult of Boone began, the Boone and Crockett Club became a leader in conservation. In addition to lobbying for the creation of national parks, forests, and wildlife refuges, the club sought to protect buffalo, elk, and antelope.[9] The club also promoted the exploration of unsettled regions of the country (such as there were), enabling members to think of themselves as American Natives in the mold of Meriwether Lewis.

Emblematic of this crusade was the campaign to save the buffalo. Shamed by the "wicked and wanton" killing of buffalo, sportsmen, legislators, and members of the American Society for the Prevention of Cruelty to Animals banded together as early as the 1860s to protect this species. The result was the passage in 1873 by both the U.S. House and Senate of a bill to protect the buffalo, "the finest wild animal in our hemisphere." President Ulysses Grant, however, apparently loyal to military men who wished to eradicate the buffalo to subjugate Plains Indians, killed the bill with a pocket veto. Though legislation was passed at the state level prohibiting the killing of buffalo merely for hides, it was almost never enforced. On an expedition to collect a few of the last buffalo for the Smithsonian Institution in 1886, William Temple Hornaday, the Smithsonian's chief taxidermist, estimated that as few as three hundred remained in the wild.[10]

At the moment that buffalo approached extinction, images of buffalo proliferated, appearing in paintings, as sculptures, on coins, and even on the ten dollar bill. A few of the last living buffalo also appeared in Buffalo Bill's Wild West Show, where they became performers in reenactments of the gallant hunts of old. Insofar as the buffalo symbolized all that was best about America—abundance, sublimity, chivalrous conquest—it symbolized the American Native. The buffalo, as zoologist J. A. Allen phrased it, was "the most characteristic and important mammal in our country."[11]

Beyond symbolizing all that was right about Americans, however, the buffalo also symbolized all that was wrong with Americans: profligacy, wantonness, and the drift away from the old virtue of self-restraint. The decline of the buffalo showed the limits of freedom and individualism. Without law to provide restraint, America would fall victim to the ungovernable passions of its citizens. Only by saving the buffalo, implored Hornaday in 1887, could Americans "in a small measure, atone for the national disgrace that attaches to the heartless and senseless extermination of the species in a wild state."[12]

To publicize this point, Hornaday made the buffalo the centerpiece of his Extermination Series. In this exhibit, transported by the Smithsonian Institution to fairs and expositions throughout the country, Hornaday displayed mounted

Images of buffalo proliferated precisely as buffalo populations reached their nadir. This ten dollar United States banknote, series 1901, shows Meriwether Lewis, William Clark, and what was then the world's record buffalo, shot by William Temple Hornaday on behalf of the Smithsonian Institution. Courtesy of the National Numismatic Collection, Smithsonian Institution, Washington, D.C.

specimens of each mammal species in danger of extinction. Alongside lifelike specimens, Hornaday added the grisly skeleton of a buffalo, made to look as though it had been killed by hide hunters and left to rot. Behind this skeleton appeared a display of the guns employed in the killing, labeled "Weapons of Destruction."[13]

Admonished by men like Hornaday and George Bird Grinnell, the second editor of *Forest and Stream*, the federal government— together with the Boone and Crockett Club, the New York Zoological Society, and numerous sport hunters and conservationists—took a new interest in saving the buffalo. This effort bore fruit as early as 1902, when the U.S. Congress appropriated $15,000 to rebuild the remnant herd of wild buffalo in Yellowstone National Park. Larger appropriations came over the next several decades, particularly after the American Bison Society teamed up with the U.S. government to establish federal herds. Whereas in 1891 only 1,091 buffalo survived in the United States (virtually all in privately owned herds), by 1933, thanks to the efforts of Roosevelt and his fellow conservationists, there were 21,707 buffalo.[14]

Elsewhere, too, hunters led the way in conservation. As early as 1874, Charles Hallock had launched a campaign for cooperative game laws, meaning the rationalization of game laws in accordance with ecological zones rather than state lines (Kentucky, Ohio, and Illinois, for example, would be subject to the same game laws because of the similarity in their game species and climates). In the same year, Hallock assisted in bringing together an ad hoc association of professional scientists who were to formulate rational guidelines for international game laws. If Hallock was not as successful or systematic a conservationist as Gifford Pinchot, he was nevertheless one of the earliest exponents of rationalized conservation.[15]

The impetus hunters gave to conservation, as John Reiger argues, was the most creditable accomplishment of their movement.[16] In the twentieth century, the conservationist cause has been distorted by the National Rifle Association, which has substituted gun for game as a symbol of American identity. But other sportsmen's organizations continue to promote conservation and outdoor recreation with or without the gun, and all have cultural roots in the last century. Nineteenth-century sport hunters found meaning and identity in their native game and in nature as a whole, and the sport hunter, often alone, cried out (with more or less consistency) against the tide of progress.

Whereas hunters had once been hardy individualists, the campaign to save American game made them organization men. Despite the Boone and Crockett Club's call for self-help and self-reliance, conservation in the Gilded Age and Progressive era required concerted action. Even the Boone and Crockett Club's requirement that prospective members take in fair chase several species of American big game made hunting not an end in itself but an ordeal for confirmation in a conservationist fraternity.

The shift from defining identity through hunting to defining identity by joining a hunting club—and then lobbying the government to protect game—underlay the modern conservation movement. Indeed, this shift prefigured the Progressive movement as a whole. Even before middle-class Americans appealed to their government to rein in market capitalism, they, as members of conservation organizations, appealed to their government to rein in the slaughter of game. The impending extinction of buffalo and other game threatened the old America of individualism and self-reliance every bit as much as the hegemony of big business. Only through organization and legislation could the old America be saved.

From the vantage point of the twenty-first century, it is easy to see how limited the vision of these hunter-conservationists was. They might wish to save buffalo and elk but not the Great Plains biome on which buffalo and elk had thrived. The rationale for saving game, moreover, was often chauvinistic (game was to be saved to protect America's frontier heritage) or petty (game was to be saved for tourists and hunters, who generated profits for railroads, guides, and local communities). Yet it is hardly fair to suggest that Progressive era conservationists should have dreamed of saving something so vast as the Great Plains biome or that they should have repudiated civilization and progress, or even the goal of profit. Conservationists worked within the constraints of the time; they were romantics insofar as they sought to save America's cultural heritage, yet necessity made them pragmatists. They had to pick and choose their battles, and they had to offer utilitarian reasons for preserving game, along with appeals to the nation's conscience and sense of greatness. They were not titans of environmentalism, but there is reason to honor them.

Even hunters who supported conservation, however, were capable of glaring acts of hypocrisy. Hunting author Charles Edward Whitehead, for instance, refused to attend the annual meetings of the New York State Society for the Protection of Game in the 1870s and 1880s because "trials with the shot gun, rifle, and pistol" would absorb most of the meeting, and just "a few moments" over dinner would be devoted "to casual and ineffectual talk upon the laws for the protection of game." The trials to which Whitehead referred were mostly trapshoots in which live passenger pigeons served as targets; nine thousand pigeons were killed at the New York State Sportsmen's Convention at Oswego in 1874.[17]

Such slaughter was by no means exceptional. At least two different companies shipped fifteen thousand pigeons per week to shooting clubs and game markets in the late nineteenth century. *Forest and Stream* defended the slaughter in 1874 because pigeons, although not "created for the express purpose of being shot from the trap, . . . break down forests and defile the face of nature" wherever they roosted. Because so few sportsmen considered the passenger pigeon a game bird, its fate was extinction.[18]

The slaughter was also conducted by sportsmen in the Midwest and Far West. Although Henry Hastings Sibley lamented the buffalo's impending extinction and called for stringent game laws, in the 1840s he had led a small party on a hunting expedition that, in twenty-two days, took 16 buffalo, 3 elk, 8 raccoons, 12 wolves, 7 geese, 244 ducks, and 80 grouse, "besides sundry other small snaps not worth recording." By blaming Indians for the extinction of buffalo, Sibley could ignore the toll taken by himself and his American Fur Company.[19]

Col. Richard Irving Dodge also campaigned for game laws (and later became a member of the Boone and Crockett Club), yet in 1872 he had taken 1,262 animals on a hunt with three English gentlemen. This total included 127 buffalo, despite the fact that Dodge would later write that the buffalo was a quarry unworthy of a novice. The following year he and the same party, minus one participant, bagged 1,141 animals. And in 1884 Theodore Roosevelt, the founder of the Boone

Fulsome kills were more common than sportsmen cared to admit. At Richard Burch (guide) house, Long Lake, 1891. Courtesy of the Adirondack Museum, Blue Mountain Lake, New York.

and Crockett Club, took 170 animals in a forty-seven-day hunt in the Dakotas, logging each day's total into his journal along with a brief description of the wounds he had inflicted.[20]

Such slaughters were not so different in spirit from the galas of Gilded Age plutocrats, who rolled cigars in $100 dollar bills or attended parties mounted on horses that ate from silver feed bags. The conspicuous consumption of life, like the conspicuous consumption of money, was the peculiar sickness of Gilded Age America.

To be fair, these men came to regret the slaughter and to endorse conservation. And however implicated they were in the extinction of the passenger pigeon, sport hunters were not the primary cause of the near extinction of buffalo and elk. Market hunters took the vast majority of game animals, and even game seasons were merely token efforts to stop what had become a massive nationwide trade. Every city had its game stalls at its open-air markets, supplied by market hunters who were recruited by posted circulars and hired on commission.[21]

With the opening of the railroads, St. Louis and Chicago became entrepôts for deer, buffalo, and every other kind of western quadruped and wildfowl even long after the decline of the fur trade. The *American Sportsman* reported on December 27, 1874, that some $500,000 worth of game had changed hands in Chicago alone in the previous year. From the Far West, the Midwest, and Maine, massive quantities of game were also shipped to New York City for sale to restaurants and hotels and for exportation overseas.[22]

One of the great ironies in sport hunting's rise to popularity was the fact that, despite the sportsman's efforts to protect the quarry from extinction, game became a culinary staple among the middle and upper classes. No longer was eating game thought to make one wild or barbaric. Judging from its abundance in fine restaurants, game became in the late nineteenth century a source of vitality. To dine on American wildlife was a gesture of patriotism, a celebration of a manly identity and the conquest of the continent. The annual Thanksgiving dinners at Drake's Grand Pacific Hotel in Chicago in the 1880s, for instance, featured no less than thirty different native species prepared to gourmet standards, plus a few exotics. The decimation of wild animal stocks was further intensified by the craze for stuffed birds in ladies' hats. One ornithologist claimed to have counted some 542 different species in seven hundred hats in a single day in New York City in the 1880s.[23]

Sport hunters formed clubs to save game and to save the sport that defined them as American Natives, yet they tended to target neither the epicures who consumed game, nor the railroads that transported it, nor the restaurateurs who served it, but the workaday men who were paid to supply it. The real pot hunters were often small farmers, lumberers, innkeepers, railroad workers, or even guides for gentlemen sportsmen who, when they ran low on money or lost their seasonal work, hunted to keep themselves solvent.[24]

In much of the West, the abundance of big game and wildfowl made market hunting a full-time occupation, but even there gentlemen hunters considered their working counterparts "lazy and shiftless" men who would kill everything in sight and then use up their earnings on a drinking spree. Market hunters were aware that respectable people saw their business as "fit only for roughs and idlers," but they viewed themselves as businessmen who were no more dishonorable than those who wore the feathers or fur or who ate the game that they provided. Yet as sport hunting generated increasing amounts of tourist spending in rural districts, market hunters found themselves pilloried by the press as the "thriftless, lazy and irresponsible class" who disobeyed the game laws, in contrast to "the educated, intelligent men from the cities" who "come by the hundreds and thousands, patronizing hotels, stables, boats, & c."[25] Market hunters also found themselves subject to increasing regulation as states, at the behest of city sportsmen, appointed game wardens whose job was to arrest those who violated game laws.

By the 1880s, tensions in Maine ran so high that several men burned down the home of a game warden, and the state's game commission reported "open resistance to the authority of the State ... by an organized band of outlaws." Despite the prosecution of the culprits, the quasi-rebellion continued when, in 1886, a market hunter shot and killed two game wardens who had accused him of illegally using a dog to hunt deer. Although the killer went to prison, he became a folk hero in rural Maine.[26]

Despite hunting's egalitarian tradition, conflicts between market and subsistence hunters, on the one hand, and gentlemen sportsmen, on the other, gave the United States more than a superficial resemblance to England. Although market and subsistence hunters were legitimate heirs of the great Kentucky long hunter, Daniel Boone, they found themselves castigated and despised by Boone's other heirs, the gentlemen hunters of the cities. The rhetorical solidarity between the middle-class hunter and his common man cousin had begun to disintegrate.

Part of the conflict between sportsmen and market hunters can be traced to common law decisions that declared wild animals the property of those who took them rather than the property of those on whose land they were taken. "Though it is the broad common law maxim, that 'everything upon a man's land is his own,'" wrote hunting author William Elliott in 1846, "yet custom, with us, fortified by certain decisions of our courts, has gone far to qualify and set limitations to the maxim."[27]

The conflict was also spurred by the fact that American abundance and American custom had made hunting the prerogative of common men since the first years of colonization. "The right to hunt wild animals," lamented Elliott, "is held by the great body of the people, whether landholders or otherwise, as one of their franchises," and "to all limitations" on that right "they submit with the worst possible grace." Rather than applauding game laws, most Americans raised "the senseless cry of aristocracy!—privileged orders!—oppression of the poor by the rich!"[28]

The cry of aristocracy was raised because Americans were constantly reminded by orators and editors of the gross inequities of the English system. In the nineteenth century, less than one Englishman in ten thousand was legally eligible to hunt. England had restricted the right to hunt to nobles and gentry since the early Middle Ages, but the eighteenth and nineteenth centuries saw particularly bitter conflict between poachers and squires. As the gentry gained control of Parliament in the early eighteenth century, it sought to defend its hunting prerogatives by making deer poaching a capital crime. In 1817 another law made seven years' transportation to a penal colony mandatory for those convicted of poaching at night, a sentence few were robust enough to survive.[29]

If some hardy soul was bold enough to defy the law, he could expect to find coverts and pheasant preserves guarded by spring guns, mantraps, armed gamekeepers, and ferocious dogs. Even these tactics did not stop poachers. In 1831 fully one-sixth of England's convicted criminals were guilty of game law violations. Deer poisonings, dog killings, the burning of ricks, and pitched battles between poachers and gamekeepers recurred throughout the first decades of the nineteenth century, particularly during the depression that followed the Napoleonic Wars. Not until 1880 could English commoners hunt legally so much as a rabbit.[30] French and German game laws were similarly harsh.

Sport hunters argued that American game laws protected the game and not a class of men, but the cry of "aristocracy!" was not so irrational as they liked to think. Though Theodore Roosevelt wrote in 1893 that he would "much regret" to see hunting confined to a "system of large private game preserves, kept for the enjoyment of the very rich," that is precisely what was happening in many parts of the country. In fact, there was nothing extraordinary about hunting author Dwight Huntington's assertion in 1900 that in the future all hunting would take place on private preserves.[31]

The drift toward private preserves had begun harmlessly enough as hunters brought sporting guns to fashionable resorts like White Sulphur Springs, Virginia, and Cape May, New Jersey. By 1842 hotels began running ads in the sporting press appealing specifically to hunters and fishermen, and by 1858 rural and seaside properties were being sold routinely as shooting resorts. Hunting clubs also built increasingly expensive clubhouses and cottages. As of 1874 the South Side Sportsmen's Club of Long Island had lavished some $126,000 on its facilities.[32]

Meanwhile, the Adirondack Mountains, like Long Island before them, continued to gain popularity as an enormous resort for wealthy sportsmen. In 1874 shooting a deer in the Adirondacks was "quite essential to the good standing of a gentleman," wrote Samuel Irenaeus Prime, adding that "the ladies enter so heartily into it that a man fancies he loses somewhat in the eyes of his own wife if he fail to assassinate one or two bucks."[33]

Paul Smith, who began his career as a guide, rode the Adirondack wave by building resorts—beginning in 1858 with Hunter's Home—that, along with real

estate speculation, made him a millionaire by the 1880s. Another resort, the Ra-
quette Lake House, built in 1857, had just forty-four guests in its first year but
saw the numbers double in each of its next few years. For Boston and Brook-
line sportsmen, the destinations of choice were Maine's Penobscot Bay, Mount
Desert Island, and Moosehead, Sebago, Kennebago, and Rangeley Lakes, while
in the Far West, hotels catered to sportsmen in California, Colorado, Montana,
and Wyoming.[34]

Nothing satisfied hunters more than returning to the hotel with evidence of success. "Return
of the Hunters to the Windsor," photograph by Seneca Ray Stoddard, 1891. Courtesy of the
Adirondack Museum, Blue Mountain Lake, New York.

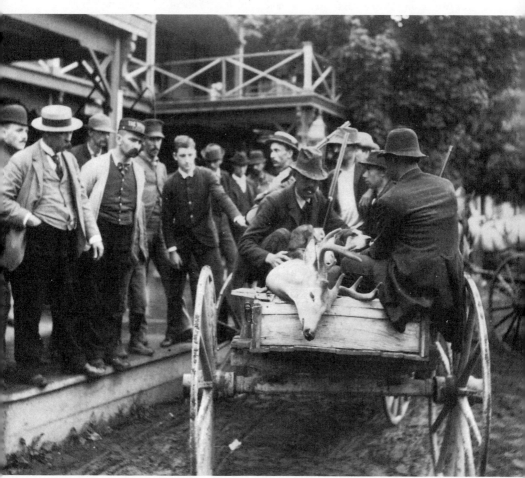

At these resorts wealthy sportsmen shot deer, grouse, and ducks baited with corn; dined on squab, filet mignon, and venison; and drank wines chilled in brooks. They also enjoyed hot and cold running water, gas heating, and "walls ... decorated by all the imaginable trophies of the hunt." Even the chairs and flower stands at Colorado's Meeker Hotel, reported one sportsman, "are made from elk and deer horns."[35] The sportsman's family, too, was invited, albeit to partake in long walks, rowing, and games rather than the chase.

Equally typical of the Gilded Age was the private game preserve. The prototype for these preserves was Blooming Grove Park in western Pennsylvania, established by a select group of sportsmen in 1870 as the Fontainbleau of America. Just over four hours from New York City via the Erie Railroad, the park consisted of twelve thousand acres of streams, lakes, uplands, lowlands, and forests.[36]

The Adirondacks also became a popular locale for Gilded Age preserves. Cornelius Vanderbilt put his Camp Sagamore there; J. P. Morgan established Camp Uncas; and T. L. Woodruff gave his Adirondack preserve the seemingly oxymoronic name Kamp Kill Kare. By the early 1900s, sixty privately owned game preserves sprawled over 791,208 Adirondack acres.[37]

Even Henry Ford, the American entrepreneur with his bedrock Jeffersonian values, established a game preserve on twenty-one hundred acres near Dearborn, Michigan. And in New Hampshire, 220 buffalo—ten times the number that existed in Yellowstone National Park—roamed on a single private preserve in 1900.[38] To own a game preserve, or to belong to a club that did, was to be an American aristocrat.

The situation was much the same in urbanized areas of the West. "Nearly every available marsh in the valleys of the Columbia and Willamette" Rivers of Oregon and Washington, reported the *Century Illustrated Monthly Magazine* in 1903, "is now controlled by clubs of sportsmen, many of whom reside in Portland." In the vicinities of Denver and Los Angeles, virtually all duck hunting grounds had been "preserved" by clubs, causing "hard feelings among the poorer classes, who like to shoot but cannot afford membership in one of these exclusive institutions." In San Francisco three hunting clubs owned or leased a combined 116,000 acres of game preserves in 1904, some of which, like English preserves, were patrolled by privately paid gamekeepers. "Game preserves," reported *Forest and Stream* in 1897, "are now as thoroughly established in this country as they are in the old world."[39]

That was how one "Pacificator" saw the situation. "A battle is now being waged" in San Francisco, he wrote in 1889, "between the patrician and plebeian gunners of this State, which has already aroused so much ill feeling that neither

Hunting clubs of Gilded Age America often built luxurious clubhouses like this one, owned by the Fox Lake Shooting and Fishing Club. From *Forest and Stream* 32, no. 1 (January 24, 1889): 7. Courtesy of the University of California, Berkeley.

party . . . would hesitate much about turning its guns upon the other." Even respectable clerks and businessmen "who do not belong to the clubs," he reported, "are stigmatized as pot-hunters, poachers, scoundrels, villains, etc." In leasing or buying waterfront properties and in courting the legislature to strengthen laws protecting these properties from trespass, "patrician" hunters had "made a strong bid for the monopoly of all shooting in the State."[40]

Conflicts—sometimes fatal—also occurred in New York and Illinois when poachers cut fences surrounding private game preserves. The Tolleston Club of Chicago found that it had to hire "officers and keepers" as well as Pinkertons to keep out "the lawless element of . . . South Chicago." "Big Pinkerton men," reported a *Forest and Stream* correspondent, "grab these rough fellows, pound them up, throw them in the river, confiscate their guns, smash their boats, and by other gentle means endeavor to convey the impression that the Tolleston Club owns the Tolleston marsh." With a "list of members . . . prominent in business and professional circles, eminent in wealth, station, and culture," the Tolleston Club, announced the correspondent, "means to fight, and has all the money it wants to fight with."[41]

In the company of one another, by contrast, club members displayed "absolute jollity and perfect congeniality." Members of the Mak-saw-ba Club, another hunting club of Chicago, were "men of means and business cares," according to *Forest and Stream*, "but at their resting place you cannot hear a word of business."[42] Elite sportsmen assumed that good humor showed them to be regular fellows, but it also marked them—like members of the Unadilla Hunt—as members of a class, friends and mates rather than laissez-faire competitors.

Perhaps understanding this reality better than the elite sportsmen themselves, "malcontent natives" who "imagine they are doing themselves good by injuring the sport of club members" routinely invaded club properties in Indiana. Sometimes these malcontents poached, whereas at other times they set fire to marsh grass to destroy the grounds. Clubs sought to prosecute trespassers whenever possible, yet found that Indiana juries would seldom convict.[43]

By the end of the nineteenth century, the triumph of American sport hunting had eroded the image of the American Native that hunting had once sustained. Leaving behind its roots in the literature of Boone and Leatherstocking, sport hunting had become so undemocratic, so imperious and chauvinistic, that the sociologist Thorstein Veblen conceived of it as a wasteful warrior ritual of a barbaric ("predatory") ruling class. The propensity to hunt, wrote Veblen, was a genetic trait of the "delicho-blond" type who retained an atavistic desire to rule by plunder and chicanery rather than accede to the dull, work-a-day industriousness of the productive classes.[44]

Like John Winthrop and Benjamin Rush before him, and like much of the urban middle class of late twentieth-century America, Veblen considered sport hunting unproductive, cruel, and of no benefit to the community. Sport hunting, he argued, diverted men from the laudable workmanship ethic that led to the production of goods and services beneficial to society. Where gentlemen sportsmen spoke of the self-reliance and good fellowship inculcated by hunting, Veblen saw "truculence and clannishness."[45]

However penetrating his analysis, by portraying sport hunting as an atavistic, predatory instinct of a ruling class, Veblen misunderstood hunting's place in American history. American sport hunters had always sought to mimic the gentility of the English elite, yet in hunting they had also sought to reclaim the simple virtues of agrarian life, to celebrate self-reliance, and to define themselves as American Natives. Perhaps because he was unfamiliar with American cultural history, Veblen overlooked the sport hunter's claim to kinship with the prototypical American Native, Daniel Boone, who had seemed to embody the indigenous virtues of American nature.

Veblen could make such an oversight because the sport hunters of his era had become imperious. Individuals like George Eastman, Cornelius Vanderbilt, and Lawrence and Leonard Jerome—not middle-class but upper-class men—had become America's most noteworthy sport hunters. In the process, they made hunting a lesson in social Darwinism, a sanguine expression of their station in life as the fittest and most predatory individuals. It was just such men—toadies of the English aristocracy—whom Veblen satirized for substituting elk and deer on the greenswards of their estates for utilitarian cows, symbols of a more agrarian, more egalitarian America.[46]

18

Friends and Foes

The Gilded Age and the Progressive era were not solely decades of conspicuous consumption, anxiety about race suicide, and game conservation. They were also decades of labor unrest, strikes, and radical activism. To recite the conflicts between labor and capital in the late nineteenth and early twentieth centuries is to realize how close America came to class warfare. In the Great Strike of 1877, railroad workers closed down much of the nation's transportation system, burned railroad property, and touched off riots and looting. The strike came to an end when President Rutherford Hayes sent in the National Guard. Then, in the Homestead strike of 1892 in Pennsylvania, workers occupied Andrew Carnegie's steel mills, engaged in a shoot-out with invading Pinkerton men, and finally succumbed to the state militia and martial law. And in 1894 occurred the Pullman strike in Pullman, Illinois, where sleeping cars were manufactured. When the American Railway Union shut down railroads all over the nation in support of the Pullman strikers, President Grover Cleveland called out troops. Again, the strikers lost.[1]

Those were the most renowned confrontations between labor and capital of the age, but they were hardly the only ones. Strikes multiplied across the United States as labor unions— those not crushed by the forces of capital and government—grew bigger and more powerful. By 1900 the American Federation of Labor (AFL), the umbrella union of skilled workers, could claim a million members. The AFL, however, refused to organize unskilled workers, a task it left to the Industrial Workers of the World (IWW), which formed in Chicago in 1905. The IWW sought to organize every worker in America, whereupon it would overthrow the wage-labor system with "One Big Strike." Though better at bluster than accomplishment, the IWW's membership peaked at 100,000 members, enough to attract the attention of government and bring about mass arrests of the union's leaders in 1917.[2]

Radical political parties, too, made headway among Americans. The People's (Populist) party, formed by hard-pressed American farmers in the early 1890s and endowed with a mildly socialistic platform, soon gained control of several state legislatures. In the 1896 presidential election, the Populists, with help from the Democrats who had nominated the same candidate, came within 600,000 votes (of 13.6 million votes cast for both major parties) of electing their candidate, William Jennings Bryan, over the Republican candidate, William McKinley. Though the appeal of Populism declined markedly after 1896, the appeal of socialistic measures did not. In 1912 Americans gave socialist candidate Eugene Debs 900,000 votes (6 percent of the electorate) in the presidential election, despite the fact that huge numbers of immigrant workers (many with socialist leanings) could not vote because they had not been naturalized.[3]

With the possible exception of the Great Depression, never has the United States experienced a more unbridgeable gulf between capitalist and worker, or between capitalist and farmer, than during the Gilded Age and the Progressive era. Never (again with the possible exception of the 1930s) has the country been closer to revolution, and never have men of means felt more anxious about their property, their power, and their relationship to the working people of America.

At first glance, none of this history relates to hunting, yet nothing could be more relevant. The same men (from President Cleveland on down) who bought stocks and broke unions were often sport hunters. On vacations these men took railroads to the Adirondacks, the Rockies, or California; hired guides; and tramped around the wilderness elbow-to-elbow with genuine working men. In the wilderness, sportsmen hoped to forget about class conflict and enter a timeless realm of frontier virtue, rough egalitarianism, and natural beauty. Because, however, sport hunters were often members of the elite, whereas guides were not, social divisions followed hunters into the wilderness.

Face to face in the wilderness, sportsmen and guides negotiated their relationships in ways seldom possible in the urban world. At times, elite hunters recaptured the lapsed solidarity between themselves and common men. Sporting journals abound with instances of friendship and good feelings between hunters and guides (recall Theodore Roosevelt's relationship with John Goff). With no office, no suit, and no management hierarchy to shield employer from employed, however, unresolved issues of status and hierarchy could cast a pall over a trip.

Should sport hunters and guides be equals in the woods? Or should city sports-men, being "children" in woodcraft, take on subordinate roles? Or should the guide be, as one sport hunter phrased it, a "valet" to the gentleman hunter?[4]

Despite some sportsmen's desire to restore harmony between themselves and common men, the latter equation often triumphed. Gentlemen hunters from the city needed guides to cook and to set up camp, as well as to locate game. Yet, having established themselves as American Natives, identifiable by their chivalry, probity, and good manners, many gentlemen hunters felt that they no longer needed the goodwill and forest wisdom of their rustic guides. The "ideal sportsman," explained a correspondent of *Forest and Stream* in 1881, "is, first, a thorough-going business man—whether his business be banker, merchant, teacher or author—and not a loafer, dead-beat, nor bummer."[5] Too often guides—despite their hunting skills—were among the latter, or so it seemed to gentlemen hunters.

Even in the antebellum era, guides had been subjected to sporadic condescen-sion by genteel authors of hunting narratives. In the Gilded Age, condescension at times gave way to mockery. Among the most popular of Adirondack guides was "Old Mountain" Phelps, who, wrote Charles Dudley Warner in 1878, cultivated his image as a "real son of the soil" by refusing to use soap. Warner, continuing in this vein, pointed out that Phelps's education as a forest philosopher came not only from nature but also from Horace Greeley's *New York Tribune.* The *Tribune,* wrote Warner, gave Phelps "a complete education in all departments of human practice and theorizing" and "the more valuable and satisfying assurance that there was nothing more to be gleaned in the universe worth the attention of man."[6]

When not caricatured, the guide might be portrayed as the barbaric back-woods hunter who continued to haunt the American imagination. The Currier and Ives lithographs of paintings by Arthur Fitzwilliam Tait, with their depic-tion of the ever-faithful and subservient guide, metamorphosed in the Gilded Age into Winslow Homer's 1891 painting *Huntsman and Dogs.* Homer portrayed an Adirondack man (presumably a guide) hefting the skin and head of a deer as he trudges through a field of tree stumps, accompanied by a pair of braying dogs. Homer may have intended to dignify the common man in his art, yet others had their own interpretations. "Every tender quality of nature seems to be frozen out of" *Huntsman and Dogs,* noted a critic, adding that the hunter "is just the sort of scoundrel . . . who hounds deer to death up in the Adirondacks for the couple of dollars the hide and horns bring in."[7]

Sensing the deterioration of relations between themselves and guides, gentlemen hunters time and again tried to restore their lapsed solidarity. The "sportsman's relation to his guide is scarcely less close, scarcely less sacred than that of child to mother," inveighed Harry Radford in 1903, urging guides to treat their charges with "tender, motherlike solicitude." Guides were "nature's noblemen," continued Radford, who had "slept under one blanket" with presidents, statesmen, generals, poets, philosophers, and scientists. Radford could but dimly express the "admiration in which the man of the city holds his brother man who has lived his life amid the ennobling environments of the forest."[8]

Yet time and again efforts at rapprochement met with frustration and irony. Radford himself, slayer of the world's record wood bison and member of the Arctic Club of America and the New York Zoological Society, failed to express his admiration for his Eskimo guides on a journey to Point Barrows, Alaska. When one of the guides attempted to back out of the expedition (his wife being sick), Radford became enraged and struck him with the handle of a whip. A fight ensued in which Radford and his hunting partner were stabbed to death.[9]

Though men like Radford preached of solidarity between guides and employers, it was becoming apparent that guides were drawn to their profession more by money than by any longing to become priests of nature. Even Nat Foster, among the first of the Adirondack guides, had earned as much as $1,250 a year in cash as a bounty hunter and guide for surveyors in the 1830s, in comparison with the $30 a year in cash earned by local farmers. As the popularity of the Adirondacks rose dramatically in the 1870s, salaries for hunting guides rose to $4–5 a day in peak season, with a $20–30 bonus tagged on at the end of a trip. Guides were also kept on salary by hotels and private estates and by the 1890s had established their own trade unions, which established uniform rates and enforced game laws.[10]

As guides came to identify themselves as working men with common interests rather than frontier individualists, sportsmen began to find them less subservient and less compelling as American Natives. Whereas guides of the 1850s "were all jolly, good-natured and pleasant people," according to Albany journalist Samuel H. Hammond, a different demeanor had appeared as early as the 1860s. Adirondack guides, reported an English sportsman, restricted their conversation to "ya" and "na" and exhibited extreme sensitivity to any hint of reproval by their employers. "We were particularly careful," he wrote, "not to use any irritating language to men who are not accustomed generally to put any restraint on their feelings." And although in 1869 William H. H. Murray believed that the guide was the keeper of nature's secrets, he recommended a caveat emptor approach to hiring a guide. Rather than being overly taciturn, Murray found

Members of the Adirondack Guides Association attend a sportsman's show in New York City, ca. 1891. Courtesy of the Adirondack Museum, Blue Mountain Lake, New York.

too many guides to be "witty," "talkative," or "lazy," and he recommended that his readers "admonish" their guide for any ill manners and, if that tack failed, "turn him mercilessly adrift."[11]

Ned Buntline embroiled himself in a bitter feud with a well-known Adirondack guide named Alvah Dunning over a more material issue: Dunning's refusal to obey game laws. Buntline referred to Dunning as an "amaroogian," a nonsensical term that another sportsman took to describe "a kind of unsophisticated woodsman, who cannot fraternize with a man of the world like Ned Buntline."[12] Though hunters like Buntline celebrated Boone-like backwoods hunters as model American Natives, they found that their middle-class sensibilities meshed poorly with those of genuine backwoodsmen.

By the Gilded Age, the gentleman hunter had established his credentials as an American Native, and it was the guide who was to be edified—and disciplined—by the gentleman hunter rather than vice versa. That, at least, was how guides and backwoodsmen interpreted the intrusive power of the game laws advocated by gentlemen hunters. The famous Adirondack guide Alvah Dunning complained,

> In the old days I could kill a little meat when I needed it, but now they're a-savin' it for them city dudes with velvet suits and pop-guns, that can't hit a deer if they see it, and don't want it if they do hit it. But they'd put me in jail if I killed a deer 'cause I was hungry. I dunno what we're a-comin' to in this 'ere free country![13]

Like Dunning, other guides, as if to even the score with their detractors, were as likely to mock their employers as to praise them. Even President Grover Cleveland suffered indignity at the hands of his guide, John Stell, who liked to tell clients that Cleveland had lacked the courage to shoot deer.[14]

To counteract this animus, sportsmen served up mixed doses of condescension and flattery. Verplanck Colvin, the man who explored and mapped the Adirondacks in the 1870s on behalf of the state of New York, praised guides for being "fearless of panther, bear or wolf" and for "battling your way forward perhaps unconsciously—but ever in the interest of mankind." Colvin, honorary president of the Adirondack Guides Association, found in guides a "body of magnificent riflemen and woodsmen" who, "should war arise," would prove "a very safeguard to the state." Colvin's ultimate point, however, was that guides should put away grievances over wages and work conditions and respect the authority of their betters.

> You have traveled . . . with capitalists, worked with them; hunted with them; fished with them; chatted with them; philosophized with them; cooked for them; camped with them; eaten with them—you are too well acquainted with capitalists to be afraid of them; and the men of fortune have, in this way, come to know you, appreciate you and like you also.[15]

What was the upshot of this talk? "If you secure wise councils from safe and conservative men," advised Colvin, men who were "the best, kindest, gentlest and noblest hearted employers, . . . you will have . . . solved the socialist or labor question of this age." Far from suggesting an unbridgeable gulf between capitalist and worker, the hunter-guide relationship revealed "a system of natural commingling of interests of employers and employed in the same organization."[16] Sport hunter and guide would restore the lost harmony between boss and worker, pointing the way to the salvation of America.

None of this rhetoric could hide the fact that guides, whatever their wages,

Guides who hunted for market and subsistence in the off-season did not always favor game laws. "An Adirondack Hunter" (Alvah Dunning), 1891. Photograph by Seneca Ray Stoddard. Courtesy of the Adirondack Museum, Blue Mountain Lake, New York.

were losing status. In the Midwest, they even lost their right to call themselves guides. Although midwestern sportsmen paid their men up to three dollars a day, they referred to guides as "pushers," meaning men who simply pushed boats and carried gear. And in the Adirondacks, the New York State Forest Commission suggested in 1894 that guides, "some of [whom] are careless as to their personal appearance," wear "some simple, characteristic costume, suitable to their work." Guides were to wear uniforms, like bellhops or waiters. Sadly, reported the commission, guides resisted this "as a sacrifice of their independence."[17]

Why was it, wondered Lt. Townsend Whelen in 1907, "that the average sportsman is held in such contempt by the guides and hunters of the backwoods?" Why, he continued, did guides invariably refer to sportsmen as "tenderfeet" and "dudes"?[18] In asking these questions, Whelen was asking for a return to the days of old when sport hunter and guide had been as one.

Whelen, by 1907 one of the foremost authorities on hunting in America, berated sportsmen for requiring guides to carry their guns and their extravagant camping accessories, saddle their horses, and even shoot their game. The sportsman who asked his guide to do all that was "a weakling come to play at a life which calls for only strong men." For Whelen the ideal hunter was a man like himself, who hired no guide but, like Boone, relied on his own strength and skill. To such a man, a guide might be a friend and a compatriot but never a hired servant.[19]

Stung by these charges, sportsmen fired back in the pages of *Outdoor Life,* the magazine in which Whelen had published his jeremiad. Leading the counterattack was Levant Fred Brown, who described Whelen's strictures as "buffoonery and impudence—rank scolding; offensive assumption to instruct, fanfare of zeal, absence of all discretion." The sport hunter, argued Brown, should bring on his hunt all the extravagant sporting paraphernalia he desired to use, regardless of what guides might think. Whelen, claimed Brown, had disparaged both gentlemen hunters and the sporting goods industry, but, worse yet, Whelen had attempted to "array sportsmen and guides against each other—to treat them as if they were enemies. Bismillah!"[20]

In response to what *Outdoor Life* dubbed the "Whelen-Brown Controversy" came a storm of letters supporting both sides. "If we condemn Mr. Whelen's article," wrote one correspondent in the April 1907 issue, "we must re-write the history of Davy Crockett and Daniel Boone; we must rescind all praise that has been accorded to our early explorers." Whelen, he insisted, was absolutely correct; real hunters wanted no stigma attached to their capacity to care for themselves in the woods. That was why so many hunting clubs were named after "Boone, Crockett, Lewis, Clarke," and other frontiersmen and explorers. Sportsmen, he wrote, "re-

GOING OUT WITH THE HEAD.
The authentic record of that glorious procession to the lake shore: Bob Jones, the guide, before he was through, felt like pitching that "gol darned" son of a dude tourist into the lake, only he was afraid it would kill all the fish.

RETURN FROM THE HUNT.
The tourist at home relates his adventures: "Had simply a ripping time, don't-cher-know. Got the biggest moose head ever taken in the district. The worst of it was, though, I had simply an awful time humping the beastly thing out to camp. Moose heads are so infernally heavy, don't-cher-know, and I had my rifle to carry, too; so you can imagine my state when I finally reached camp, quite fagged out. Big game hunting is really awfully exhausting work!"

The solidarity between sportsman and guide often broke down in the late nineteenth and early twentieth centuries, as these illustrations from the October 1907 issue of *Outdoor Life* show. Photograph courtesy of the Library of Congress, Washington, D.C.

vere them as men who were natural hunters and nature-lovers, imbued with the natural love of the woods and waters." Such men had learned "to work their way through" the forests "unassisted, making their own fires and beds, cooking their own meals, packing their own outfits, and killing their own game."[21]

After months of charge and countercharge, the Whelen-Brown Controversy showed no sign of abating. Countless letters had flooded the offices of *Outdoor Life*, announced the editors, too many to print. No further letters on this issue were sought; the animus on both sides must subside.[22]

The larger significance of the controversy, however, did not subside. In hiring guides to do camp chores, carry guns, and saddle horses, elite sport hunters betrayed the egalitarian, individualistic tradition of their forebears. Indeed, they betrayed their status as American Natives. All America, it seemed, was endangered.

A second great conflict flared between gentlemen hunters and another breed of virtuous American—farmers. Since the rise of their sport in the 1830s, gentlemen hunters had attempted to constitute themselves as American Natives and to recapture old virtues attributed to the farming life. And just as the success of gentlemen hunters in this campaign led to conflict with guides, so it also led to conflict with farmers, who found themselves denounced as poachers and beset with game laws.

Henry William Herbert had appealed to farmers by arguing, somewhat disingenuously, that game laws only protected game from an "idle, worthless and dissipated crew, *who lurk in the purlieus of large towns,* [emphasis added] or hang about the bar-rooms of village taverns." This argument, however, did not alter the fact that it was often the farmer who benefited from market hunting between growing seasons, nor did it alter the fact that farmers considered restrictions on their right to hunt on their own lands a form of tyranny. Herbert was more honest when he commented that "no man, boy or fool, *in the country,* abstains from killing game, in or out of season, for fear of the law."[23]

From as early as the 1790s, when JERSEY FARMER condemned fox hunters who trespassed on his lands, farmers and sport hunters had begun to clash. In the antebellum era, the contest took on greater immediacy. One group of "highly respectable farmers" in the vicinity of Newburgh, New York, sent a petition to the state legislature in the 1840s declaring it "stupendously absurd" that a farmer had no right to take game on his own land during the closed season and comparing American game laws with the unjust laws of England. But farmers were not concerned strictly with hunting rights; they were attacking the hubris of an increasingly powerful class of urban men. Game laws are "the more vexatious," wrote the petitioners,

> on account of the impudence, and uncivility of persons calling themselves sportsmen. On the first day that the law permits, they issue in droves from the dens and groggeries of our towns and villages, and not unlike the predatory Vandals, who sacked and pillaged Rome, they ride down fences, grain and grass, killing game in useless, and unnecessary quantities.

The petitioners added that the only reason game was protected in winter was because city sportsmen refused to hunt in cold weather.[24]

Henry William Herbert suggested that the problem could be solved if farmers would set aside part of their lands as game preserves and charge sportsmen for the privilege of hunting. That, however, smacked of elitism, making farmers into gamekeepers.[25]

In the mid-Atlantic states, where Elisha Jarrett Lewis hunted, the same tensions appeared. Though worried that he might widen the rift between "farmers and citizens," Lewis took to task "headstrong and selfish farmers" who, although they did not hunt, refused to allow sportsmen on their property. Lewis admitted that game laws protecting woodcock were purely for the benefit of city sportsmen because when the season began in July, farmers were "housing" their crops and had no time to hunt, and by the time they had finished, most of the mature birds had been taken. (Indeed, in 1856 Massachusetts moved up its open-season date on woodcocks from September 1 to July 4 to give city sportsmen a chance to hunt when they were "less crowded with business calls.") To remedy this conflict, Lewis proposed extending the off-season until August, when farmers had time to hunt. But that was a partial solution, since farmers bore a grudge against city sportsmen that transcended their dislike of game laws.[26]

After the Civil War, relations between farmers and hunters grew more bitter. In 1874 an author calling himself "Mohawk" warned in *Forest and Stream* that farmers were deeply upset by the intrusion of hunters on their lands and had taken up the "war-cry" in Ohio for stiffer trespass laws. Mohawk observed that "it is usual to picture the farmer as a gouty, unaccommodating individual, actuated by mercenary motives in not allowing shooting on his land," but hoped that stiffer trespass laws would be passed to appease farmers, as long as farmers would be restrained from trapping and snaring wildfowl. Another correspondent in the *American Sportsman* attempted to deflect the charge of "special privilege" back on farmers, accusing them of exercising the "feudal" right of taking game out of season on their lands.[27]

Similar wars of words and occasionally deeds erupted in Indiana. The Evansville Sportsman's Club reported in 1891 that "matters have reached such a pitch among the farmers that no matter how gentlemanly in deportment we are, we are ordered (often with curses and all kinds of foul abuse) from nearly every farm in this section." When verbal abuse failed, farmers took their case to court. Hence, while Indiana sportsmen lobbied their legislature for laws to prevent farmers from killing and selling game out of season, farmers lobbied the same legislature to stiffen laws against trespass by sportsmen on farms and to relax laws against trespass on marshes owned or leased by sportsmen. That the legislature, with its "petty . . . politico-granger wisdom," complied with the latter demand represented a "slap in the face" to members of Chicago hunting clubs, according to *Forest and Stream*, since these men often owned or leased Indiana preserves.[28]

In 1881 the *Chicago Field* observed that farmers and sport hunters "have become accustomed to the belief that the interests of these two classes clash, and that a certain amount of antagonism must exist between them." Indeed, in Michigan and in Ohio, sport hunters reported that locals had poisoned their dogs; the Ohio hunter thus victimized went so far as to burn down the barn of the farmer he thought responsible. Although the *Chicago Field* proudly cited the case of a St. Paul hunting club that awarded $100 and an interest-free loan to an impoverished farm family on whose lands members had hunted, this gesture reeked of charity. Far from suggesting camaraderie between hunters and farmers, it suggested the noblesse oblige of a superior class.[29]

"In America," an Englishman observed in the 1880s, "the owners of game and the men who shoot it belong . . . to two distinct and almost antagonistic sections of the community—the plain farmer on the one hand, and the better class of townsfolk on the other." Farmers, added a *Forest and Stream* correspondent in 1880, had begun to refer to sportsmen derisively as "town gentry," and not without reason. Another correspondent in the same issue conceded that game laws—by barring landowners from hunting game on their own lands for most of the year and by barring them altogether from marketing game—had made farmers into gamekeepers for city sportsmen. Indeed, wrote a *Forest and Stream* correspondent in 1893, one might conclude from a perusal of popular sporting journals "that it was a crime to live in the country, and own land and farm the same."[30]

Time and again, sportsmen spoke anxiously of the breach between themselves and farmers, yet rapprochement seemed impossible. As late as 1923, one hunter reported having "had the posted property thing thrust at us, glaringly, damnably and imperatively, on every milestone of our journey." In some states, he reported, it had become impossible to hunt unless one "places himself in the middle of the public highway and risks a shot between glares of the observant farmer on either side of the fence."[31]

For all its semblance to English class struggles, the conflict between farmers and sportsmen in the United States had American dimensions. As Richard Hofstadter pointed out in the *Age of Reform*, the farmer had long been held up by politicians and writers as the cornerstone of American virtue, the ideal republican.[32] The farmer represented an earlier sort of "citizen of nature" who took rightful possession of the continent by cultivating it. But as the nineteenth century wore on, farmers found themselves not only at the mercy of international markets and corrupt railroads but also at the mercy of city men who exercised ever greater power in politics, law, and finance. The gentleman sportsman was only a figurehead for this growing urban power, but he served well as the farmer's target of resentment.

Exacerbating the feud were demographic and cultural trends that few of those involved fully comprehended. Even though it was only in 1920 that the U.S. Census officially declared that more Americans lived in cities than in the country, rural communities throughout the Midwest had been in decline throughout the second half of the nineteenth century. While farm productivity rose due to mechanization and the opening of new lands, the price of agricultural produce often fell due to greater supply, causing economic stagnation and a net loss of jobs. As a result, fully half the rural townships of Ohio, Indiana, and Illinois lost population between 1880 and 1890, and Iowa was not far behind. The same trend had occurred in rural New England earlier in the century. Meanwhile the farmer, far from being idolized as the cornerstone of the Republic, was accused by urbanites of being feebleminded, illiterate, and backward, the product of generations of inbreeding and provincialism.[33]

In response to this rural decline, Progressives launched the Country Life Movement. Led by professors, clergymen, and educators—but not by farmers—the Country Life Movement pressed for better rural schools, more training for rural ministers, and improved agricultural productivity. As G. Walter Fiske put it in 1913, the "challenge" of the nation was to "teach [residents of] the country . . . the social efficiency of urban life." To accomplish this goal, urban managers and professionals sought to pave country roads, to consolidate country schools, to promote studies of agricultural technology, and even to train rural clergymen. In the process, they eroded the cultural traditions and authority of agrarian communities.[34]

To the consternation of reformers, farmers continued to prefer one-room schoolhouses, unpaved roads, and untrained fundamentalist ministers. Most of all, they preferred local autonomy and self-government. As farmers saw it, they were model citizens of the Republic. Like their Jeffersonian forebears, they continued to view urbanites—particularly stock jobbers and speculators, but also small-town merchants—as lazy and unscrupulous men who lived by wits rather than work.

None of that meant that farmers were hidebound traditionalists; they did not reject all that was urban or new, nor did they reject the idea of free enterprise. Yet neither were they modern in the strictest sense. Their loyalties, according to Hal Barron, were first and foremost to local community, kin, and the continuity of the family farm. They were more likely than urbanites to be blood relatives of their neighbors, and they were less likely to have migrated from somewhere else. Set apart from urban Americans by work, values, kinship, and community, farmers gradually developed their own rural culture in the late nineteenth and early twentieth centuries.[35]

It was hardly surprising that farmers and hunters came to blows. The game regulations so resolutely backed by gentlemen sportsmen were but one more net of control for urbanites to throw over their rural brethren. More important, in hunting for sport, urban gentlemen displayed their ethic of chivalrous individualism,

Animus between gentlemen hunters and farmers peaked in the late nineteenth century. A. B. Frost, *Ordered Off,* ca. 1903 (watercolor, 16 × 23½ inches). Collection of Henry M. Reed. Photograph by Peter S. Jacobs, Fine Arts Photography.

their loyalty to class, and their social hegemony—everything that made them different from, and supposedly superior to, farmers. In scolding hunters for their impudence, farmers proved to be well aware of sport hunting's cultural implications.

Not incidentally, the clash coalesced around the issue of trespass. Gentlemen sportsmen inverted the old doctrine of *vacuum domicilium,* the farmer's right to the vacant land he cleared and planted. At one time, the hunter had been conceived of as too indolent and savage to clear and plant and therefore held no rightful claim to the land. Now the hunter offered his sport as justification for trespass on the land of the very citizen who had evicted him, figuratively, in an earlier era. If hunting had replaced agrarian expansionism with a logic of empire based on

Forest and Stream's hunter's cabin, one of the most popular exhibits at the 1876 Philadelphia Centennial International Exhibition, seemed intended to reaffirm the notion of hunting as a tradition of the common man. Another hunter's cabin was erected by the Boone and Crockett Club at the World's Columbian Exposition in Chicago in 1893. From John Filmer and George C. Bell, *The Illustrated Catalogue of the Centennial Exhibition, Philadelphia, 1876.* Photograph by Terry Firman Jr.

notions of chivalry, science, and individual enterprise, sport hunting now seemed to justify the requisition of the lands of the farmer himself.

Since the beginning of the cult of Boone, hunters and farmers had uneasily coexisted as heirs of nature, heroes of expansion, and model citizens, but they could peaceably coexist no longer. The clash between sport hunters and farmers pitted an older, Jeffersonian set of values, political interests, and lifestyles against a newer way of life of a modern, urban, middle class. From the inception of the cult of Boone, the hunter had become the hero and alter ego of the middle-class man and had begun to replace the farmer in the middle-class imagination as the true citizen of nature. Though the farmer continued to enjoy a vaunted image as producer and settler, it was clear by the late nineteenth century—particularly after big-game hunter and naturalist Theodore Roosevelt assumed the presidency—that the United States had become in many respects a nation of hunters.

That America had become a nation of hunters, however, did not necessarily mean that it had become a nation given over entirely to oligarchy and arrogance. Just when hunting seemed ripe to become the sport of would-be aristocrats, men like Roosevelt and Whelen sought to reclaim it on behalf of the common man. Through their efforts—and those of thousands of others who recalled the tradition of Daniel Boone and Natty Bumppo—hunting was redefined as a bastion of individualism and egalitarianism. In later decades, sport hunting would achieve new heights of popularity among common men in America. At the same time, men like Roosevelt and Whelen ensured that hunting would remain a badge of ethnic identity for white Americans, a badge that, though tarnished, is still worn.

Epilogue

 We live in a world that Theodore Roosevelt and his fellow sportsmen both salvaged and created in the early twentieth century. Far from becoming the sport of the aristocratic few, hunting has remained the pastime of the democratic many. Though its popularity slips a bit with each decade, it represents for thousands of men (and increasing numbers of women) the essence of American tradition, even a way of life.[1] The American Native, the man or woman who finds meaning and identity in nature and in hunting, and who clings to the self-reliance and manliness of the pioneer past, survives. Even today hunters seem more likely than others to embrace a conservative or libertarian worldview, with its emphasis on self-reliant individualism. In turn, like Theodore Roosevelt, hunters are torn between their desire to protect wildlife and habitat and their dislike of government intervention.

Yet the hunters of the late nineteenth century are not the hunters of today. The middle-class or patrician sportsman has fallen by the wayside of late. Hunting still appeals to businessmen who hobnob within the confines of private hunting clubs (particularly in Texas), but such clubs are scarcer than they once were.

According to the U.S. Fish and Wildlife Service's publication *National Survey of Fishing, Hunting, and Wildlife-Associated Recreation,* the typical American hunter of 1996 had twelve years of schooling or less and came from a household with a yearly income of under $50,000. Thus the average hunter was neither rich nor poor, neither highly educated nor poorly educated. Fifty-six percent lived in metropolitan areas with populations of over 50,000, and the remaining 44 percent lived outside major metropolitan areas. These data indicate that ruralites—though a minority of the hunting population—were more likely than urbanites to hunt. The vast majority of these hunters (95 percent) were white, and their favored target was overwhelmingly the deer.[2]

We can surmise from these facts that hunting appeals to blue-collar men (and lesser numbers of women) in both urban and rural locales. These hunters still square off against property owners on whose land they hunt, but the class distinctions are often reversed. The person behind the no hunting sign is in some areas more likely to own an expensive ranchette than a farm, whereas the person behind the gun is more likely to be of rural, working-class, or lower middle-class background.

The reasons for this shift are many, but perhaps the most important is the success of conservation campaigns of old. In creating bag limits, game seasons, and game wardens, conservationists abolished pot hunting and market hunting. By the early twentieth century, all hunters, with rare exceptions, were sport hunters. That did not mean that the pot-hunting tradition truly died out; it simply meant that even those who paid little attention to sportsmanship, men not of middle-class or elite rank, counted as sportsmen. Arms and ammunition companies assisted this transition by embracing these hunters in order to reach the widest possible market. The companies' sales representatives, called "missionaries," ventured in the early twentieth century "to the utmost rural sectors," where they found hardware and grocery stores eager to sell hunting wares and shooters eager to buy them. At the same time, firearms prices continued to drop, as they had since the antebellum era. In 1920 rifles and shotguns were produced at half their pre–World War I cost.[3]

With a push from gun makers and their missionaries, sport hunting surged in popularity in the early twentieth century; the number of hunting licenses sold in America doubled between 1910 and 1920. Part of this surge came with the success of the automobile. Cheap cars like the Model T made it possible for men of modest means to seek out distant hunting grounds. This mobility, in conjunction with legislation mandating longer weekends, more holidays, and paid vacations, allowed Americans to engage in the chase as never before. By 1945 fully one-quarter of American men were sport hunters.[4]

Yet as thousands of rural and working-class men took up hunting, they vitiated the idea of the sport hunter as a man of integrity, honor, and a strict code of ethics. The nonhunting public—wrongly, for the most part—came to see sportsmen not as eminently respectable but as reckless, beer-swilling, violent men. This image of the redneck hunter recalls the savage hunters of colonial imagination rather than the true sportsmen of the nineteenth century.

As an index of changing attitudes toward hunting since World War II, consider the fate of William Temple Hornaday's National Collection of Heads and Horns. Hornaday projected that the collection, housed in the 1920s in a building intended to accommodate 60,000 visitors per day, would last two hundred years. What Hornaday presumed would remain a popular exhibition, however, turned stale in the Vietnam era. "Just dead animals," visitors would utter. In the mid-1970s, the collection was closed for lack of public interest.[5]

Hunters assume that negative stereotypes arose as Americans became more urban, affluent, and, ipso facto, antihunting. There is truth in this assumption. Middle-class urbanites no longer embrace hunting as they once did in part because gentility has been redefined. Though Protestant and Enlightenment conceptions of the ideal citizen—the man of rationality and restraint—were eclipsed in the nineteenth century, they returned in the late twentieth. To be middle class in modern America is, generally speaking, to be a restrained and domesticated citizen, not to be a chivalrous slayer of wild beasts.

Meanwhile, many Americans have entered the middle class from the ranks of immigrants who lacked a hunting tradition and saw no reason to adopt one. Hunting's popularity has declined still further as the popularity of sports like football, basketball, and baseball—sports that have been more accessible to urban immigrant and minority groups than hunting—has risen. Because these sports emphasize team cooperation, they are far more representative of today's corporate culture than is hunting with its emphasis on self-reliance.

Negative stereotypes of hunting have appeared, finally, not because Americans as a whole have become more urban, affluent, and divorced from nature but because hunters themselves have become less urban and affluent. The popularity of sport hunting surged in the nineteenth century because of its association with the social elite (and, of course, frontier heroes like Daniel Boone), whereas it loses popularity today—at least among middle-class men—because of its association with working-class and rural folk. Hunting, to be blunt, seems backward.

In an attempt to reclaim the moral high ground, respectable hunters chide their irresponsible brethren (much as true sportsmen chided pot hunters a century ago), but with little success in the realm of public relations. To cite one example, Safari Club International, a society of responsible hunters and conservationists with a membership of thirty-two thousand (mostly American), complains of a computer game called "Deer Hunter Avenger." According to a 1999 newspaper article, club members whose children had received the game as Christmas gifts "were appalled [that] the presentation of hunting included references to bazookas, drinking and sex. They contend the video game urges violence against hunters."[6]

Far from being the miscreants portrayed in the computer game, points out Alfred "Skip" Donau, president of Safari Club International, members of his group "pride themselves in promoting hunter safety and ethics." His organization calls on members to share game with the needy and has teamed up with the National Rifle Association and the Lakeshore Foundation to promote hunting and shooting activities among the disabled.

Simon and Schuster, marketer of "Deer Hunter Avenger," counters that its game is a parody, yet the fact that a parody of hunters is popular in American markets shows how far the reputation of hunters has fallen. Even educated, virtuous sportsmen who belong to Safari Club International share the stigma attached to hunters.

Perhaps the biggest factor working toward the depopularization of hunting has been the camera. Although at the turn of the century, *Outdoor Life* recommended that hunters carry cameras to record kills, it was not long before the camera was presented as an alternative to the gun. To shoot an animal with film was as much a triumph as to shoot it with a bullet. Soon the photograph began to replace the trophy, threatening to make taxidermy obsolete. As a portable form of technology, the camera harmonized with nature every bit as much as the gun yet did not require the death of sentient beings.

The camera permitted individuals—particularly those of the middle and upper classes—to venture into the wilderness to practice the virtue of self-reliance without breaching the ethic of domesticity. Roosevelt hoped in 1906 that the camera would supplant the rifle as a tool for capturing wild game, though adding that "it is highly undesirable that the rifle should be wholly laid by."[7] Roosevelt got his wish and then some. Thousands of children grow up today with the ambition of becoming not Daniel Boones but wildlife photographers. Yet the gun has not been "wholly laid by," as continuing debates over gun control demonstrate.

The camera also undermined hunting from a different direction, allowing Walt Disney and his progeny to project anthropomorphic images of animals to the millions. Once exposed to Bambi and similar depictions of cheerful, innocent, infantlike animals in films—in addition to nature specials showing real animals playing, cuddling, and mothering their young—children are less likely to grow up to be hunters. Indeed, they are likely to oppose hunting altogether. Big-city zoos, too, continue to teach the ethic of domesticity; zoo animals seem cute, friendly, fascinating, and occasionally fierce but seldom truly threatening (they are, after all, caged). Meanwhile, other outdoor sports—rock climbing, mountaineering, kayaking, and skiing—have replaced hunting as ways for middle-class and elite Americans to test their mettle against the forces of nature.

Hunters remain loyal to a sport they consider traditional and unchanging, yet hunters have changed with the times. Battered and embarrassed by humanitarians and advocates of gun control, some have embraced the shibboleths of the National Rifle Association, whereas others have bent in the opposite direction, creating new, more sensitive personae for themselves. Whereas nineteenth-century hunters proclaimed their chivalrous defeat of the wild beast, many of today's hunters portray themselves as nature lovers who kill reluctantly (with "mingled sadness and elation," writes hunter Richard Nelson), and who show infinite respect for their prey. "Other beings," writes poet Gary Snyder in *The Practice of the Wild*, speaking for hunters, "do not mind being killed and eaten as food, but they expect us to say please, and thank you, and they hate to see themselves wasted."[8]

With respect as their watchword, hunters have come to see themselves as heirs to the animistic Indian hunters of old (little realizing how much their new personae reflect those of their true sportsmen ancestors). Many of today's hunters are reluctant to call themselves sport hunters; in fact, they are coached not to describe hunting as sport because that denotes killing for pleasure. Hunters insist that they kill not to gain pleasure but to become one with nature. "Hunting . . . deepens my sense of connection to the surrounding natural world," writes Richard Nelson, "and sharpens my awareness that I am an animal, not separate from my fellow creatures but twisted together with them in one great braidwork of life. Hunting brings me into the wild and brings the wild into me."[9] Hunters like Nelson enter the wild to become part of it, not to prove their superiority over other forms of life. This return to nature allows hunters to regain sanity (and saintliness) in a world divorced from nature.

Despite hunting's declining popularity since World War II, Nelson's idea of hunting as sacred rite resonates with many Americans. Indeed, jeremiads that call on Americans to return to hunting have reappeared in the past several decades with some frequency. In 1995 James A. Swan, a California psychologist, produced a fascinating apologia titled *In Defense of Hunting* that described hunting as psychotherapy. In 1997 Mary Zeiss Stange, director of the Women's Studies Program at Skidmore College in Saratoga Springs, New York, made a comparable argument in *Woman the Hunter*, contending that women have hunted for millennia and urging modern women to hunt to empower themselves.[10] These tracts in turn recall the seminal work of Paul Shepard, a naturalist (recently deceased) who sought to refashion Americans into a hunting people.

When Shepard began publishing in the 1960s and 1970s, American hunters were already on the defensive. It had become fashionable in intellectual circles to decry hunting as humanity's most ancient sin, the source of human (or at least human male) bloodlust. This idea, though as old as the Enlightenment, had been sanctioned in the twentieth century by Australian anatomist Raymond Dart who, in the 1920s, had had the good fortune of identifying in South Africa some of the earliest hominid fossils then known. From these fossils, Dart conjectured that hominids had evolved into big-brained bipeds precisely because they were hunters. Dart's idea—known as the "hunting hypothesis"—achieved wide acceptance among paleontologists, anthropologists, philosophers, and poets, particularly after World War II, when thinkers sought to identify the source of human brutality. As instinctive hunters—given to rapine, war, and genocide—humans represented "the eventual hell of life, the animal / Toward which all evolution toiled and was damned / From the beginning," wrote American poet Robinson Jeffers.[11]

Many Americans, however, with their unique hunting tradition, have been reluctant to equate hunting with original sin. Hence in *The Tender Carnivore and the Sacred Game*, published in 1973, Paul Shepard revised Dart's hunting hypothesis. In combing the recesses of history and prehistory to determine where humans had gone wrong, Shepard decided that hominids had evolved as hunters but that agriculture had made them degenerate. With agriculture and pastoralism had come the idea of perpetual progress, along with social hierarchy, tyranny, incessant war, overpopulation, drudgery, neuroses, and ecological crisis.[12]

Hunting peoples ("cynegetic man," in Shepard's idiom) were by contrast peaceful, gregarious, healthy, and fulfilled. The answer to modern woes, suggested Shepard, was not to reject technology or urbanization but to recast men as hunters (women were to become gatherers). To accomplish this transformation, Shepard suggested that the interior of each continent be set aside as hunting refuges and that cities be limited to seaboard areas.[13]

It is easy to snicker at Shepard's vision, yet much of his logic is compelling. Few have thought more deeply about the evolutionary origins of humanity than Shepard or about the place of humans in nature. Few have proposed a more sweeping plan for wilderness preservation (or, more accurately, wilderness creation). And few have offered social prescriptions more redolent of the American Native.

In Shepard's thought, hunters had replaced farmers as ideal citizens of nature. Not surprisingly, Shepard, like Roosevelt, looked to urbanites to implement his vision. "Urban man today is less deformed," he wrote, "in spite of his lack of nature contact, than the peasants, farmers, and their small-town collaborators who have predominated in the agricultural era." In the future foreseen by Shepard, small bands of urban hunters bearing bows or spears would venture periodically beyond the pale of technology and cities to achieve true humanity in the wilderness.[14] How different is this vision—apart from the bows and spears—from that of nineteenth-century sport hunters? Not very different at all.

The ideas of Paul Shepard, Richard Nelson, James Swan, and Mary Zeiss Stange are not precisely those of Theodore Roosevelt, yet those ideas derive from America's hunting tradition. Each theorist suggests that hunting is psychologically healthy and that hunters belong to, and on, the land. Gone are odes of triumph over the beast; gone are overt associations between hunting and empire; gone—in the case of Stange, at least—are connections between hunting and patriarchy. Stripped of these sins, what remains is the bonelike outline of the American Native, the man or woman who hunts because he or she loves land and animals and because he or she is heir to a mystical and ancient hunting tradition. Hunters hunt, to quote Jimmy Carter, because "my father and all my ancestors did it before me."[15]

One doubts that all Jimmy Carter's ancestors, or even the males among them, hunted before him. There has probably never been a time in American history when the majority of adult white males hunted regularly either for subsistence or sport. Dig into a hunter's past, and you will find male ancestors who did not hunt. It is the ancestors who did hunt, however, whom hunters choose to remember.

What hunters of today should also remember is that even in America, with its abundance of game and its frontier past, hunting was an "invented tradition," in the words of Eric Hobsbawm.[16] True, there were genuine backwoods hunters in America, men who for generations hunted for subsistence, for profit, or for an escape from the drudgery of farming. But the meaning that Americans attached to backwoods hunters was far more important than their simple existence.

America's hunting tradition was invented first by colonial promoters who painted the New World as a place of fantastic abundance, a place where all men could indulge in leisure pursuits enjoyed by the elite few in Europe. This initial celebration of hunting, however, soon gave way to a repudiation of hunters, who seemed too Indian or, at times, too aristocratic. The farmer—who might hunt occasionally, but not as a way of life—became the paragon of colonial virtue. Hunters, by contrast, were perceived as men who had rejected civilization, observing no authority but their own.

During the American Revolution, this Hobbesian hunter who was at war with nature and society was transformed into a symbol of the jealous defense of natural rights. This incipient celebration of hunters in buckskins, however, was muted by the continuing popularity of agrarian doctrine. To men of the Enlightenment, farmers were ideal citizens of the Republic. Farmers were disinterested because they had no need to manipulate government to benefit themselves, yet they were educated enough to make political choices. As men with property, moreover, they had an interest in society that roving hunters lacked. Farmers represented honesty, integrity, and civilization; hunters represented the savagism of the frontier.

Despite its Revolutionary heritage, America's hunting tradition did not come into its own until the market revolution. During the Age of Jackson—the age of go-ahead individualism—middle-class men sought new rituals of self-sufficiency and moral rectitude. In celebrating heroes like Boone and in taking up the rural sport of hunting, clerks, merchants, ministers, teachers, lawyers, doctors, and planters hoped to recapture the spartan, republican virtues of their forebears and—despite the contradiction—to associate themselves with the English gentry. "Our tastes are rural and our habits of the simplest," announced *Forest and Stream* in its inaugural issue of August 1873, recapitulating an idea that had emerged in the earliest Jacksonian sporting literature.[17] Whether these rural tastes and simple habits were those of English country gentlemen, American yeomen farmers, or frontiersmen like Boone was left unsaid.

In professing loyalty to rural virtues of old, hunters ironically distanced themselves from the founding generation. In identifying themselves as heirs to a hunting tradition, Americans forgot or neglected the fact that the nation's founders had praised farming and farmers—not hunting and hunters—as cornerstones of republicanism. They also forgot or neglected an older definition of Americanness—and manliness—based on duty to community, church, and polis. In its place, they embraced the ethic of laissez-faire individualism and self-reliance, an ethic born of market revolution rather than republicanism. It was this ethic that hunting conveyed.

In turn, the predatory individualism of the hunter translated into the predatory nationalism of Manifest Destiny. Hunting did not cause Manifest Destiny or the Civil War, but it exemplified—and fed—the national obsession with chivalry, guns, and martial valor. That did not mean that all hunters were expansionists, or that all embraced war, or that all rejected community and commonwealth in favor of unrestrained individualism. Hunters were, and are, diverse people with diverse ideas. Taken as a whole, however, the celebration of hunters and hunting in nineteenth-century America represented—and contributed to—sea changes in American culture, changes that the founding generation might not have endorsed.

The hunting tradition was again reinvented in the late nineteenth and early twentieth centuries by Progressives like Theodore Roosevelt, George Bird Grinnell, and William Temple Hornaday. Such men sought to segregate true Americans from insolent hordes of racial and ethnic others, while guarding the old America of individualism and self-help from the excesses of Gilded Age capitalism. To save hunting as a rite of Americanness, however, hunters had to save game, and to save game they had to rely on government. The alternative was either the extirpation of game or the privatization of hunting, neither of which were palatable to most Americans. Consequently, the individualism so cherished by hunters gave way to organization as hunters formed clubs and lobbied government.

In accepting the challenge of saving game, hunters made themselves stewards of the American environment. Stewardship, indeed, had been implicit in sport hunting from its Jacksonian inception. In identifying Americanness with wild animals and wilderness, hunters had made themselves American Natives, men with a special appreciation for the continent's fauna, geography, and sublime scenery. Demanding government aid to protect wilderness and wildlife was a way to reaffirm this identity and to save hunting as a rite (and right) of the democratic many.

Nonetheless, there was ambiguity in the hunter's ethical vision. As heirs to an agrarian tradition that for centuries had equated predators with evil, sport hunters developed little appreciation for wolves, coyotes, or cougars. Predators were especially reviled for being "fiendish" because they killed deer or "cowardly" because they refused to do battle with gun-toting humans. Far from comprehending the irony of calling an animal that hunts for food "fiendish," while calling one that hunts for sport "courageous," hunters of the early twentieth century routinely supported predator eradication programs conducted by the government. Deer and other game were to be reserved for human predators.[18]

Nor did sport hunters appreciate the idea that nongame species—even small ones, like snail darters and spotted owls—fulfill unique roles within ecosystems and deserve salvation as much as elk or buffalo. When Americans did come to appreciate the concepts of ecosystems and ecology in the second half of the twentieth century (and the role of predators within them), their appreciation was sparked by scientists rather than hunters.[19]

As hunters ignored nongame species and waged war on predators, they also battled fellow hunters. In saving hunting as a sport (a relatively new American tradition), conservationists abolished an older and equally democratic tradition of hunting for subsistence and market. Soon, in the national parks, forests, and game preserves of the West, as well as in the public hunting grounds of the East, wardens and rangers began arresting a new sort of criminal—the poacher who hunted game out of season or without a license. In turn, wardens and rangers met with hostility and retaliatory poaching by hunters who—whether they were immigrants, Indians, or Anglo-Americans—resented the replacement of what Louis Warren calls a "local commons" by a "state" or "national commons." For impoverished Indians, whose hunting rights on undeveloped federal lands were guaranteed in treaties, the curtailment of hunting rights was particularly galling. In some cases, such as when park rangers and deputized locals ambushed a party of Bannock hunters in Jackson Hole, Wyoming, in 1895, American Indians were killed in the name of game preservation.[20]

A dark truth stood behind conservation: it displaced the weak to benefit the strong. Just as the price for enclosure in England had been paid by commoners, so in America the price for saving game was paid by those too poor, or too "other," to gain the ear of the U.S. Congress and state legislatures. The lesson to be learned, however, is not that the creation of national or state commons was wrong or elitist; the creation of those commons permitted millions of working-class and rural people to become sport hunters in subsequent decades. What was wrong and elitist was the creation of national and state commons without compensation or concern for those injured by it.

The conflicts that resulted from the creation of national and state commons were, as Louis Warren shows, callous and in most cases unnecessary. Yet assuming the country was going to maintain hunting as a democratic sport, state and federal oversight of lands and game populations was necessary. Undoubtedly, market and subsistence hunters, together with habitat reduction caused by ranching, farming, logging, and mining, would have wiped out game species had sport hunters not crusaded for conservation. Beaver, buffalo, and grizzly, as well as elk and antelope in many locales, had fallen victim to progress by 1900; only a few decades more would have brought the annihilation of deer and waterfowl and perhaps dozens of other species. If hunters had not campaigned to save game, there would have been no local—or national—commons worthy of the name.

Without conservation, hunting would not have disappeared; it simply would have been the province of elite and arrogant men (recall the actions of the Tolleston Club) who owned game preserves. Many Gilded Age hunters would have been perfectly at ease with that outcome. As one hunter wrote in 1909,

> Until all of the wild game is shot off and the public has no further interest in its protection, it is absolutely impossible to have decent shooting or much game. Free public shooting is a delusion anyway. When there is no more wild game to be protected, and men of wealth, whose tastes run in that direction, are permitted to breed and

kill and sell anything they want to, whenever they want to, without a lot of red tape, there will be no end of big preserves created, and more game . . . than this generation of sportsmen has ever seen.[21]

Sentiments like those make the accomplishments of other hunters and conservationists all the more remarkable.

In the end, the men who banned together to protect America through Progressive reforms—the mugwumps, middle-class and upper-class men of Anglo-Saxon, Protestant, American descent—also banned together to protect game. Although their efforts redounded to their own benefit as hunters, they transcended special interests. One can deride sport hunters for their elitism, yet one must praise them for their foresight. After all, would we be better off if men like Theodore Roosevelt, George Bird Grinnell, and William Temple Hornaday had not enlisted government in the cause of saving wildlife?

The most important legacy of the American Native is not the preservation of hunting but the creation of an ethic of stewardship. Those Americans who call themselves environmentalists—and I count myself among them—do not have to be hunters to appreciate what nineteenth- and early twentieth-century sport hunters accomplished. Their love for American fauna, their fascination with natural history, and their appreciation for the sublime contributed to our own sensibilities.

These meanings for nature were socially constructed from America's imperialist and patriarchal past (there may also be a biological basis for them, but I will leave biologists to speculate on that). To admit that American ideas about nature come from the past, however, does not mean that we should categorically reject old premises. Culture is built by accretion, not by revolution. The best one can do is evaluate one's worldview and reform it to accord with the ideals of fairness, tolerance, egalitarianism, and respect for life.

That evaluation has long been under way in America, proceeding by fits and starts. It will continue in the future, one hopes, alongside the ethic of stewardship that emerged in the nineteenth century. This ethic of stewardship transcended, and transcends, the radical individualism—the denial of community—embedded in the nineteenth-century romance of hunting. The ethic of stewardship must also transcend, however, the limitations within the persona—the American Native—that gave it birth.

In identifying themselves with American fauna and geography, nineteenth-century sport hunters developed a unique ethnic identity. In the era of Theodore Roosevelt, hunting separated true Americans from alien peoples who encroached from without. There was magnificent irony in this ethnic identity. At one time, white Americans had identified themselves as hard-working farmers destined to replace the brave, yet indolent, dark-skinned hunters who were indigenous to the continent. By the late nineteenth century, white Americans identified themselves as indigenous hunters who—if they did not preserve their hunting tradition—would be displaced by dark-skinned folk from other continents.

Given that 95 percent of today's American hunters are white and that many of them see hunting as a profoundly American pastime, one can surmise that hunting has not entirely shed its affiliation with ethnic, or tribal, identity. That does not mean that hunters are uniquely ethnocentric. One might argue that members of Recreational Equipment Incorporated or the Sierra Club are every bit as tied to Anglo-American ethnic heritage as members of Ducks Unlimited.[22] Many modern environmentalists—from Sierra Club executive director David Brower to Earth First! founder Dave Foreman—deserve to be called American Natives as much as or more than sport hunters.

Neither hunters nor environmentalists deliberately cling to an ethnic identity, yet cultural legacies are hard to erase. What is to be done about that? Neither hunters nor environmentalists should repudiate their reverence for American wildlife and wilderness (even if those are cultural constructs), yet they must bring others within the collective tent, especially those who are not white. Failure to do so is to risk marginalization and irrelevancy in the twenty-first century.

What sport hunters and environmentalists must also do is learn to share their tent with one another. If environmentalists can recognize traditional Indian hunters as legitimate, they should recognize modern hunters as equally legitimate, especially hunters who espouse a philosophy of minimal impact and conservation. There is no reason that hunters should play lesser roles in modern ecosystems than in ancient ones; hunters are and always have been integral components of wilderness.

The trick is to permit humans to interact with wilderness without polluting it out of existence. Some hunters, oblivious to the concept of impact, drive all-terrain vehicles wherever they wish, strewing the ground with sardine tins and bullet shells, not to mention corpses of deer half-dismembered. Other hunters slip quietly into the forest, leaving hardly a footprint behind. Edward Abbey appreciated them, and so should others.

But is America still a nation of hunters? On the face of it, no. As of 1996, only about 7 percent of Americans over the age of fifteen purchased hunting licenses (the total number of hunters in America had fallen by more than half a million since 1985).[23]

Even if the number of hunters is declining, Americans remain—more than citizens of other nations—individualists. Perhaps they are not as self-reliant as they once were (though there was never a time when Americans wholly determined their own fates), but they are equally ambitious for individual success. Moreover, Americans continue to reject measures like national health care that emphasize communal rather than individual responsibility. And they continue to view nature—like society—as a realm of struggle and strife in which only the strong prevail. Leaf through any outdoor magazine—not just *Field and Stream* or *Outdoor Life*, but *Outside, Backpacker, National Geographic,* or *Sierra*—and you will find (at least occasionally) a nature red in tooth and claw.

Consider the crusade to bring back predators—wolves, grizzlies, and cougars—to the wilderness. How different is the current fascination for these predatory animals from the earlier fascination for predatory men? Though idolizers of wolves and bears do not necessarily idolize human hunters, they tend to accept the hunter's view of wilderness as a Darwinian realm of struggle and strife, a testing ground for the fittest.

Or consider the Darwinian realm of the American highway, where Safaris, Defenders, Explorers, and Pathfinders contest the road with Blazers, Broncos, Troopers, and Discoverers. The popularity of these sturdy vehicles among affluent Americans who seldom drive off-road suggests that even today middle-class Americans feel compelled to advertise themselves as hardy pioneers. One wonders whether these vehicles represent a subtle form of nativism in a time of affirmative action and renewed immigration.

Side by side with Darwinian images appear images based on John Muir's vision of wilderness as church, in which hunting is sacrilege, or images based on Edward Hicks's vision of nature as Eden, where all is harmony. These images (which nineteenth-century domesticators would have approved) also appear in all the outdoor magazines, including those purchased by hunters.

The same contradictory images of nature that existed in nineteenth-century America—and the same contradictory images of society—exist in today's America. Often these contradictory images exist in the same mind, exemplifying the paradoxes of which consciousness is capable. On balance, however, our images of nature have shifted more toward the domestic ideal than the Darwinian as we enter the new millennium. "It's a good thing," as Martha Stewart might say. Yet I, for one, hope that American individualism and hunting, to echo the sentiment of Theodore Roosevelt, are never "wholly laid by."

Notes

All quotes have been reproduced as found in the sources. When both original and reprint editions are given, page citations are to the reprint edition.

Prologue

1. John Smith, *The Generall Historie of Virginia, New England & the Summer Isles together with the True Travels, Adventures and Observations, and a Sea Grammar,* vol. 1 (Glasgow, 1907), 155. Smith's *Generall Historie* was first published in London in 1624. John Smith, *A Description of New England: or the Observations and Discoveries of Captain John Smith (Admirall of that Country) in the North of America, in the Year of Our Lord 1614 . . .*, in *Tracts and Other Papers relating principally to the Origin, Settlement, and Progress of the Colonies in North America, from the Discovery of the Country to the Year 1776,* comp. Peter Force, vol. 2 (Washington, D.C., 1836; reprint, Gloucester, Mass., 1963), document no. 1, 22. Smith's *Description of New England* was first published in London in 1616.

2. Elisha Jarrett Lewis, *The American Sportsman: Containing Hints to Sportsmen, Notes on Shooting, and the Habits of Game Birds and Wild Fowl of America* (Philadelphia, 1855), unnumbered leaf 7. Lewis's *American Sportsman* was first published as *Hints to Sportsmen* in Philadelphia in 1851.

3. D. H. Lawrence, *Studies in Classic American Literature* (New York, 1964), 62; Richard Slotkin, *Regeneration through Violence: The Mythology of the American Frontier, 1600–1860* (Middletown, Conn., 1973); Richard Slotkin, *The Fatal Environment: The Myth of the Frontier in the Age of Industrialization, 1800–1890* (New York, 1985); Richard Slotkin, *Gunfighter Nation: The Myth of the Frontier in Twentieth-Century America* (New York, 1992).

4. Joseph Campbell, *The Hero with a Thousand Faces* (New York, 1949).

5. Mann Butler, "Details of Frontier Life," *Register of the Kentucky Historical Society* 62, no. 3 (1964): 207. Butler's commentary on frontier life was first published in the St. Louis periodical *The Western Journal and Civilian* between February 1853 and December 1855 under the title "Valley of the Ohio: Its Conquest and Settlement by Americans."

Matthew Patten, *The Diary of Matthew Patten of Bedford, New Hampshire from 1754 to 1788* (Camden, Maine, 1993), 33.

6. James Kirby Martin and Mark Edward Lender, *A Respectable Army: The Military Origins of the Republic, 1756–1789* (Arlington Heights, Ill., 1982), 20, 208.

7. On the intellectual currents within the Revolution, see, for instance, Bernard Bailyn, *The Ideological Origins of the American Revolution* (Cambridge, Mass., 1967); Ruth H. Bloch, *Visionary Republic: Millennial Themes in American Thought, 1756–1800* (Cambridge, England, 1985); and Henry F. May, *The Enlightenment in America* (New York, 1976).

8. Cotton Mather, *Magnalia Christi Americana*, ed. Kenneth B. Murdock (London, 1977), 179. Mather's *Magnalia* was first published in London in 1702. Samuel Latham Mitchill, *A Discourse on the Character and Services of Thomas Jefferson, More Especially as a Promoter of Natural and Physical Science. Pronounced, by Request, Before the New-York Lyceum of Natural History, on the 11th October, 1826* (New York, 1826), 16.

9. Lee Clark Mitchell, *Witnesses to a Vanishing America: The Nineteenth-Century Response* (Princeton, N.J., 1981).

10. "Wheaton and the Panther," *Spirit of the Times* 9, no. 3 (March 23, 1839): 26, cols. 2–3. Anthropologist Alan Dundes argues that hunting involves the symbolic victory of man over nature. The hunter who mounts or stuffs a game animal or who cuts off its antlers, tusks, or tail, contends Dundes, symbolically castrates the prey ("Traditional Male Combat: From Game to War," in *Gewalt in der Kultur, Vorträge des 29, Deutscher Volkskundekongresses, Passau 1993*, ed. Rolf W. Brednich and Walter Hartinger [Passau, Germany, 1994], 159). Whether or not one accepts Dundes's proposition that all sports and games, including war, amount to symbolic castration, it is certainly true that sport hunting allowed American men to demonstrate their psychic and cultural mastery of nature.

11. See Michel Foucault, *The Archaeology of Knowledge*, trans. A. M. Sheridan Smith (London, 1972).

12. Mark Catesby, quoted in Robert Henry Welker, *Birds and Men: American Birds in Science, Art, Literature, and Conservation, 1800–1900* (Cambridge, Mass., 1955), 12; Patricia Tyson Stroud, *Thomas Say: New World Naturalist* (Philadelphia, 1992), 100–101.

13. Reverend Israel Acrelius, *Account of the Swedish Churches in New Sweden*, in *Narratives of Early Pennsylvania, West New Jersey and Delaware, 1630–1707*, ed. Albert Cook Myers (New York, 1912; reprint, New York, 1959), 71.

14. Thomas Jefferson, *Notes on the State of Virginia*, ed. William Peden (New York, 1954; reprint, New York, 1982), 164–65. Jefferson's *Notes* was first published in Paris in 1785.

15. Perry Miller, *Nature's Nation* (Cambridge, Mass., 1967).

1. Paradise

1. Beauchamp Plantagenet, *A Description of the Province of New Albion. And a Direction for Adventurers . . . to Live Plentifully*, in *Tracts and Other Papers relating principally to the Origin,*

Settlement, and Progress of the Colonies in North America, from the Discovery of the Country to the Year 1776, comp. Peter Force, vol. 2 (Washington, D.C., 1836; reprint, Gloucester, Mass., 1963), document no. 7, 6. Plantagenet's tract was first published in 1648. [Robert Johnson], *Nova Britannia. Offering the Most Excellent Fruites by Planting in Virginia. Exciting All Such as Be Well Affected to Further the Same,* in Force, *Tracts,* vol. 1, document no. 6, 10. Johnson's *Nova Britannia* was first published in London in 1609. Michael Drayton, *Ode to the Virginia Voyage,* quoted in Arthur K. Moore, *The Frontier Mind* (Lexington, Ky., 1957; reprint, New York, 1963), 36. Drayton's *Ode* was first published in 1606. John Hammond, *Leah and Rachel, or, the Two Fruitfull Sisters Virginia, and Mary-Land: Their Present Condition, Impartially Stated and Related . . . ,* in Force, *Tracts,* vol. 3, document no. 14, 13. Hammond's *Leah and Rachel* was first published in London in 1656.

2. Samuel Wilson, *An Account of the Province of Carolina,* in *Narratives of Early Carolina, 1650–1708,* ed. Alexander S. Salley Jr. (New York, 1911; reprint, New York, 1959), 170. Wilson's *Account* was first published in London in 1682. T.A. [Thomas Ashe], *Carolina,* quoted in Verner W. Crane, *The Southern Frontier, 1670–1732* (Ann Arbor, Mich., 1929; reprint, Ann Arbor, Mich., 1956), 111. Ashe's *Carolina* was first published in 1682.

3. William Wood, *New England's Prospect,* ed. Alden T. Vaughan (Amherst, Mass., 1977), 38, 53. Wood's *Prospect* was first published in London in 1634. Francis Higginson to his friends at Leicester, September 1629, *Letters from New England: The Massachusetts Bay Colony, 1629–1638,* ed. Everett Emerson (Amherst, Mass., 1976), 35. Higginson's letter was published as *New-Englands Plantation; Or, A Short and True Description of the Commodities and Discommodities of that Countrey* in London in 1630. Thomas Morton, *New English Canaan or New Canaan* (New York, 1972), 67. Morton's *New English Canaan* was first published in London in 1637.

4. John Josselyn, *A Critical Edition of Two Voyages to New-England,* ed. Paul J. Lindholdt (Hanover, N.H., 1988), 71. Josselyn's *Two Voyages* was first published in London in 1674.

5. See Phineas Pratt, "Narrative," in *A Declaration of the Affairs of the English People that First Inhabited New England,* Massachusetts Historical Society Collections, 4th ser., vol. 4 (1858), 479.

6. Stephen J. Pyne, *Fire in America: A Cultural History of Wildland and Rural Fire* (Princeton, N.J., 1982), 71–83; William Cronon, *Changes in the Land: Indians, Colonists, and the Ecology of New England* (New York, 1983), 28, 49–51, 90–91.

7. Gary Nash, *Red, White, and Black: The Peoples of Early America* (Englewood Cliffs, N.J., 1974), 37.

8. Alexander Pope, *Essay on Man,* Epistle 3, in *The Best of Pope,* ed. George Sherburn (New York, 1931), 4.151–154. Pope's *Essay on Man* was first published in 1733–34. As late as 1791 one writer speculated that the "ante-diluvian paradise" existed "near the northwest boundary of the United States" (*The American Museum, or, Universal Magazine* 10, no. 6 [December 1791]: 262).

9. Roderick Nash, *Wilderness and the American Mind* (Cambridge, Mass., 1968), 1–22; John Stilgoe, *Common Landscapes of America, 1580 to 1845* (New Haven, Conn. 1982), 7–12.

10. William Bradford, *Of Plymouth Plantation: The Pilgrims in America,* ed. Harvey Wish (New York, 1962), 60. Bradford's *Of Plymouth Plantation* was first published in 1897.

11. Dwight B. Heath, ed., *A Journal of the Pilgrims at Plymouth; Mourt's Relation, a relation or journal of the English plantation settled at Plymouth in New England, by certain English adventurers, both merchants and others* (New York, 1963), 82. *Mourt's Relation* was first published in London in 1622.

12. Patrick M. Malone, *The Skulking Way of War: Technology and Tactics among the New England Indians* (New York, 1991), 31–33, 57.

13. William Wood, quoted in Malone, *Skulking Way of War,* 18; John Gorham Palfrey, *A Compendious History of New England: from the Discovery by Europeans to the First General Congress of the Anglo-American Colonies,* vol. 1 (Boston, 1873), 72; Nicholas Wolfe Proctor, "Bathed in Blood: Hunting in the Antebellum South" (Ph.D. diss., Emory Univ., 1998), 5.

14. Nash, *Red, White, and Black,* 78; Joyce Lee Malcolm, *To Keep and Bear Arms: The Origins of an Anglo-American Right* (Cambridge, Mass., 1994), 139; John Russell Bartlett, ed., *Records of the Colony of Rhode Island and Providence Plantations, in New England,* vol. 1, *1636–1663* (Providence, R.I., 1856; reprint, New York, 1968), 94; *The Statutes at Large: Being A Collection of All the Laws of Virginia from the First Session of the Legislature, in the Year 1619 . . . ,* ed. William Waller Hening, vol. 1 (Richmond, 1823), 127, nos. 24, 25, 27, 28; 174, Act 51.

15. Carolyn Merchant, *The Death of Nature: Women, Ecology, and the Scientific Revolution* (San Francisco, 1980), 172–90; Max Weber quoted in Arthur Mitzman, *The Iron Cage: An Historical Interpretation of Max Weber* (New York, 1970), 226; Francis Bacon, *The Advancement of Learning and New Atlantis,* ed. Arthur Johnson (Oxford, England, 1974). Bacon's *New Atlantis* was first published in 1627 as an appendix to *Sylva Sylvarum; or, A Naturall Historie.*

16. Malcolm, *To Keep and Bear Arms,* 134.

17. Roger B. Manning, *Hunters and Poachers: A Social and Cultural History of Unlawful Hunting in England, 1485–1640* (Oxford, England, 1993), 3; Thomas Cockaine, *A Short Treatise of Hunting, 1591,* Shakespeare Association Facsimiles No. 5 (Oxford, England, 1932), A3. Cockaine's *Treatise* was first published in 1573.

18. Manning, *Hunters and Poachers,* 4, 5, 37; Ben Jonson, *Every Man in His Humour,* ed. Robert N. Watson (New York, 1988), 11. Jonson's play, first performed in 1598, was rewritten and performed a number of times between 1605 and 1612.

19. *The Institucion of a Gentleman. Anno Domini MD.LXVIII* (London, 1568), fol. 45r–v, quoted in Manning, *Hunters and Poachers,* 4.

20. W. R. Halliday, introduction to *Short Treatise of Hunting,* by Thomas Cockaine, xvii.

21. Nicholas Cox, *The Gentleman's Recreation, in Four Parts; (viz.) Hunting, Hawking, Fowling, Fishing. Collected from Ancient and Modern Authors Forrein and Domestick, and Rectified by the Experience of the Most Skilfull Artists of these Times* (London, 1674), 3–6; Matt Cartmill, *A View to a Death in the Morning: Hunting and Nature through History* (Cambridge, Mass., 1994), 64–65. Even the cries of the prey demanded discrimination: "The Hart *belloweth;*

the Buck *groaneth;* the Roe *belleth;* the Fox *barketh;* the Wolf *houleth;* the Goat *rattleth;* the Boar *freameth;* the Badger *shrieketh;* and the Otter *whineth"* (Cox, *Gentleman's Recreation,* 6).

22. Desiderius Erasmus, *The Praise of Folly,* trans. John Wilson (New York, 1942), 158–59. Erasmus's *In Praise of Folly* was first published in English in London in 1668. See also Cockaine, *Short Treatise of Hunting,* C2.

23. Manning, *Hunters and Poachers,* 5, 7, 10–12, 18; P. B. Munsche, *Gentlemen and Poachers: The English Game Laws, 1671–1831* (Cambridge, England, 1981), 29.

24. Manning, *Hunters and Poachers,* 60.

25. Munsche, *Gentlemen and Poachers,* 7, 53–54.

26. John Smith, *The Generall Historie of Virginia, New England & the Summer Isles together with the True Travels, Adventures and Observations, and a Sea Grammar,* vol. 1 (Glasgow, 1907), 178. John Lawson, quoted in Stuart A. Marks, *Southern Hunting in Black and White: Nature, History, and Ritual in a Carolina Community* (Princeton, N.J., 1991), 29.

27. Thomas Gabriel, *An Historical and Geographical Account of Pennsylvania and of West-New-Jersey,* in *Narratives of Early Pennsylvania, West New Jersey and Delaware, 1630–1707,* ed. Albert Cook Myers (New York, 1912; reprint, New York, 1959), 322. Gabriel's *Account* was first published in London in 1698. James A. Tober, *Who Owns the Wildlife? The Political Economy of Conservation in Nineteenth-Century America* (Westport, Conn., 1981), 19; William Penn, *Some Account of the Province of Pennsylvania,* in *Narratives of Early Pennsylvania,* 204. Penn's *Account* was first published in 1681. *Governor Nicholls' Answer to the Severall Queries Relative to the Planters in the Territories of His Royal Highness the Duke of Yorke in America,* in *Documents Relative to the Colonial History of the State of New York,* ed. E. B. O'Callaghan and B. Fernow, vol. 1 (Albany, N.Y., 1853), 88.

28. Terry G. Jordan and Matti Kaups, *The American Backwoods Frontier: An Ethnic and Ecological Interpretation* (Baltimore, 1989), 211, 213.

29. Grady McWhiney, *Cracker Culture: Celtic Ways in the Old South* (Tuscaloosa, Ala., 1988), 144–45, 238–40, 264; James Hall, *The Romance of Western History; or, Sketches of History, Life, and Manners in the West* (Cincinnati, 1885), 247. Hall's *Romance of Western History* was first published in Cincinnati in 1857.

30. Robert Beverley, *The History and Present State of Virginia,* ed. Louis B. Wright (Chapel Hill, N.C., 1947), 269. Beverley's *History* was first published in London in 1705. William Blathwayt quoted in Edmund S. Morgan, *American Slavery, American Freedom: The Ordeal of Colonial Virginia* (New York, 1975), 240.

31. Michael A. Bellesiles, *Arming America: The Origins of a National Gun Culture* (New York, 2000), 71, 107; Beverley, *History and Present State of Virginia,* xv; Judith A. McGaw, "'So Much Depends upon a Red Wheel Barrow': Agricultural Tool Ownership in the Eighteenth-Century Mid-Atlantic," in *Early American Technology: Making and Doing Things from the Colonial Era to 1850,* ed. Judith A. McGaw (Chapel Hill, N.C., 1994), 332.

32. Beverley, *History and Present State of Virginia,* 308–12.

33. Beverley, *History and Present State of Virginia,* 291–92.

34. By using secondary literature and colonial primary sources and by making inferences from early national sources (called "upstreaming" by anthropologists), one gains an appreciation for the diverse and pragmatic hunting methods employed by settlers. See Jennie Holliman, *American Sports (1785–1835)* (Durham, N.C., 1931), 37–38; Gerald Carson, *Men, Beasts and Gods: A History of Cruelty and Kindness to Animals* (New York, 1972), 63–65; Pyne, *Fire in America,* 71–83; Henry W. Shoemaker, comp., *A Pennsylvania Bison Hunt; . . .* (Middleburg, Pa., 1915), 26–27; Beverley, *History and Present State of Virginia,* 308–11; Louis Booker Wright, ed., *The Prose Works of William Byrd of Westover: Narratives of a Colonial Virginian* (Cambridge, Mass., 1966), 139; Philip Tome, *Pioneer Life; or, Thirty Years a Hunter. Being Scenes and Adventures of the Life of Philip Tome, Fifteen Years Interpreter for Cornplanter and Gov. Blacksnake, Chiefs on the Allegany River* (Buffalo, N.Y., 1854; reprint, Salem, N.H., 1989), 107; Thaddeus Mason Harris, *Journal of a Tour into the Territory Northwest of the Allegheny Mountains; April 7–July 1, 1803,* in *Early Western Travels, 1748–1846,* ed. Reuben Gold Thwaites, vol. 3 (Cleveland, 1904), 327; Oliver Taylor, *Historic Sullivan: A History of Sullivan County, Tennessee, with brief Biographies of the Makers of History* (Bristol, Tenn., 1909), 249; Mrs. George A. Perkins [Julia Anna (Shepard)], *Early Times on the Susquehanna* (Binghamton, N.Y., 1870; reprint, Binghamton, N.Y., 1906), 181–85; Samuel Griswold Goodrich, *Recollections of a Lifetime* (Auburn, N.Y., 1856), 100–102; Walter F. Peterson, "Rural Life in Antebellum Alabama," *Alabama Review* 19, no. 2 (April 1966): 143–45; and Dwight M. Smith, "An Antebellum Boyhood: Samuel Escue Tillman on a Middle Tennessee Plantation," *Tennessee Historical Quarterly* 47, no. 1 (1988): 8; D. Griffiths, *Two Years' Residence in the New Settlements of Ohio, North America; with Directions to Emigrants* (London, 1835), 72–74; Crisfield Johnson, *History of Washington Co., New York. With Illustrations and Biographical Sketches of Some of Its Prominent Men and Pioneers* (Philadelphia, 1878), 69–70.

35. Daniel H. Usner Jr., *Indians, Settlers, and Slaves in a Frontier Exchange Economy: The Lower Mississippi Valley before 1783* (Chapel Hill, N.C., 1992), 246, 248; Crane, *The Southern Frontier,* 111–12; Valerie M. Fogleman, "American Attitudes towards Wolves: A History of Misconception," *Environmental Review* 10, no. 4 (winter 1988): 63–94; David Hardin, "Laws of Nature: Wildlife Management Legislation in Colonial Virginia," in *The American Environment: Interpretations of Past Geographies,* ed. Larry Dilsaver and Craig Colten (Lanham, Md., 1992), 137–62. On furs and skins as barter, see also Matthew Patten, *The Diary of Matthew Patten of Bedford, New Hampshire from 1754 to 1788* (Camden, Maine, 1993), 10, 12, 33.

36. Lyman Copeland Draper, *The Life of Daniel Boone,* ed. Ted Belue (Mechanicsburg, Pa., 1998), 229.

37. Sir Robert Mountgomry, *A Discourse Concerning the Design'd Establishment of a New Colony to the South of Carolina, in the Most Delightful Country of the Universe,* in Force, *Tracts,* vol. 1, document no. 1, 8. Mountgomry's *Discourse* was first published in London in 1717.

38. Mountgomry, *Discourse Concerning . . . a New Colony to the South of Carolina,* in Force, *Tracts,* vol. 1, document no. 1, 7.

39. Louis B. Wright, *The First Gentlemen of Virginia: Intellectual Qualities of the Early Colonial Ruling Class* (San Marino, Calif., 1940), 11–12, 29, 85–86, 89; Thomas A. Lund, *American Wildlife Law* (Berkeley, Calif., 1980), 26.

40. Lund, *American Wildlife Law,* 24–25.

41. Manning, *Gentlemen and Poachers,* 59.

2. Hunting as a Religious Problem

1. My account of the Pomfret wolf hunt is based on Ellen D. Larned, *History of Windham County, Connecticut,* vol. 1 (Chester, Conn., 1976), 360–62; and David Humphreys, *The Miscellaneous Works of David Humphreys* (New York, 1804; reprint, Gainesville, Fla., 1968), 251–54. Larned's *History*—though drawn from earlier sources (chiefly Humphreys, it seems)—was first published in Worcester, Massachusetts, in 1874 and 1880; Humphreys's biographical treatise on Putnam was first published in 1788.

2. Larned, *History of Windham County,* vol. 1, 360; Barry Holstun Lopez, *Of Wolves and Men* (New York, 1978), 56; Larned, *History of Windham County,* vol. 1, 360.

3. Humphreys, *Miscellaneous Works,* 252.

4. Larned, *History of Windham County,* vol. 1, 361–62; Humphreys, *Miscellaneous Works,* 252.

5. Larned, *History of Windham County,* vol. 1, 361; Humphreys, *Miscellaneous Works,* 252.

6. Humphreys, *Miscellaneous Works,* 253.

7. Larned, *History of Windham County,* vol. 1, 360; Philip H. Smith, *Legends of the Shawangunk (Shon-Gum) and Its Environs. Including Historical Sketches, Biographical Notices, and Thrilling Border Incidents and Adventures Relating to Those Portions of the Counties of Orange, Ulster and Sullivan Lying in the Shawangunk Region* (Syracuse, N.Y., 1965), 181.

8. Humphreys, writing shortly after the Revolution, was eager to point out Putnam's credentials as a simple, virtuous farmer, never mentioning Putnam's credentials as a hunter (Humphreys, *Miscellaneous Works,* 251). Larned, writing in 1874, noted that Putnam was an experienced hunter (Larned, *History of Windham County,* vol. 1, 361).

9. Richard Slotkin describes Benjamin Church, the seventeenth-century frontiersman who defeated the forces of Metacomet ("King Philip"), as the precursor of the Daniel Boone hero. Though Church mentions in his narrative killing and feasting on a deer during his pursuit of Indians, he became famous as a hunter of men, not beasts. For brief tales of hunting predators in Connecticut, see Theron Wilmot Crissey and Rev. Joseph Eldridge, comps., *History of Norfolk, Litchfield County, Connecticut* (Everett, Mass., 1900), 219.

10. The term "half-horse, half-alligator" became popular in the Jacksonian and antebellum eras to describe rough-and-tumble hunter-heroes like Davy Crockett. The term seems to have been invented by Samuel Woodworth in his poem *Hunters of Kentucky.* See Samuel Woodworth, *Hunters of Kentucky* (Boston, [1815?]). The poem celebrates Andrew Jackson's victory over the English in the Battle of New Orleans. According to the poem, each of the hunters from Kentucky who had come to defend New Orleans was "half a horse, / And half an alligator."

11. John Winthrop, "John Winthrop's Experiencia, entry c. 1610," in *Winthrop Papers,* vol. 1, *1498–1628* (Boston, 1929), 165.

12. Max Weber, *The Protestant Ethic and the Spirit of Capitalism,* trans. Talcott Parsons (New York, 1930). Weber's *Protestant Ethic* was first published in 1904–1905.

13. Robert W. Malcolmson, *Popular Recreations in English Society, 1730–1850* (Cambridge, England, 1973), 45–46, 55–56, 68, 71.

14. Thomas Babington Macaulay, *The History of England from the Accession of James II,* vol. 1 (London, 1856), 161. Macaulay's *History of England* was first published in 1848 (vols. 1–2) and 1855 (vols. 3–4).

15. Macaulay, *History of England,* vol. 1, 81. On English poaching in the seventeenth and eighteenth centuries, see Roger B. Manning, *Hunters and Poachers: A Social and Cultural History of Unlawful Hunting in England, 1485–1640* (Oxford, England, 1993); and E. P. Thompson, *Whigs and Hunters: The Origins of the Black Act* (New York, 1975). On Puritanism, see Michael Walzer, "Puritanism as a Revolutionary Ideology," *History and Theory* 3 (1961): 59–90; Michael Walzer, *The Revolution of the Saints: A Study in the Origins of Radical Politics* (Cambridge, Mass., 1965); and David Little, *Religion, Order, and Law: A Study in Pre-Revolutionary England* (New York, 1969).

16. Richard H. Thomas, *The Politics of Hunting* (Aldershot, England, 1983), 17.

17. Patrick M. Malone, *The Skulking Way of War: Technology and Tactics among the New England Indians* (New York, 1991), 53–54; John Josselyn, *A Critical Edition of Two Voyages to New-England,* ed. Paul J. Lindholdt (Hanover, N.H., 1988), 62; Thomas Dudley to Lady Bridget, Countess of Lincoln, March 12 and 28, 1630[/31], *Letters from New England: The Massachusetts Bay Colony, 1629–1638,* ed. Everett Emerson (Amherst, Mass., 1976), 75; [?] Pond to William Pond, in *Winthrop Papers,* vol. 3, *1631–1637,* 18.

18. William Bradford, "Governor Bradford's History of Plymouth Colony," in *Chronicles of the Pilgrim Fathers of the Colony of Plymouth from 1602 to 1625,* ed. Alexander Young (Boston, 1841), 231; James Deetz, "The Reality of the Pilgrim Fathers," *Natural History* 78, no. 9 (November 1969): 43.

19. Joyce Lee Malcolm, *To Keep and Bear Arms: The Origins of an Anglo-American Right* (Cambridge, Mass., 1994), 70–72; Alexander E. Bergstrom, "English Game Laws and Colonial Food Shortages," *The New England Quarterly: An Historical Review of New England Life and Letters* 12, no. 4 (December 1939): 686.

20. Phineas Pratt, "Narrative," in *A Declaration of the Affairs of the English People that First Inhabited New England,* Massachusetts Historical Society Collections, 4th ser., vol. 4 (1858), 479.

21. See Michael Zuckerman, "Identity in British America: Unease in Eden," in *Colonial Identity in the Atlantic World, 1500–1800,* ed. Nicholas Canny and Anthony Pagden (Princeton, N.J., 1987), 126, 143–45; and William S. Simmons, "Cultural Bias in the New England Puritans' Perception of Indians," *William and Mary Quarterly,* 3d ser., no. 38 (1981): 56–72.

22. [John White], *The Planters Plea. Or, the Grounds of Plantations Examined, and Usual Objections Answered. Together with a Manifestation of the Causes Mooving such as have Lately Undertaken a Plantation in New-England: for the Satisfaction of those that Question the Lawfulnesse of the Action*, in *Tracts and Other Papers relating principally to the Origin, Settlement, and Progress of the Colonies in North America, from the Discovery of the Country to the Year 1776*, comp. Peter Force, vol. 2 (Washington, D.C., 1836; reprint, Gloucester, Mass., 1963), document no. 3, 3. White's *Planters Plea* was first published in London in 1630.

23. [White], *Planters Plea*, in Force, *Tracts*, vol. 2, document no. 3, 3.

24. Robert Cushman, *Reasons and Considerations Touching the Lawfulness of Removing Out of England into . . . America*, in *Mourt's Relation: A Journal of the English Plantation Settled at Plymouth in New England, by Certain English Adventurers Both Merchants and Others*, ed. Dwight B. Heath (New York, 1963), 91–93. *Mourt's Relation* was first published in London in 1622.

25. *The Revolution in New-England Justified: and the People There Vindicated from the Aspersions Cast Upon Them by Mr. John Palmer . . .* (Boston, 1691), in *Tracts and Other Papers relating principally to the Origin, Settlement, and Progress of the Colonies in North America, from the Discovery of the Country to the Year 1776*, comp. Peter Force, vol. 4 (Washington, D.C., 1847; reprint, Gloucester, Mass., 1963), document no. 8, 18; William Hubbard, *A General History of New England, from the Discovery to MDCLXXX* (Cambridge, Mass., 1815), 168, 210. For a fuller elaboration of the legal basis of land appropriation, see Alden T. Vaughan, *New England Frontier: Puritans and Indians, 1620–1675* (Boston, 1965), 110–14; and Wilcomb E. Washburn, "The Moral and Legal Justifications for Dispossessing the Indians," in *Seventeenth-Century America: Essays in Colonial History*, ed. James Morton Smith (Chapel Hill, N.C., 1959), 15–32.

26. Roger Williams, *Bloudy Tenent of Persecution* (1644), in *The Complete Writings of Roger Williams*, ed. Samuel L. Caldwell, vol. 3 (New York, 1963), 416; and Roger Williams, *Bloody Tenent Yet More Bloody* (1652), in *Complete Writings*, vol. 4, 29. On the Massachusetts Bay Colony's response to Williams's arguments, see John Winthrop to John Endecott, January 3, 1633[/34], *Winthrop Papers*, vol. 3, *1631–1637*, 148; and William Cronon, *Changes in the Land: Indians, Colonists, and the Ecology of New England* (New York, 1983), 100.

27. Hubbard, *General History of New England*, 209.

28. Samuel Eliot Morison, ed., *Of Plymouth Plantation, 1620–1647, by William Bradford, Sometime Governor Thereof* (New York, 1967), 187–88, 333. On Puritan attitudes toward the wilderness, see Peter N. Carroll, *Puritanism and the Wilderness: The Intellectual Significance of the New England Frontier, 1629–1700* (New York, 1969).

29. Josselyn, *Two Voyages to New-England*, 66.

30. Cronon, *Changes in the Land*, 100, 101, 105; John Russell Bartlett, ed., *Records of the Colony of Rhode Island and Providence Plantations, in New England*, vol. 1, *1636–1663* (Providence, R.I., 1856; reprint, New York, 1968), 84, 85; *The Public Records of the Colony of Connecticut [1636–1776]*, vol. 3, *May, 1678, to June, 1689* (Hartford, Conn., 1859; reprint, New York, 1968), 31.

31. William Bradford, quoted in Malone, *Skulking Way of War*, 61; Cronon, *Changes in the Land*, 54–81, 108–56. The New England colonist "was not much of a hunter," Alden Vaughan reminds us. Vaughan, *New England Frontier*, 108.

32. Timothy Dwight, *Travels in New England and New York [1795–1815]*, ed. Barbara Solomon and Patricia M. King, vol. 1 (Cambridge, Mass., 1969), 33. Dwight's *Travels* was originally published in New Haven in 1821–22.

33. Humphreys, *Miscellaneous Works*, 249.

34. William Penn, quoted in Richard Bridgman, "Jefferson's Farmer before Jefferson," *American Quarterly* 14, no. 4 (winter 1962): 570; John James Audubon, "Myself," in *Audubon and His Journals. With Zoological and Other Notes by Elliott Coues*, ed. Maria R. Audubon (New York, 1897), 16.

35. Patricia U. Bonomi, *Under the Cape of Heaven: Religion, Society, and Politics in Colonial America* (Oxford, England, 1986), 188.

36. Moravian diary, quoted in Albert H. Tillson Jr., *Gentry and Common Folk: Political Culture on the Virginia Frontier, 1740–1789* (Chapel Hill, N.C., 1991), 10.

3. Hunting as a Social Problem

1. William Byrd of Westover, *Secret History of the Line*, in *The Prose Works of William Byrd of Westover: Narratives of a Colonial Virginian*, ed. Louis Booker Wright (Cambridge, Mass., 1966), 118, 141; William Byrd of Westover, *The History of the Dividing Line*, in *Prose Works*, 278.

2. Byrd, *Secret History of the Line*, 140–41; Byrd, *History of the Dividing Line*, 230.

3. J. Hector St. John de Crèvecoeur, *Letters from an American Farmer and Sketches of Eighteenth-Century America* (New York, 1963), 70–71. Crèvecoeur's *Letters* was first published in London in 1782.

4. Richard Bernheimer, *Wild Men in the Middle Ages: A Study in Art, Sentiment, and Demonology* (Cambridge, Mass., 1952), 1–3, 9, 12, 73.

5. Devereux Jarratt, *The Life of Devereux Jarratt, Rector of Bath Parish, Dinwiddie County, Virginia, Written by Himself, in a Series of Letters Addressed to the Rev. John Coleman . . .* (Baltimore, 1806; facsimile reprint, New York, 1969), 16.

6. Rachel Klein, *Unification of a Slave State: The Rise of the Planter Class in the South Carolina Backcountry, 1760–1808* (Chapel Hill, N.C., 1990), 52, 63; Charles Woodmason, *The Carolina Backcountry on the Eve of the Revolution*, ed. Richard J. Hooker (Chapel Hill, N.C., 1953), 226; Pennsylvania *Gazette*, June 7, 1770, January 2, 1772, May 28, 1772. Accessible Archives CD-ROM Edition of the Pennsylvania *Gazette* with Additions from the Pennsylvania *Packet*. The American Revolution, Folio III, 1766–1783.

7. Woodmason, *Carolina Backcountry*, 226.

8. Aedanus Burke, quoted in Klein, *Unification of a Slave State*, 240.

9. Klein, *Unification of a Slave State*, 53–54; Woodmason, *Carolina Backcountry*, 245, n. 53; Stuart A. Marks, *Southern Hunting in Black and White: Nature, History, and Ritual in a*

Carolina Community (Princeton, N.J., 1991), 29–30; Nicholas Wolfe Proctor, "Bathed in Blood: Hunting in the Antebellum South" (Ph.D. diss., Emory Univ., 1998), 15.

10. Patrick Campbell, *Travels in the Interior Inhabited Parts of North America in the Years 1791 and 1792* (Toronto, 1937), 46. Campbell's *Travels* was first published in Edinburgh in 1793. J. H. Battle, *History of Bucks County, Pennsylvania* (Philadelphia, 1887), 280–90; James Habersham, quoted in Grady McWhiney, *Cracker Culture: Celtic Ways in the Old South* (Tuscaloosa, Ala., 1988), unnumbered leaf vii. On the anxiety aroused by backcountry hunters, see Klein, *Unification of a Slave State,* 52–54, 240; Marks, *Southern Hunting in Black and White,* 29–30; Drew Cayton, *The Frontier Republic: Ideology and Politics in the Ohio Country, 1780–1825* (Kent, Ohio, 1986), 3–11; Alan Taylor, *Liberty Men and Great Proprietors: The Revolutionary Settlement on the Maine Frontier, 1760–1820* (Chapel Hill, N.C., 1990); and James Habersham, *A proclamation . . . : Whereas his most gracious majesty . . . is determined . . . to support and protect the Indians in amity and alliance with him in their just rights and possessions* (Savannah, Ga., 1772).

11. New York *Gazette,* quoted in Pennsylvania *Gazette,* August 15, 1771. Accessible Archives CD-ROM Edition of the Pennsylvania *Gazette* with Additions from the Pennsylvania *Packet.* The American Revolution, Folio III, 1766–1783.

12. Peter S. Onuf, "Liberty, Development, and Union: Visions of the West in the 1780s," *William and Mary Quarterly,* 3d ser., 43, no. 2 (April 1986): 188, 189, 195. See also Peter Onuf, *Statehood and Union: A History of the Northwest Ordinance* (Bloomington, Ill., 1987); and Robert F. Berkhofer, "The Northwest Ordinance and the Principle of Territorial Evolution," in *The American Territorial System,* ed. John Porter Bloom (Athens, Ohio, 1973).

13. Onuf, "Liberty, Development, and Union," 188, 189, 195, 197–98.

14. Other four-stages theorists included Lord Kames, Sir John Dalrymple, and John Millar in Great Britain and Jean-Jacques Rousseau, Marie-Jean-Antoine-Nicolas de Caritat, Marquis de Condorcet, Helvétius, François Quesnay, Antoine-Yves Goguet, and Anne-Robert-Jacques Turgot, Baron de l'Aulne, in France.

15. Ronald Meek, *Social Science and the Ignoble Savage* (New York, 1976), 119; Thomas Hobbes, *Leviathan,* ed. Richard Tuck (Cambridge, England, 1991), 88. Hobbes's *Leviathan* was first published in London in 1651.

16. Hobbes, *Leviathan,* 88, 89; Hobbes (man as "arrant wolf"), quoted in Richard Ashcraft, "Leviathan Triumphant: Thomas Hobbes and the Politics of Wild Men," in *The Wild Man Within: An Image in Western Thought from the Renaissance to Romanticism,* ed. Edward Dudley and Maximillian E. Novak (Pittsburgh, 1972), 151.

17. Meek, *Social Science and the Ignoble Savage,* 6, 119–21, 129–30, 227. On the four-stages theory in the American context, see Drew R. McCoy, *The Elusive Republic: Political Economy in Jeffersonian America* (Chapel Hill, N.C., 1980), 19–20.

18. François Quesnay (restating a sentiment as old as Xenophon and Hesiod), quoted in Tamara Plakins Thornton, *Cultivating Gentlemen* (New Haven, Conn., 1989), 3. See also Chester E. Eisinger, "The Influence of Natural Rights and Physiocratic Doctrines on

American Agrarian Thought during the Revolutionary Period," *Agricultural History* 21, no. 1 (1947): 20–21; and Richard Bridgman, "Jefferson's Farmer before Jefferson," *American Quarterly* 14, no. 4 (winter 1962): 567–77.

19. Roy Harvey Pearce, *Savagism and Civilization: A Study of the Indian and the American Mind* (Baltimore, 1953; reprint, Berkeley, Calif., 1988), 70–71.

20. Benjamin Rush, *Essays, Literary, Moral and Philosophical*, 2d ed. (Philadelphia, 1806), 221.

21. On four-stages theory and the observations of American travelers, see Frederick Jackson Turner, "The Significance of the Frontier in American History," *The Frontier in American History* (New York, 1921), 12–22; and Henry Nash Smith, *Virgin Land: The American West as Symbol and Myth* (Cambridge, Mass., 1950), 219.

22. *American Museum, or, Universal Magazine* 10, no. 6 (December 1791): 262; William Newnham Blane, *An Excursion through the United States and Canada during the Years 1822–23. By an English Gentleman* (London, 1824), 178–79.

23. Thomas Jefferson, *The Writings of Thomas Jefferson*, ed. H. A. Washington, vol. 7 (Philadelphia, 1868–71), 377–78; Thomas Jefferson, *Notes on the State of Virginia*, ed. William Peden (New York, 1954; reprint, New York, 1982), 164–65. Jefferson's *Notes* was first published in Paris in 1785. Crèvecoeur, *Letters*, 70–72. On praise for farmers, see also Bridgman, "Jefferson's Farmer before Jefferson," 566.

24. Crèvecoeur, *Letters*, 70–72; G.B., "Letter from a Gentleman in Kentucky to His Friend in this State," *The Boston Magazine* 2, no. 12 (September 1785): 344; "Account of the Mode of Settlement, & c. & c. of the Inhabitants of Kentucky," *The New-York Magazine; or, Literary Repository* 4, no. 9 (Sept. 1793): 547.

25. François-André Michaux, *Travels to the West of the Alleghany Mountains, in the States of Ohio, Kentucky, Tennessee, and Back to Charleston by the Upper Carolines, etc.; September 24, 1801–March 26, 1803*, in *Early Western Travels, 1748–1846*, ed. Reuben Gold Thwaites, vol. 3 (Cleveland, 1904), 190. Michaux's *Travels* was first published in London in 1805. George W. Ogden, *Letters from the West, Comprising a Tour through the Western Country, and a Residence of Two Summers in the States of Ohio and Kentucky; 1821–1823*, in *Early Western Travels, 1748–1846*, ed. Reuben Gold Thwaites, vol. 19 (Cleveland, 1905), 33. Ogden's *Letters* was first published in New Bedford, Massachusetts, in 1823. Edward Augustus Kendall, *Travels through the Northern Parts of the United States in the Years 1807 and 1808*, vol. 3 (New York, 1809), 74–75. See also Fortescue Cuming, *Sketches of a Tour to the Western Country, through the States of Ohio and Kentucky; a Voyage down the Ohio and Mississippi Rivers, and a Trip through the Mississippi Territory, and part of West Florida; January 8, 1807–April 11, 1809*, in *Early Western Travels, 1748–1846*, ed. Reuben Gold Thwaites, vol. 4 (Cleveland, 1904), 175 (Cuming's *Sketches* was first published in Pittsburgh in 1810); Friedrich Gerstaecker, *Wild Sports in the Far West* (London, 1854), 164; Morris Birkbeck, *Notes on a Journey in America, from the Coast of Virginia to the Territory of Illinois* (London, 1818), 119; Frances [D'Arusmont] Wright, *Views of Society and Manners in America; in a Series of Letters from that Country to a Friend in England, during the Years 1818, 1819, and 1820. By an Englishwoman* (London, 1821), 294; William Bingley,

Travels in North America, from Modern Writers with Remarks and Observations Exhibiting a Connected View of the Geography and Present State of that Quarter of the Globe (London, 1821), 76; and Elias Pym Fordham, *Personal Narratives of Travels in Virginia, Maryland, Pennsylvania, Ohio, Indiana, Kentucky; and a Residence in the Illinois Territory: 1817–1818*, ed. Frederic Austin Ogg (Cleveland, 1906), 125–27.

26. Alexis de Tocqueville, *Democracy in America. The Henry Reeve Text as Revised by Francis Bowen Now Further Corrected and Edited with a Historical Essay, Editorial Notes, and Bibliographies by Phillips Bradley*, vol. 1 (New York, 1945), 356. Tocqueville's study was first published in Paris in 1835 (part 1) and 1840 (part 2). William Elliott, *Carolina Sports, by Land and Water: Including Incidents of Devil-Fishing, Wild-Cat, Deer, and Bear Hunting, &c.* (Charleston, S.C., 1846), 283.

4. Hunting as a Way of Life

1. Henry Nash Smith, *Virgin Land: The American West as Symbol and Myth* (Cambridge, Mass., 1950), 66.

2. Virtually all the pioneer hunters of the early- to mid-nineteenth century in the Kankakee River region of Ohio, for instance, seem to have hunted for market. See J. Lorenzo Werich, *Pioneer Hunters of the Kankakee* (n.p., 1920), 33–45. See also Henry Rowe Schoolcraft, *Rude Pursuits and Rugged Peaks: Schoolcraft's Ozark Journal, 1818–1819* (Fayetteville, Ark., 1996), 64.

3. Ted Franklin Belue, *The Long Hunt: Death of the Buffalo East of the Mississippi* (Mechanicsburg, Pa., 1996), 86, 110, 125; Walter F. Peterson, "Rural Life in Antebellum Alabama," *Alabama Review* 19, no. 2 (April 1966): 140; Guy Humphrey McMaster, *History of the Settlement of Steuben County, New York* (New York, 1853), 252.

4. Joseph Doddridge, *Notes on the Settlement and Indian Wars of the Western Parts of Virginia and Pennsylvania* (Wellsburg, Va., 1824), 123–24.

5. McMaster, *History of the Settlement of Steuben County*, 45.

6. Ibid., 40; Lyman Copeland Draper, *The Life of Daniel Boone*, ed. Ted Belue (Mechanicsburg, Pa., 1998), 417.

7. Mann Butler, "Details of Frontier Life," *Register of the Kentucky Historical Society* 62, no. 3 (1964): 207. Butler's commentary on frontier life was first published in the St. Louis periodical *The Western Journal and Civilian* between February 1853 and December 1855 under the title "Valley of the Ohio: Its Conquest and Settlement by Americans." Schoolcraft, *Rude Pursuits and Rugged Peaks*, 63; Henry W. Shoemaker, *Pennsylvania Deer and Their Horns* (Reading, Pa., 1915), 40.

8. Samuel E. Edwards, *The Ohio Hunter; or, a Brief Sketch of the Frontier Life of Samuel E. Edwards, the Great Bear and Deer Hunter of the State of Ohio* (Battle Creek, Mich., 1866), 33.

9. Doddridge, *Notes on the Settlement*, 113–16; Belue, *Long Hunt*, 90–92; Neal O. Hammon, ed., *My Father, Daniel Boone: The Draper Interviews with Nathan Boone* (Lexington, Ky., 1999), 36–37; Elias Pym Fordham, *Personal Narrative of Travels in Virginia, Maryland,*

Pennsylvania, Ohio, Indiana, Kentucky; and a Residence in the Illinois Territory: 1817–1818, ed. Frederic Austin Ogg (Cleveland, 1906), 128; William Newnham Blane, *An Excursion through the United States and Canada during the Years 1822–23. By an English Gentleman* (London, 1824), 111. The calibers of Kentucky rifles varied, but because powder was scarce and lead expensive, the average rifle was about a .38. See *1976 NRA Hunting Annual* (Washington, D.C., 1976), 4.

10. Theodore Roosevelt, *The Winning of the West. Homeward Bound Edition,* vol. 1 (New York, 1910), 130, 146. Roosevelt's *Winning of the West* was first published in New York in 1889.

11. Elliott West, "American Frontier," in *The Oxford History of the American West,* ed. Clyde A. Milner, Carol A. O'Connor, and Martha A. Sandweiss (New York, 1994), 140.

12. Patrick Campbell, *Travels in the Interior Inhabited Parts of North America in the Years 1791 and 1792* (Toronto, 1937), 68–70. Campbell's *Travels* was first published in Edinburgh in 1793. Draper, *Life of Daniel Boone,* 208, 214; Belue, *Long Hunt,* 89–90; West, "American Frontier," 140.

13. On bear hunting as a rite of passage, see, for instance, Captain C. B. Marryat, *Diary in America. With Remarks on Its Institutions* (New York, 1839), 116–17. The great nimrod discussed by Marryat, one Captain Scott of the United States army, indicated that the hunting of the bear was actually an unusual and hence much celebrated occurrence in his native Vermont of the early nineteenth century.

14. Shoemaker, *Pennsylvania Deer,* 41, 63, 71–72.

15. Edwards, *Ohio Hunter,* 122, 145; Doddridge, *Notes on the Settlement,* 22–23, 127, 161–66. Shoemaker, former ambassador to Bulgaria, newspaper owner, and author of stories about werewolves, had a penchant for the weird and wonderful tale. Some of Shoemaker's stories of hunting in early Pennsylvania were clearly fabricated, although there is no reason to doubt that he had interviewed hunters and their descendants. See Belue, *Long Hunt,* 136.

16. Werich, *Pioneer Hunters of the Kankakee,* 50.

17. Philip Tome, *Pioneer Life; or, Thirty Years a Hunter. Being Scenes and Adventures of the Life of Philip Tome, Fifteen Years Interpreter for Cornplanter and Gov. Blacksnake, Chiefs on the Allegany River* (Buffalo, N.Y., 1854; reprint, Salem, N.H., 1989), 114.

18. Ibid, 161.

19. Alice Morse Earle, *Customs and Fashions in Old New England* (New York, 1893), 238; Jennie Holliman, *American Sports (1785–1835)* (Durham, N.C., 1931), 21–23; Samuel Griswold Goodrich, *Recollections of a Lifetime* (Auburn, N.Y., 1856), 101; John James Audubon, *Delineations of American Scenery and Character* (New York, 1926), 59–63; Isaac Weld, *Travels through the States of North America,* vol. 1 (New York, 1968), 118–19. Weld's *Travels* was first published in 1799.

20. Blane, *Excursion through the United States and Canada,* 88, 173–74, 302; Fordham, *Personal Narrative of Travels,* 125–26; Philip Gosse, *Letters from Alabama* (London, 1859), 130–31; Fortescue Cuming, *Sketches of a Tour to the Western Country, through the States of Ohio and Kentucky; a Voyage down the Ohio and Mississippi Rivers, and a Trip through the Mississippi*

Territory, and part of West Florida. Commenced at Philadelphia in the Winter of 1807, and Concluded in 1809 (Pittsburgh, 1810), 30.

21. Alan Taylor, "'Wasty Ways': Stories of American Settlement," *Environmental History* 3, no. 3 (July 1998): 304; Edwards, *Great Deer and Bear Hunter,* 69; John Mack Faragher, *Daniel Boone: The Life and Legend of an American Pioneer* (New York, 1992), 76–77. Benjamin Patterson, the great hunter of Steuben County, New York, although forced to move farther into the forest as farmers cleared land, was said to be (like Daniel Boone) a "Moses to despairing emigrants" (McMaster, *History of the Settlement of Steuben County,* 40).

22. Draper, *Life of Daniel Boone,* 263.

23. Shepard Krech III, *The Ecological Indian: Myth and History* (New York, 1999), 170–71.

24. James Axtell, "The First Consumer Revolution," in *Beyond 1492: Encounters in Colonial North America* (New York, 1992), 125–51.

25. The best study of Indian involvement in market hunting is Krech, *The Ecological Indian.* See also Calvin Martin, *Keepers of the Game: Indian-Animal Relationships and the Fur Trade* (Berkeley, Calif., 1978); and Shepard Krech III, ed., *Indians, Animals, and the Fur Trade: A Critique of Keepers of the Game* (Athens, Ga., 1981). On the involvement of southern tribes in the deerskin trade, see Charles H. Hudson Jr., "Why the Southeastern Indians Slaughtered Deer," in *Indians, Animals, and the Fur Trade,* 155–76; and Kathryn E. Holland Braund, "Mutual Convenience—Mutual Dependence: The Creeks, St. Augustine, and the Deerskin Trade, 1733–1783" (Ph.D. diss., Florida State Univ., 1986). As early as 1705 Robert Beverley reported that Indians killed deer only for the skins, leaving the meat to rot (Robert Beverley, *The History and Present State of Virginia* [Chapel Hill, N.C., 1947], 155). Such reports were frequent on the eighteenth- and nineteenth-century frontiers as Indians became dependent on European trade goods. In Ohio, it was said, Indians wiped out deer—taking skins and leaving carcasses to rot—only to deny white settlers a useful food source (S. P. Hildreth, *Pioneer History: Being an Account of the First Examinations of the Ohio Valley, and the Early Settlement of the Northwest Territory* [Cincinnati, 1848], 220).

26. Belue, *Long Hunt,* 151.

27. Ibid., 109, 163–64.

28. Hammon, *My Father, Daniel Boone,* 33.

29. N. E. Jones, *The Squirrel Hunters of Ohio or Glimpses of Pioneer Life* (Cincinnati, 1898), 173, 190–92.

30. William Clinkenbeard, quoted in Belue, *Long Hunt,* 132.

31. Campbell, *Travels in the Interior,* 229; Hildreth, *Pioneer History,* 358, 402; Reginald Horsman, *The Frontier in the Formative Years, 1783–1815* (New York, 1970), 116; Eugene T. Peterson, *Hunters' Heritage: A History of Hunting in Michigan* (Lansing, Mich., 1979), 19; Michael A. Bellesîles, "The Origins of Gun Culture in the United States, 1760–1865," *Journal of American History* 83, no. 2 (September 1996): 426–28, 435; Michael A. Bellesiles, *Revolutionary Outlaws: Ethan Allen and the Struggle for Independence on the Early American*

Frontier (Charlottesville, 1993), 56. On the market price for game on the Ohio Valley frontier, see John Stillman Wright, *Letters from the West; or a Caution to Emigrants* (Ann Arbor, Mich., 1966). Wright's *Letters* was first published in Salem, New York, in 1819.

32. Michael A. Bellesiles, *Arming America: The Origins of a National Gun Culture* (New York, 2000), 106–9.

33. Ibid., 106; Francis Baily, *Journal of a Tour in the Unsettled Parts of North America, in 1796 & 1797. With a Memoir of the Author* (London, 1856), 134. As late as the 1830s, a Norwegian immigrant wrote that in America a good rifle cost between fifteen and twenty dollars. Ole Rynning, *Ole Rynning's True Account of America*, ed. and trans. Theodore C. Blegen (Freeport, N.Y., 1976), 99.

34. George R. Carroll, *Pioneer Life in and Around Cedar Rapids, Iowa, 1839–1849* (Cedar Rapids, Iowa, 1895), 45; Fordham, *Personal Narrative of Travels*, 126; William Cooper Howells, *Recollections of Life in Ohio, from 1813 to 1840* (Cincinnati, 1895), 67.

35. William Priest, *Travels in the United States of America; Commencing in the Year 1793 and Ending in 1797. With the Author's Journal of His Voyage across the Atlantic* (London, 1802), 91; Samuel Griswold Goodrich, *Recollections of a Lifetime* (Auburn, N.Y., 1856), 98–101; Henry W. Shoemaker, comp., *A Pennsylvania Bison Hunt* (Middleburg, Pa., 1915), 59; Gottfried Duden, *Report on a Journey to the Western States of North America and a Stay of Several Years Along the Missouri (During the Years 1824, '25, '26, and 1827)*, ed. and trans. George H. Kellner, Elsa Nagel, Adolf E. Schroeder, and W. M. Senner (Columbia, Mo., 1980), 180; William Lewis Manly, *Death Valley in '49: An Important Chapter in California Pioneer History* (San Jose, Calif., 1894; reprint, New York, 1929), 14–15; Carroll, *Pioneer Life*, 42; Hildreth, *Pioneer History*, 496; James Flint, *Flint's Letters from America, 1818–1820*, in *Early Western Travels, 1748–1846*, ed. Reuben Gold Thwaites, vol. 9 (Cleveland, 1904), 120. Flint's *Letters* was first published in Edinburgh in 1822.

36. William Cobbett, *A Year's Residence in the United States* (New York, 1818), 260, 263; Shoemaker, *Pennsylvania Bison Hunt*, 59.

37. Timothy Flint, "The Kentuckian in New York," *Western Monthly Review* 1 (1827): 88; Timothy Flint, *The First White Man of the West, or the Life and Exploits of Col. Daniel Boone, the First Settler of Kentucky* (Cincinnati, 1847), 107. Flint's biography of Boone was first published in Cincinnati in 1833 under the title *Biographical Memoir of Daniel Boone, the First Settler of Kentucky: Interspersed with Incidents in the Early Annals of the Country.*

38. Flint, *First White Man*, 107; Timothy Flint, *The Personal Narrative of James Ohio Pattie*, ed. William Goetzmann (New York, 1962), 3. Pattie's *Personal Narrative* was first published in Cincinnati in 1831.

39. Doddridge, *Notes on the Settlement*, vi. On Doddridge's ministerial career, see Narcissa Doddridge, "Memoir of the Rev. Dr. Joseph Doddridge," in Joseph Doddridge, *Notes on the Settlement and Indian Wars of the Western Parts of Virginia and Pennsylvania . . .* (Pittsburgh, 1912), 243–72 (on Doddridge's conversion from Methodism to Episcopacy, 248; on Doddridge as opponent of "enthusiastic raptures," 257; on Doddridge as a Freemason, 266).

40. Doddridge, *Notes on the Settlement*, viii–x.

41. Mann Butler, *A History of the Commonwealth of Kentucky* (Louisville, Ky., 1834), 136–37.

42. Jeptha R. Simms, *Trappers of New York, or a Biography of Nicholas Stoner & Nathaniel Foster; together with Anecdotes of Other Celebrated Hunters, and some account of Sir William Johnson, and His Style of Living* (Albany, N.Y., 1851), 6, 112, 146. Simms's book was first published in 1850 and went through four more editions before 1872.

5. The Problem with Sport Hunting

1. Louis Booker Wright, *The First Gentlemen of Virginia; Intellectual Qualities of the Early Colonial Ruling Class* (San Marino, Calif., 1940), 11; Matt Cartmill, *A View to a Death in the Morning: Hunting and Nature through History* (Cambridge, Mass., 1994), 77–78.

2. Cartmill, *View to a Death*, 78–79; Desiderius Erasmus, *The Praise of Folly*, trans. John Wilson (New York, 1942), 158–59. Erasmus's *Praise of Folly* was written in 1511 and published in London in 1549.

3. James Turner, *Reckoning with the Beast: Animals, Pain, and Humanity in the Victorian Mind* (Baltimore, 1980), 10–11.

4. Soame Jenyns, "Disquisition on Cruelty to Inferior Animals," reprinted in *Massachusetts Magazine: or, Monthly Museum of Knowledge and Rational Entertainment* 6, no. 1 (January 1794): 37.

5. This survey included each periodical from the American Periodical Series microfilm collection (1750–1800). Antihunting tracts include Benjamin Rush, "Thoughts Upon the Amusements and Punishments Which Are Proper for Schools. Addressed to George Clymer, Esq., by Benjamin Rush, M.D.," *The Universal Asylum, and Columbian Magazine* 4, no. 8 (August 1790): 68; Jenyns, "Disquisition on Cruelty to Inferior Animals," 34–37; *The Boston Magazine* 1 (October 1785): 412–14; *The American Universal Magazine* 3, no. 4 (November 1797): 435–42; *The New Hampshire Magazine: or the Monthly Repository of Useful Information* 1, no. 4 (September 1793): 241; and *The Lady's Magazine and Repository of Entertaining Knowledge* 1 (November 1792): 61–64. Jenyns was British, but his thoughts on hunting clearly resonated among Revolutionary era Americans, as witnessed by the praise bestowed on his disquisition by a reviewer in *The American Monthly Review; or, Literary Journal* 2, no. 5 (May 1795): 720.

Antihunting poems include Andrew Marvell, "The Wounded Fawn," *The Literary Miscellany, Containing Elegant Selections of the Most Admired Fugitive Pieces and Extracts from Works of the Greatest Merit, with Originals* 1, no. 5 (1795): 24–27 (a reprint of a seventeenth-century poem); "A Loving and Panegyrical Epistle on Certain Fox Hunters," *The Weekly Magazine* 1, no. 10 (April 7, 1798): 315–16; A Young Lady, "On Fowling," *The Weekly Magazine* 2, no. 26 (July 28, 1798): 411; "To a Frighted Hare," *Juvenile Magazine* 2, no. 1 (1802): 136–38; and Gottfried Augustus Bürger, "The Chase," *The Weekly Magazine* 2, no. 25 (July 21, 1798): 413–14. Bürger's poem was translated from the German original. "On

Fowling," by a Young Lady, shows how the natural rights logic of republicanism could be used to strike a blow against hunting:

> 'Tis true, no future ills [game animals] know,
> Nor does prescience strike the blow,
> Before the destined hour;
> Yet still to murder every joy,
> Their unoffending lives employ,
> Proclaims despotic power.

I have not included the many discussions of animal intelligence that appeared in eighteenth-century periodicals, although they often contained implicit messages opposing sport hunting. Nor have I included strictures on the indolence or cruelty of frontier hunters.

Unambiguous celebrations of sport hunting include two poems ("Engraved Upon a Hunting Horn," *The American Universal Magazine* 3, no. 5 [September 1797]: 388; and "The Sportsman: A Sonnet," *The Boston Magazine* 3 [November–December 1786]: 425–26) and two songs ("A Hunting Song. Set to Music by Mr. Roth, of Philadelphia," *The Universal Asylum, and Columbian Magazine* 4, no. 4 [April 1790]: 254–56; and "The Hill Tops; A New Hunting Song," *The Royal American Magazine* 1, no. 8 [August 1774]): 152–53.

On William Bartram, see Thomas P. Slaughter, *The Natures of John and William Bartram* (New York, 1996), xvi.

6. Benjamin Rush, *Thoughts Upon the Amusements and Punishments Which are Proper for Schools. Addressed to George Clymer, Esq. by Benjamin Rush, M.D.* (Philadelphia, 1790), 2. (Rush's original magazine article by the same name was printed subsequently as a pamphlet.)

7. See Edmund Morgan, "The Puritan Ethic of the American Revolution," *In Search of Early America: The William and Mary Quarterly, 1943–1993* (Richmond, 1993), 78–108; Pennsylvania *Gazette*, May 31, 1775, September 3, 1778. Accessible Archives CD-ROM Edition of the Pennsylvania *Gazette* with Additions from the Pennsylvania *Packet*. The American Revolution, Folio III, 1766–1783. See also Robert Means Lawrence, *New England Colonial Life* (Cambridge, Mass., 1927), 252.

8. Benjamin Franklin, *The Autobiography of Benjamin Franklin* (New York, 1986), 73. Franklin's *Autobiography* has a complex publishing history. The first full version was edited by John Bigelow and published in Philadelphia in 1868.

9. *The Hare; or, Hunting Incompatible with Humanity. Written as a Stimulus to Youth Towards a Proper Treatment of Animals* (Philadelphia, 1802), 46; *A Peep into the Sport of Youth* (Philadelphia, 1809), entry no. 27.

10. Turner, *Reckoning with the Beast*, 5; Keith Thomas, *Man and the Natural World: A History of the Modern Sensibility* (New York, 1983), 176; Jeremy Bentham, *An Introduction to the Principles of Morals and Legislation*, ed. Wilfrid Harrison (Oxford, England, 1948), 412 n. On seventeenth- and eighteenth-century studies of anatomy, see Turner, *Reckoning with the Beast*, 4.

11. On the Enlightenment celebration of reason, rationality, and pacifism, I rely on Peter Gay, *The Enlightenment: An Interpretation*, vol. 2, *The Science of Freedom* (New York, 1969), 34–55.

12. Robert Beverley, *The History and Present State of Virginia* (London, 1705), 308–12; John Davis, *Travels of Four Years and a Half in the United States of America; during 1798, 1799, 1800, 1801, and 1802* (London, 1803), 81; J. H. Easterby, ed., "The St. Thomas Hunting Club, 1785–1801," *South Carolina Historical and Genealogical Magazine* 48 (1947): 42; Kenneth S. Greenberg, *Honor and Slavery: Lies, Duels, Noses, Masks, Dressing as a Woman, Gifts, Strangers, Humanitarianism, Death, Slave Rebellions, the Proslavery Argument, Baseball, Hunting, and Gambling in the Old South* (Princeton, N.J., 1996), 133. See also Nancy L. Struna, "Sport and the Awareness of Leisure," in *Of Consuming Interests: The Style of Life in the Eighteenth Century*, ed. Cary Carson, Ronald Hoffman, and Peter J. Albert (Charlottesville, 1994), 406–43; and Nancy L. Struna, "The Formalizing of Sport and the Formation of an Elite: The Chesapeake Gentry, 1650–1720," *Journal of Sport History* 13, no. 3 (1986): 212–34.

13. John Russell Young, ed., *Memorial History of the City of Philadelphia; From Its First Settlement to the Year 1895*, vol. 2 (New York, 1898), 118; J. Thomas Scharf and Thompson Westcott, *History of Philadelphia, 1609–1884*, vol. 2 (Philadelphia, 1884), 1092; David Hackett Fischer, *Paul Revere's Ride* (Oxford, England, 1994), 19; Pennsylvania *Gazette*, December 17, 1778, January 1, 1779. Accessible Archives CD-ROM Edition of the Pennsylvania *Gazette* with Additions from the Pennsylvania *Packet*. The American Revolution, Folio III, 1766–1783.

14. Robert Elman, "Introduction," *The Great American Shooting Prints* (New York, 1972), unnumbered page 2; William Dering (active ca. 1735–1751), *George Booth*, n.d., oil on canvas, 50 × 40 inches, Colonial Williamsburg Foundation, Williamsburg.

15. Elman, "Introduction," unnumbered page 2.

16. "The Hill Tops; A New Hunting Song," 152–53.

17. *The Sportsman's Companion, or, An Essay on Shooting* (Burlington, N.J., 1791), 76. *The Sportsman's Companion* was first published in New York in 1783.

18. Herbert Manchester, *Four Centuries of Sport in America, 1490–1890* (New York, 1931), 63; Elman, "Introduction," unnumbered page 3.

19. Pennsylvania *Gazette*, January 25, 1770.

20. Jennie Holliman, *American Sports (1785–1835)* (Durham, N.C., 1931), 389; D. B. Updike, *Hunt Clubs and Country Clubs in America* (Boston, 1928), 12.

21. Fairfax Harrison, "The Genesis of Foxhunting in Virginia," *The Virginia Magazine of History and Biography* 37 (1929): 155–57. See also D. C. Itzkowitz, *Peculiar Privilege—A Social History of English Fox-hunting* (Hassock, Sussex, England, 1977); Updike, *Hunt Clubs and Country Clubs*, xiv, xiii, 5; Foster Rhea Dulles, *America Learns to Play: A History of Popular Recreation, 1607–1940* (New York, 1940), 60.

22. Pennsylvania *Gazette*, January 25, 1770.

23. "A Loving and Panegyrical Epistle on Certain Fox Hunters," *The Weekly Magazine* 1, no. 9

(March 31, 1798): 315–16; "Fox Hunting in America," *Spirit of the Times* 26, no. 31 (September 13, 1856): 363, col. 3; Manchester, *Four Centuries of Sport,* 68.

24. Updike, *Hunt Clubs and Country Clubs,* xiv; William H. Schreiner, *Schreiner's Sporting Manual. A Complete Treatise on Fishing, Fowling and Hunting, as Applicable to this Country; with Full Instructions for the Management of the Dog* (Philadelphia, 1841), unnumbered; John T. Faris, *Old Roads Out of Philadelphia* (Philadelphia, 1917), 85–86. On the discontinuation of fox hunting after the Revolution in New York, see A. Henry Higginson and Julian Ingersoll Chamberlain, *Hunting in the United States and Canada* (Garden City, N.J., 1928), 100. Bayard Taylor indicates that fox hunting did, however, survive in at least one part of rural Pennsylvania. See Bayard Taylor, *The Story of Kennett* (New York, 1903), iii–v, 1–24. Taylor's *Story of Kennett* was copyrighted in 1866.

6. Hunters Ascendant

1. Israel Ralph Potter, *Life and Remarkable Adventures of Israel R. Potter, (a Native of Cranston, Rhode-Island,) Who Was a Soldier in the American Revolution . . . after which He Was Taken Prisoner by the British, Conveyed to England, Where for 30 Years He Obtained his Livelihood . . . by Crying "Old Chairs to Mend"* (Providence, R.I., 1824), 8–15.

2. David Chacko and Alexander Kulcsar, "Israel Potter: Genesis of a Legend," *William and Mary Quarterly,* 3d ser., 41, no. 3 (July 1984): 374.

3. George Washington Parke Custis, *Recollections and Private Memoirs of Washington, by His Adopted Son, George Washington Parke Custis, with a Memoir of the Author, by His Daughter; and Illustrative and Explanatory Notes, by Benson J. Lossing* (New York, 1860), 264–69; Pennsylvania *Gazette,* September 6, 1775; September 10, 1777. Accessible Archives CD-ROM Edition of the Pennsylvania *Gazette* with Additions from the Pennsylvania *Packet.* The American Revolution, Folio III, 1766–1783.

4. Pennsylvania *Gazette,* August 16, 1775. On the "amazing hardihood" of 6,000 Virginia militiamen who had lived "so long in the woods," see James C. Ballagh, ed., *Letters of Richard Henry Lee,* vol. 1 (New York, 1912–14), 130–31.

5. "Tommyhawk or Scalping Knife," quoted in Rhys Isaac, *Transformation of Virginia, 1740–1790* (Chapel Hill, N.C., 1982), 258; Georgia Bill of Exchange, 1777, National Numismatic Collection, Smithsonian Institution. On the hunting outfits of backwoodsmen, see also Carolyn R. Shine, "Hunting Shirts and Silk Stockings: Clothing Early Cincinnati," *Queen City Heritage: The Journal of the Cincinnati Historical Society* 45, no. 3 (1987): 23–48; and Joseph Doddridge, *Notes on the Settlement and Indian Wars of the Western Parts of Virginia and Pennsylvania* (Wellsburg, Va., 1824), 113–16.

6. See, for instance, Alan Taylor, *Liberty Men and Great Proprietors: The Revolutionary Settlement on the Maine Frontier, 1760–1820* (Chapel Hill, N.C., 1990); Michael Bellesiles, *Revolutionary Outlaws: Ethan Allen and the Struggle for Independence on the Early American Frontier* (Charlottesville, 1993); Rachel Klein, *Unification of a Slave State: The Rise of the Planter Class in the South Carolina Backcountry, 1760–1808* (Chapel Hill, N.C., 1990), 52–54,

240; Stuart A. Marks, *Southern Hunting in Black and White: Nature, History, and Ritual in a Carolina Community* (Princeton, N.J., 1991), 29–30; and Drew Cayton, *The Frontier Republic: Ideology and Politics in the Ohio Country, 1780–1825* (Kent, Ohio, 1986), 3–11.

7. Elias Pym Fordham, *Personal Narrative of Travels in Virginia, Maryland, Pennsylvania, Ohio, Indiana, and Kentucky; and a Residence in the Illinois Territory: 1817–1818* (Cleveland, 1906), 81–82.

8. For my discussion of republicanism and Jeffersonian liberalism, I have relied on Joyce Appleby, *Liberalism and Republicanism in the Historical Imagination* (Cambridge, Mass., 1992), particularly chapter 10, "The 'Agrarian Myth' in the Early Republic." On the transition from a monarchical to a republican society, and from a republican to a democratic society, see Gordon Wood, *The Radicalism of the American Revolution* (New York, 1992).

9. Isaac, *Transformation of Virginia*, 258.

10. Isaac, *Transformation of Virginia*, 267; Henry Stephen Randall, *The Life of Thomas Jefferson*, vol. 1 (New York, 1858), 40.

11. David Humphreys, "A Poem on the Industry of the United States of America," *The Miscellaneous Works of David Humphreys* (New York, 1804), 107; Samuel Williams, *Natural and Civil History of Vermont*, 2d ed., cor. and enl., vol. 2 (Burlington, Vt., 1809), 359; Joel Barlow, *The Columbiad* (Philadelphia, 1807), 389.

7. The Hunter's Empire

1. Gary E. Moulton, ed., *The Journals of the Lewis and Clark Expedition*, vol. 3 (Lincoln, Nebr., 1987), 80; Ibid., vol. 4, 111.

2. Ibid., vol. 3, 80–81.

3. Ibid., 81.

4. Ibid., 81–82.

5. Ibid., 82.

6. Paul Russell Cutright, *Lewis and Clark: Pioneering Naturalists* (Urbana, Ill., 1969; reprint, Lincoln, Nebr., 1989).

7. John C. Greene, *American Science in the Age of Jefferson* (Ames, Iowa, 1984), 196; Thomas Jefferson, *Notes on the State of Virginia*, ed. William Peden (New York, 1954; reprint, New York, 1982); Thomas Jefferson to Dr. Benjamin Smith Barton, Washington, D.C., February 27, 1803, *The Writings of Thomas Jefferson*, ed. A. A. Lipscomb and A. E. Bergh, vol. 10 (Washington, D.C., 1907), 366–67.

8. Moulton, *Journals of the Lewis and Clark Expedition*, vol. 4, 85, 132.

9. Richard White, "Are You an Environmentalist or Do You Work for a Living?: Work and Nature," in *Uncommon Ground: Rethinking the Human Place in Nature*, ed. William Cronon (New York, 1995), 175. On Lewis and Clark as claimants of the Far West, see also Albert Furtwangler, *Acts of Discovery: Vision of America in the Lewis and Clark Journals* (Urbana, Ill., 1993).

10. J. Hector St. John de Crèvecoeur, *Letters from an American Farmer and Sketches of Eighteenth-Century America* (New York, 1963), 70–71. Crèvecoeur's *Letters* was first published in London in 1782. Thomas Hobbes, *Leviathan*, ed. Richard Tuck (Cambridge, England, 1991), 88. Hobbes's *Leviathan* was first published in London in 1651. Jean-Jacques Rousseau, *Discours sur l'origine et les fondements de l'inégalité parmi les hommes* (Discourse on the origin of inequality), trans. Franklin Philip (Oxford, England, 1994). Rousseau's *Discours* was first published in 1754.

11. Arthur O. Lovejoy, "The Supposed Primitivism of Rousseau's *Discourse on Inequality*," *Essays in the History of Ideas* (Baltimore, 1948), 16, 20–21.

12. Thomas Jefferson, quoted in Donald Jackson, *Thomas Jefferson and the Stony Mountains: Exploring the West from Monticello* (Norman, Okla., 1993), 12.

13. Charles Willson Peale, *Introduction to a Course of Lectures on the Science of Nature; with Original Music, Composed for, and Sung on, the Occasion, Delivered in the Hall of the University of Pennsylvania, Nov. 8, 1800* (Philadelphia, 1800), 39–40; Charles Willson Peale to Thomas Jefferson, Philadelphia, January 29, 1808, *Selected Papers of Charles Willson Peale and His Family,* ed. Lillian B. Miller, vol. 2, *Charles Willson Peale: The Artist as Museum Keeper, 1791–1810* (Washington, D.C., 1988), pt. 2, 1055–56. On relations between Lewis and Clark and the Indians of the Far West, see James P. Ronda, *Lewis and Clark among the Indians* (Lincoln, Nebr., 1984).

14. Thomas Jefferson to Paul Allen, Monticello, August 18, 1813, *Letters of the Lewis and Clark Expedition,* ed. Donald Jackson, vol. 2 (Urbana, Ill., 1962; reprint, Urbana, Ill., 1978), 591.

15. Citizens of Fincastle, Virginia, to Lewis and Clark, January 8, 1807, *Letters of the Lewis and Clark Expedition,* vol. 1, 358; Lewis to the citizens of Charlottesville, Virginia, December 15, 1806, *Letters of the Lewis and Clark Expedition,* vol. 2, 693; Federalist reaction cited in Jerry W. Knudson, "Newspaper Reaction to the Louisiana Purchase," *Missouri Historical Review* 63, no. 1 (October 1968): 198–99, 209.

16. Thomas Jefferson to Paul Allen, Monticello, August 18, 1813, *Letters of the Lewis and Clark Expedition,* vol. 2, 587.

17. Thomas Jefferson to Paul Allen, Monticello, August 18, 1813, *Letters of the Lewis and Clark Expedition,* vol. 2, 587; Thomas Jefferson, "Biographical Sketch of Lewis [ca. August 18, 1813]," *Letters of the Lewis and Clark Expedition,* vol. 2, 593.

18. Thomas Jefferson to Paul Allen, Monticello, August 18, 1813, *Letters of the Lewis and Clark Expedition,* vol. 2, 590–91.

19. Silvio A. Bedini, *Thomas Jefferson: Statesman of Science* (New York, 1990), 437. Of the many contemporary descriptions of Jefferson's collections, perhaps the best is the translation of Baron de Montlezun's journal entry of September 20, 1816, in J. M. Carrière and L. G. Moffat, "A Frenchman Visits Albemarle, 1816," *Magazine of the Albemarle County Historical Society* 4 (1943–44): 39–55. On the fate of specimens sent back by Lewis and Clark, see Cutright, *Lewis and Clark: Pioneering Naturalists,* 349–92.

20. Jefferson, *Notes on the State of Virginia,* 53–54.

21. Ibid., 47; Lillian B. Miller, ed., *Selected Papers of Peale,* vol. 2, pt. 1, 408.

22. Jefferson, *Notes on the State of Virginia,* 43.

23. Jackson, *Thomas Jefferson and the Stony Mountains,* 30, 76; Greene, *American Science in the Age of Jefferson,* 196; Thomas Jefferson, *The Anas, Writings,* vol. 1, 362. For a discussion of Jefferson's identification of the megalonyx as a carnivore, see Julian P. Boyd, "The Megalonyx, the Megatherium, and Thomas Jefferson's Lapse of Memory," *Proceedings of the American Philosophical Society* 52, no. 5 (October 1958): 420–35.

24. Moulton, *Journals of the Lewis and Clark Expedition,* vol. 4, 141.

25. John Quincy Adams, quoted in Anthony DeWolfe Howe, "The Capture of Some Fugitive Verses," *Proceedings of the Massachusetts Historical Society,* 3rd ser., 43 (October 1909–June 1910): 237–38.

26. E. P. Wild, quoted in Anna Clark Jones, "Antlers for Jefferson," *New England Quarterly* 12, no. 2 (June 1939): 333.

27. Charles Willson Peale, "Introduction to a Course of Lectures on Natural History Delivered in the University of Pennsylvania, November 16, 1799," *Selected Papers,* vol. 2, pt. 1, 270; Charles Willson Peale to George Washington, Philadelphia, December 31, 1786, *Selected Papers,* vol. 1, *Charles Willson Peale: Artist in Revolutionary America, 1735–1791,* 464. On Peale and his museum, see David Brigham, "'A World in Miniature': Charles Willson Peale's Philadelphia Museum and Its Audience" (Ph.D. diss., Univ. of Pennsylvania, 1992).

28. Charles Willson Peale to Andrew Ellicott, Philadelphia, February 28, 1802, *Selected Papers,* vol. 2, pt. 1, 411; Charles Willson Peale to John W. Cunningham, Germantown, Pennsylvania, March 17, 1811, *Selected Papers,* vol. 3, 86; Charles Coleman Sellers, *Mr. Peale's Museum: Charles Willson Peale and the First Popular Museum of Natural Science and Art* (New York, 1980), 15, 153. On the relationship between natural history and republicanism, see also Christopher Looby, "The Constitution of Nature: Taxonomy as Politics in Jefferson, Peale, and Bartram," *Early American Literature* 22, no. 3 (1987): 252–73; and Ralph N. Miller, "American Nationalism as a Theory of Nature," *William and Mary Quarterly,* 3d ser., 12, no. 1 (January 1955): 82–83, 91.

29. Charles Willson Peale to Thomas Jefferson, Philadelphia, November 3, 1805, *Letters of the Lewis and Clark Expedition,* vol. 1, 268; Charles Willson Peale to the American Philosophical Society, Philadelphia, October 29, 1805, *Selected Papers,* vol. 2, pt. 2, 904; Charles Willson Peale to John Hawkins, Philadelphia, May 5, 1807, *Letters of the Lewis and Clark Expedition,* vol. 2, 411.

30. Sellers, *Mr. Peale's Museum,* 29. On Titian Ramsay Peale as a hunter in the Far West, see Edwin James, *Account of an Expedition from Pittsburgh to the Rocky Mountains, performed by order of the Hon. J. C. Calhoun, Secretary of War, . . . compiled from the Notes of Maj. S. H. Long, Mr. T. Say, and other Gentlemen of the Party; March 31, 1819–November 22, 1820,* in *Early Western Travels, 1748–1846,* ed. Reuben Gold Thwaites, vol. 15 (Cleveland, 1905). James's *Account* was first published in Philadelphia in 1822–23. See also Kenneth Haltman, "Figures in a Western Landscape: Reading the Art of Titian Ramsay Peale from the Long Expedition to the Rocky Mountains, 1819–1820" (Ph.D. diss., Yale Univ., 1992).

31. Lillian B. Miller, *The Collected Papers of Charles Willson Peale and His Family: A Guide and Index to the Microfiche Edition* (Millwood, N.Y., 1980), 17; Bernard, Duke of Saxe-Weimar-Eisenach, *Travels through North America during the Years 1825 and 1826,* vol. 2 (Philadelphia, 1828), 101–2; Henry Rowe Schoolcraft, *A View of the Lead Mines of Missouri* (New York, 1819), 241. See also John C. Ewers, "William Clark's Indian Museum in St. Louis," *A Cabinet of Curiosities: Five Episodes in the Evolution of American Museums,* ed. Whitfield J. Bell Jr. (Charlottesville, 1967), 52.

8. Daniel Boone

1. I wish to acknowledge the intellectual debt that this chapter and the ensuing chapter owe to four pioneering works of American cultural history: John William Ward, *Andrew Jackson: Symbol for an Age* (Oxford, England, 1955); Marvin Meyers, *The Jacksonian Persuasion: Politics and Belief* (Stanford, Calif., 1957); Henry Nash Smith, *Virgin Land: The American West as Symbol and Myth* (Cambridge, Mass., 1950); and R. W. B. Lewis, *The American Adam: Innocence, Tragedy, and Tradition in the Nineteenth Century* (Chicago, 1955). In my interpretation of Daniel Boone as an American Adam, as a symbol for a new age, and as a symbol for an old age, readers will note the influence of each of these scholars. My purpose here has not been to challenge my predecessors so much as to add new dimensions to their ideas. In particular, I seek to distinguish the agrarian worldview that was often associated with Jefferson and Jackson from the middle-class worldview that Boone epitomized. This chapter appeared in somewhat different form under the title "The Other Daniel Boone: The Nascence of a Middle-Class Hunter Hero, 1784–1860," *Journal of the Early Republic* 18, no. 3 (fall 1998): 429–57.

2. John Mack Faragher, *Daniel Boone: The Life and Legend of an American Pioneer* (New York, 1992), 211; Reuben Gold Thwaites, *Daniel Boone* (New York, 1903), 110.

3. Stephen Anthony Aron, *How the West Was Lost: The Transformation of Kentucky from Daniel Boone to Henry Clay* (Baltimore and London, 1996), 14–16, 23–26, 33; Faragher, *Daniel Boone: The Life and Legend,* 61–62; John Bakeless, *Daniel Boone: Master of the Wilderness* (Lincoln, Nebr., 1939), 143; Thwaites, *Daniel Boone,* 32.

4. Bakeless, *Daniel Boone: Master of the Wilderness,* 59–60; Faragher, *Daniel Boone: The Life and Legend,* 39, 170, 300.

5. Thwaites, *Daniel Boone,* 133, 209; Bakeless, *Daniel Boone: Master of the Wilderness,* 143, 342.

6. Bakeless, *Daniel Boone: Master of the Wilderness,* 380–82.

7. On the publishing history of Filson's Boone text, see Richard Slotkin, *Regeneration through Violence: The Mythology of the American Frontier, 1600–1860* (Middletown, Conn., 1973); and Michael A. Lofaro, "The Eighteenth Century 'Autobiographies' of Daniel Boone," *Register of the Kentucky Historical Society* 76 (1978): 85–97. Even Trumbull's Boone, though deprived of his philosophical aphorisms, describes the "inconceivable grandeur" and "sylvan pleasures" of the wilderness, thus turning the Puritan concept of wilderness on its head. [John Filson], *The Adventures of Colonel Daniel Boon,* ed. John

Trumbull (Norwich, Conn., 1786), 5.

8. John Filson, *Filson's Kentucke. A Facsimile Reproduction of the Original Wilmington Edition of 1784, with Paged Critique, Sketch of Filson's Life and Bibliography* (Louisville, 1930), 55, 65. Filson's *Kentucke* was first published in Wilmington, Delaware, in 1784.

9. Timothy Flint, *The First White Man of the West, or the Life and Exploits of Col. Daniel Boone, the First Settler of Kentucky* (Cincinnati, 1847), 57, 249. Flint's book was first published in Cincinnati in 1833 as *Biographical Memoir of Daniel Boone, the First Settler of Kentucky: Interspersed with Incidents in the Early Annals of the Country.* W. H. Bogart, *Daniel Boone, and the Hunters of Kentucky* (Auburn and Buffalo, N.Y., 1854), 194.

10. Patrick M. Malone, *The Skulking Way of War: Technology and Tactics among the New England Indians* (New York, 1991), 60–61; Thomas Jefferson, *Notes on the State of Virginia,* in *The Life and Selected Writings of Thomas Jefferson,* ed. Adrienne Koch and William Peden (New York, 1944; reprint, New York, 1993), 198; William Guthrie, *A New Geographical, Historical, and Commercial Grammar, and Present State of the Several Kingdoms of the World* (London, 1771), 614.

11. Filson, *Kentucke,* 53–54; John Mason Peck, *Life of Daniel Boone, the Pioneer of Kentucky,* in *The Library of American Biography,* 2d ser., vol. 13, ed. Jared Sparks (Boston, 1847), 19; Cecil B. Hartley, *Life of Daniel Boone, the Great Western Hunter and Pioneer* (Philadelphia, 1865), 44. Hartley's *Life of Daniel Boone* was first published in Philadelphia in 1859 under the title *Life and Times of Colonel Daniel Boone, Comprising a History of the Early Settlement of Kentucky.* Bogart, *Daniel Boone, and the Hunters of Kentucky,* 40. On the middle-class concern with athleticism and the body, see E. Anthony Rotundo, *American Manhood: Transformations in Masculinity from the Revolution to the Modern Era* (New York, 1993), 226–46.

12. Flint, *First White Man,* 236.

13. Bingham titled his 1851–52 painting *Daniel Boone Escorting Settlers through the Cumberland Gap;* Greenough titled his 1851 statue *The Rescue Group.* On Boone's interment and the monument placed over his grave in 1860, see Faragher, *Daniel Boone: The Life and Legend,* 354–59. The best assessment of Boone in art is J. Gray Sweeney, *The Columbus of the Woods: Daniel Boone and the Typology of Manifest Destiny* (St. Louis, 1992).

14. William Harvey Miner, *Daniel Boone: Contribution Toward a Bibliography of Writings Concerning Daniel Boone* (New York, 1901); Faragher, *Daniel Boone: The Life and Legend,* 323.

15. Flint, preface to *First White Man;* George Canning Hill, *Daniel Boone, The Pioneer of Kentucky* (New York, 1889), 16.

16. William Newnham Blane, *An Excursion through the United States and Canada during the Years 1822–23. By an English Gentleman* (London, 1824), 292–93.

17. Faragher, *Daniel Boone: The Life and Legend,* 54. For an accurate portrait of backwoods masculinity, see Elliott J. Gorn, "'Gouge and Bite, Pull Hair and Scratch': The Social Significance of Fighting in the Southern Backcountry," *American Historical Review* 90 (February 1985): 18–43.

Slotkin, Faragher, and others assume that the Boone legend originated in frontier oral tradition and subsequently was discovered by the publishing industry. In my view the process worked in reverse. Had Filson not made the world aware of Boone in 1784, Boone probably would have remained obscure. Other hunters would have come to the fore, but not necessarily Boone.

Consider the so-called fire-hunt myth, cited by Slotkin and others in his train as sterling evidence of Boone's folk culture origins. As the story goes, Boone first glimpsed his wife-to-be, Rebecca, while on a fire-hunt, a practice in which the hunter carried a torch through the forest at night, searching for the gleam in the eyes of his dazzled prey. While thus engaged, Boone ostensibly mistook his future wife's shining eyes for those of a deer but refrained from shooting (Flint, *First White Man*, 26). Rebecca, thinking Boone was a "painter" (panther), turned and fled, and Boone pursued his unlikely prey to her home, discovering his "deer" to be a "dear."

Because the fire-hunt tale appeared in oral histories and correspondence collected by Lyman Draper decades after Boone's death, modern scholars presume that the tale—and hence the larger Boone legend to which it was attached—originated in frontier oral tradition. "The fire-hunt legend is crucial to any understanding of Boone as a myth-hero," testifies Slotkin, adding—without citation—that the tale "was well known to the Boones themselves, and they often repeated it to their children (who refused to believe it)." Filson omitted the tale in *Kentucke,* explains Slotkin, only because he wished to present a mannered, literary narrative rather than the "original, primitive, experiential" frontier myth (Slotkin, *Regeneration through Violence,* 299–308, 420).

Yet Filson probably neglected the fire-hunt tale because it did not exist—in fact or fancy—until thirteen years after Boone's death, when Flint invented it. Slotkin's sole source for the fire-hunt tale is Timothy Flint, who claimed to have interviewed those who knew Boone but gave no attribution for the fire-hunt tale per se. Even if Flint could rest his conscience in the knowledge that he had "put down the facts," he was cognizant of the sentimental tastes of his middle-class reading public, and he was heir to a literary tradition dating from the Middle Ages that equated deer hunting with erotic pursuit. Flint's fellow hagiographer, W. H. Bogart, called attention to Flint's fraud (Bogart, *Daniel Boone, and the Hunters of Kentucky,* 30). Matt Cartmill, *A View to a Death in the Morning: Hunting and Nature through History* (Cambridge, Mass., 1994), 70, 74.

18. Cathy Davidson, *Revolution and the Word: The Rise of the Novel in America* (New York, 1986), 27–29; David Donald Hall, "Introduction: The Uses of Literacy in New England, 1600–1850," *Printing and Society in Early America,* ed. William L. Joyce et al. (Worcester, Mass., 1983), 7–9; William J. Gilmore, "Elementary Literacy on the Eve of the Industrial Revolution: Trends in Rural New England, 1760–1830," *Proceedings of the American Antiquarian Society* 92 (1982): 124, 159; Ronald J. Zboray, *A Fictive People: Antebellum Economic Development and the American Reading Public* (New York, 1993), 11–12, 106. Although Connecticut wit Timothy Dwight noted that he had only once met a bookish farmer, some farmers of the early republic, ambitious for social status, did learn to read extensively (Richard D. Brown, *Knowledge Is Power: The Diffusion of Information in Early*

America, 1700–1865 [Oxford, England, 1989], 142, 153). William Gilmore has argued that reading had become "a necessity of life" by the 1820s for residents of Vermont's rural Windsor District. Gilmore's rural readers, however, were concentrated in a web of growing townships and were caught up in the get-ahead spirit of the market revolution (William J. Gilmore, *Reading Becomes a Necessity of Life: Material and Cultural Life in Rural New England, 1780–1835* [Knoxville, Tenn., 1989], 5, 8, 18, 21–22, 107, 109). On the increasing cosmopolitanism of the middle class, Ronald Zboray detects a "new cultural nationality" in the 1840s, whereas John Kasson notes that antebellum etiquette books characterized localisms in speech as the sure sign of a person who was "underbred" (Zboray, *Fictive People,* 191–92; Kasson, *Rudeness and Civility,* 55).

Some scholars—most notably Richard Slotkin—describe Boone as a contested figure, a cultural cipher capable of relaying diverse and contradictory political and sectional meanings. Slotkin thus distinguishes a tension between the active, adventurous Boone who ostensibly appeared in the literature of the frontier West, the philosophical Boone who appeared in the literature of the Yankee North, and the chivalric Boone who appeared in the literature of the planter South (Slotkin, *Regeneration through Violence,* 324, 409, 458–59). Remarkable in the Boone literature, however, is not its variety and complexity but its homogeneity and consistency. Slotkin's thesis succeeds only by ignoring the ubiquity of such Boone traits as chivalry, moral integrity, self-reliance, self-control, and dedication to the hunt, traits that are woven throughout the literature regardless of its sectional origins.

19. Charles Sellers, *The Market Revolution: Jacksonian America, 1815–1846* (Oxford, England, 1991), 43. On the technological and transportation advances that produced the market revolution, see David Freeman Hawke, *Nuts and Bolts of the Past: A History of American Technology, 1776–1860* (New York, 1988); Brooke Hindle and Steven Lubar, *Engines of Change: The American Industrial Revolution, 1790–1860* (Washington, D.C., 1986); David A. Hounshell, *From the American System to Mass Production, 1800–1932: The Development of Manufacturing Technology in the United States* (Baltimore, 1984); George Rogers Taylor, *The Transportation Revolution, 1815–1860* (New York, 1951); Carter Goodrich, ed., *Canals and American Economic Development* (New York, 1961); Ronald E. Shaw, *Canals for a Nation: The Canal Era in the United States, 1790–1860* (Lexington, Ky., 1990); and Albert Fishlow, *American Railroads and the Transformation of the Ante-Bellum Economy* (Cambridge, Mass., 1965).

20. The slogan "Go Ahead!" appeared at the head of each cover title of the first series of Crockett almanacs. See *The Crockett Almanacs, Nashville Series, 1835–1838* (Chicago, 1955).

21. See, for instance, James Willard Hurst, *Law and the Conditions of Freedom in the Nineteenth-Century United States* (Madison, Wisc., 1967), 6–7.

22. Ellwood C. Parry III, "Thomas Cole's *The Hunter's Return*," *The American Art Journal* 17, 3 (summer 1985): 15.

23. Mann Butler, *A History of the Commonwealth of Kentucky,* 2d ed. (Cincinnati, 1836), 19; Hill, *Daniel Boone, The Pioneer of Kentucky,* 10.

24. Joseph Kett, *Rites of Passage: Adolescence in America, 1790 to the Present* (New York, 1977), 95, 108; Sellers, *Market Revolution,* 156; Karen Halttunen, *Confidence Men and Painted Women: A Study of Middle-Class Culture in America, 1830–1870* (New Haven, Conn., 1982), 35. Many historians have noted that colonial patriarchy was undermined as young men moved away from their families in search of new opportunities rather than learning their fathers' trades. The market revolution produced a further breakdown of patriarchal authority—and a concomitant anxiety over social order—as middle-class men established autonomous urban business districts separate from homes and factories. Paul Johnson, *A Shopkeeper's Millennium: Society and Revivals in Rochester, New York, 1815–1837* (New York, 1978), 32–36, 42–55; Halttunen, *Confidence Men and Painted Women,* 12–13; Mary P. Ryan, *Cradle of the Middle Class: The Family in Oneida County, New York, 1790–1865* (Cambridge, England, 1981), 13, 64, 152, 232. My discussion of urban migration and etiquette books is drawn from Halttunen, *Confidence Men and Painted Women,* 1–55, 92–123; and John Kasson, *Rudeness and Civility: Manners in Nineteenth-Century Urban America* (New York, 1990), 35–69. Works concentrating on the formation of a middle class in the early Republic include Ryan, *Cradle;* Stuart M. Blumin, "The Hypothesis of Middle-Class Formation in Nineteenth-Century America: A Critique and Some Proposals," *American Historical Review* 90 (1985): 299–338; Stuart Blumin, *The Emergence of the Middle Class: Social Experience in the American City, 1760–1900* (Cambridge, England, 1989); and Richard Bushman, *The Refinement of America: Persons, Houses, Cities* (New York, 1992).

25. Flint, *First White Man,* 23, 29, 31, 41; Bogart, *Daniel Boone, and the Hunters of Kentucky,* 22. The title of Cecil B. Hartley's etiquette manual was *The Gentlemen's Book of Etiquette and Manual of Politeness: Being a Complete Guide for a Gentleman's Conduct in All His Relations towards Society: Containing Rules for the Etiquette To Be Observed in the Street, at Table, in the Ball Room, Evening Party, and Morning Call: With Full Directions for Polite Correspondence, Dress, Conversation, Manly Exercises, and Accomplishments: From the Best French, English, and American Authorities* (Boston, 1860).

26. William Henry Milburn, *The Rifle, Axe, and Saddle-Bags, and Other Lectures* (New York, 1857), 28, 30, 42.

27. Milburn, *Rifle, Axe, and Saddle-Bags,* xi, xiii, xv. It is difficult to say how popular Milburn's lectures were, yet they were popular enough to be published in book form. The Boone lecture appeared first in the aforementioned anthology. The book also included a biographical entry on Milburn written by the well-known humorist and hunting author Thomas Bangs Thorpe.

28. The terms "self-possession" and "peculiar self-possession" recur several times in Flint's descriptions of Boone (*First White Man,* 21, 68, 79, 236). Alexis de Tocqueville, quoted in Sellers, *Market Revolution,* 251. Art critic Robert Mills similarly praised Causici's relief of Boone for showing the hero's "cool resolution and self-possession," whereas George Canning Hill commented that Boone "felt the peculiar glory there was in trusting to himself, in relying on his own exertions" (Robert Mills, quoted in Vivien Green Fryd,

Art and Empire: The Politics of Ethnicity in the United States Capitol, 1815–1860 [New Haven, Conn., 1992], 35; Hill, *Daniel Boone, The Pioneer of Kentucky,* 23). Still others praised Boone for his prudence (John McClung, *Sketches of Western Adventure* [Maysville, Ky., 1832; reprint, Covington, Ky., 1872], 86). On the power of individuality and self-reliance in Jacksonian America, see also Rotundo, *American Manhood,* 13, 19.

29. Hartley, *Life of Daniel Boone, the Great Western Hunter and Pioneer,* 4; Peck, *Life of Daniel Boone, the Pioneer of Kentucky,* 18; Flint, preface to *First White Man.*

30. Flint, *Biographical Memoir,* 29–30, quoted in Slotkin, *Regeneration through Violence,* 424; Michael Kimmel, *Manhood in America* (New York, 1995), 26; John Cawelti, *Apostles of the Self-Made Man* (Chicago, 1965), 40–41; Charles C. B. Seymour, *Self-Made Men* (New York, 1858).

31. Peck, *Life of Daniel Boone, the Pioneer of Kentucky,* 18, 174; Thwaites, *Daniel Boone,* 114; Faragher, *Daniel Boone: The Life and Legend,* 327 (citing New York *American,* quoted in *Niles Weekly Register* 24 [May 17, 1823]: 19–23); Flint, *First White Man,* 64.

32. Anthony F. C. Wallace, *Rockdale: The Growth of an American Village in the Early Industrial Revolution* (New York, 1978), 19; Bogart, *Daniel Boone, and the Hunters of Kentucky,* 39; Peck, *Life of Daniel Boone, the Pioneer of Kentucky,* 22, 142.

33. Peck, *Life of Daniel Boone, the Pioneer of Kentucky,* 15; Halttunen, *Confidence Men and Painted Women,* 11; Kasson, *Rudeness and Civility,* 112–46.

34. Compare Jared Waterbury's advice to urban young men of the antebellum era ("Insidious foes lurk around your path. A dangerous enemy lies in ambush") with an earlier description of Boone's Indian foes ("enemies the most daring, insidious, and cruel"). Waterbury, quoted in Kett, *Rites of Passage,* 95. Boone's foes are described in U.S. Senate, *Report of the Committee to Whom was Referred the Petition of Daniel Boon, Together with the Bill for His Relief* (Washington, D.C., 1810). Boone's daughter enters her father's masculine realm only when she is captured by Indians and must be rescued. This was a standard Boone anecdote.

35. Carroll Smith-Rosenberg, *Disorderly Conduct: Visions of Gender in Victorian America* (Oxford, England, 1985), 90.

36. Sellers, *Market Revolution,* 246.

37. Boone, quoted in Faragher, *Daniel Boone: The Life and Legend,* 302; Bogart, *Daniel Boone, and the Hunters of Kentucky,* 13, 284.

38. Francis Lister Hawks [Uncle Philip, pseud.], *The Adventures of Daniel Boone, the Kentucky Rifleman* (New York, 1844), 2. James Oakes, among others, convincingly argues that planters adopted a bourgeois worldview *(The Ruling Race: A History of American Slaveholders* [New York, 1983]). On the market and middle-class values among western farmers and townspeople, see Andrew R. L. Cayton and Peter S. Onuf, *The Midwest and the Nation: Rethinking the History of an American Region* (Bloomington, Ill., 1990), 63, 84, 103, 118; and John Mack Faragher, *Sugar Creek: Life on the Illinois Prairie* (New Haven, Conn., 1986), 199–215. Several scholars contend that Jacksonian and antebellum political and social struggles in frontier states hinged on how to control forces unleashed by the

market revolution—and how to shape community in an individualistic, egalitarian society—rather than whether to accept the market. See Don Harrison Doyle, *The Social Order of a Frontier Community: Jacksonville, Illinois, 1825–1870* (Urbana, Ill., 1978), 3, 15; and Harry Watson, *Jacksonian Politics and Community Conflict: The Emergence of the Second American Party System in Cumberland County, North Carolina* (Baton Rouge, La., 1981), 322. Charles Sellers's voluminous and elegant—yet perhaps oversimplified—treatment of the market revolution, on the other hand, offers a neo-Progressive analysis of the Jacksonian era as a great cultural and political clash between bourgeois men-on-the-make (the "interests") and pre-industrial farmers (the "people"). See Sellers, *Market Revolution.*

Much of Appalachia—where the Boone myth supposedly began—was itself embroiled in the market revolution in the Jacksonian and antebellum eras. Only after the Civil War did parts of Appalachia become the backwater societies that we identify as traditional. Hence, even if the Boone myth did blossom in Appalachian oral tradition, its meaning may well have lain in its reevaluation of masculinity in the context of the market revolution. See Robert D. Mitchell, ed., *Appalachian Frontiers: Settlement, Society, and Development in the Preindustrial Era* (Lexington, Ky., 1991). In Mitchell's book, of particular relevance are Robert D. Mitchell, "Introduction: Revisionism and Regionalism," 1–22; Tyrel G. Moore, "Economic Development in Appalachian Kentucky, 1800–1860," 222–34; Mary Beth Pudup, "Social Class and Economic Development in Southeastern Kentucky, 1820–1880," 235–60; and Paul Salstrom, "The Agricultural Origins of Economic Dependency, 1840–1880," 261–83. See also Mary Beth Pudup, Dwight B. Billings, and Altina L. Waller, eds., *Appalachia in the Making: The Mountain South in the Nineteenth Century* (Chapel Hill, N.C., 1995); and Henry D. Shapiro, *Appalachia on Our Mind: The Southern Mountains and Mountaineers in the American Consciousness, 1870–1920* (Chapel Hill, N.C., 1978).

39. Daniel Bryan, *The Mountain Muse. Comprising the Adventures of Daniel Boone; and the Power of Virtuous and Refined Beauty* (Harrisonburg, Va., 1813), 137; Davidson, *Revolution and the Word,* 27.

40. Bogart, *Daniel Boone, and the Hunters of Kentucky,* iii, 59, 335; Bakeless, *Daniel Boone: Master of the Wilderness,* 394. Despite Boone's reputation as the "First White Man of the West," hundreds of whites had preceded him into Kentucky. See Clarence Alvord, "The Boone Myth," *Journal of the Illinois State Historical Society* 19 (April–July 1926): 22.

41. William Truettner, ed., *The West as America: Reinterpreting Images of the Frontier* (Washington, D.C., 1991), 98. On Andrew Jackson Grayson's career, see Juliette Mouron Hood, "Andrew J. Grayson: The Audubon of the Pacific," *The Auk* 50, no. 4 (October 1933): 396–402.

9. A Pantheon of Hunter-Heroes

1. John Jack Faragher, *Daniel Boone: The Life and Legend of an American Pioneer* (New York,

1903), 335; Samuel Woodworth, *Hunters of Kentucky* (broadside) (Boston, [1815?]). John William Ward points out that the poem became "a 'folk-song' only in the sense that its popularity was so great it was eventually taken over by the folk." John William Ward, *Andrew Jackson—Symbol for an Age* (New York, 1955; reprint, New York, 1971), 13–33, 217. This chapter appeared in somewhat different form under the title "The Other Daniel Boone: The Nascence of a Middle-Class Hunter Hero, 1784–1860," *Journal of the Early Republic* 18, no. 3 (fall 1998): 429–57.

2. George Bancroft, quoted in Ward, *Andrew Jackson—Symbol*, 73; Mark Derr, *The Frontiersman: The Real Life and Many Legends of Davy Crockett* (New York, 1993), 211; "Davy Crockett's Rifle," *Forest and Stream* 20 (April 26, 1883): 246; Carroll Smith-Rosenberg, *Disorderly Conduct: Visions of Gender in Victorian America* (Oxford, England, 1985), 50. On Crockett, see also Michael A. Lofaro, *Davy Crockett: The Man, the Legend, the Legacy* (Knoxville, Tenn., 1985); and Michael A. Lofaro and Joe Cummings, eds., *Crockett at Two Hundred: New Perspectives on the Man and the Myth* (Knoxville, Tenn., 1989).

3. James Atkins Shackford, *David Crockett: The Man and the Legend* (Chapel Hill, N.C., 1956; reprint, Chapel Hill, N.C., 1986), 52–53, 64.

4. David Crockett, *The Autobiography of David Crockett* (New York, 1923), 125; Shackford, *David Crockett*, 131. On Crockett as a savvy politician rather than a dupe of the Whigs, see Thomas E. Scruggs, "Davy Crockett and the Thieves of Jericho: An Analysis of the Shackford-Parrington Conspiracy Theory," *Journal of the Early Republic* 19, no. 3 (fall 1999): 481–98.

5. Quoted in Catharine L. Albanese, *Nature Religion in America, from the Algonkian Indians to the New Age* (Chicago, 1990), 75.

6. James Strange French, quoted in Derr, *Frontiersman*, 198. On Mike Fink, see Walter Blair and Franklin J. Meine, *Half Horse Half Alligator: The Growth of the Mike Fink Legend* (New York, 1977).

7. James Fenimore Cooper, *The Pioneers, or the Sources of the Susquehanna; a Descriptive Tale*, in *The Leatherstocking Tales*, vol. 1 (New York, 1985), 84, 265. Cooper's *The Pioneers* was first published in 1823.

8. Ibid., 362, 375–76, 161, 462.

9. Ibid., 248–50.

10. Ibid., 23, 445–49.

11. Alan Taylor, *William Cooper's Town: Power and Persuasion on the Frontier of the Early American Republic* (New York, 1995), 418–20; Faragher, *Daniel Boone: The Life and Legend*, 331.

12. "The 'Leatherstocking' Tales," *Forest and Stream* 33, no. 10 (September 26, 1889): 181, cols. 2–3.

13. Cooper, *Pioneers*, vol. 1, 214, 449.

14. Ibid., 202.

15. Charles Burdett, *The Life and Adventures of Christopher Carson, the Celebrated Rocky Mountain Hunter, Trapper, and Guide* (Philadelphia, 1860), 4; Reuben Gold Thwaites,

Daniel Boone (New York, 1903), 231; *Broadway Journal* (January 4, 1845): 35, quoted in Carol Clark, "Charles Deas," in *American Frontier Life: Early Western Paintings and Prints,* by Ron Tyler et al. (New York, 1987), 60. The full title of Deas's 1844 painting is *Long Jakes (Long Jakes, The Rocky Mountain Man).* Henry Eugene Davies, *Ten Days on the Plains by* ** (New York, n.d.), 29.

16. Theodore Roosevelt, *The Winning of the West. Homeward Bound Edition,* vol. 1 (New York, 1910), 137.

17. Francis Parkman, *The California and Oregon Trail* (New York, 1898), 14, 291. Parkman's *California and Oregon Trail* was first published in New York in 1849. Charles Lanman, *Adventures in the Wilds of the United States and British American Provinces* (Philadelphia, 1856), 229. Lanman's book was first published in London in 1854 under the title *Adventures in the Wilds of North America.*

18. Estwick Evans, *A Pedestrious Tour of Four Thousand Miles, through the Western States and Territories, February 2–July, 1818,* in *Early Western Travels, 1748–1846,* ed. Reuben Gold Thwaites, vol. 8 (Cleveland, 1904), 102. Evans's *Pedestrious Tour* was first published in Concord, New Hampshire, in 1819. Washington Irving, quoted in Michael Kimmel, *Manhood in America* (New York, 1995), 19; Washington Irving, *The Rocky Mountains; or, Scenes, Incidents, and Adventures in the Far West; digested from the Journal of Capt. B. L. E. Bonneville . . . and illustrated from various other sources* (Philadelphia, 1837).

19. Robert Johannsen, *To the Halls of the Montezumas: The Mexican War in the American Imagination* (Oxford, England, 1985), 74–77.

20. Timothy Flint, *The First White Man of the West, or the Life and Exploits of Col. Daniel Boone, the First Settler of Kentucky* (Cincinnati, 1847), 227–28. Flint's book was first published in Cincinnati in 1833 as *Biographical Memoir of Daniel Boone, the First Settler of Kentucky: Interspersed with Incidents in the Early Annals of the Country.*

21. Benjamin G. Rader, *American Sports: From the Age of Folk Games to the Age of Spectators* (Englewood Cliffs, N.J., 1983), 34. See also Drew R. McCoy, *The Elusive Republic: Political Economy in Jeffersonian America* (Chapel Hill, N.C., 1980).

22. Charles Wilkins Webber, *The Hunter-Naturalist: Romance of Sporting; or, Wild Scenes & Wild Hunters,* vol. 1 (Philadelphia, 1851), 30–31.

10. *The Sport Hunter's Awakening*

1. Alan Taylor, "The Unadilla Hunt Club" (paper presented at the annual conference of the Society of Historians of the Early American Republic, Nashville, Tenn., July 19, 1996), 15. I wish to thank Professor Taylor for granting me permission to publish this account of the Unadilla Hunt, which is entirely based on his paper.

2. Ibid., 20.

3. Ibid., 15.

4. Ibid., 9.

5. Ibid., 25.

6. Charles Fenno Hoffman, *A Winter in the West. By a New-Yorker,* vol. 1 (n.p., 1977), 133. Hoffman's *Winter in the West* was first published in New York in 1835.

7. B., "Cincinnati Shooting Club," *American Turf Register and Sporting Magazine* 4, no. 12 (August 1833): 637; GWG, "The St. Louis Hunting Club," *Spirit of the Times* 21, no. 1 (February 22, 1851), 1, col. 3, through 3, col. 1; [William Barrows], *The General; or, Twelve Nights in the Hunters' Camp. A Narrative of Real Life* (Boston, 1869), 14. Middle-class and elite men of Cleveland, Ohio, likewise formed their own sporting and natural history club in the 1830s, known as "the Ark." See Oliver Hazard Perry, *Hunting Expeditions of Oliver Hazard Perry,* ed. John E. Howard (DeForest, Wisc., 1994), 8–10.

8. Patricia R. Click, *The Spirit of the Times: Amusements in Nineteenth-Century Baltimore, Norfolk, and Richmond* (Charlottesville, 1989), 75; *Spirit of the Times* 18, no. 1 (February 26, 1848): 7, col. 3; 9, no. 46 (January 18, 1840): 546, col. 2; 18, no. 7 (April 4, 1848): 79, col. 3.

   For reports on hunting club activities, see *Spirit of the Times* 26, no. 21 (July 5, 1856): 246, col. 2; 18, no. 20 (July 8, 1848): 235, col. 3; 27, no. 8 (April 4, 1857): 91, col. 2; 18, no. 21 (July 15, 1848): 246, col. 2; 20, no. 14 (May 25, 1850): 157, col. 3; 19, no. 7 (April 7, 1849): 73, cols. 2–3; 19, no. 12 (May 12, 1849): 138, cols. 2–3; 19, no. 51 (February 9, 1850): 608, col. 1; 29, no. 7 (March 26, 1859): 80, col. 3; 27, no. 3 (February 28, 1857): 27, col. 2; 10, no. 37 (November 14, 1840): 438, col. 1; 27, no. 3 (February 28, 1857): 27, col. 2; 17, no. 50 (February 5, 1847): 585, col. 3; and *American Turf Register* 6, no. 5 (January, 1835): 234–7; 9, no. 3 (March 1838): 98.

   On rifle clubs, see S.L., "Rifle Shooting," *Spirit of the Times* 18, no. 8 (April 15, 1848): 90, col. 1; "The Rifle Shooting Challenge," *Spirit of the Times* 18, no. 11 (May 6, 1848): 132, col. 2; "Rifle Shooting at Cincinnati and New Orleans," *Spirit of the Times* 18, no. 14 (May 27, 1848): 59, cols. 1–2; "The Rifle Challenge," *Spirit of the Times* 18, no. 15 (June 3, 1848): 174, cols. 1–2; Horace E. Dimick, "Proposition to Eastern Riflemen from the Western," *Spirit of the Times* 18, no. 16 (June 10, 1848): 186, col. 2; John R. Chapman, "Remarks on the Rifle and Riflemen," *Spirit of the Times* 18, no. 8 (June 24, 1848): 210, col. 2; E. Wesson, "Reply to the Rifle Challenge of the West," *Spirit of the Times* 18, no. 18 (June 24, 1848): 210, col. 3; "Central N.Y. Rifle Club," *Spirit of the Times* 18, no. 48 (January 20, 1849): 576, col. 3; and Boon Club, "Rifle Shooting in Kentucky," *Spirit of the Times* 18, no. 7 (April 8, 1848): 79, col. 3. See also Russell S. Gilmore, "'Another Branch of Manly Sport': American Rifle Games, 1840–1900," in *Guns in America: A Reader,* ed. Jan E. Dizard, Robert Merrill Muth, and Stephen P. Andrews Jr. (New York, 1999), 105–21. Gilmore concentrates on the Creedmore matches of the postbellum era, but rifle clubs were numerous in earlier decades.

9. Nicholas Wolfe Proctor, "Bathed in Blood: Hunting in the Antebellum South" (Ph.D. diss., Emory Univ., 1998), 205.

10. Taylor, "Unadilla Hunt Club," 30–31.

11. Ibid., 5.

12. [Jervis McEntee], "The Lakes of the Wilderness," *The Great Republic. A Monthly National*

Magazine (April 1859), 335, Adirondack Museum Vertical Files (AMVF). Though detailing a real hunting excursion, and though expressing the sentiments of real sportsmen, this article is a classic of antebellum parody.

13. Michael A. Bellesîles, "The Origins of Gun Culture in the United States, 1760–1865," *Journal of American History* 83, no. 2 (September 1996): 439; Henry William Herbert [Frank Forester, pseud.], *The Complete Manual for Young Sportsmen: with Directions for the Handling of the Gun, the Rifle, and the Rod; the Art of Shooting on the Wing; the Breaking, Management, and Hunting of the Dog; the Varieties and Habits of Game; River, Lake, and Sea Fishing. Etc. Etc. Etc. Prepared for the Instruction and Use of the Youth of America* (New York, 1848; reprint, New York, 1868), 26.

14. George Bird Grinnell, quoted in John Reiger, *American Sportsmen and the Origins of Conservation* (New York, 1975), 25; George Bird Grinnell, "American Game Protection: A Sketch," in *Hunting and Conservation,* ed. George Bird Grinnell and Charles Sheldon (New Haven, Conn., 1925; reprint, New York, 1970), 225; "Value of Outdoor Sports," *Outdoor Life* 6, no. 2 (August 1900).

15. "A Discourse Against Laziness in Sportsmen," in *Classics of the American Shooting Field; A Mixed Bag for the Kindly Sportsman, 1783–1926,* ed. John C. Phillips and Lewis Webb Hill (Boston, 1930), 21–26. The discourse appeared originally in [J. Davis], *Essays on Various Subjects. Written for the Amusement of Everybody, by One Who Is Considered Nobody* (New York, 1835).

16. Several historians have traced changing definitions of gender to the Age of Jackson and the market revolution. See E. Anthony Rotundo, *American Manhood: Transformations in Masculinity from the Revolution to the Modern Era* (New York, 1993); Mark C. Carnes, *Secret Ritual and Manhood in Victorian America* (New Haven, 1989); Peter N. Stearns, *Be a Man! Males in Modern Society* (New York, 1990); and Michael Kimmel, *Manhood in America* (New York, 1995). Also helpful are John Cawelti, *Apostles of the Self-Made Man* (Chicago, 1965); Mark C. Carnes and Clyde Griffen, eds., *Meanings for Manhood: Constructions of Masculinity in Victorian America* (Chicago, 1990); Joe L. Dubbert, *A Man's Place* (Englewood Cliffs, N.J., 1979); Rupert Wilkinson, *American Tough: The Tough-Guy Tradition and American Character* (Westport, Conn., 1984); and David G. Pugh, *Sons of Liberty: The Masculine Mind in Nineteenth-Century America* (Westport, Conn., 1983).

17. On the differences between monarchical and republican societies, see Gordon Wood, *The Radicalism of the American Revolution* (New York, 1992), parts 1 and 2. N.S.J., "The Sporting Journal of N.S.J., Esq.," *American Turf Register and Sporting Magazine* 1, no. 1 (September 1829): 46. "Six deer in six shots," bragged another hunter in 1850, "is not bad shooting, dear *Spirit*" ("Deer Hunting in South Carolina," *Spirit of the Times* 20, no. 3 [March 9, 1850]: 26, col. 1).

18. "Discourse," *Classics of the American Shooting Field,* 23.

19. *American Farmer,* 1st ser., vol. 7 (1825): 175.

20. Harry Worcester Smith, *A Sporting Family of the Old South* (Albany, N.Y., 1936), 9, 26; Donald William Klinko, "Antebellum American Sporting Magazines and the De-

velopment of a Sportsman's Ethic" (Ph.D. diss., Washington State Univ., 1986), 29, 36; Ernest R. Gee, *Early American Sporting Books 1734 to 1844. A Few Brief Notes* (New York, 1928), 2.

21. "Introduction," *American Turf Register and Sporting Magazine* 1, no. 1 (September 1829): 1.

22. Wilson G. Duprey, "Introduction," in *Cabinet of Natural History and American Rural Sport,* ed. Gail Stewart (Barre, Mass., 1973), ix–x.

23. Frank H. Goodyear, *Thomas Doughty 1793–1856: An American Pioneer in Landscape Painting.* Selection and Catalogue by Frank H. Goodyear Jr. (Philadelphia, 1973), 12, 13; John Alan Walker, *Fine Art Source Material Newsletter* 1, no. 1 (January 1971): 1.

24. Nathaniel Parker Willis and the *Knickerbocker* magazine, quoted in Goodyear, *Thomas Doughty,* 11, 15, 30.

25. *Cabinet of Natural History and American Rural Sport* 1 (1830): vii; Goodyear, *Thomas Doughty,* 15–16.

26. Francis Brinley, *Life of William T. Porter* (New York, 1860), 20; Izaak Walton, *The Compleat Angler, or the Contemplative Man's Recreation* (London, 1653).

27. Klinko, "Antebellum American Sporting Magazines," 64.

28. "New Volume, with New Correspondents, New Subscribers, AND A NEW DRESS!" *Spirit of the Times* 23, no. 1 (February 19, 1853): 1, col. 1.

29. Frank Luther Mott, *A History of American Magazines,* vol. 2 (Cambridge, Mass., 1957), 11; "Letter from an Officer of the U.S. Dragoons. Fort Leavenworth, Mo., March 16th, 1844," *Spirit of the Times* 14, no. 7 (April 13, 1844): 78, col. 3.

30. "Partridge Shooting," *American Turf Register* 6, no. 3 (November 1834): 140–42; Samuel H. Hammond, *Hills, Lakes, and Forest Streams: or, A Tramp in the Chateaugay Woods* (New York, 1854), 14; Vale, "Memories of Two Weeks' Encampment in the Woods of Pennsylvania," *Spirit of the Times* 17, no. 34 (August 7, 1847): 447, col. 1.

31. N.S.J., "Copy of the Sporting Journal of N.S.J., Esq.," *American Turf Register* 1, no. 2 (October 1829): 78; I.T.S., "The Usefulness of Sporting," in *Cabinet of Natural History and American Rural Sport,* ed. Gail Stewart (Barre, Mass., 1973), 1:16; Joel Tyler Headley, *Letters from the Backwoods and the Adirondac* (New York, 1850), 71. "The Usefulness of Sporting" was reprinted from time to time by other papers. One 1837 version in the *Spirit of the Times* included an advertisement for a gunsmith, showing the growing popularity and commercialization of hunting: "If citizens who are closely confined for most part of the day . . . would *shoulder their guns,* (if they have them—otherwise step into E. P. Tabb's SPORTING ESTABLISHMENT, where there is a large and beautiful assortment just opened, and select one of the real *Simon's*) *and march away;* occasionally even for a few hours, it would produce a renovation of strength, as well as spirits for business."

32. *Hunt's Merchants' Magazine,* 1855, quoted in Stuart Blumin, *The Emergence of the Middle Class: Social Experience in the American City, 1760–1900* (Cambridge, England, 1989), 78.

33. Oliver Wendell Holmes, quoted in Roberta J. Park, "Biological Thought, Athletics,

and the Formation of a 'Man of Character': 1830–1900," *Manliness and Morality: Middle-Class Masculinity in Britain and America, 1800–1940* (Manchester, England, 1987), 15, 19; Horace Mann, quoted in Fred Somkin, *Unquiet Eagle: Memory and Desire in the Idea of American Freedom, 1815–1860* (Ithaca, N.Y., 1967), 45. On the fear of emasculation, see also Francis Parkman to the *Boston Daily Advertiser,* June 30, July 4, and July 14, 1863, in *Letters of Francis Parkman,* ed. Wilbur R. Jacobs, vol. 1 (Norman, Okla., 1960), 159–60.

34. Ann Douglas, *The Feminization of American Culture* (New York, 1977), 17 (quote from Henry James Sr.), 8, 62.

35. Mark C. Carnes, *Secret Ritual and Manhood in Victorian America* (New Haven, Conn., 1989), 65, 78–79, 116, 124–27; Ronald J. Zboray, *A Fictive People: Antebellum Economic Development and the American Reading Public* (Oxford, England, 1993), 88.

36. Ralph Waldo Emerson, quoted in David E. Shi, *The Simple Life: Plain Living and High Thinking in American Culture* (New York, 1985), 131.

37. Carnes, *Secret Ritual and Manhood,* 65, 78–79, 116, 124–27.

38. R. D. McE., "Our Game," *Spirit of the Times* 20, no. 21 (July 13, 1850): 241, col. 2.

39. Lyman Beecher, "The Gospel the Only Security for Eminent and Abiding National Prosperity," *National Preacher* 3 (March 1829), 147, quoted in John Kasson, *Civilizing the Machine: Technology and Republican Values in America, 1776–1900* (New York, 1976), 37.

40. John Adams to Thomas Jefferson, December 21, 1819, *The Adams-Jefferson Letters,* ed. Lester J. Cappon, vol. 2 (Chapel Hill, N.C., 1959), 551.

41. *American Turf Register* 1, no. 1 (September 1829): 31.

42. F. S. Stallknecht, "An August Sporting Tour," *Frank Leslie's New Family Magazine* 6, no. 4 (April 1860): 338.

43. Henry William Herbert, "Long Jakes, the Prairie Man," in *Life and Writings of Frank Forester. (Henry William Herbert.),* ed. David W. Judd, vol. 2 (New York, 1882), 207. Failure to obey the codes of sportsmanship, by extension, was "subversive of all the chivalric spirit which should animate the true sportsman." See "Sketch of a True Sportsman," *American Turf Register* 6, no. 1 (January 1833): 14–15.

44. Elisha Jarrett Lewis, *Hints to Sportsmen, Containing Notes on Shooting; the Habits of the Game Birds and Wild Fowl of America; the Dog, the Gun, the Field, and the Kitchen* (Philadelphia, 1851), 246. See also Lewis's enlarged edition of the aforementioned title, *The American Sportsman: Containing Hints to Sportsmen, Notes on Shooting, and the Habits of the Game Birds, and Wild Fowl of America* (Philadelphia, 1855), viii.

45. Ralph Ranger, "Sporting at the South: Or a Week on the Cooper River," *Spirit of the Times* 15, no. 52 (February 21, 1846): 609–10, quoted in Nicholas Wolfe Proctor, "Bathed in Blood: Hunting in the Antebellum South" (Ph.D. diss., Emory Univ., 1998), 143.

46. Tamara Plakins Thornton, *Cultivating Gentlemen: The Meaning of Country Life among the Boston Elite, 1785–1860* (New Haven, Conn., 1989), 46. Rural retirement in eighteenth-century England, writes Maren-Sofie Røstvig, represented an attempt "to transform man from a local and temporary creature, swayed by importunate passions and popular

superstitions, into an immortal soul rejoicing in the full possession of the eternal sphere of pure and undefiled reason and in the exercise of all the virtues." Maren-Sofie Røstvig, *The Happy Man: Studies in the Metamorphosis of a Classical Ideal*, vol. 2, *1700–1760* (Oslo, 1958), 28.

47. Thornton, *Cultivating Gentlemen*, 45–46, 49, 57, 66, 73.

48. On passion and aggression as traits of middle-class men in Jacksonian and antebellum America, see E. Anthony Rotundo, *American Manhood: Transformations in Masculinity from the Revolution to the Modern Era* (New York, 1993), 10–25.

49. Richard Bushman, *The Refinement of America: Persons, Houses, Cities* (New York, 1993); John F. Kasson, *Rudeness and Civility: Manners in Nineteenth-Century America* (New York, 1990).

50. "Pigeon Shooting," *American Turf Register* 1, no. 7 (March 1830): 338.

51. *Forest and Stream* 1, no. 1 (August 14, 1873): 8; [J.C.?] Beltrami, "Indian Hunters," in *Cabinet of Natural History and American Rural Sport*, ed. Gail Stewart (Barre, Mass., 1973), 1:159.

11. Manliness and Its Constraints

1. The account that follows is from "My First Deer Hunt," *Spirit of the Times* 24, no. 9 (April 15, 1854): 100, cols. 1–3.

2. Dickey Jones, "A Tour through the Adirondack.—No. 2," *Spirit of the Times* 23, no. 1 (February 19, 1853): 5.

3. Here resumes the account of "My First Deer Hunt," *Spirit of the Times* 24, no. 9 (April 15, 1854): 100, cols. 1–3.

4. Sportsman, "Rejoinder to I.T.S.," in *Cabinet of Natural History and American Rural Sport*, ed. Gail Stewart (Barre, Mass., 1973), 1:116.

5. Boon Club, "Rifle Shooting in Kentucky," *Spirit of the Times* 18, no. 7 (April 8, 1848): 79, col. 3.

6. *American Turf Register and Sporting Magazine*, quoted in Michael A. Bellesîles, "The Origins of Gun Culture in the United States, 1760–1865," *Journal of American History* 83, no. 2 (September 1996): 447.

7. Bellesîles, "Origins of Gun Culture," 426–28, 435; Michael A. Bellesiles, *Arming America: The Origins of a National Gun Culture* (New York, 2000), 263, 267.

8. Ibid., 427–28.

9. Timothy Flint, *Indian Wars of the West* (Cincinnati, 1833), 51.

10. S.L.C., "A Hunting Article," *Southern Literary Messenger* 17, no. 1 (January 1851): 44–49, quoted in Nicholas Wolfe Proctor, "Bathed in Blood: Hunting in the Antebellum South" (Ph.D. diss., Emory Univ., 1998), 82.

11. John Kasson, *Civilizing the Machine: Technology and Republican Values in America, 1776–1900* (New York, 1976), 47; "Deer Shooting in Northern New York," *Spirit of the Times* 18, no. 50 (February 3, 1849): 595, col. 1; Saranac, "American Rifles and Deer Shooting," *Spirit of the Times* 18, no. 42 (December 9, 1848): 499, col. 3. On Kentucky rifles as folk art, see Richard F. Rosenberger and Charles Kaufman, *The Longrifles of Western Pennsylvania:*

Allegheny and Westmoreland Counties, Bill Owen (photographer) (Pittsburgh, 1993); Joe Kindig Jr., *Thoughts on the Kentucky Rifle in Its Golden Age,* ed. Mary Ann Cresswell (Mechanicsburg, Pa., 1960; reprint, n.p., 1976); John G. W. Dillin, *The Kentucky Rifle,* ed. Kendrick Scofield (York, Pa., 1975). Dillin's *The Kentucky Rifle* was first published in 1924. On later rifles as folk art, see George Madis, *The Winchester Book* (Dallas, 1961).

12. Leo Marx, *The Machine in the Garden: Technology and the Pastoral Idea in America* (New York, 1964), 204.

13. "Facts from a Georgia Friend," *Spirit of the Times* 31, no. 20 (June 22, 1861): 305, cols. 1–2; Donald William Klinko, "Antebellum American Sporting Magazines and the Development of a Sportsman's Ethic" (Ph.D. diss., Washington State Univ., 1986), 209, 212; "The Old Family," *Turf, Field, and Farm* 5, no. 20 (November 16, 1867): 312, cols. 1–2.

14. Marcus Cunliffe, *Soldiers and Civilians: The Martial Spirit in America, 1775–1865* (Boston, 1968), 335–84. On hunting as a manly art of planters who sought to segregate themselves from Northerners, urbanites, and poor whites, see Scott C. Martin, "Don Quixote and Leatherstocking: Hunting, Class, and Masculinity in the American South, 1800–40," *The International Journal of the History of Sport* 12, no. 3 (December 1995): 61–79; and Proctor, "Bathed in Blood." There is no doubt that by the Age of Jackson hunting had become popular among Southerners. To say that the South harbored "the most enthusiastic devotees of [hunting] in the United States," as Clarence Gohdes claims, however, is to ignore equally enthusiastic devotees in the North and the West. See Clarence Gohdes, ed., *Hunting in the Old South: Original Narratives of the Hunters* (Baton Rouge, La., 1967), ix.

15. "Prospectus of the *Turf, Field, and Farm,*" *Turf, Field, and Farm. Sportsman's Oracle and Country Gentleman's Newspaper* 1, no. 8 (September 23, 1865): 127, col. 4; "The Old Family," *Turf, Field, and Farm* 5, no. 20 (November 16, 1867): 312, cols. 1–2; Klinko, "Antebellum American Sporting Magazines," 219; John Rickards Betts, "Sporting Journalism in Nineteenth-Century America," *American Quarterly* 5, no. 1 (spring 1953): 48; [George Bird Grinnell], "No Latitude nor Longitude," *Forest and Stream* 41, no. 1 (July 8, 1893): 1, col. 1. For another tale of rapprochement between the gentlemen hunters of South and North, see Charles Austin Fosdick [Harry Castlemon, pseud.], *The Sportsman's Club Among the Trappers* (Philadelphia, 1874).

16. Horace Mann, quoted in David Shi, *The Simple Life: Plain Living and High Thinking in American Culture* (New York, 1985), 122.

17. Henry David Thoreau, *Walden; or, Life in the Woods* (New York, 1962), 207–8. Thoreau's *Walden* was first published in Boston in 1854.

18. Thoreau, *Walden,* 209, 213. See also Thomas L. Altherr, "'Chaplain to the Hunters': Henry David Thoreau's Ambivalence Toward Hunting," *American Literature, A Journal of History, Criticism, and Bibliography* 56, no. 3 (October 1984): 351.

19. William Elliott, *Carolina Sports by Land and Water. Including Incidents of Devil-Fishing, Wild-Cat, Deer, and Bear Hunting, & c.* (Charleston, S.C., 1846), 281–82.

20. Catharine L. Albanese, *Nature Religion in America, from the Algonkian Indians to the New*

Age (Chicago, 1990), 4, 10. For Thoreau's notions of spirituality, see Thoreau, *Walden*, 215–16.

21. Thomas Doughty, "The Characteristics of a True Sportsman," *Cabinet of Natural History and American Rural Sport* 1 (1830): 8. Unfortunately, many sportsmen continued to brag of their fulsome kills. In 1857, long after the code of sportsmanship had been popularized, a correspondent of the *Spirit of the Times* reported that two midwestern hunters had taken 505 pinnated grouse in a two-week excursion, in addition to five Canada geese, nine turkeys, several sandhill cranes, and an assortment of bitterns, rails, ducks, and ruffed grouse. Another sport hunter, Henry Hastings Sibley of Minnesota, took 1,798 ducks in three years. Such scores were by no means unusual in the sporting press. John T. Flanagan, "Hunting in Early Illinois," *Journal of the Illinois State Historical Society* 72, no. 1 (1979): 9–12.

22. Elisha Jarrett Lewis, *The American Sportsman: Containing Hints to Sportsmen, Notes on Shooting, and the Habits of the Game Birds, and Wild Fowl of America* (Philadelphia, 1855), 62. Lewis's *American Sportsman* was first published in Philadelphia in 1851 as *Hints to Sportsmen, Containing Notes on Shooting; the Habits of the Game Birds and Wild Fowl of America; the Dog, the Gun, the Field, and the Kitchen.* Thoreau, *Walden*, 208.

23. "Sportsmen," in *Classics of the American Shooting Field; A Mixed Bag for the Kindly Sportsman, 1783–1926*, ed. John C. Phillips and Lewis Webb Hill (Boston and New York, 1930), 13, 15. "Sportsmen" was first published in [Davis], *Essays on Various Subjects* in New York in 1835.

24. "Sportsmen," *Classics of the American Shooting Field*, 15, 17.

25. Ibid., 16.

26. Lewis, *The American Sportsman*, 84.

27. Charles Fenno Hoffman, *Wild Scenes in the Forest and Prairie*, 2 vols. (London, 1839), vol. 2, 19; vol. 1, 92; Samuel H. Hammond, *Hills, Lakes, and Forest Streams: or, A Tramp in the Chateaugay Woods* (New York, 1854), 71.

28. Edmund Flagg, *The Far West: or, a Tour beyond the Mountains; June–Autumn, 1836*, in *Early Western Travels, 1748–1846*, ed. Reuben Gold Thwaites, vol. 26 (Cleveland, 1906), 366; and Friedrich Gerstaecker, *Wild Sports in the Far West* (London, 1854), 363. Flagg's *Wild Sports in the Far West* was first published in 1838. Captain Flack, "Turkey Hunts in Texas," in Clarence Gohdes, ed., "Hunting in the Old South," *Georgia Review* 23, no. 4 (winter 1964): 478. Captain Flack's narrative was first published in London in 1866 under the title *Hunter's Experiences in the Southern States of America, Being an Account of the Natural History of the Various Quadrupeds and Birds which are the Objects of the Chase in Those Countries.*

29. For a description of "floating," see Alfred B. Street, *Woods and Waters, or the Saranacs and Racket* (New York, 1860), 82–84.

30. Elliott, *Carolina Sports*, 244–59, 285.

31. Thomas Bangs Thorpe, "The American Deer: Its Habits and Associations" *Harper's New Monthly Magazine* 17 (October 1858): 613; Henry William Herbert [Frank Forester,

pseud.], *Frank Forester's Field Sports of the United States, and British Provinces of North America*, vol. 2 (New York, 1849), 250.

32. Charles Dudley Warner, *In the Wilderness* (Boston, 1878), 59; Richard Irving Dodge, *The Hunting Grounds of the Great West; A Description of the Plains, Game, and Indians of the Great North American Desert* (London, 1877), 113; Dwight W. Huntington, *Our Big Game: A Book for Sportsmen and Nature Lovers* (New York, 1904), 118.

33. John James Audubon, *Ornithological Biography, or An Account of the Habits of the Birds of the United States of America; Accompanied by Descriptions of the Objects Represented in the Work Entitled The Birds of America, and Interspersed with Delineations of American Scenery and Character*, vol. 1 (Edinburgh, 1831), 335; Thomas Bangs Thorpe, "Sporting in Louisiana," *Spirit of the Times* 10, no. 48 (January 30, 1841): 571, cols. 2–3; Hoffman, *Wild Scenes*, vol. 1, 87–88.

34. John Cheney, quoted in Charles Lanman, *Adventures in the Wilds of the United States and British American Provinces*, vol. 2 (Philadelphia, 1856), 232. Lanman's book was first published under the title *Adventures in the Wilds of North America* in London in 1854. "Sketch of a True Sportsman," *American Turf Register* 1, no. 6 (September 1829): 14–15.

35. Herbert, *Frank Forester's Field Sports*, vol. 1, 44; vol. 2, 241, 245–47.

36. Audubon, *Ornithological Biography*, vol. 1, 335; Huntington, *Our Big Game*, 141; Herbert, *Frank Forester's Field Sports*, vol. 2, 245–46.

37. Huntington, *Our Big Game*, 97, 118, 137; Dwight W. Huntington, "Field Sports of To-Day," *The Century Illustrated Monthly Magazine* 66, no. 6 (October 1903): 890. On the history of New York's game laws, see Donald Wharton, "The Lawless Years," *The Conservationist* 37, no. 3 (November–December 1982): 10–13.

38. *Porter's Spirit of the Times* 1, no. 8 (October 25, 1856): 126, col. 2.

39. Elliott J. Gorn, *The Manly Art: Bare-Knuckle Prize Fighting in America* (Ithaca, N.Y., 1986), 62; *Forest and Stream* 1, no. 1 (August 14, 1873): 8.

40. Gorn, *Manly Art*, 66.

41. *American Sportsman* editorial, quoted in John G. Mitchell, "Gentlemen Afield," *American Heritage* 29, no. 6 (October–November 1978): unnumbered page.

12. American Natives

1. Washington Irving, preface to *Adventures in the Wilds of the United States and British American Provinces*, by Charles Lanman, vol. 1 (Philadelphia, 1856), v, 481. Lanman's book was first published under the title *Adventures in the Wilds of North America* in London in 1854.

2. "The Writings of 'J. Cypress, Jr.,'" *American Turf Register and Sporting Magazine* 13, no. 11 (November 1842): 630–33; *Spirit of the Times* 21, no. 39 (November 15, 1851): 458, cols. 1–2.

3. "Introduction," *American Turf Register and Sporting Magazine* 1, no. 1 (September 1829): 1.

4. *Cabinet of Natural History and American Rural Sport* 1 (1830): unnumbered leaf 3v.

5. Ibid., 9; "Scenes in the West," *American Turf Register* 5, no. 3 (January 1834): 141; "Scenes

in the West—the Platte, & c.," *American Turf Register* 8, no. 10 (July 1837): 454; "Mr. Catlin," *American Turf Register* 7, no. 12 (August 1836): 554. The full citations of the works abstracted in the *Cabinet* are William Darby, *A Geographical Description of the State of Lousiana . . . with an account of the character and manners of the inhabitants: being an accompaniment to the map of Louisiana* (Philadelphia, 1816); and Timothy Flint, *The History and Geography of the Mississippi Valley. To which is appended a condensed physical geography of the Atlantic United States, and the whole American continent* (Cincinnati, 1832).

6. The eighth installment appeared in the *Spirit of the Times* 16, no. 2 (March 7, 1846): 19, col. 5; "New-Mexico—Its Animals and Game," *Spirit of the Times* 26, no. 14 (May 17, 1856): 159, cols. 2–3.

7. "Naturalist and Sportsman," *American Sportsman: Devoted Exclusively to Shooting, Fishing, and Natural History* 2, no. 9 (June 1873): 136, cols. 2–3.

8. *Forest and Stream* 1, no. 1 (August 14, 1873): 8; "Natural History," *Forest and Stream* 6, no. 11 (April 20, 1876): 163, col. 2; "U.S. Geological Survey," *Forest and Stream* 1, no. 3 (August 28, 1873): 35, col. 2; "Exploration West of the 100th Meridian," *Forest and Stream* 2, no. 11 (April 23, 1874): 168, cols. 1–2.

9. "Hurst's Stereoscopic Studies of Natural History for Object Teaching in Schools, and Parlor Entertainment" [advertisement], *Forest and Stream* 4, no. 10 (April 15, 1875): 161, col. 4; "Stereoscopic Studies of Natural History, for Schools and Parlor Entertainments" [advertisement], *American Sportsman* 2, no. 6 (March 1873): 93, col. 2; "Works on the Horse, Dog, Natural History, Taxidermy, & c. for Sale by the Forest and Stream Publishing Co." [advertisement], *Forest and Stream* 2, no. 14 (May 14, 1874): 224, col. 3; "What the People Say," *Forest and Stream* 1, no. 3 (August 28, 1873): 46.

10. "Forest and Stream Geography," *Forest and Stream* 7, no. 8 (September 28, 1876): 120, col. 3.

11. Dr. Herman Ellenbogen, M.D., "Discovery of Two Remarkable Animals in the Rocky Mountains," *Spirit of the Times* 25, no. 52 (February 9, 1856): 617, cols. 1–2. This was a reprint of an article that originally appeared in the *San Francisco Herald*. See also "The Gyasticutus. Major Twigg's Story," *Spirit of the Times* 20, no. 46 (January 4, 1851): 548, cols. 1–2.

12. William B. O. Peabody, *The Life of Alexander Wilson*, ed. Jared Sparks, vol. 2 of *The Library of American Biography* (New York, 1848), 3–4.

13. "Wild Turkey," *American Turf Register* 5, no. 2 (October 1833): 57–59; "Audubon," *American Turf Register* 9, no. 8 (August 1838): 359–60; *Spirit of the Times* 16, no. 2 (March 7, 1846): 18, col. 2; *Spirit of the Times* 19, no. 51 (February 10, 1850): 602, cols. 1–2; *Wilkes' Spirit of the Times. A Chronicle of the Turf, Field Sports, and the Stage* 17, no. 19 (December 28, 1867): 335, col. 1; "Adventure on the Alleghenies, or Pheasant Shooting in Pennsylvania," *Spirit of the Times* 11, no. 36 (November 6, 1841): 1, cols. 2–3; "Audubon and His Associates," *Spirit of the Times* 17, no. 4 (March 20, 1847): 43, cols. 1–2.

14. [George Bird Grinnell], "A Monument to Audubon," *Forest and Stream* 30, no. 9 (March 22, 1888): 161, cols. 1–2.

15. John James Audubon, *Ornithological Biography, or An Account of the Habits of the Birds of the United States of America; Accompanied by Descriptions of the Objects Represented in the Work Entitled The Birds of America, and Interspersed with Delineations of American Scenery and Character,* vol. 1 (Edinburgh, 1831), 10. John James Audubon to Lucy Bakewell Audubon, Liverpool, November 25, 1827, *Letters of John James Audubon, 1826–1840,* ed. Howard Corning, vol. 2 (Boston, 1930), 51.

16. John James Audubon and John Bachman, *The Viviparous Quadrupeds of America* (New York, 1851), Plate 78; Ann Shelby Blum, "Science and Sentiment: American Birds from Audubon to the Audubon Society" (seminar paper, Univ. of California at Berkeley, fall 1989).

17. Audubon, *Ornithological Biography,* vol. 1, 503; Alice Ford, *John James Audubon* (New York, 1988), 89.

18. Maria R. Audubon, ed., *Audubon and His Journals. With Zoological and Other Notes by Elliott Coues,* vol. 1 (New York, 1897), frontispiece, 48, 132, 206, 348, 454, 532; [Parke Godwin], "Audubon," *Homes of American Authors: Comprising Anecdotal, Personal, and Descriptive Sketches by Various Writers* (New York, 1853), 5, 10. On Audubon in portraiture, see Helena E. Wright, "A 'Transatlantic Stranger': Portrait Prints of John James Audubon," *Imprint: Journal of the American Historical Print Collectors Society* 23, no. 1 (spring 1998): 9–17.

19. *Forest and Stream* 2, no. 9 (April 9, 1874): 141, col. 3; Theodore Roosevelt, quoted in Thomas L. Altherr, "The American Hunter-Naturalist and the Development of the Code of Sportsmanship," *Journal of Sport History* 5, no. 1 (spring 1978): 16.

20. *Forest and Stream* 2, no. 8 (April 2, 1874): 124, col. 3; *Forest and Stream* 2, no. 5 (March 12, 1874): 76, col. 1; *Forest and Stream* 2, no. 6 (March 19, 1874): 91, col. 2; William Temple Hornaday, "The Passing of the Buffalo—I," *The Cosmopolitan* 4, no. 2 (October 1887): 9. On the cultural significance of taxidermy, see also the works of Charles Austin Fosdick [Harry Castlemon, pseud.], particularly *Frank, the Young Naturalist* (Philadelphia, 1860), *The Sportsman's Club Among the Trappers* (Philadelphia, 1874), and *Two Ways of Becoming a Hunter* (Philadelphia, 1892).

21. Dr. R. W. Shufeldt, "Mounted Game Birds in the U.S. National Museum," *Forest and Stream* 41, no. 8 (August 26, 1893): 161, cols. 2–3. John Norval, "Taxidermy" [advertisement], *Spirit of the Times* 17, no. 7 (April 10, 1847): 83, col. 1.

22. Francis Brinley, *Life of William T. Porter* (New York, 1860), 86, 197.

23. John MacKenzie, *The Empire of Nature: Hunting, Conservation, and British Imperialism* (Manchester, England, 1988), 28–31; Transit, "Mounting Deer Feet," *Forest and Stream* 1, no. 25 (January 29, 1874): 387, col. 3; Ruth Irwin Weidner, "Images of the Hunt in Nineteenth Century America and Their Sources in British and European Art" (Ph.D. diss., Univ. of Delaware, 1988), 113.

24. Samuel Irenaeus Prime, *Under the Trees* (New York, 1874), 105.

25. William Cullen Bryant, "Thanatopsis," in *The Poetical Works of William Cullen Bryant* (New York, 1878), 21–23; Ralph Waldo Emerson, "Nature," in *Selected Writings of Emerson,* ed. Donald McQuade (New York, 1981), 6. Bryant's "Thanatopsis" was first

published in the *North American Review* in 1817. Emerson's "Nature" was first published in 1836.

26. Alfred B. Street, *Woods and Waters; or, The Saranacs and Racket* (New York, 1860), 95–96.

27. John F. Sears, *Sacred Places: American Tourist Attractions in the Nineteenth Century* (Oxford, England, 1989), 5; Perry Miller, "Nature and the National Ego," *Errand into the Wilderness* (Cambridge, Mass., 1964), 207, 210, 211.

28. Charles Wilkins Webber, *The Hunter-Naturalist: Romance of Sporting; or, Wild Scenes & Wild Hunters,* vol. 1 (Philadelphia, 1851), 171.

29. Perry Miller, *Nature's Nation* (Cambridge, Mass., 1967); [William Barrows], *The General; or, Twelve Nights in the Hunters' Camp. A Narrative of Real Life* (Boston, 1869), 18, 219, 267.

30. [Barrows], *The General,* 19, 221.

31. Ibid., 12; Samuel H. Hammond, quoted in John Reiger, *American Sportsmen and the Origins of Conservation* (New York, 1975), 88.

32. Charles Hallock, quoted in Philip G. Terrie, *Contested Terrain: A New History of Nature and People in the Adirondacks* (Syracuse, N.Y., 1997), 94; ibid., 97.

33. [Charles Hallock], *Forest and Stream* 1, no. 1 (August 14, 1873): 8; [Charles Hallock], "What Two Advertisers Say," *Forest and Stream* 7, no. 4 (August 31, 1876): 57, col. 2.

34. Louis Warren, *The Hunter's Game: Poachers and Conservationists in Twentieth-Century America* (New Haven, Conn., 1997), 1–3; "Notice from Jackson Hole, Wyoming," *Outdoor Life* 4, no. 1 (July 1899); "Annual Indian Game Hunt," *Outdoor Life* 4, no. 6 (December 1899); "Indian and American Game Butchers Should Be Checked," *Outdoor Life* 7, no. 3 (March 1901); Mountaineer, "Indians and the Big Game," *Forest and Stream* 40, no. 16 (April 20, 1893): 337, cols. 1–2. See also Mark David Spence, *Dispossessing the Wilderness: Indian Removal and the Making of the National Parks* (Oxford, England, 1999).

35. Thomas Cole, quoted in Alan Wallach, "Thomas Cole: Landscape and the Course of American Empire," in *Thomas Cole: Landscape into History,* ed. William H. Truettner and Alan Wallach (New Haven, Conn., 1994), 67. On the contradictory and multivalent meanings of "wilderness" and "sublime," see William Cronon "The Trouble with Wilderness; or, Getting Back to the Wrong Nature," in *Uncommon Ground: Rethinking the Human Place in Nature,* ed. William Cronon (New York, 1995), 69–90; and Kenneth R. Olwig, "Reinventing Common Nature: Yosemite and Mount Rushmore—A Meandering Tale of a Double Nature," in *Uncommon Ground: Rethinking the Human Place in Nature,* ed. William Cronon, (New York, 1995), 379–408.

13. Disciples of Sport Hunting

1. "Herbert's Personal Characteristics," in *Life and Writings of Frank Forester. (Henry William Herbert.),* ed. David W. Judd, vol. 1 (New York, 1882), 10.

2. [Thomas Picton], "Henry William Herbert. [Frank Forester.] The Story of His Life," in *Life and Writings of Frank Forester. (Henry William Herbert.),* ed. David W. Judd, vol. 1 (New York, 1882), 14–16.

3. Ibid., 14.

4. Ibid., 17, 23; Harry Worcester Smith, "Henry William Herbert. Frank Forester," in *The Deerstalkers*, by Henry William Herbert [Frank Forester, pseud.], *The Hitchcock Edition of Frank Forester*, vol. 4 (New York, 1930), 143; Luke White, *Henry William Herbert and the American Publishing Industry, 1831–1858* (Newark, 1943), 27.

5. [Picton], "Henry William Herbert. [Frank Forester.] The Story of His Life," 42, 44, 65; Henry William Herbert [Frank Forester, pseud.], *Frank Forester's Field Sports of the United States and British Provinces of North America*, vol. 1 (New York, 1849), 22.

6. Herbert, *Frank Forester's Field Sports*, vol. 1, v, 26–27.

7. Henry William Herbert, "The Woodcock," in *Life and Writings of Frank Forester. (Henry William Herbert.)*, ed. David W. Judd, vol. 2 (New York, 1882), 62.

8. Henry William Herbert [Frank Forester, pseud.], *The Complete Manual for Young Sportsmen: with Directions for Handling the Gun, the Rifle, and the Rod; the Art of Shooting on the Wing; the Breaking, Management, and Hunting of the Dog; the Varieties and Habits of Game; River, Lake, and Sea Fishing. Etc. Etc. Etc. Prepared for the Instruction and Use of the Young of America* (New York, 1868), 22.

9. Herbert, *Frank Forester's Field Sports*, vol. 1, 24; Henry William Herbert [Frank Forester, pseud.], "The Game of North America; Its Nomenclature, Habits, Haunts, and Seasons; with Hints on the Science of Woodcraft," *Spirit of the Times* 15, no. 51 (February 14, 1846): 604, col. 3; Henry William Herbert, "Quail," in *Life and Writings of Frank Forester. (Henry William Herbert.)*, ed. David W. Judd, vol. 2 (New York, 1882), 70.

10. Henry William Herbert, "Memoir of the Smelt of the Passaic River," in *Life and Writings of Frank Forester. (Henry William Herbert.)*, ed. David W. Judd, vol. 2 (New York, 1882), 98, 105; Henry William Herbert, *Frank Forester's Sporting Scenes and Characters. Embracing "The Warwick Woodlands," "My Shooting Box," "The Quorndon Hounds," and "The Deerstalkers,"* vol. 1 (Philadelphia, 1881), 27.

11. Henry William Herbert, "Long Jakes, the Prairie Man," *New York Illustrated Magazine of Literature and Art* 2 (July 1846): 169–74. See also Carol Clark, "Charles Deas," in *American Frontier Life: Early Western Paintings and Prints*, by Ron Tyler et al. (New York, 1987), 60–62.

12. Henry William Herbert, *The Deerstalkers*, in *The Hitchcock Edition of Frank Forester*, vol. 4 (New York, 1930), 133.

13. Ibid., 138.

14. [Picton], "Henry William Herbert. [Frank Forester.] The Story of His Life," 5, 75.

15. William Southworth Hunt, *Frank Forester [Henry William Herbert]: A Tragedy in Exile* (Newark, N.J., 1933), 73, 75; [Picton], "Henry William Herbert. [Frank Forester.], The Story of His Life," 10, 86–89. For a description of hunting lodges in the United Kingdom, see John MacKenzie, *Empire of Nature: Hunting, Conservation, and British Imperialism* (Manchester, England, 1988), 28.

16. Hunt, *Forester*, 75; [Picton], "Henry William Herbert. [Frank Forester.], The Story of His Life," 7, 99; White, *Herbert and the American Publishing Industry*, 64; Henry William

Herbert to "The Press of the United States of America," in Newark *Daily Advertiser,* May 18, 1858, 2, quoted in White, *Herbert and the American Publishing Industry,* 66.

17. Herbert, *Deerstalkers,* in *The Hitchcock Edition of Frank Forester,* vol. 4, 42; Beckford, "Fox Hunting in the South," *Spirit of the Times* 18, no. 48 (January 20, 1849): 571, col. 3; "Angling in the United States," *Spirit of the Times* 20, no. 2 (March 2, 1850): 15, col. 1, through 17, col. 1; Saranac, "American Rifles and Deer Shooting," *Spirit of the Times* 18, no. 42 (December 9, 1848): 499, col. 3.

18. Henry William Herbert, "Trouting Along the Catasauqua," in *Life and Writings of Frank Forester. (Henry William Herbert.),* ed. David W. Judd, vol. 1 (New York, 1882), 272; "Deer Hunting on Long Island," *Spirit of the Times* 19, no. 13 (May 19, 1849): 151, col. 3.

19. C.E., "Letter to Frank Forester," *Spirit of the Times* 15, no. 5 (March 29, 1845): 45, cols. 2–3. It is unclear whether the article refers to the Cedars or to some small hunting retreat Herbert had erected elsewhere.

20. Newark Herbert Association, *Newark Herbert Association to "Frank Forester." In Memorium, May 19, 1876* (Newark, 1876), 12; [Picton], "Henry William Herbert. [Frank Forester.], The Story of His Life," 7–8.

21. Newark Herbert Association, *In Memorium,* 5, 26; Hunt, *Forester,* 97.

22. Francis Brinley, *Life of William T. Porter* (New York, 1860), 77; Charles Lanman, *The Private Life of Daniel Webster* (New York, 1852), 78.

23. Lanman, *Private Life,* 89.

24. John Rickards Betts, *America's Sporting Heritage: 1850–1950* (Reading, Mass., 1974), 43.

25. Lanman, *Private Life,* 141; A., "How Daniel Webster Thought It Was a Squirrel," *Forest and Stream* 15, no. 3 (August 19, 1880): 50, col. 1; Stephen Anthony Aron, "How the West Was Lost: The Transformation of Kentucky from Daniel Boone to Henry Clay" (Ph.D. diss., Univ. of California at Berkeley, 1990), 280; Theodore Roosevelt, *The Wilderness Hunter. Homeward Bound Edition* (New York, 1910), 279. Roosevelt's *Wilderness Hunter* was first published in 1893.

26. Lanman, *Private Life,* 80, 92, 135.

27. O., "Sportsmen in Congress," *Forest and Stream* 14, no. 2 (February 12, 1880): 31, col. 1, through 32, col. 2; Ruth Irwin Weidner, "Images of the Hunt in Nineteenth Century America and Their Sources in British and European Art" (Ph.D. diss., Univ. of Delaware, 1988), 153; Edward Comstock Jr. and Mark C. Webster, eds. and comps., *The Adirondack League Club, 1890–1990* (Old Forge, N.Y., 1990), 132.

28. Jay Monaghan, *The Great Rascal: The Life and Adventures of Ned Buntline* (Boston, 1952), 65.

29. Monaghan, *Great Rascal,* 123; Fred E. Pond [Will Wildwood, pseud.], *Life and Adventures of "Ned Buntline" with Ned Buntline's Anecdote of "Frank Forester" and Chapter of Angling Sketches* (New York, 1919), 4–8.

30. Pond, *Life and Adventures of "Ned Buntline,"* 45.

31. Ibid., 12.

32. Monaghan, *Great Rascal,* 4.

33. Ibid., 7.

34. Pond, *Life and Adventures of "Ned Buntline,"* 50; Monaghan, *Great Rascal,* 16.

35. Pond, *Life and Adventures of "Ned Buntline,"* 46, 55, 56, 119.

36. Alfred L. Donaldson, *A History of the Adirondacks,* vol. 2 (New York, 1921), 121; Pond, *Life and Adventures of "Ned Buntline,"* 62.

37. Pond, *Life and Adventures of "Ned Buntline,"* 65, 93, 125.

38. Quoted in George Baxter Ward III, "Bloodbrothers in the Wilderness: The Sport Hunter and the Buckskin Hunter in the Preservation of the American Wilderness Experience" (Ph.D. diss., Univ. of Texas at Austin, 1980), 174.

14. Adirondacks and Aesthetics

1. "The Easy Chair," *Harper's New Monthly Magazine* 25 (October 1862): 706–7.

2. Samuel H. Hammond, *Hills, Lakes and Forest Streams: or, a Tramp in the Chateaugay Woods* (New York, 1854), 59, 191; Charles Fenno Hoffman, *Wild Scenes in the Forest and Prairie,* vol. 1 (London, 1839), 35, 39, 88; Charles Lanman, *Adventures in the Wilds of the United States and British American Provinces,* vol. 2 (Philadelphia, 1856), 232. Part of Lanman's *Adventures* was first published in Philadelphia in 1848 under the title *A Tour to the River Saguenay, in Lower Canada.*

3. Alfred L. Donaldson, *A History of the Adirondacks,* vol. 2 (New York, 1921), 83; Joel Tyler Headley, *The Adirondacks: or, Life in the Woods* (New York, 1869), 253. Headley's *Adirondacks* was first published in New York in 1849.

4. Samuel H. Hammond, quoted in Philip G. Terrie, *Contested Terrain: A New History of Nature and People in the Adirondacks* (Syracuse, N.Y., 1997), 53. On the guide as Leatherstocking, see Charles Fenno Hoffman, "Scenes at the Source of the Hudson," *The New-York Mirror: Devoted to Literature and the Fine Arts* 16 (October 14, 1837): 335; Paul Martindale, "A Deer-Hunt on the Bouquet," *Knickerbocker* 20 (June 1855): 578; "The Sportsman's Camping Ground," *Fur, Fin, and Feather: A Compilation of Game Laws of the Principal States and Provinces of the United States and Canada; Together with a List of Hunting and Fishing Localities and Other Useful Information for Gunners and Anglers* (New York, 1871), iv.

5. John J. Duquette, "The Philosophers' Camp," *Adirondack Life* 3 (spring 1972): 47, 48; William Stillman, "The Philosophers' Camp. Emerson, Agassiz, Lowell and Others in the Adirondacks," *Century Magazine* 46, no. 4 (August 1893): 599.

6. Ralph Waldo Emerson, "The Adirondacs," *The Poems of Ralph Waldo Emerson,* ed. Louis Untermeyer (New York, 1945), 125.

7. Stillman, "Philosophers' Camp," 599; Emerson, "The Adirondacs," 127.

8. Emerson, "The Adirondacs," 131, 133.

9. Stillman, "Philosophers' Camp," 603; Emerson, "The Adirondacs," 129.

10. "Agassiz as a Sportsman—the Microscope and the Gun," *Spirit of the Times* 28, no. 45 (December 18, 1858): 534, col. 1; Stillman, "Philosophers' Camp," 601–2; Emerson, "The Adirondacs," 125.

11. Duquette, "Philosophers' Camp," 51.

12. Warder H. Cadbury and Henry F. Marsh, *Arthur Fitzwilliam Tait: Artist in the Adirondacks / An Account of His Career by Warder H. Cadbury, A Checklist of His Works by Henry F. Marsh* (Newark, 1986), 29; see also Warder H. Cadbury, "Arthur F. Tait," in *American Frontier Life: Early Western Paintings and Prints,* by Ron Tyler et al. (New York, 1987), 109–30.

13. Cadbury and Marsh, *Arthur Fitzwilliam Tait,* 34, 50, 52.

14. Warder H. Cadbury, "Biographical Sketch," *A. F. Tait: Artist in the Adirondacks. An Exhibition of Paintings and Other Works by the Sporting and Animal Artist Arthur Fitzwilliam Tait (1819–1905)* (The Adirondack Museum, June 15–October 15, 1974)(Blue Mountain Lake, N.Y.), 10; Cadbury and Marsh, *Arthur Fitzwilliam Tait,* 68; Ruth Irwin Weidner, "Images of the Hunt in Nineteenth Century America and Their Sources in British and European Art" (Ph.D. diss., Univ. of Delaware, 1988), 21. Louis Prang and Company also marketed lithographs of Tait's works. Richard H. Saunders, *Collecting the West: The C.R. Smith Collection of Western American Art* (Austin, Tex., 1988), 184. See also *Sporting Prints by N. Currier and Currier and Ives, Being a Pictorial Check List and Collation, with Many Intimate Facts Regarding the Prints* (New York, 1930).

15. John Doughty, "American Feathered Game" [advertisement], *Spirit of the Times* 1, no. 15 (March 3, 1832): 3; Weidner, "Images of the Hunt," 21. The hunting lithographs of both Currier and Ives and their competitors can be found in the Whitney Collection at the Yale University Art Gallery.

16. *Cosmopolitan Art Journal* 3 (1858–59), quoted in Cadbury and Marsh, *Arthur Fitzwilliam Tait,* 38, 50, 57.

17. Cadbury and Marsh, *Arthur Fitzwilliam Tait,* 18.

18. Weidner, "Images of the Hunt," 133.

19. Cadbury and Marsh, *Arthur Fitzwilliam Tait,* 102. On late nineteenth-century hunting artists, see James Allen Young, "An Artist-Sportsman's Portfolio," *American Heritage* 29, no. 6 (1978): 101–5; and Robert Elman, *The Great American Shooting Prints* (New York, 1972). On Frost, see Henry M. Reed, *The A. B. Frost Book* (Rutland, Vt., 1967). On dead-game still lifes, see Alfred Frankenstein, *After the Hunt: William Harnett and Other American Still Life Painters, 1870–1900* (Berkeley, Calif., 1969), Plates 67–72, 74.

20. Elman, *Great American Shooting Prints,* text for Plate 13; Weidner, "Images of the Hunt," 2.

21. Kenneth L. Ames, *Death in the Dining Room and Other Tales of Victorian Culture* (Philadelphia, 1992), 57–62.

22. Ames, *Death in the Dining Room,* 73–76.

23. Harriett Prescott Spofford, *Art Decoration Applied to Furniture* (New York, 1878), 15, quoted in Ames, *Death in the Dining Room,* 92–93.

24. Harry V. Radford, *Adirondack Murray: A Biographical Appreciation* (New York, 1906), 13.

25. Warder H. Cadbury, introduction to *Adventures in the Wilderness,* by William H. H.

Murray, ed. William K. Verner (Syracuse, N.Y., 1970), 40, 52, 58, 63. Murray's *Adventures* was first published in New York in 1869. Radford, *Adirondack Murray*, 15.

26. Cadbury, introduction to *Adventures in the Wilderness*, 15; Radford, *Adirondack Murray*, 53.

27. Cadbury, introduction to *Adventures in the Wilderness*, 17, 32.

28. Radford, *Adirondack Murray*, 56, 57; Cadbury, introduction to *Adventures in the Wilderness*, 53.

29. Thomas Bangs Thorpe, quoted in Cadbury, introduction to *Adventures in the Wilderness*, 48.

30. Radford, *Adirondack Murray*, 67. The character John Norton first appeared in various tales written by Murray for a newspaper he edited, *The Golden Rule. An Independent, Religious, Family Journal*, in 1876. The Norton tales were collected in William H. H. Murray, *Adirondack Tales* (New York, 1877).

31. Radford, *Adirondack Murray*, 32.

15. The Far West

1. George Rutledge Gibson, *Over the Chihuahua and Santa Fe Trails, 1847–1848: George Rutledge Gibson's Journal*, ed. Robert W. Frazer (Albuquerque, 1981), 84.

2. Ibid., 84–86.

3. Richard Irving Dodge, *The Hunting Grounds of the Great West: A Description of the Plains, Game, and Indians of the Great North American Desert* (London, 1877), 2.

4. Theodore Roosevelt, *Hunting the Grisly and Other Sketches, Homeward Bound Edition* (New York, 1910), 50. Roosevelt's *Hunting the Grisly* was first published in New York in 1893. "Monarch of the Plains," from *Wichita Eagle*, March 20, 1873, quoted in Wayne Gard, *The Great Buffalo Hunt* (New York, 1960), 210.

5. William Clark Kennerly, as told to Elizabeth Russell, *Persimmon Hill: A Narrative of Old St. Louis and the Far West* (Norman, Okla., 1948), 147–48; Henry Marie Brackenridge, *Journal of a Voyage up the River Missouri; April 2–August, 1811* in *Early Western Travels, 1748–1846*, ed. Reuben Gold Thwaites, vol. 6 (Cleveland, 1904), 110. Brackenridge's *Journal* was first published in 1816.

6. Franklin Langworthy, *Scenery of the Plains, Mountains and Mines*, ed. Paul C. Phillips (Ogdensburgh, N.Y., 1855; reprint, Princeton, 1932), 53.

7. Charles Edward Pancoast, *A Quaker Forty-Niner: The Adventures of Charles Edward Pancoast on the American Frontier*, ed. Anna Paschall Hannum (Philadelphia, 1930), 187; Heinrich Lienhard, *From St. Louis to Sutter's Fort in 1846*, trans. and ed. Erwin G. and Elisabeth K. Gudde (Norman, Okla., 1961), 49.

8. William Audley Maxwell, *Crossing the Plains, day of '57: A Narrative of Early Emigrant Travel to California by the Ox-Team Method* (San Francisco, 1915), 16, 18.

9. Mary Stuart Bailey, "A Journal of Mary Stuart Bailey," in *Ho for California! Women's Overland Diaries from the Huntington Library*, ed. Sandra Myres (San Marino, Calif., 1980), 60.

10. George Frederick Augustus Ruxton, *Life in the Far West,* quoted in John I. Merritt, *Baronets and Buffaloes: The British Sportsman in the American West* (Missoula, Mont., 1985), 65. Ruxton's *Life in the Far West* was first published in New York in 1849. Merritt, *Baronets and Buffaloes,* 93–94.

11. Merritt, *Baronets and Buffaloes,* 99.

12. "Captain Marcy, U.S.A., and the Hon. G.F. Berkeley," *Spirit of the Times* 30, no. 1 (February 4, 1860): 1, col. 2. See also George Charles Grantley Fitzhardinge Berkeley, *The English Sportsman in the Western Prairies* (London, 1861).

13. "Hunting Exploits of the Hon. G. Berkeley," *Spirit of the Times* 30, no. 4 (March 3, 1860): 42, col. 2.

14. "A Wolf Hunt in Texas," *Spirit of the Times* 19, no. 51 (January 26, 1850): 585, cols. 1–2; see also "Kentucky Shooting," *Spirit of the Times* 11, no. 2 (March 13, 1841): 19, col. 1. "A Wolf Hunt in Texas," 585, cols. 1–2.

15. Edwin James, *Account of an Expedition from Pittsburgh to the Rocky Mountains, performed by order of the Hon. J.C. Calhoun, Secretary of War, . . . compiled from the Notes of Maj. S.H. Long, Mr. T. Say, and other Gentlemen of the Party; March 31, 1819–November 22, 1820,* in *Early Western Travels, 1748–1846,* ed. Reuben Gold Thwaites, vol. 15 (Cleveland, 1905), 257. James's *Account* was first published in Philadelphia in 1822–23. Kennerly, *Persimmon Hill,* quoted in Merritt, *Baronets and Buffaloes,* 43.

16. Quoted in Tom McHugh, *The Time of the Buffalo* (New York, 1972), 249.

17. Dan Flores, "Bison Ecology and Bison Diplomacy: The Southern Plains from 1800 to 1850," *Journal of American History* 78 (September 1991): 465–85; Josiah Gregg, *Commerce of the Prairies: or, the Journal of a Santa Fe Trader, during Eight Expeditions across the Great Western Prairies, and a Residence of Nearly Nine Years in Northern Mexico; 1831–1839,* in *Early Western Travels, 1748–1846,* ed. Reuben Gold Thwaites, vol. 19 (Cleveland, 1905), 244. Gregg's *Commerce* was first published in New York in 1844. Gard, *Great Buffalo Hunt,* 56.

18. Gard, *Great Buffalo Hunt,* 90–92, 128. There are a number of outstanding studies of the American buffalo and its decline. The most recent of these is Andrew Isenberg, *The Destruction of the Bison* (Cambridge, England, 2000). See also Flores, "Bison Ecology"; Frank Gilbert Roe, *The North American Buffalo: A Critical Study of the Species in Its Wild State* (Toronto, 1951); Tom McHugh, *The Time of the Buffalo* (New York, 1972); Francis Haines, *The Buffalo* (New York, 1970); David Dary, *The Buffalo Book: The Full Saga of the American Animal* (Chicago, 1974); and J. Albert Rorabacher, *The American Buffalo in Transition: A Historical and Economic Survey of the Bison in America* (St. Cloud, Minn., 1970). The classic study of the destruction of the bison is still William T. Hornaday, *The Extermination of the American Bison* (Washington, D.C., 1889).

19. William Post Hawes [J. Cypress, Jr., pseud.], *Sporting Scenes and Sundry Sketches. Being the Miscellaneous Writings of J. Cypress, Jr.,* ed. Henry William Herbert [Frank Forester, pseud.] (New York, 1842), 150; Gregg, *Commerce of the Prairies,* in *Early Western Travels,* vol. 19, 282.

20. Quoted in Tracy I. Storer and Lloyd P. Trevis Jr., *California Grizzly* (Lincoln, Nebr., 1978), 216.

21. On bears and bear hunters, see Storer and Trevis, *California Grizzly,* 195–96, 216; Daniel J. Gelo, "The Bear," in *American Wildlife in Symbol and Story,* ed. Angus K. Gillespie and Jay Mechling (Knoxville, Tenn., 1987), 133–62; Roosevelt, *Hunting the Grisly;* Charles B. Coale, *The Life and Adventures of Wilburn Waters, the Famous Hunter and Trapper of White Top Mountain; Embracing Early History of Southwestern Virginia, Sufferings of the Pioneers, Etc.* (Richmond, 1878); George Nidever, *The Life and Adventures of George Nidever, 1802–1883* (Santa Barbara, Calif., 1984), 53; Cecil B. Hartley, *Hunting Sports in the West, Comprising Adventures of the Most Celebrated Hunters & Trappers* (Philadelphia, 1865), 27; and James Ohio Pattie, *Personal Narrative during an Expedition from St. Louis through the Vast Regions between that place and the Pacific Ocean, and thence back through the City of Mexico to Vera Cruz, etc.; June 20, 1824–August 30, 1830,* in *Early Western Travels, 1748–1846,* ed. Reuben Gold Thwaites, vol. 18 (Cleveland, 1905), 93, 141. Pattie's *Personal Narrative* was first published in Cincinnati in 1831.

22. Theodore Henry Hittell, *The Adventures of James Capen Adams, Mountaineer and Grizzly Bear Hunter of California* (San Francisco, 1860), 87.

23. Hittell, *The Adventures of James Capen Adams,* 18, 57, 100; James Capen Adams, *The Life of J. C. Adams, Known as Old Adams, Old Grizzly Adams, Containing a Truthful Account of His Bear Hunts, Fights with Grizzly Bears, etc.* (New York, 1860), 30, 33–34.

24. Hittell, *The Adventures of James Capen Adams,* 206.

25. Henry Brown, *The History of Illinois, from Its First Discovery and Settlement to the Present Time* (New York, 1844), 14.

26. Brown, *History of Illinois,* 14.

27. Charles Alston Messiter, *Sport and Adventures among the North-American Indians* (London, 1890), 247; Richard Irving Dodge, *Our Wild Indians: Thirty-Three Years' Personal Experience Among the Red Men of the Great West . . .* (Hartford, Conn., 1883), 574.

28. Nathaniel West, *The Ancestry, Life, and Times of Hon. Henry Hastings Sibley . . .* (St. Paul, Minn., 1889), v.

29. Ibid., iv, v, 407.

30. Ibid., 58; Henry Hastings Sibley, *The Unfinished Autobiography of Henry Hastings Sibley Together with a Selection of Hitherto Unpublished Letters from the Thirties,* ed. Theodore C. Blegen (Minneapolis, n.d.), 33.

31. Henry Hastings Sibley [Hal A. Dacotah, pseud.], "Hunting on the Western Prairies," *Spirit of the Times* 12, no. 7 (April 10, 1847): 87, cols. 1–3.

32. Henry Hastings Sibley [Hal A. Dacotah, pseud.], "Sketches of Two Hunting Parties," *Spirit of the Times* 12, no. 7 (April 16, 1842): 74, col. 3.

33. The best analysis of the nexus between British hunting and imperialism is John MacKenzie, *The Empire of Nature: Hunting, Conservation, and British Imperialism* (Manchester, England, 1988), 28–31.

34. West, *The Ancestry . . . of Hon. Henry Hastings Sibley,* 78. See, for instance, Henry Hastings Sibley [Hal A. Dacotah, pseud.], "Hunting in the Northwest," *Spirit of the Times* 18, no. 6 (April 1, 1848): 66, col. 3.

35. West, *The Ancestry . . . of Hon. Henry Hastings Sibley*, 152, 154. Another hunter, trader, politician, conservationist, and occasional Indian benefactor in the Sibley mold was James R. Mead. See James R. Mead, *Hunting and Trading on the Great Plains, 1859–1875*, ed. Schuyler Jones (Norman, Okla., 1986), 70.

36. John Gregory Bourke, *On the Border with Crook* (Glorieta, N.Mex., 1969), 110. Bourke's *On the Border* was first published in New York in 1892. George A. McCall, *Letters from the Frontiers. Written During a Period of Thirty Years' Service in the Army of the United States* (Philadelphia, 1868), 216; George Armstrong Custer [Nomad, pseud.], "On the Plains," *Turf, Field, and Farm* 1, no. 15 (October 12, 1867): 230, cols. 1–4. On army officers as hunters, see also William T. Sherman, *Memoirs of Gen. W.T. Sherman, Written by Himself, with an Appendix Bringing His Life Down to its Closing Scenes, Also a Personal Tribute and Critique of the Memoirs, by Hon. James G. Blaine*, vol. 1 (New York, 1891), 61; and Philip H. Sheridan, *Personal Memoirs of P.H. Sheridan. General United States Army*, vol. 1 (New York, 1888), 20.

37. William H. Emory, *Notes of a Military Reconnaissance, from Fort Leavenworth, in Missouri, to San Diego, in California, including part of the Arkansas, Del Norte, and Gila Rivers* (Washington, D.C., 1848), 49.

38. Randolph Barnes Marcy, *The Prairie Traveller, A Hand-Book for Overland Expeditions . . .* , ed. Richard Francis Burton (London, 1863), 173.

39. Ibid.

40. Custer, "On the Plains," 230, cols. 1–4; Elizabeth Bacon Custer, *Following the Guidon* (New York, 1890), 33; Frances M. A. Roe, *Army Letters from an Officer's Wife* (New York, 1909), 40.

41. Evan S. Connell, *Son of the Morning Star: Custer and the Little Bighorn* (San Francisco, 1984), 121, 254; Officer of the U.S. Army, "Field Sports in the West," *Spirit of the Times* 14, no. 52 (February 22, 1845): 618, col. 3.

42. Brian W. Dippie, ed., *Nomad: George A. Custer in Turf, Field, and Farm* (Austin, Tex., 1980), xiii; Custer, "On the Plains," 230, cols. 1–4.

43. Connell, *Son of the Morning Star*, 141; George Armstrong Custer, *My Life on the Plains, or, Personal Experience with Indians* (New York, 1874), 49. For a slightly different version, see Custer, "On the Plains," 182, col. 2, through 183, col. 1.

44. Custer, *Following the Guidon*, 55; Dippie, *Nomad*, xi; Connell, *Son of the Morning Star*, 244.

45. Connell, *Son of the Morning Star*, 244.

46. Custer, *Following the Guidon*, 216; Connell, *Son of the Morning Star*, 232.

47. Sherman, *Memoirs*, vol. 1, 61; Nelson Appleton Miles, *Personal Recollections and Observations of General Nelson A. Miles* (New York, 1969), 131. Miles's *Recollections* was first published in Chicago and New York in 1896. Sheridan, *Personal Memoirs*, vol. 1, 20, vol. 2, 353.

48. George Crook, *General George Crook: His Autobiography*, ed. Martin F. Schmitt (Norman, Okla., 1946), 21; Crook, *His Autobiography*, 21; Bourke, *On the Border with Crook*, 108, 110; John S. Collins, *Across the Plains in '64* (Omaha, 1904), 100; Dippie, *Nomad*, xi.

49. Bourke, *On the Border with Crook*, 112.

50. Ibid., 487; Crook, *His Autobiography*, 289.

51. Bourke, *On the Border with Crook*, 111, 295, 299.

52. Connell, *Son of the Morning Star*, 234, 245; Sheridan, *Personal Memoirs*, vol. 1, 30.

53. Custer, *Following the Guidon*, 71.

54. Randolph Barnes Marcy, *Thirty Years of Army Life on the Border. Comprising Descriptions of the Indian Nomads of the Plains; Explorations of New Territory; A Trip Across the Rocky Mountains in the Winter; Descriptions of the Habits of Different Animals Found in the West, and the Methods of Hunting Them; with Incidents in the Life of Different Frontier Men* (New York, 1866), 353; Dodge, *Our Wild Indians*, 424.

55. Collins, *Across the Plains in '64*, 96, 100, 114; [Henry Eugene Davies], *Ten Days on the Plains by *** (New York, n.d.), 15, 29.

56. George Baxter Ward III, "Bloodbrothers in the Wilderness: The Sport Hunter and the Buckskin Hunter in the Preservation of the American Wilderness Experience" (Ph.D. diss., Univ. of Texas at Austin, 1980), 77, 80; *The Grand Duke Alexis in the United States of America* (New York, 1972), 152. *The Grand Duke Alexis* was first published under the title *His Imperial Highness the Grand Duke Alexis in the United States of America during the winter of 1871–72* in Cambridge, Massachusetts, in 1872.

16. Manly Men and Manly Women

1. Edmund Morris, *The Rise of Theodore Roosevelt* (New York, 1979), 47; Thomas L. Altherr, "The American Hunter-Naturalist and the Development of the Code of Sportsmanship," *Journal of Sport History* 5, no. 1 (spring 1978): 16. On Roosevelt's passion for natural history, see also Paul Russell Cutright, *Theodore Roosevelt: The Naturalist* (New York, 1956); Theodore Roosevelt, "My Life as a Naturalist," *American Museum Journal* 18, no. 5 (May 1918): 321.

2. Morris, *Rise of Theodore Roosevelt*, 131–32; George Baxter Ward III, "Bloodbrothers in the Wilderness: The Sport Hunter and the Buckskin Hunter in the Preservation of the American Wilderness Experience" (Ph.D. diss., Univ. of Texas at Austin, 1980), 348.

3. Morris, *Rise of Theodore Roosevelt*, 733–34; William Chapman White, *Adirondack Country*, ed. Erskine Caldwell (New York, 1954), 159.

4. James B. Trefethen, *An American Crusade for Wildlife* (New York, 1961; reprint, New York, 1975), 110, 118; John Reiger, *American Sportsmen and the Origins of Conservation* (New York, 1975), 142–51. See also Paul Russell Cutright, *Theodore Roosevelt: The Making of a Conservationist* (Urbana, Ill., 1985).

5. Theodore Roosevelt, *The Wilderness Hunter. Homeward Bound Edition* (New York, 1910), 146, 147. For an interesting comparison of Roosevelt's *Winning of the West* with Frederick Jackson Turner's frontier thesis, see Richard Slotkin, *Gunfighter Nation: The Myth of the Frontier in Twentieth-Century America* (New York, 1992), 56.

6. Theodore Roosevelt, "The Main Object of the Roosevelt Foundation for the Conservation of Wild Life," Smithsonian Institution Archives (SIA), Record Unit (RU)

7364, Box 8, Folder 9; Theodore Roosevelt, "The Strenuous Life," in *The Strenuous Life. Homeward Bound Edition* (New York, 1910), 9, 29.

7. Theodore Roosevelt, "Manhood and Statehood," in *The Strenuous Life. Homeward Bound Edition* (New York, 1910), 205; Roosevelt's favorite hunters included not only Boone and Crockett but also an Englishman, Frederick Courteney Selous, who had gained fame in Africa.

8. Kermit Roosevelt, *The Long Trail* (New York, 1921), 25–26.

9. Edgar A. Mearns to F. W. True, memorandum, May 31, 1911, SIA, RU 192, Box 82, no. 34193.

10. See, for instance, Gerrit S. Miller Jr., Curator of Mammals, to Dr. Stejneger, memorandum, March 29, 1912, SIA, RU 192, Box 89, no. 36938; Professor Theodore Lyman to Dr. C. D. Walcott, January 20, 1912, Cambridge, Massachusetts, SIA, RU 192, Box 85, no. 36120; and George Mixter to Richard Rathbun, Assistant Secretary in Charge of the United States National Museum, January 28, 1913, SIA, RU 192, Box 99, no. 39253. See also "John Charles Phillips (1876–1938)," obituary in *Proceedings of the American Academy of Arts and Sciences* 74, no. 6 (1940), SIA, RU 7252, Box 2.

11. Theodore Roosevelt to Elihu Root, Juju Farm, Africa, May 17, 1909, *The Letters of Theodore Roosevelt*, ed. Elting E. Morison, vol. 7, *The Days of Armageddon, 1909–1914* (Cambridge, Mass., 1954), 11; Theodore Roosevelt to William Loeb Jr., in camp on the 'Nzoi River, near Mt. Elgon, November 12, 1909, *Letters*, vol. 7, 38. See also Theodore Roosevelt, *African Game Trails: An Account of the African Wanderings of an American Hunter-Naturalist* (New York, 1910).

12. An excellent example of the literature of international hunting expeditions is John B. Burnham, *The Rim of Mystery: A Hunter's Wanderings in Unknown Siberian Asia* (New York, 1929). Here Burnham describes his search for a rare mountain sheep in Siberia on behalf of the Smithsonian Institution, meeting in the process "Eskimos, Chukchis, Japanese, Bolshevists and the traders from many ports."

13. Theodore Roosevelt, *The Winning of the West. Homeward Bound Edition*, vol. 1 (New York, 1910), 130–31. Roosevelt's *Winning of the West* was first published in New York in 1889. Andrew Isenberg, *The Decline of the Bison* (Cambridge, England, 2000), 182.

14. Theodore Roosevelt, *Hunting Trips of a Ranchman; Hunting Trips on the Prairie and in the Mountains. Homeward Bound Edition* (New York, 1910), 23–24. Roosevelt's *Hunting Trips of a Ranchman* was first published in New York in 1885.

15. Roosevelt, *Long Trail*, 45–47.

16. John B. Goff, "The Roosevelt Lion Hunt," *Outdoor Life* 7, no. 5 (May 1901).

17. Theodore Roosevelt, "National Life and Character," *Strenuous Life*, 310.

18. On industrial and corporate growth in the Gilded Age, see Edward Chase Kirkland, *Industry Comes of Age: Business, Labor, and Public Policy, 1860–1897* (New York, 1961); Alfred D. Chandler Jr., *The Visible Hand: The Managerial Revolution in American Business* (Cambridge, Mass., 1977); David F. Noble, *America by Design: Science, Technology, and the Rise of Corporate Capitalism* (New York, 1977); Samuel P. Hays, *The Response to Industrialism,*

1885–1914 (Chicago, 1957); Robert H. Wiebe, *The Search for Order, 1877–1920* (New York, 1967); and Alan Trachtenberg, *The Incorporation of America: Culture and Society in the Gilded Age* (New York, 1982).

19. Henry Adams, *The Education of Henry Adams* (New York, 1931), 379–90. Adams's *Education* was first published in 1906.

20. Theodore Roosevelt, *The Wilderness Hunter, Homeward Bound Edition* (New York, 1910), 29, 270; Reiger, *American Sportsmen,* 93–151; Trefethen, *American Crusade,* 122–28.

21. Emma A. Preston, "A Woman Scores on a Deer," *Field and Stream* (October 1906): unnumbered pages, xerox, Adirondack Museum Vertical Files (AMVF). On women as deer hunters, see also Josephine Wilhelm Hard, "My First Deer: The Story of a Sportswoman in the Adirondacks," *Four Track News: An Illustrated Magazine of Travel and Education* 8, no. 3 (September 1904): 149–51, AMVF.

22. Preston, "A Woman Scores on a Deer."

23. Nellie Bennett, "My First Deer Hunt," *Outdoor Life* 11, no. 2 (February 1903).

24. Mrs. Arthur F. Rice, "A Woman's Telling Shot," *Amateur Sportsman* 5 (August 1896): 84–85, AMVF.

25. "Women Becoming Expert Trap Shooters—Team Issues Defy," *St. Paul News* (August 20, 1915), Hagley Museum, Accession 1207, Item 1 (Nemours Gun Club for Women).

26. On the popularity of trapshooting among men, see D. R. Rutter, "Why is Trapshooting So Popular?" *Country Club Life* (July 4, 1914), Hagley Museum, Accession 1207, Item 1. On women as trapshooters, see George Frank Lord, "Why Women Are Learning to Shoot," *Illustrated Sunday Magazine* [*Philadelphia Record?*] (July 12, 1914): 14, Hagley Museum, Accession 1207, Item 1.

27. John Mack Faragher, *Daniel Boone: The Life and Legend of an American Pioneer* (New York, 1992), 50; William C. Smith, *Indiana Miscellany: Consisting of Sketches of Indian Life, the Early Settlement, Customs, and Hardships of the People and the Introduction of the Gospel and of Schools; together with Biographical Notices of the Pioneer Methodist Preachers of the State* (Cincinnati, 1867), 77–78; Livonia Stanton Emerson, *Early Life at Long Lake, New York,* typescript copy of manuscript, Adirondack Museum, Blue Mountain Lake, N.Y.

28. Frances M. A. Roe, *Army Letters from an Officer's Wife, 1871–1888* (New York, 1909), 22, 42.

29. On changing gender roles and the decline of agrarian patriarchy in late eighteenth- and early nineteenth-century America, see Linda Kerber, *Women of the Republic: Intellect and Ideology in Revolutionary America* (Chapel Hill, N.C., 1980); Mary Beth Norton, *Liberty's Daughters: The Revolutionary Experience of American Women, 1750–1800* (Boston, 1980); Joan M. Jensen, *Loosening the Bonds: Mid-Atlantic Farm Women, 1750–1850* (New Haven, Conn., 1986); Mary P. Ryan, *Cradle of the Middle Class: The Family in Oneida County, New York, 1790–1865* (Cambridge, England, 1981); Barbara Leslie Epstein, *The Politics of Domesticity: Women, Evangelism, and Temperance in Nineteenth-Century America* (Middletown, Conn., 1981); and Keith Melder, *Beginnings of Sisterhood: The American Women's Rights Movement, 1800–1850* (New York, 1977).

30. Wilson Flagg, *Atlantic Monthly* 27 (1871), quoted in Elizabeth B. Keeney, *The Botanizers: Amateur Scientists in Nineteenth-Century America* (Chapel Hill, N.C., 1992), 69–71, 72.

31. On the "new women" of the late nineteenth and early twentieth centuries, see Carroll Smith-Rosenberg, *Disorderly Conduct: Visions of Gender in Victorian America* (New York, 1985), 176–77; Patricia Marks, *Bicycles, Bangs, and Bloomers: The New Woman in the Popular Press* (Lexington, Ky., 1990); Martha Banta, *Imaging American Women: Idea and Ideals in Cultural History* (New York, 1987), chapter 1; and Anna Firor Scott, "What Then, Is This New Woman?" *Journal of American History* 65 (December 1978): 679–703.

32. Maxine Benson, *Martha Maxwell: Rocky Mountain Naturalist* (Lincoln, Nebr., 1986), 128–40.

33. Thomas Bangs Thorpe, quoted in Warder H. Cadbury, introduction to *Adventures in the Wilderness,* by William H. H. Murray, ed. William K. Verner (Syracuse, N.Y., 1970), 48.

34. Elizabeth Bacon Custer, *Following the Guidon* (New York, 1890), 190, 204. On women as occasional spectators and participants in antebellum hunts, see Nicholas Wolfe Proctor, "Bathed in Blood: Hunting in the Antebellum South" (Ph.D. diss., Emory Univ., 1998), 114–25.

35. Harvey Green, "Scientific Thought and the Nature of Children in America, 1820–1920," in *A Century of Childhood: 1820–1920,* ed. Mary Lynn Stevens Heininger et al. (Rochester, N.Y., 1984), 132; Gail Bederman, *Manliness and Civilization: A Cultural History of Gender and Race in the United States, 1880–1917* (Chicago, 1995), 200–201. On neurasthenia, see F. G. Gosling, *Before Freud: Neurasthenia and the American Medical Community, 1870–1910* (Urbana, Ill., 1987); T. J. Jackson Lears, *No Place of Grace: Antimodernism and the Transformation of American Culture, 1880–1920* (New York, 1981), 49–57; and Tom Lutz, *American Nervousness, 1903: An Anecdotal History* (Ithaca, N.Y., 1991).

36. Theodore Roosevelt, quoted in Roderick Nash, *Wilderness and the American Mind* (New Haven, Conn., 1967; reprint, New Haven, Conn., 1982), 150. See also Mrs. Francis Trevelyan Miller, "The American Tendency to Dwarf Life," *Outdoor Life* 8, no. 1 (January 1904). Mrs. Miller reported that as Americans "accumulate[d]" in cities they tended to forget the virtues of country life. "Herded life stunts nature and dwarfs the character," forcing Americans to imbibe the "purity or impurity" of those around them. An illustration accompanying this article shows a man and woman in the forest, each holding a gun, with the caption "The Gun an Important Factor in the Saving of the American Race."

37. G. Stanley Hall, *Adolescence,* vol. 1 (New York, 1904), x; Hall, quoted in Bederman, *Manliness and Civilization,* 90.

38. D. C. Beard, *The American Boys Handy Book: What to Do and How to Do It* (New York, 1910; reprint, New York, 1917), 209, 232; "Early American Impressions," *The American Field: The Sportsman's Journal* 61, no. 17 (April 23, 1904): 389.

39. Thomas W. Knox, *The Young Nimrods in North America. A Book for Boys,* Hunting Adventures on Land and Sea, part 1 (New York, 1881).

40. Ibid., preface.

41. On James Fenimore Cooper and other authors inspiring men to hunt, see Anthony W.

Dimock, *Wall Street and the Wilds* (New York, 1915), 235; H. N. Curtis, "My First Deer," *Outing* (January 1888): 372, AMVF; and H. M. Lee, "My First Bear Hunt," *Outdoor Life* 5, no. 1 (January 1900). On adults taking up hunting, see G. A. Warburton, "Can a Novice Get a Deer?" *Recreation* 21 (September 1904): 165; George F. Doll, "Two Adirondack Deer and How the Greenhorn of the Party Chanced to Bring Them into Camp," *Field and Stream* (January 1909): 781–85, AMVF; A. D. Gibbs, "A Trip to the Adirondacks and a Few Deductions Drawn Therefrom," *The Sportsmen's Review* 36, no. 18 (October 30, 1909): 1031–32, AMVF; and "My First Buck," *Shooting and Fishing* (November 17, 1904): 109, AMVF.

42. William Temple Hornaday, *Our Vanishing Wildlife: Its Extermination and Preservation* (New York, 1913), 101–2; Thomas R. Dunlap, "Sport Hunting and Conservation, 1880–1920," *Environmental Review* 12, no. 1 (spring 1988): 60 n. 32; Donna Haraway, "Teddy Bear Patriarchy: Taxidermy in the Garden of Eden, New York City, 1908–1936," *Social Text* 11 (winter 1984/85): 56. On the contest between Italian immigrant hunters, American farmers, and game wardens, see Louis Warren, *The Hunter's Game: Poachers and Conservationists in Twentieth-Century America* (New Haven, Conn., 1997), 21–47.

The Italian folk tradition of hunting songbirds was neither less praiseworthy nor more blameworthy than American sport hunting. One suspects that Americans recoiled at the idea of hunting small birds in part because that seemed to be a parody of their own hunting tradition, with its emphasis on courageous man versus noble beast. More important, Americans—taking cues from Audubon and others—had come to identify songbirds with middle-class conceptions of home, family, and the cult of domesticity, all of which were considered inviolate.

43. G. L. Lehle, "Military Rifle Shooting," *Outdoor Life* 21, no. 4 (April 1908).

44. William Temple Hornaday, *The National Collection of Heads and Horns* (New York, 1907), 2, 5. For a description of the wild fauna displayed at the 1876 Centennial International Exhibition, see J. S. Ingram, *The Centennial Exposition Described and Illustrated . . .* (Philadelphia, 1876), 121–22.

45. Hornaday, *National Collection of Heads and Horns,* 5, 6.

17. Conservation and Conflict

1. "Wild Animals in Art, with Illustrations from the Sculptures of Edward Kemeys," *The Century Illustrated Monthly Magazine* 28, no. 2 (May 1884–October 1884): 215.

2. William T. Hornaday, "The New York Plan for Zoological Parks," *Scribner's Magazine* 46, no. 69 (1909): 595, Smithsonian Institution Archives (SIA), Record Unit (RU) 74, Box 115, Folder 9; George Baxter Ward III, "Bloodbrothers in the Wilderness: The Sport Hunter and the Buckskin Hunter in the Preservation of the American Wilderness Experience" (Ph.D. diss., Univ. of Texas at Austin, 1980), 360; Leonidas Hubbard Jr., "What a Big Zoo Means to the People," *Outing, An Illustrated Monthly Magazine of Recreation* (September 1904): 670, SIA, RU 74, Box 115, Folder 9. On the Boone and

Crockett Club's role in the creation of the Bronx Zoo, see William Bridges, *Gathering of Animals: An Unconventional History of the New York Zoological Society* (New York, 1974), 1–19. See also William Temple Hornaday, *Popular Official Guide to the New York Zoological Park*, 9th ed. (New York, 1907); and "The Boone and Crockett Club," *Forest and Stream* 62, no. 5 (January 30, 1904): 81, cols. 1–2.

3. *American Sportsman*, quoted in John Reiger, *American Sportsmen and the Origins of Conservation* (New York, 1975), 40–41; Fred E. Pond [Will Wildwood, pseud.], *The Sportsman's Directory* (Milwaukee, 1891), 9–32. In counting the clubs listed in Pond's directory, I defined regions as follows: the Northeast includes New York (79 clubs), Pennsylvania (68), New Jersey (48), Connecticut (31), Massachusetts (31), Delaware (7), and Maine (1); the Midwest includes Illinois (158), Iowa (80), Kansas (76), Indiana (59), Ohio (50), Kentucky (47), Missouri (29), Michigan (23), Nebraska (15), and Wisconsin (14); the West includes the Dakotas (32), Colorado (27), California (24), Montana (2), Nevada (1), Oregon (1), and Washington (1); and the South includes Alabama (17), Georgia (10), Florida (9), and Louisiana (1).

4. "Missionary Work Among the Gunners," *Forest and Stream* 4, no. 1 (February 11, 1875): 8, cols. 2–3; "Important Legal Decision," *Spirit of the Times* 17, no. 13 (May 22, 1847): 147, col. 1.

5. William Cronon, *Changes in the Land: Indians, Colonists, and the Ecology of New England* (New York, 1983), 100–105; James B. Trefethen, *An American Crusade for Wildlife* (New York, 1961; reprint, New York, 1975), 106. On a similar New York law passed in 1795 to protect other game bird species, see Jennie Holliman, *American Sports (1785–1835)* (Durham, N.C., 1931), 53; and *American Turf Register and Sporting Magazine* 1, no. 11 (July 1830): 547. Discussions of hunting clubs' campaigns for game laws saturate the sporting periodicals; for one example, see Scolopax, "Game and the Game Laws," *Spirit of the Times* 30, no. 28 (August 18, 1860): 337, col. 3.

6. Thomas R. Dunlap, "Sport Hunting and Conservation, 1880–1920," *Environmental Review* 12, no. 1 (spring 1988): 51; James A. Tober, *Who Owns the Wildlife? The Political Economy of Conservation in Nineteenth-Century America* (Westport, Conn., 1981), 27.

7. *Spirit of the Times* 29, no. 35 (October 8, 1859): 444, col. 2; "The 'National Sportsmen's Association,'" *Forest and Stream* 3, no. 6 (September 17, 1874): 89, cols. 2–3.

8. George Baxter Ward III, "Bloodbrothers in the Wilderness: The Sport Hunter and the Buckskin Hunter in the Preservation of the American Wilderness Experience" (Ph.D. diss., Univ. of Texas at Austin, 1980), 352.

9. See Trefethen, *American Crusade for Wildlife*; Paul Russell Cutright, *Theodore Roosevelt, The Naturalist* (New York, 1956); and George Bird Grinnell, ed., *Brief History of the Boone and Crockett Club, with Officers, Constitution and List of Members for the Year 1910* (New York, 1910).

10. Wayne Gard, *The Great Buffalo Hunt* (New York, 1960), 207 ("finest animal"), 212; William T. Hornaday, "The Last Buffalo Hunt," *Washington (D.C.) Evening Star*, March 5, 1887; William Temple Hornaday, "Progress Report of Explorations for Buffalo in the

Northwest, Spring of 1886," SIA, RU 201, Box 17, Folder 9. As of January 1, 1889, Hornaday estimated that 285 buffalo survived in the wild in the United States, including 200 in Yellowstone National Park. William T. Hornaday, *The Extermination of the American Bison* (Washington, D.C., 1889), 525.

11. J. A. Allen to G. B. Goode, New York City, March 2, 1888, SIA, RU 201, Box 17, Folder 1.

12. William Temple Hornaday to G. B. Goode, Assistant Secretary of the Smithsonian Institution, Washington, D.C., December 2, 1887, SIA, RU 201, Box 17, Folder 10.

13. *Official Guide for Centennial Exposition of the Ohio Valley and Central States* (Cincinnati, 1888), SIA, RU 70, Box 29, Folder 1; R. E. Earle, *Report Upon the Participation of the Smithsonian Institution, in the Ohio Valley and Central States Centennial Exposition*, SIA, RU 70, Box 29, Folder 5, Item 7.

14. Trefethen, *American Crusade for Wildlife*, 138–42; Charles Banks Bellt, comp., *History of the Committee on Conservation of Forest and Wildlife of the Camp Fire Club of America 1909–1989 and the Camp Fire Conservation Fund 1977–1989*, updated and republished by the Camp Fire Club of America and the Camp Fire Conservation Club (Dobbs Ferry, N.Y., 1989), 33. On saving the buffalo, see also Martin S. Garretson, *The American Bison: The Story of Its Extermination as a Wild Species and Its Restoration under Federal Protection* (New York, 1938); Wayne C. Lee, *Scotty Philip: The Man Who Saved the Buffalo* (Caldwell, Idaho, 1975); Charles Jesse Jones, *Buffalo Jones' Forty Years of Adventure; a Volume of Facts Gathered from Experience* (Topeka, Kans., 1899); and Robert Olney Eason, *Lord of the Beasts: The Saga of Buffalo Jones* (Tucson, 1961).

15. "Cooperative Game Laws," *Forest and Stream* 2, no. 5 (March 12, 1874): 74, col. 1; "International Game Laws," *Forest and Stream* 4, no. 9 (April 8, 1875): 136, col. 2. On hunters as conservationists, see also Reiger, *American Sportsmen*; Trefethen, *American Crusade for Wildlife*; Theodore Whaley Cart, "The Struggle for Wildlife Protection in the United States, 1870–1900: Attitudes and Events Leading to the Lacey Act" (Ph.D. diss., Univ. of North Carolina at Chapel Hill, 1971); and T. S. Palmer, *Chronology and Index of the More Important Events in American Game Protection, 1776–1911*, U.S. Department of Agriculture, Bureau of Biological Survey, Bulletin 41 (Washington, D.C., 1912). For an argument against the idea that sport hunters led the way in conservation, see Thomas R. Dunlap, "Sport Hunting and Conservation, 1880–1920," *Environmental Review* 12, no. 1 (spring 1988): 51–60.

16. John Reiger, *American Sportsmen and the Origins of Conservation* (New York, 1975).

17. Charles E. Whitehead, Letter to the Editor, *Forest and Stream* 14, no. 22 (July 1, 1880): 435, col. 2; "Protection of Game," *Forest and Stream* 2, no. 21 (July 2, 1874): 328.

18. Arlie William Schorger, *The Passenger Pigeon, Its Natural History and Extinction* (Madison, Wisc., 1955), 151; "The Shooting Tournament at Niagara," *Forest and Stream* 3, no. 3 (August 27, 1874): 41, col. 3; Schorger, *Passenger Pigeon*, 29.

19. Henry Hastings Sibley [Hal A. Dacotah, pseud.], "A Buffalo and Elk Hunt in 1842," *Spirit of the Times* 16, no. 7 (April 11, 1846): 73, cols. 1–3; Henry Hastings Sibley [Hal A. Dacotah, pseud.], "Game in the West," *Porter's Spirit of the Times* 1, no. 8 (October 25, 1856): 126, cols. 1–2.

20. Richard Irving Dodge, *The Hunting Grounds of the Great West; A Description of the Plains, Game, and Indians of the Great North American Desert* (London, 1877), 118; Edmund Morris, *The Rise of Theodore Roosevelt* (New York, 1979), 286.

21. Tober, *Who Owns the Wildlife,* 79.

22. *American Sportsman,* cited in Tober, *Who Owns the Wildlife,* 77; Ibid., 79.

23. Tober, *Who Owns the Wildlife,* 76, 80. The menu at Drake's Grand Pacific Hotel included white-tailed deer (soup, boiled tongue, roast saddle, broiled steak, cutlet), black-tailed deer (roast), mountain sheep (boiled leg, roast), black bear (boiled ham, roast, ragout "Hunter style"), cinnamon bear (roast), buffalo (boiled tongue, roast loin, broiled steak), antelope (steak), elk (roast leg), opposum (roast), raccoon (roast), rabbit (broiled, "Braise, Cream sauce"), jackrabbit (roast), English hare (roast), goose (roast), redhead duck (roast), canvasback duck (roast), bluewing teal (roast, broiled), widgeon (roast), mallard (roast, broiled), wood duck (roast), butterballs (broiled), wild turkey (roast), quail (roast), pheasant (roast, broiled), prairie chicken (roast, "en Socle," file "with Truffles," salad), spotted grouse (roast), sandhill crane (roast), jacksnipe (broiled), English snipe (broiled), blackbirds (broiled), reed birds (broiled), trout (broiled), and black bass (baked), and other "ornamental dishes" including "Red-Wing Starling on Tree," "The Coon out at Night," and "Pyramid of Game en Bellevue." "Chicago and the West," *Forest and Stream* 31, no. 19 (November 29, 1888): 365, col. 1; see also Peter Mattheissen, *Wildlife in America* (New York, 1959), 166. For the amount and variety of game marketed in the 1860s, see Thomas F. DeVoe, *The Market Assistant, Containing a Brief Description of Every Article of Human Food Sold in the Public Markets of the Cities of New York, Boston, Philadelphia, and Brooklyn* (New York, 1866). See also William Temple Hornaday, "Extermination of Birds for Women's Hats," *Our Vanishing Wildlife: Its Extermination and Preservation* (New York, 1912), 114–36.

24. Edward Ives, "The Poacher as Hero: The Graves Case as Exemplar," *Forest and Conservation History* 35, no. 1 (1991): 24–28; Edward Ives, *George Magoon and the Down East Game War: History, Folklore, and the Law* (Urbana, Ill., 1988), 58.

25. Dodge, *Hunting Grounds,* 116; David W. Cartwright, *Natural History of Western Wild Animals and Guide for Hunters, Trappers, and Sportsmen; . . . Written by Mary F. Bailey, A.M.* (Toledo, 1875), 3; "The Pot Hunter," *Forest and Stream* 2, no. 21 (July 2, 1874): 326, col. 1; *Machias (Maine) Union,* September 1, 1874, quoted in Ives, *George Magoon,* 63.

26. Ives, *George Magoon,* 71, 72; Ives, "Poacher as Hero," 27.

27. William Elliott, *Carolina Sports by Land and Water. Including Incidents of Devil-Fishing, Wild-Cat, Deer, and Bear Hunting, & c.* (Charleston, S.C., 1846), 286.

28. Elliott, *Carolina Sports,* 285; *The American Farmer,* 3d ser., 3 (1841): 25.

29. Henry William Herbert [Frank Forester, pseud.], *Frank Forester's Field Sports of the United States and British Provinces of North America,* vol. 1 (New York, 1849), 19; Derek Ernest Johnson, *Victorian Shooting Days: East Anglia 1810–1910* (Woodbridge, Suffolk, England, 1981), 39; Richard H. Thomas, *The Politics of Hunting* (Aldershot, England, 1983), 17; Johnson, *Victorian Shooting Days,* 39. On the costs of game parks and the popularity of

hunting among the English landed elite in the nineteenth century, see F. M. L. Thompson, *English Landed Society in the Nineteenth Century* (London, 1963), 136–50. On the history of poaching in England, see Roger B. Manning, *Hunters and Poachers: A Social and Cultural History of Unlawful Hunting in England, 1485–1640* (Oxford, England, 1993); P. B. Munsche, *Gentlemen and Poachers: The English Game Laws, 1671–1831* (Cambridge, England, 1981); E. P. Thompson, *Whigs and Hunters: The Origin of the Black Act* (New York, 1975); and Charles Chenevix Trench, *The Poacher and the Squire: A History of Poaching and Game Preservation in England* (London, 1967).

30. Roger Longrigg, *The English Squire and His Sport* (New York, 1977), 180, 248, 260; Thomas, *Politics of Hunting,* 15–25; Johnson, *Victorian Shooting Days,* 36, 39.

31. Theodore Roosevelt, *The Wilderness Hunter. Homeward Bound Edition* (New York, 1910), 270. Roosevelt's *Wilderness Hunter* was published in 1893. Dwight W. Huntington, *Our Big Game: A Book for Sportsmen and Nature Lovers* (New York, 1904), 35.

32. Donald William Klinko, "Antebellum American Sporting Magazines and the Development of a Sportsman's Ethic" (Ph.D. diss., Washington State Univ., 1986), 76; C., "Cape May and Some of Its Amusements," *American Turf Register and Sporting Magazine* 7, no. 1 (September 1835): 23–25; B., "Deer Hunting at the White Sulphur," *Spirit of the Times* 9, no. 30 (September 28, 1839): 349, col. 2; "Agawam Hotel, East Wareham, Mass." [advertisement], *Spirit of the Times* 12, no. 5 (April 2, 1842): 58, col. 2 ("To sportsmen, in pursuit of hunting and fishing, this place offers unrivalled inducements, it being in the immediate vicinity of the far famed Plymouth woods, abounding in deer, and streams and ponds abounding in trout, pike, perch, & c., and contiguous to the celebrated Cape Cod trout streams at Marshpee, Sandwich, Falmouth, Rochester, & c. . . . It is the only legitimate place for 'Head-quarters' in this region, and here good guides may be found to point out to sportsmen the most favorite places for sport"). *Forest and Stream* 2, no. 2 (February 19, 1874): 44, col. 2.

33. Samuel Irenaeus Prime, *Under the Trees* (New York, 1874), 108.

34. Richard Patrick Roth, "The Adirondack Guide (1820–1919): Hewing Out an American Occupation" (Ph.D. diss., Syracuse Univ., 1990), 94; Maitland C. De Sormo, *The Heydays of the Adirondacks* (Saranac Lake, N.Y., 1974), 233; Alfred L. Donaldson, *A History of the Adirondacks,* vol. 2 (New York, 1921), 89; John G. Mitchell, "Gentlemen Afield," *American Heritage* 29, no. 6 (October/November 1978): 99.

35. Mitchell, "Gentlemen Afield," no page number; J. A. Ricker, "An Outing in Colorado," *Outdoor Life* 4, no. 5 (November 1899).

36. "Blooming Grove Park," *Harper's Weekly* 14, no. 729 (December 17, 1870): 815, 820. On private game preserves generally, see Theodore S. Palmer, *Private Game Reserves and Their Future in the United States.* U.S. Biological Survey Circular 72 (Washington, D.C., 1910).

37. Huntington, *Our Big Game,* 26; William Temple Hornaday, *Our Vanishing Wildlife,* 360.

38. Eugene T. Peterson, *Hunters' Heritage: A History of Hunting in Michigan* (Lansing, Mich., 1979), 44; Huntington, *Our Big Game,* 174.

39. Dwight W. Huntington, "Field Sports of To-Day," *The Century Illustrated Monthly Magazine* 66, no. 6 (October 1903): 896; "That 'Duck Preserve' Question," *Outdoor Life* 7, no. 2 (February 1901); Huntington, *Our Big Game,* 34; "American Game Parks. The 'Forest and Stream's' Fourth Annual Report on Game in Preserves. Part One—Fenced Parks," *Forest and Stream* 49, no. 5 (July 31, 1897): 85, col. 2. For an additional listing of privately owned preserves, see the sequel to this article, "Part Two—Unfenced Parks," *Forest and Stream* 49, no. 6 (August 7, 1897): 104, col. 3, through 106, col. 3. See also William Henry Atherton, "The 'Rich' and the 'Poor,'" *Forest and Stream* 48, no. 16 (April 17, 1897): 306, col. 2, through 307, col. 1.

40. Pacificator, "The War in California," *Forest and Stream* 32, no. 10 (March 28, 1889): 191. A response to Pacificator came from Club Man, "California Sportsmen's Rights," *Forest and Stream* 32, no. 15 (May 2, 1889): 296–99.

41. Huntington, *Our Big Game,* 29; Hornaday, *Our Vanishing Wildlife,* 360; Emerson Hough, "The Shooting Clubs of Chicago. V. The Tolleston Club," *Forest and Stream* 32, no. 3 (February 7, 1889): 44.

42. E[merson?] Hough, "The Shooting Clubs of Chicago. IV. The Mak-saw-ba Club," *Forest and Stream* 32, no. 4 (February 14, 1889): 64.

43. E[merson?] Hough, "Shooting Clubs of Chicago. IV. The Mak-saw-ba Club," 65, 87; E[merson?] Hough, "The Cumberland Club," *Forest and Stream* 32, no. 6 (February 28, 1889): 87.

44. Thorstein Veblen, *The Theory of the Leisure Class: An Economic Study of Institutions* (New York, 1890; reprint, New York, 1912), 40–41.

45. Ibid., 40–41, 258, 263, 270.

46. Ibid., 134.

18. Friends and Foes

1. The literature on Gilded Age strikes is voluminous. A few important sources are R. V. Bruce, *1877: Year of Violence* (Indianapolis, Ind., 1959); Paul Arvich, *The Haymarket Tragedy* (Princeton, 1984); Leon Wolff, *Lockout: The Story of the Homestead Strike of 1892; A Study of Violence, Unionism, and the Carnegie Steel Empire* (New York, 1965); Almont Lindsey, *The Pullman Strike: The Story of a Unique Experiment and of a Great Labor Upheaval* (Chicago, 1942); and Stanley Buder, *Pullman: An Experiment in Industrial Order and Community Planning, 1880–1930* (New York, 1967).

2. On Gilded Age and Progressive era labor, see three works by David Montgomery: *Citizen Worker: The Experience of Workers in the United States with Democracy and the Free Market during the Nineteenth Century* (Cambridge, England, 1993); *The Fall of the House of Labor: The Workplace, the State, and American Labor Activism, 1865–1925* (Cambridge, England, 1987); and *Workers' Control in America: Studies in the History of Work, Technology, and Labor Struggles* (Cambridge, England, 1979). See also Peter N. Stearns and Daniel J. Walkowitz, eds., *Workers in the Industrial Revolution: Recent Studies of Labor in the United*

States and Europe (New Brunswick, N.J., 1974); James H. Drucker, *Men of the Steel Rails: Workers on the Atchison, Topeka and Santa Fe Railroad, 1869–1900* (Lincoln, Nebr., 1983); Walter Licht, *Working for the Railroad: The Organization of Work in the Nineteenth Century* (Princeton, 1983); Herbert G. Gutman, *Work, Culture, and Society in Industrializing America: Essays in American Working-Class and Social History* (New York, 1977); and John A. Garraty, ed., *Labor and Capital in the Gilded Age: Testimony Taken by the Senate Committee upon Relations between Labor and Capital, 1883* (Boston, 1968). On labor unions, see Harold C. Livesay, *Samuel Gompers and Organized Labor in America* (Boston, 1978); and Melvin Dubofsky, *We Shall Be All: A History of the Industrial Workers of the World* (Chicago, 1969).

3. On the Populists, I have consulted Lawrence Goodwyn, *Democratic Promise: The Populist Moment in America* (New York, 1976). See also John D. Hicks, *The Populist Revolt: A History of the Farmer's Alliance and the People's Party* (Minneapolis, 1931); Richard Hofstadter, *The Age of Reform: From Bryan to F.D.R.* (New York, 1955); Norman Pollack, *The Just Polity: Populism, Law, and Human Welfare* (Urbana, Ill., 1987); and Walter T. K. Nugent, *The Tolerant Populists: Kansas, Populism, and Nativism* (Chicago, 1963). On the 1896 presidential election, see Robert W. Cherney, *A Righteous Cause: The Life of William Jennings Bryan* (Boston, 1985); Paul W. Glad, *The Trumpet Soundeth: William Jennings Bryan and His Democracy, 1896–1912* (Lincoln, Nebr., 1960); and Stanley L. Jones, *The Presidential Election of 1896* (Madison, 1964). On the appeal of socialism, see Nick Salvatore, *Eugene V. Debs: Citizen and Socialist* (Urbana, Ill., 1982); and Aileen S. Kraditor, *The Radical Persuasion, 1890–1917: Aspects of the Intellectual History and the Historiography of Three American Radical Organizations* (Baton Rouge, La., 1981).

4. W. H. Boardman, quoted in Edward Comstock Jr. and Mark C. Webster, eds. and comps., *The Adirondack League Club, 1890–1990* (Old Forge, N.Y., 1990), 58; Harry Radford, "The Sportsman and His Guide; Address Delivered by Harry V. Radford at the Annual Banquet of the Brown's Trace Guides' Association, Held in the Historic Old Forge House, at Old Forge, N.Y., January 8, 1903," *Woods and Waters* 7, no. 1 (spring 1904): 16.

5. H.P.U., "The Ideal Sportsman," *Forest and Stream* 18, no. 22 (December 29, 1881): 429, col. 1.

6. Charles Dudley Warner, *In the Wilderness* (Boston, 1878), 88, 95.

7. Alfred Trumble, quoted in Lloyd Goodrich, *Winslow Homer* (New York, 1945), 112.

8. Radford, "The Sportsman and His Guide," 18.

9. "Three Years Trip in Barren Lands," *Edmonton Journal*, August 17, 1910, Smithsonian Institution Archives (SIA), Record Unit (RU) 208, Box 47, Folder 5; "Bare Arctic Tragedy," *Washington Post*, January 1, 1915, SIA, RU 7252, Box 3; "Wood Bison Hunter Here," *Edmonton Capital*, July 29, 1910, SIA, RU 208, Box 47, Folder 5.

10. Richard Patrick Roth, "The Adirondack Guide (1820–1919): Hewing Out an American Occupation" (Ph.D. diss., Syracuse Univ., 1990), 29; Warder H. Cadbury, introduction to *Adventures in the Wilderness*, by William H. H. Murray, ed. William K. Verner (Syracuse, N.Y., 1970), 25; William Chapman White, *Adirondack Country*, ed. Erskine Caldwell (New York, 1954), 156, 160.

11. Samuel H. Hammond, quoted in Philip G. Terrie, *Contested Terrain: A New History of Nature and People in the Adirondacks* (Syracuse, N.Y., 1997), 53; F. Trench Townshend, *Ten Thousand Miles of Travel, Sport, and Adventure* (London, 1869), 43; Cadbury, introduction to *Adventures in the Wilderness*, 35.

12. Fred Mather, "Men I Have Fished With: L.—Edward Zane Carroll Judson (Ned Buntline)," *Forest and Stream* 49, no. 4 (July 24, 1897): 69, col. 1, through 70, col. 2.

13. Alvah Dunning, quoted in Alfred L. Donaldson, *A History of the Adirondacks*, vol. 2 (New York, 1921), 111.

14. Comstock and Webster, *Adirondack League Club*, 58.

15. Verplanck Colvin, "Address of Verplanck Colvin at the First Annual Meeting of the Adirondack Guides Association, Held at Saranac Lake, March 2, 1892," Adirondack Museum Vertical Files (AMVF).

16. Ibid.

17. "The Shooting Clubs of Chicago. III.—The Fox Lake Shooting and Fishing Club," *Forest and Stream* 32, no. 1 (January 24, 1889): 7; "Adirondack Guides," *New York State Forest Commission Annual Report*, 1894, AMVF.

18. Townsend Whelen, "The Sportsman and His Guide," *Outdoor Life* 19, no. 2 (February 1907): 173–74.

19. Ibid.

20. Levant Fred Brown, "Antagonizing Guides and Sportsmen—A Protest," *Outdoor Life* 19, no. 3 (March 1907): 283–88.

21. "Levant Fred Brown Severely Criticized," *Outdoor Life* 19, no. 4 (April 1907): 391–92.

22. "Notice to Readers and Correspondents," *Outdoor Life* 19, no. 5 (May 1907): 609–11.

23. Henry William Herbert [Frank Forester, pseud.], "Proposed Alteration of the Game Laws," *Spirit of the Times* 15, no. 51 (February 14, 1846): 603, col. 1; David W. Cartwright, *Natural History of Western Wild Animals and Guide for Hunters, Trappers, and Sportsmen; . . . Written by Mary F. Bailey, A.M.* (Toledo, 1875), 5; Henry William Herbert [Frank Forester, pseud.], *Frank Forester's Field Sports of the United States and British Provinces of North America*, vol. 1 (New York, 1849), 19.

24. Herbert [Forester, pseud.], "Proposed Alteration of the Game Laws," 603, cols. 1–3. Because the states claimed ownership of wildlife, farmers could not kill game on their own lands during closed seasons. They could, however, kill protected animals (presumably including deer) that threatened their property. Henry Austin, *The Law Concerning Farms, Farmers and Farm Laborers together with the Game Laws of All the States* (Boston, 1886), 46.

25. Henry William Herbert [Frank Forester, pseud.], "The Quail," *Life and Writings of Frank Forester. (Henry William Herbert.)*, ed. David W. Judd, vol. 2 (New York, 1882), 97.

26. Elisha Jarrett Lewis, *The American Sportsman: Containing Hints to Sportsmen, Notes on Shooting, and the Habits of the Game Birds, and Wild Fowl of America* (Philadelphia, 1855), 156, 167. Lewis's *American Sportsman* was first published in Philadelphia in 1851 as *Hints to Sportsmen, Containing Notes on Shooting; the Habits of the Game Birds and Wild Fowl of America;*

the Dog, the Gun, the Field, and the Kitchen. "Game and Game Laws of Massachusetts," *Spirit of the Times* 26, no. 4 (March 8, 1856): 42, col. 2. As early as 1823, a character in James Fenimore Cooper's novel *The Pioneers* observes that "I have known a farmer, in Pennsylvania, order a sportsman off his farm, with as little ceremony as I would order [my servant] to put a log in the stove." James Fenimore Cooper, *The Pioneers, or the Sources of the Susquehanna; a Descriptive Tale,* in *The Leatherstocking Tales,* vol. 2 (New York, 1985), 92. Cooper's *The Pioneers* was first published in 1823.

27. "Farmers vs. Sportsmen," *Forest and Stream* 2, no. 14 (May 14, 1874): 210, col. 2; *American Sportsman* 2, no. 9 (June 1873): 136, col. 1.

28. E[merson?] Hough, "The Shooting Clubs of Chicago. IV. The Mak-saw-ba Club," *Forest and Stream* 32, no. 4 (February 14, 1889): 64.

29. *The Chicago Field* 15, no. 7 (March 26, 1881): 104; Eugene T. Peterson, *Hunters' Heritage: A History of Hunting in Michigan* (Lansing, Mich., 1979), 27.

30. James A. Tober, *Who Owns the Wildlife? The Political Economy of Conservation in Nineteenth-Century America* (Westport, Conn., 1981), 119; C.G., letter to editor, *Forest and Stream* 15, no. 18 (December 9, 1880): 368, col. 3; Practical, "Sportsmen and Farmers," *Forest and Stream* 15, no. 21 (December 23, 1880): 408, col. 3; M. U. Skrat, "Farmers and Town Sportsmen," *Forest and Stream* 41, no. 5 (August 5, 1893): 95, col. 1.

31. Frank Winch, *Hunting Posted Property* (Wilmington, Del., 1923), 1.

32. Hofstadter, *The Age of Reform,* 23–36.

33. Hal Barron, *Those Who Stayed Behind: Rural Society in Nineteenth-Century New England* (Cambridge, England, 1984), 39.

34. Ibid., 41, 46–49; G. Walter Fiske, quoted in Barron, *Those Who Stayed Behind,* 47; Hal Barron, *Mixed Harvest: The Second Great Transformation in the Rural North, 1870–1930* (Chapel Hill, N.C., 1997), 8.

35. Barron, *Those Who Stayed Behind,* 105; Barron, *Mixed Harvest,* 220–25.

Epilogue

1. As of 1995 only about 7 percent of the American population hunted. Between 1980 and 1995 the number of hunters in the United States declined by 8 percent. The largest decrease in the number of hunters was in the Northwest (18 percent), followed by the South (12 percent) and the West (6 percent). The decrease occurred among both ruralites and urbanites in all parts of the country except the Midwest, where the number of ruralites who hunted rose. While the number of male hunters declined by 9 percent in this period, the number of female hunters increased slightly. Decreases in the number of women hunters in most parts of the country were offset by a marked increase in the Midwest, where the number of women hunters rose by an astonishing 55 percent. Richard Aiken [U.S. Fish and Wildlife Service], *1980–1995 Participation in Fishing, Hunting, and Wildlife Watching; National and Regional Demographic Trends,* Report 96-5 (Washington, D.C., 1999), 6, 9, 39–42.

2. According to the U.S. Fish and Wildlife Service's 1996 survey titled *National Survey of Fishing, Hunting, and Wildlife-Associated Recreation,* those Americans aged sixteen years and older who were likeliest to hunt came from households with yearly incomes of between $40,000 and $49,999. In general, the further one was above or below this income level, the less likely one was to hunt. Of fourteen million hunters, only three million had four or more years of college. The overwhelming majority (95 percent) of hunters were white. Hunters were more likely than the general population to come from rural areas, though 56 percent of all hunters came from metropolitan areas with populations of fifty thousand or more (*National Survey of Fishing, Hunting, and Wildlife-Associated Recreation* [Washington, D.C., 1997], 26, 30–31.

3. Nash Buckingham, "Comment on the Use of Magazine Guns (Pump and Automatic Shotguns) on Migratory Wild Fowl and Upland Game Resources in the United States" (April 1929), Smithsonian Institution Archives (SIA), Record Unit (RU) 7364, Box 1, Folder 10; John G. Mitchell, "Gentlemen Afield," *American Heritage* 29, no. 6 (October/November 1978): 100.

4. Mitchell, "Gentlemen Afield," 100; James A. Swan, *In Defense of Hunting* (New York, 1995), 2.

5. William Bridges, *Gathering of Animals: An Unconventional History of the New York Zoological Society* (New York, 1974), 307–8.

6. Jerry Gandy, "Hunting Organization Takes Aim at New CD-ROM Game," *Contra Costa Times,* January 16, 1999.

7. Theodore Roosevelt, introduction to *Camera Shots at Big Game,* by Mr. and Mrs. A. G. Wallihan (New York, 1906), 11. See also William S. Thomas, *Hunting Big Game with Gun and with Kodak. A Record of Personal Experiences in the United States, Canada, and Mexico* (New York, 1906).

8. Richard K. Nelson, "Introduction: Finding Common Ground," in *A Hunter's Heart: Honest Essays on Blood Sport,* ed. David Petersen (New York, 1996), 6; Gary Snyder, *The Practice of the Wild* (San Francisco, 1990), 20.

9. Nelson, "Introduction," *Hunter's Heart,* 2.

10. See Swan, *In Defense of Hunting;* Mary Zeiss Stange, *Woman the Hunter* (Boston, 1997).

11. Robinson Jeffers, quoted in Matt Cartmill, *A View to a Death in the Morning: Hunting and Nature through History* (Cambridge, Mass., 1993), 21. On the hunting hypothesis, see Cartmill, *View to a Death,* 1–27.

12. Paul Shepard, *The Tender Carnivore and the Sacred Game* (New York, 1973), 1–36.

13. Shepard, *Tender Carnivore,* 269–78.

14. Ibid., 277, 271.

15. Jimmy Carter, "A Childhood Outdoors," *Hunter's Heart,* 35.

16. Eric Hobsbawm, "Introduction: Inventing Traditions," in *The Invention of Traditions,* ed. Eric Hobsbawm and Terence Ranger (Cambridge, England, 1983; reprint, Cambridge, England, 1989), 1–14.

17. *Forest and Stream* 1, no. 1 (August 14, 1873): 8.

18. William A. Allen, *Adventures with Indians and Game; or Twenty Years in the Rocky Mountains* (Chicago, 1903), 115.

19. Thomas R. Dunlap, *Saving America's Wildlife* (Princeton, 1991).

20. Louis Warren, *The Hunter's Game: Poachers and Conservationists in Twentieth-Century America* (New Haven, Conn., 1997), 1–3.

21. Quoted in *History of the Committee on Conservation of Forest and Wildlife of the Camp Fire Club of America 1909–1989 and The Camp Fire Conservation Fund 1977-1989,* comp. Charles Banks Bellt (Dobbs Ferry, N.Y., 1989), 9.

22. See Dan Flores, "Environmentalism and Multiculturalism," in *Reopening the American West,* ed. Hal K. Rothman (Tucson, 1998), 27–28.

23. Swan, *In Defense of Hunting,* 3.

Index